INTAGLIO

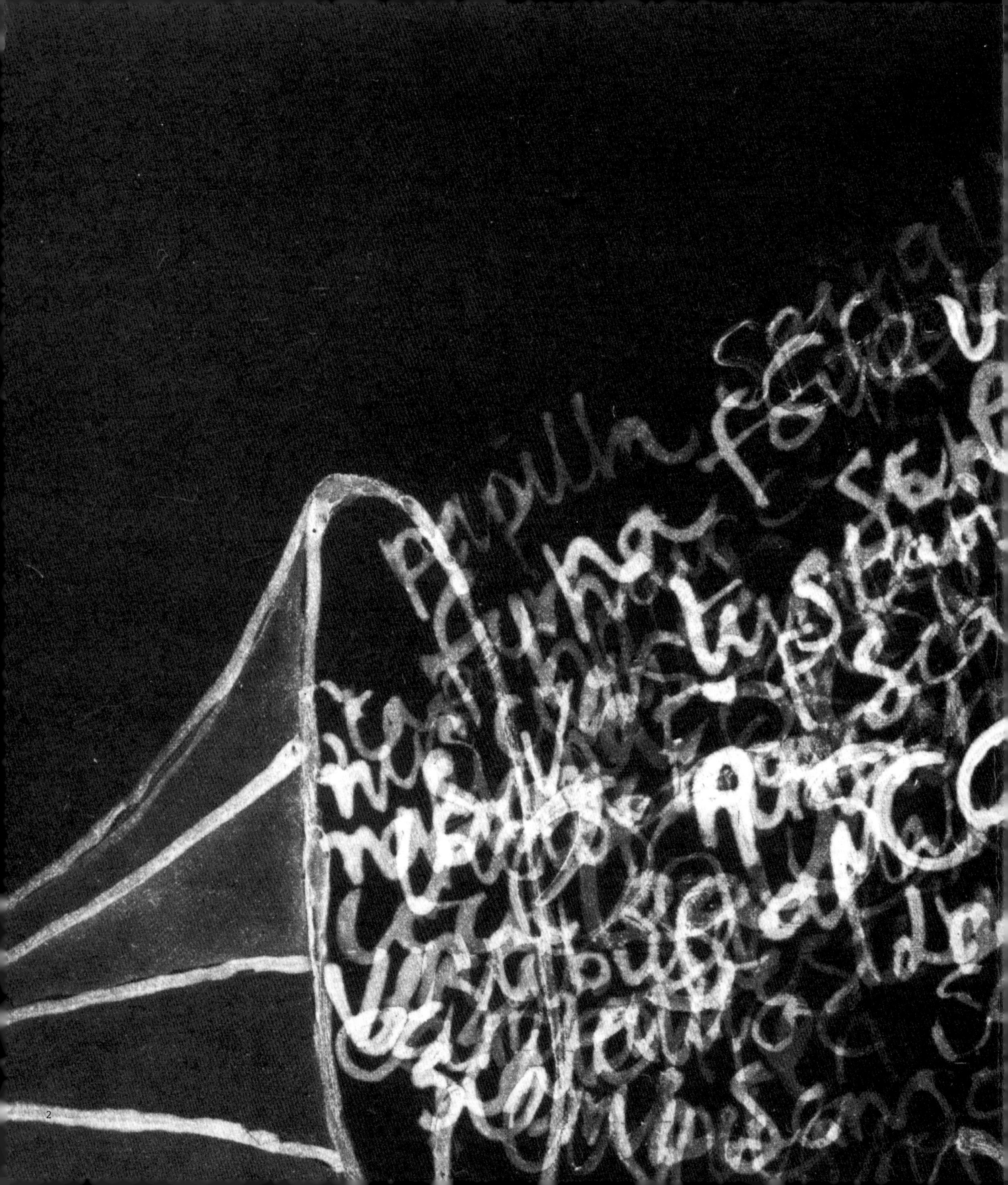

ROBERT ADAM
CAROL ROBERTSON

INTAGLIO

ACRYLIC-RESIST ETCHING
COLLAGRAPHY
ENGRAVING
DRYPOINT
MEZZOTINT

the complete safety-first system
for creative printmaking

with 229 illustrations, 199 in colour

Thames & Hudson

Frontispiece: Lucy Cobb (UK), *Drawing on Sound*, mezzotint and collagraph, co-published by Graal Press, 12 x 15 cm (4¾ x 5⅞ in.), 2004 (magnified detail). The pale tones were created by painting three different dilutions of Lascaux Hard Resist onto a pre-rocked mezzotint plate. After the resist had dried the plate was printed (see plate on p. 64 and print on p. 175).

First published in the United Kingdom in 2007 by
Thames & Hudson Ltd, 181A High Holborn, London WC1V 7QX

www.thamesandhudson.com

First published in the United States of America in 2007 by
Thames & Hudson Inc., 500 Fifth Avenue, New York, New York 10110

thamesandhudsonusa.com

A catalogue record for this book is available from the British Library
Library of Congress Catalog Card Number 2006908246

Hardback ISBN-13: 978-0-500-51343-9
ISBN-10: 0-500-51343-0

Paperback ISBN-13: 978-0-500-28661-6
ISBN-10: 0-500-28661-2

Printed and bound in China by C&C Offset Printing Co., Ltd.

contents

DIRECT INTAGLIO METHODS

ETCHING

HOW INTAGLIO PRINTMAKING DEVELOPED

THE ORIGINS OF INTAGLIO

The term 'intaglio' (pronounced in-tal' yo) is derived from the Italian word *intagliare* (*in* – into, *tagliare* – to cut). Patterns and images have been scratched and cut into hard materials since prehistory and the earliest known examples date from about 77,000 years ago. These were carved into pieces of red ochre which were found recently in Blombos Cave, on the Southern Cape coast of South Africa.

Many incised artworks from the Paleolithic period have been discovered in America, Australia, Africa, Asia and Europe. These petroglyphs are generally stylized representations and patterns but recent discoveries include ancient portraits scratched on cave floors in southern France which have an extraordinarily contemporary lifelike quality.

As aesthetic, communication and financial systems developed in civilizations across the world, the art of engraving on semi-precious stone and metal became important. This skill was applied in the earliest forms of writing and as part of the process of creating coinage; engraving was also used in the making of seals representing authority and ownership. Fine examples of decorated armour, weapons, household items and jewelry have been preserved, including bronze hand-mirrors made in the fifth century BC by Etruscans who engraved the metal and filled the indentations with a white paste.

THE INNOVATORS AND THEIR TECHNIQUES

1400 TO 1650

Medieval goldsmiths were the first to ink up their engraved decorative designs and take rubbings onto cloth or paper to document their work. Maso Finiguerra is known to have taken a print onto dampened paper as early as 1440. The first known artist's engravings to be printed on paper were made in Europe from metal plates and date from the mid-fifteenth century. Copper plates were probably used and the image was inscribed using tools such as burins and drypoint needles. The technique of applying ink to an incised plate, wiping the ink off the surface but leaving it in the recesses, then running the plate and dampened paper through a press remains largely unchanged to the present day. The characteristic quality of this intaglio printing creates prominent inky lines and rich velvety tones. The printed image on the paper is always a reversal of the image on the plate (as if seen in a mirror).

One celebrated group of engravings consists of a deck of cards depicting animals, birds, people and flowers, and these brought fame to the artist known as the Master of the Playing Cards. The Master E.S., who was probably his pupil, worked from 1450 to 1467 and introduced crosshatching and a dotting technique. Towards the end of the fifteenth century the Master of the Housebook was the first to use drypoint engraving.

The German painter Martin Schongauer made ambitious engravings on copper plates. With his burin he inscribed a wide range of marks, such as long sensitive strokes, short dashes and crosshatching. In Italy Andrea Mantegna based his personal engraving style of short lines of varying width on the tonal drawing technique he used in his figurative work. Albrecht Dürer, like Schongauer, had a father who was a goldsmith. He was influenced by the working methods of Schongauer and the prints of Mantegna. It is known that he experimented with drypoint but probably found that the plates wore out, preventing him from printing large editions. He chose to concentrate on engraving, as this meant that he could produce intricately detailed plates which could withstand long print runs, with the result that his visual ideas would be seen widely.

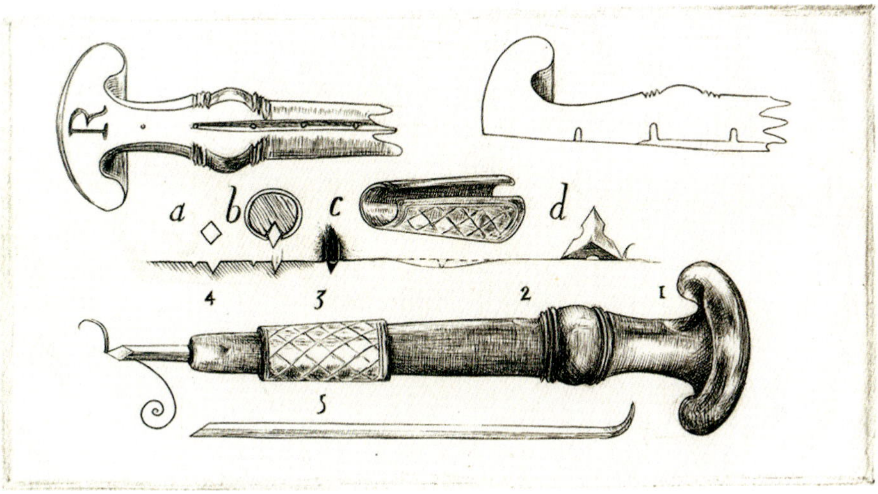

Richard Årlin (Sweden), *Burin*, engraving, 8.8 x 16.5 cm (3½ x 6½ in.), 1985. Årlin is inspired by fifteenth-century printmaking and, as well as making prints, fashions his own tools, presses and fonts to traditional specifications.

Raphael was so influenced by the way Dürer was disseminating his engravings that he employed the specialist engraver Marcantonio Raimondi, who from his studio in Venice had been pirating Dürer's woodcuts successfully as engravings. Raimondi had developed an important engraving technique consisting of even, parallel lines which described forms in curves. Raphael produced drawings from which Raimondi would work and the prints were then published.

The Flemish engraver Cornelius Cort, who worked in Italy, was employed by Titian. Cort was a master of crosshatching and developed a tonal engraving technique known as *schwellende taille*. This involved handling the burin to create lines which varied in their depth and thickness, introducing tone without the need for further lines. A fine example of this is the engraving *Head of Christ on the Sudarium* by Claude Mellan. In this image a single engraved line spirals outwards from the tip of the nose, swelling and thinning to describe the features and tonalities of the entire face.

At this time many distinguished artists formed professional relationships with engravers and their prints were widely disseminated. As a result innovations of style spread rapidly and this had a profound subsequent effect on the development of European art.

Daniel Hopfer, an Augsburg artist and armourer, is credited with the invention of the process of etching. He discovered that he could inhibit the natural rusting of iron shields and dagger blades by painting them with wax. He then drew through this waxy coating to expose the metal in the form of a design. When vinegar and vitriol were applied to the plate, the waxy areas resisted the action of the acids but the exposed metal was eroded: indentations in the form of the drawing were thus etched into the metal. Hopfer used his technique to make a number of printed etchings, including a portrait of Pope Alexander VI. This principle of applying a resist, drawing through it and etching the plate with a mordant remains unchanged today. After etching, the wax resist is removed and the etched image is filled with ink and printed (in the same way that an engraving would be printed). There is some evidence that Dürer began to experiment with etching after seeing Hopfer's prints.

Initially iron or steel plates were used for etching but by the middle of the sixteenth century knowledge had increased so that the technical difficulties of etching on copper had been overcome. Copper is still considered to be the finest metal for etching, as the bite is more accurate and the plates do not rust. Etched plates were often worked with engraving and drypoint tools to reinforce the lines and to add extra emphasis.

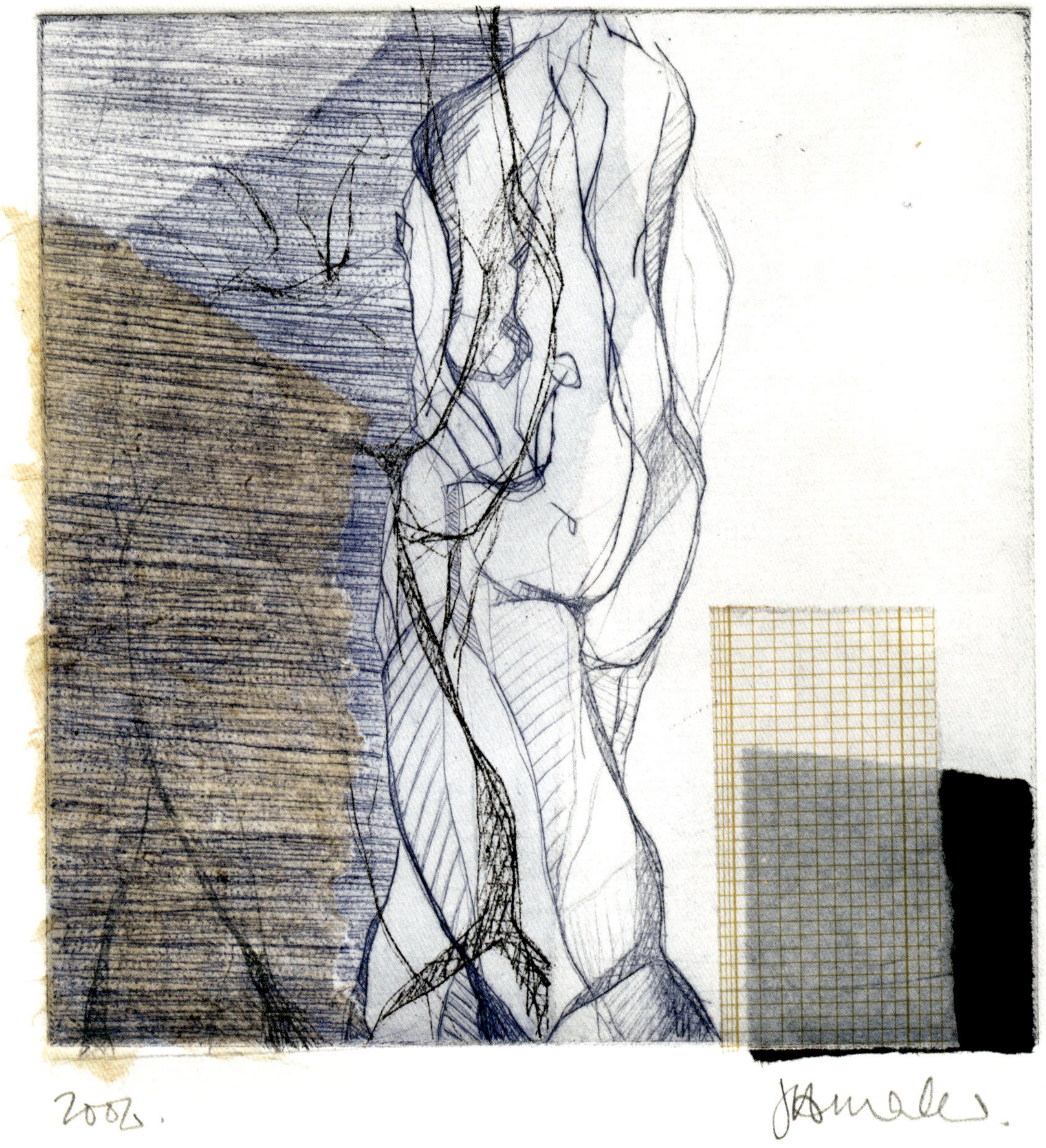

The medium of etching spread rapidly and by around 1600 Dietrich Meyer is credited with developing a soft ground which was used for making drawings on the plate. The resulting printed line was more like the effect created with a pencil or crayon than an incised line.

In the early decades of the century Jacques Callot began to establish his reputation as an important, prolific and innovative etcher. His influence became enormous and Abraham Bosse's 1645 treatise on prints recorded and promoted his crucial contributions to the technical development of the medium.

opposite Julie Arnall (UK), *Untitled,* drypoint with chine collé, 15 x 15 cm (5⅞ x 5⅞ in.), 2002. A print was taken from the plate and an enlarged photocopy made of this. The photocopy and other elements were then incorporated as chine collé in this print from the plate.

Callot experimented with lutemakers' hard varnishes and created a new acid-resistant material made from mastic and linseed oil. This hard ground was strong, long-lasting, adhered successfully to the plate and performed consistently. This development was important as the waxy ground of the time was unreliable, fairly soft and easily damaged by the artist during the drawing and etching stages, leading to foul bite (unwanted etching).

Callot also invented an etching needle known as the échoppe. This drawing tool has a sliced, angled, oval tip and when turned between the fingers describes a line of varying width in the etching ground. Callot was the first to explore the possibilities of repeated and multiple biting in order to control a wide variety of printed tones within the image. He did this by etching an image for a timed period, then removing the plate from the acid and, after cleaning, rinsing and drying the plate, painting stop-out varnish over selected lines and marks to prevent any further biting. When the plate was dry, it was etched again and the process repeated. The finished plate had a variety of depths of etch and so, when inked up, some etched areas would hold more ink than others and the resulting print would show a range of tone. Callot combined his techniques to create images of complex tonality with sharp modulated lines close to those achieved by engraving and his deeply bitten plates were able to withstand long printed editions.

In the north major publishing houses were established in Antwerp, which became the centre for engraving. Peter Paul Rubens set up a workshop for reproducing his paintings, and Anthony Van Dyck experimented with the process of etching, employing professional engravers to make and print his plates.

A completely different approach is evident in the experimental etchings of Hercules Seghers, who worked with a sugar-based lift solution to make painterly lines and used some kind of granular material to create tone. His printing methods were very creative and he was the first etcher to use colour. He printed on tinted paper, linen and canvas with pigments rather than inks, and he sometimes painted on the substrate before printing or laid washes of pigment over the finished prints.

Rembrandt van Rijn admired the experimental approach of Seghers and he in turn broke through traditional constraints by experimenting with softer grounds, as well as drawing with nails and other sharp implements to create ragged active lines and areas of deep tone. He also created tonal areas by etching with powdered flours of sulphur. Surviving stage proofs of Rembrandt's images illustrate his working methods and demonstrate his direct approach to the medium, including his use of scraping and burnishing. He made etchings and drypoints of extraordinary atmosphere and, although he did not print with colour, he altered his inking and wiping techniques, creating variants within editions.

The tonal technique of mezzotint engraving was invented during Rembrandt's lifetime and within two decades the method had achieved massive popularity. Its invention is attributed to Ludwig von Siegen, who used roulettes (spiked rollers) and heavy hand tools with toothed edges to indent the surface of the plate, creating pitted areas. These textured surfaces printed with a deep velvety tone, and artists used the process to work from light to dark.

Prince Rupert of the Rhine improved the method by employing more effective roulettes and by fixing a drypoint tool to a hinged arm in order to generate regular parallel scores across the surface of the plate in a variety of directions. This criss-crossed burred surface held the ink and printed as a dense tone. Later in the development of the mezzotint method, artists worked from dark to light by removing and smoothing areas of the previously scored surface with a scraping and burnishing tool. The smoothed areas print as glowing whites and pale tones. It was not long before the mezzotint method was used as a reproductive process alongside engraving. Etching also began to be used for reproduction and the lines of a bitten plate would often be reinforced with the engraver's burin to create an engraved appearance.

1650 TO 1800

Around 1650 a tonal etching process (later known as aquatint) was invented by Jan van de Velde IV in Amsterdam. This technique began to be used but artists were secretive about their methods and as a result the process did not gain popularity for another hundred years. Another tonal technique was to sprinkle sand over a plate coated in ground and then to run the plate through the press. The resulting 'punctured' resist was etched to form a pitted ink-holding surface.

A new printing process later referred to as monotyping was developed by the Italian etcher Giovanni Benedetto Castiglione. This method of creating a unique print involves applying a layer of ink to the entire surface of an unused etching plate. The image is formed by drawing into the ink with rags, brushes, fingers and blunt sticks. The plate is then run through an etching press to make a single print. The process is repeated for each new print.

Robert Callender (UK), detail of the copper etching plate for *Coastal Collection*, 1999 (see embossed print on p. 199). The artist used modern Lascaux resists and Photec on this plate, which was etched deeply using ferric chloride.

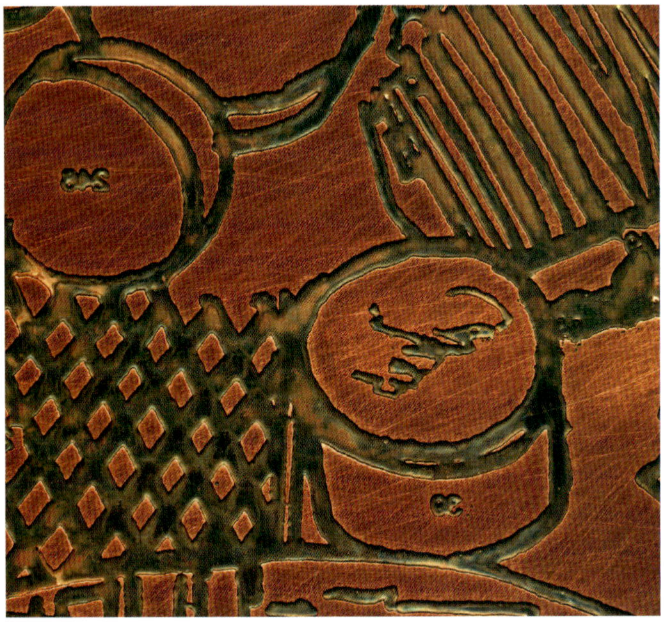

In the 1670s Abraham Blooteling invented the mezzotint rocker, a heavy tool with a curved toothed blade. When the rocker is worked methodically across the plate surface in a variety of directions, a complex burred grid is created. This grid holds the ink and prints as a dense dark tone.

The German artist Jacob Christoph Le Blon used the mezzotint process and claimed to have independently invented a three-colour printing process based on the primary colours (Isaac Newton's colour theory had recently been published). Resulting prints such as *Narcissus* are rich and glowing. His student Jacques-Fabien Gautier-Dagoty refined the process by adding a fourth plate which was printed in black or brown. He made many complex prints of scientific subjects such as dissections and botanical illustrations. However, the use of mezzotinting was expensive and the changes caused by the French Revolution brought the commercial use of the process to an end.

In the meantime knowledge of etching techniques swept across Europe and many artists experimented with the medium. In Italy Giovanni Antonio Canale, known as Canaletto, made evocative etchings of Venice scenes which he sold to English visitors. He etched long thin sensitive lines to suggest the delicate light and atmosphere of the city and its surrounding lagoon. In Rome the approach of Giovanni Battista Piranesi was quite different. The plates for his large-scale series 'Carceri D'Invenzione' (Imaginary Prisons) were vigorously worked using a variety of techniques including open bite, etching with sulphur, rough lines, engraving and burnishing.

English politics and social mores were satirized and caricatured by William Hogarth, whose popular etchings and engravings were widely disseminated. By contrast William Blake was not celebrated in his lifetime and his exact printing techniques remain unknown. Blake's imagery was uniquely visionary and he was an accomplished painter, engraver, etcher and poet. He sensitively unified texts and images in illuminated volumes such as *Songs of Innocence* and *Songs of Experience.* He developed a personal working method which involved biting plates deeply and printing them as relief prints (he said that the process was revealed to him by his dead brother in a dream). He sometimes painted watercolour washes over his prints and experimented with monotype and transfer methods by painting on millboard plates in order to introduce colour.

In 1773 an explanation of Jan van de Velde's tonal process was published in France by Stapart and a few years later by Jean Baptiste Le Prince (1780). The articles described how particles of rosin were scattered over a dry metal plate and melted to form acid-resistant dots which adhered to the surface. When the plate was immersed in the acid bath the remaining exposed network of metal etched away, creating an indented area around each particle. The depth of the etch determined the amount of ink which would be held in the reticulated structure and the tonal value of the printed area.

Yvonne Jacquette (US), *Docking (Hong Kong)*, mezzotint, printed at Yama Prints, 35 x 24 cm and 24.5 x 17 cm ($13\frac{3}{4}$ x $9\frac{7}{16}$ in. and $9\frac{5}{8}$ x $6\frac{11}{16}$ in.), 1993. An edition of 62 prints on Hahnemühle paper was taken from the two copper plates.

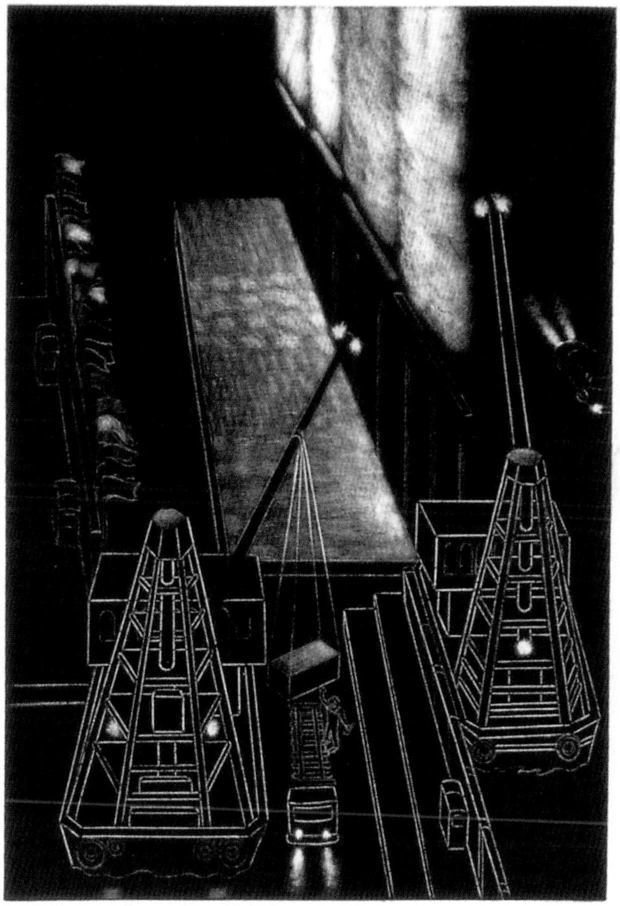

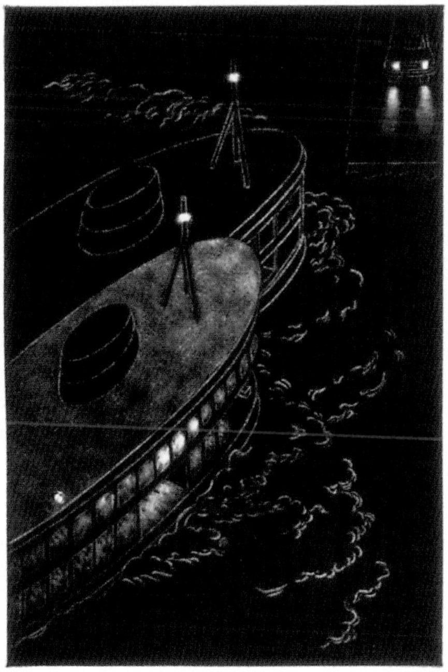

The artist Paul Sandby popularized the method in England and invented the term 'aquatint' (water tint or tone). This described the resemblance of the printed effect to painted watercolour washes. Sandby had an experimental approach to his work and is recorded as using a camera obscura. He experimented with the aquatint technique by dissolving the particles of rosin in alcohol so that he could make painted tonal marks. He also used a resist to paintbrush marks which protected ('stopped out') areas of the plate from the action of the mordant. By painting on his stop-out varnish between etching stages, Sandby was able to generate a controlled tonal range. This process became known as 'stage biting' or 'step biting'. The artist skilfully used repeated applications of sugar lift in conjunction with aquatint to create the effect of tonally varying brush marks.

Another English artist, Alexander Cozens, was an innovative educationalist who made a series of etchings which demonstrated aquatints, soft ground and lift techniques. He encouraged students to use accidental marks such as blots as starting points for drawings and compositions.

In Spain in the final quarter of the eighteenth century Francisco José de Goya y Lucientes began to produce prints which are a potent and haunting expression of the social and political circumstances of his time. Goya documented Napoleon's invasion of Spain in his series of 82 etchings, 'Los Desastres de la Guerra' (The Disasters of War). These show a deep understanding of the medium, and he was the first artist to explore the tonal drama of aquatint by laying down and biting successive aquatints to achieve rich dense blacks. Sometimes he formed the image solely from marks painted on with stop-out varnish.

By 1800 intaglio prints were being manufactured commercially to satisfy popular demand throughout Europe and by this time each of the methods had its own firmly established tradition. Mezzotints became so widely available in England that the method became known as 'la manière anglaise'. There was even a trend to transfer mezzotint images by gluing them onto sheets of glass. The paper would be dissolved with water and the transferred image would then be coloured from the back.

In France the popularity of sanguine drawings (in red or brown chalk on rough paper) led printmakers to seek a method of reproducing these marks. In 1757 an engraver, J. C. François, invented the crayon manner which solved this problem. His method involved laying a hard ground and drawing into it with new types of roulette. The resulting dotted image was etched, producing a softer effect than using the roulette directly on the plate.

In England William Wynn Ryland introduced the new method of 'stipple engraving', which was derived from the crayon manner. This process involves making a dotted image on a hard ground with an etching needle. After etching the individual dots are reinforced by engraving with a burin. By the 1770s this combined etching and engraving method started to replace mezzotint as a commercial reproduction method. Stipple engraving was successful because the plates could withstand long editioning runs and could be printed in colour 'à la poupée' (small pads or 'dolls' are used to dab coloured ink onto selected areas of the plate). In response to the fashion for stipples, mezzotinters tried new working methods to win back their audience. Richard Earlom was notable in that he made line etchings and then used a mezzotint rocker to introduce tone in selected areas. J. M. W. Turner employed mezzotint engravers and followed Earlom in combining etching and mezzotint.

1800 TO 1900

At the beginning of the century artists began to experiment with the planographic printing process of lithography, which was invented by Alois Senefelder in 1798. The innovator Joseph Nicéphore Niépce was fascinated by the new process and his experiments with it led him to create the first recorded photographic image, 'View from the window at Le Gras' (1826). He made the surface of a variety of materials such as lithographic stones, glass, copper and pewter plates sensitive to light and exposed his image onto them using a type of camera obscura.

Around this time Niépce had perfected his photo-etching process and was etching his images on copper plates. He called the resulting prints 'heliographs', from the Greek *helios* (sun) and *graphos* (to draw). To make a heliograph he would coat a pewter plate with a thin layer of light-sensitive asphaltum (bitumen of Judea), and in order to create a positive he oiled prints of engravings to make the paper translucent. He then positioned the positive in contact with the plate and exposed them to the sun for several hours. The ink in the translucent paper shielded the coated plate, and the asphaltum in these shielded areas was later dissolved with oil of lavender and turpentine, exposing the metal of the plate in the form of the image, which could then be etched. The exposed asphaltum was altered by the ultraviolet light and remained on the plate, behaving as an acid resist when the plate was etched. After etching, the asphaltum was removed from the plate and the image inked up (intaglio) and printed.

Louis Jacques Mandé Daguerre made contact with Niépce and later they formed a partnership. The 'daguerreotype' was launched in 1839 a few years after Niépce's death. In this particularly toxic process copper plates were exposed to iodine and the fumes formed light-sensitive silver iodide. The plate was placed in contact with a positive and exposed for around fifteen minutes. Then the plate was developed over heated mercury to cause the mercury to amalgamate with the silver. The image was fixed with salt and rinsed with water. As a result the copper plate showed a reversed but positive image.

In the same year William Henry Fox Talbot revealed his 'photogenic drawings' in England and in 1852 took out a patent for making photo-etchings on steel using gelatin and potassium bichromate. His later experiments with bichromatized gelatin led to the development of photogravure, which he patented in 1858 as photoglyphic engraving. Photogravure is a tonal method of reproduction and involves coating copper plates with a light-sensitive gelatin solution, allowing this thin layer to dry, exposing the plate with a positive to sunlight, and then etching the plate in ferric chloride. During etching the soft unexposed gelatin (forming the darker areas of the image) breaks down and etches first; then the mid-tone and lighter areas of the image are etched as the remainder of the resist slowly dissolves. This gradual breakdown generates a range of tones.

Talbot later applied an aquatint (melted powder type) to the surface of the plate to enhance the tonal range and began to use carbon tissue to support the potassium bichromate.

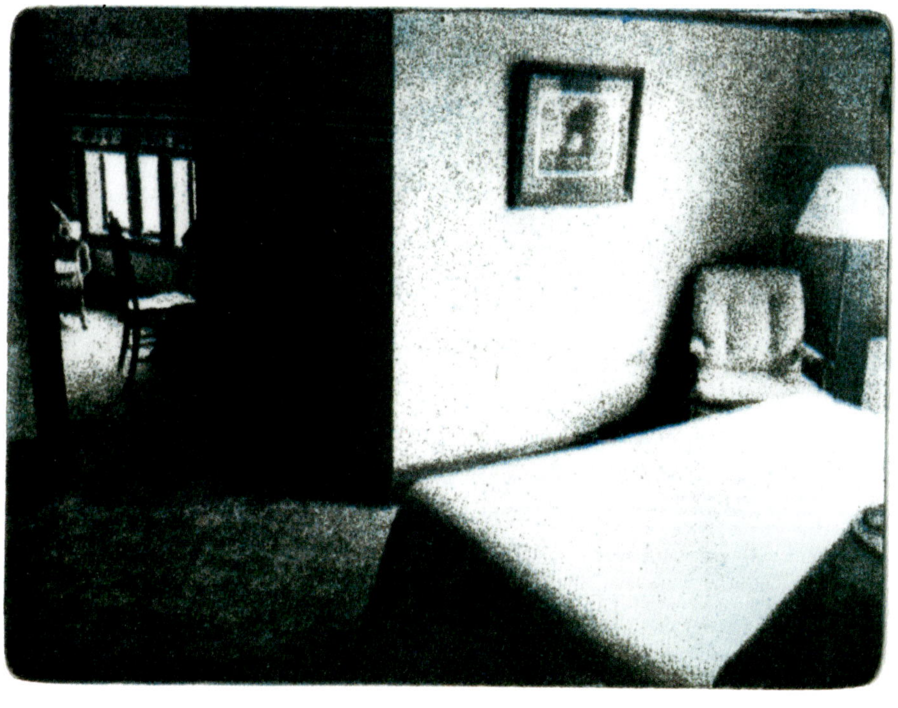

Carrie Clingan (US), *Room*, photocollagraph, 7.5 x 10 cm (3 x 4 in.), 2003. The artist used Adobe Photoshop to create two separations from a photograph (a colour field and a black). The images were output onto transparent film with an inkjet printer. These positives were then exposed to plates coated with a modern, light-sensitive, acid-resistant material. The plates were developed, dried and printed in register onto Hahnemühle copperplate paper.

Carbon tissue, invented by Joseph Wilson Swan in 1864, is a paper layered with gelatin which has been heavily pigmented. Talbot found that he could sensitize this tissue, expose it to the positive and then adhere it to the plate surface. The plate was then developed in hot water to wash away the paper backing and the unexposed areas of gelatin. The coloured layer of gelatin varied in its thickness depending on how much light had passed through the positive. The method was improved by Karl Klic and was soon used for high-quality commercial printing. Instead of an aquatint to create tonal effects, Klic used a half-tone screen which had a grid of clear lines on an opaque ground.

In the 1850s the artists Jean-Baptiste Corot and Jean-François Millet experimented with the new process of cliché-verre. This drawing method is considered to be a hybrid between etching and photography. The first stage is to smoke a piece of flat glass with a tallow taper (a similar process to the darkening of hard etching grounds). The sooty deposit is then drawn into with an etching needle or other tools. In a later development of the technique the glass was painted with etching ink and powdered with pigment to ensure a clean line. The glass and its drawing are then placed in close contact with a sheet of photosensitive paper and exposed to sunshine. The light passes through the areas where the soot has been removed from the glass and affects the photosensitized paper. This reaction causes the paper to darken and forms a black line image.

The advent of photographic processes deeply affected the way in which artists and the general public perceived artwork and the appearance of the world around them. At this time intaglio processes were considered to be a mainly commercial industry until the prints of Charles Meryon generated a revival of interest in etching as a creative process for artists. This new tide of interest began in the 1850s and influenced contemporary and later generations of artists in Europe and America. Artists who experimented with intaglio processes for themselves and were also interested in the new photographic images and processes included Edouard Manet, Camille Pissarro, Edgar Degas, Pierre-Auguste Renoir, Berthe Morisot, Auguste Rodin, Pierre Bonnard, Suzanne Valadon, Edouard Vuillard, Lovis Corinth, James Ensor and Edward Hopper.

Philip Hamerton's handbook on etching techniques published in 1868 was also influential in disseminating technical information about the medium. Amongst many other methods Hamerton describes how to colour grounds white so that the drawn lines appear dark, and he explains a means of creating deliberate foul bite by adding dust and salt to grounds. He promoted a new aesthetic for the medium, based on the concept of 'learned omission', which is clearly demonstrated in the white spaces integral to the etchings of his friend James Abbott McNeill Whistler. This American artist lived and worked in Europe and had a strong influence on later generations of artists. He made and printed his own plates, using skilful plate-wiping techniques to enhance the tonality of his images.

The idea of creative and experimental plate-wiping was introduced to Degas by his friend Vicomte Ludovic Napoléon Lepic, who used a printing process he called 'variable etchings'. He once generated 85 different images of a landscape from a single etched plate. Lepic also devised the retroussage method of inking. In this wiping technique a ball of scrim is flicked over the surface of the inked-up plate. This action drags a little ink from the indentations and the resulting print has a soft, veiled appearance. Degas used rags, brushes and fingers to displace the ink on his plates. He printed with coloured inks and drew on finished etchings with pastels. His many surviving stage proofs reveal how he employed soft ground, sandpaper, aquatint, varnishes, drypoints, scrapers and steel points to work his plates.

Degas, like many artists of his period, was attracted to immediate and direct processes and became interested in monotyping. He made several hundred 'printed drawings', as he called them, and also collaborated with Pissarro and Mary Cassatt. Cassatt was influenced by the Japanese artist Kitagawa Utamaro and revived multi-plate colour etching in her own prints.

Paul Gauguin developed his own method, which is now practised as 'trace monotype'. In this process the entire surface of a sheet of paper is painted with gouache and immediately a second sheet is laid over it. The drawing is made on the back of the second sheet, and the paint offsets onto it forming the image. These images have characteristic broken lines and textured smudges. This monotyping method was developed further by Paul Klee, who would often add watercolour to the prints. Bonnard inked up etching plates or sheets of glass rather than paper to create his richly coloured monotypes. In the 1890s Frank Duveneck introduced monotyping to America and soon the process became widely used and popular with artists who experimented with different types of plate (Masonite and plastic), with colour and with printing on canvas. Maurice Prendergast became well known for his monotypes, which had a similar appearance to watercolour painting.

At the end of the nineteenth century the Norwegian artist Edvard Munch was living in Berlin and experimenting with etching and drypoint. The process of electro-plating copper plates with steel had been discovered and Munch's drypointed plates were strengthened in this way so that they would sustain longer print runs. In order to learn more about etching he travelled to Paris, which was becoming a centre of excellence for graphic art. He found that the new fashion of creating an image by burnishing into an aquatinted surface (rather than a mezzotinted plate) suited him well. Munch purchased pre-aquatinted zinc plates on which to make his images, inking up his finished plates à la poupée.

1900 TO 1970

By the start of the twentieth century a number of enthusiastic and enterprising print publishers such as Ambroise Vollard, Daniel-Henry Kahnweiler and Albert Skira, along with the expert etchers Paul Haasen, Georges Leblanc, Auguste Delâtre, Roger Lacourière and Jacques Villon (half-brother of Marcel Duchamp and an original member of the Cubist group) encouraged and aided the finest painters and sculptors in France to make etchings. Many of their print projects and books were financially unsuccessful at the time but the works

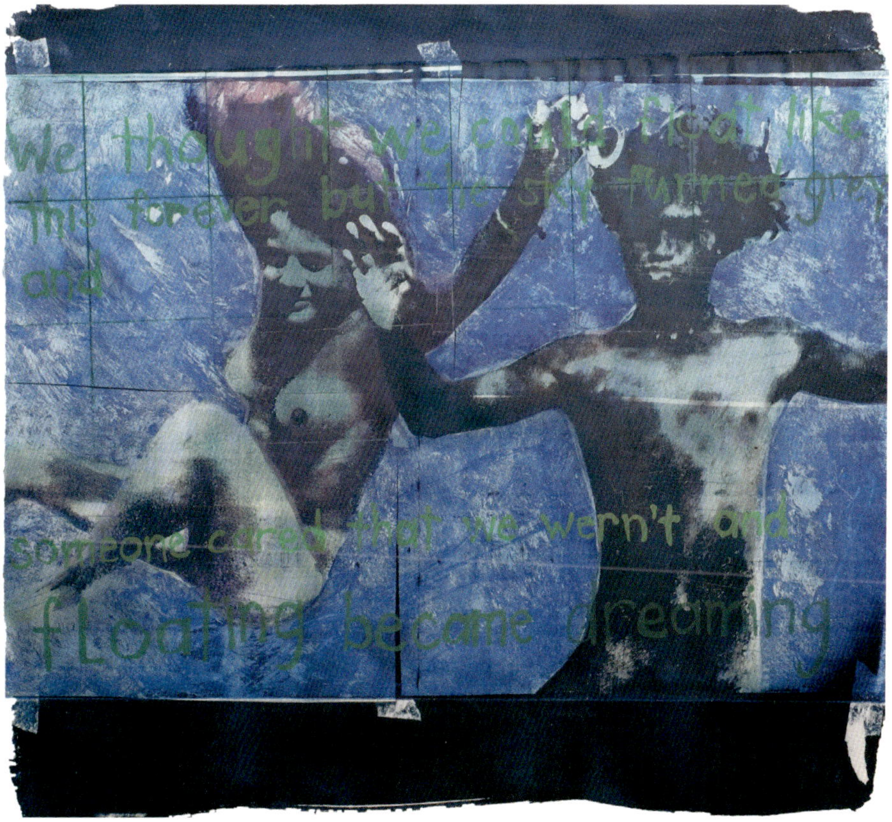

Rebecca Mayo (Australia), *Dreaming across the Atlantic*, etching, cyanotype and water-based screenprinting, 66 x 72.5 cm (26 x 28½ in.), printed by the artist at Edinburgh Printmakers, 1994. Lascaux acrylic varnish, acrylic paints and Photec were used as resists to generate an etching plate that was printed onto a cyanotype of the underwater figures. The green text was screenprinted on top with Lascaux acrylic paints.

are now considered to be of historical importance. The artists involved with Vollard included Bonnard, Marc Chagall, Degas, Raoul Dufy, Pablo Picasso and Georges Rouault. Vollard persuaded Rouault to make the suite of etchings 'Misérère et Guerre' (Misery and War). These bold and powerful statements took nine years to make and were completed in 1927. The plates were started by exposing a gouache painting (made into a positive probably by oiling the paper) to a plate coated with a photoresist. After the autographic image was etched, Rouault worked the plate further with spit bite, aquatint, drypoint line, roulette and scraping.

Kahnweiler set up a gallery and published the work of young artists including Picasso. After the First World War he continued to bring together poets and printers with artists such as Fernand Léger, Juan Gris, Georges Braque, Maurice de Vlaminck, André Derain and André Masson.

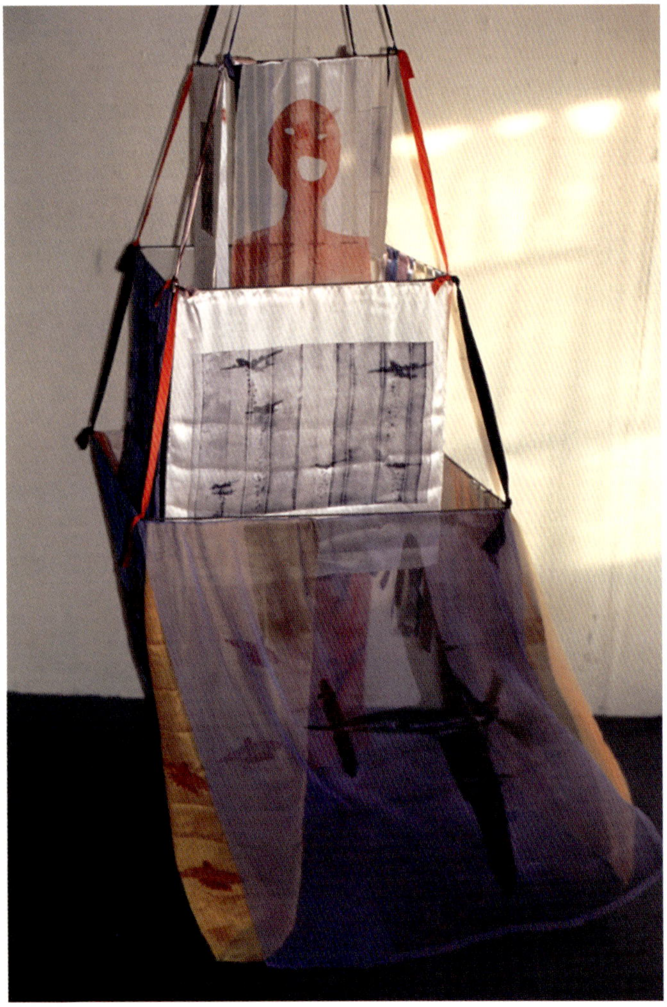

Henri Matisse made etchings with Skira. Other studios published the first etchings of Joan Miró in 1933 and Salvador Dalí in 1934. In Germany the Expressionist group Die Brücke, the Bauhaus and other etching studios published work by Corinth, Franz Marc, Ernst Ludwig Kirchner, Erich Heckel, Klee, Max Beckmann, Emil Nolde, Oskar Kokoschka, Käthe Kollwitz, George Grosz and Kurt Schwitters. Many of these bold prints were drypoints.

In Norway in 1925 the sculptor and printmaker Rolf Nesch, who had studied under Kirchner, first made his 'metal prints'. On a textured base plate he assembled compositions of found objects and shapes made from wire netting, welded pieces of metal and other elements which he sewed to the plate with metal wire. He was the first printmaker to fashion holes in his plates as an image-making device and would chisel and hammer his plates to create lines and textures. He made his own coloured ink and printed varied editions. Nesch's printmaking methods are now considered to be the precursors of collagraphy.

Boris Margo invented the 'cellocut' in 1931 and continued to develop the process by increasing the relief of the plate. He dissolved sheet celluloid in acetone to form a fluid which could be poured onto a plate made of metal, compressed wood or cardboard. Textures could then be made in the soft coating by laying fabrics, cord, other materials and shallow objects on the surface before running the plate through the press. The celluloid would then harden and the plate could be used for relief printing, inked-up intaglio, colour viscosity printing or embossing.

In the 1930s the English etcher and engraver Stanley William Hayter established Atelier 17 in Paris and created a revival of interest in engraving as a means of original expression. New inking and printing methods were devised, such as printing in plaster and the viscosity colour printing technique developed by Krishna Reddy. During the Second World War the studio moved to New York but had limited success and returned to Paris in the 1950s.

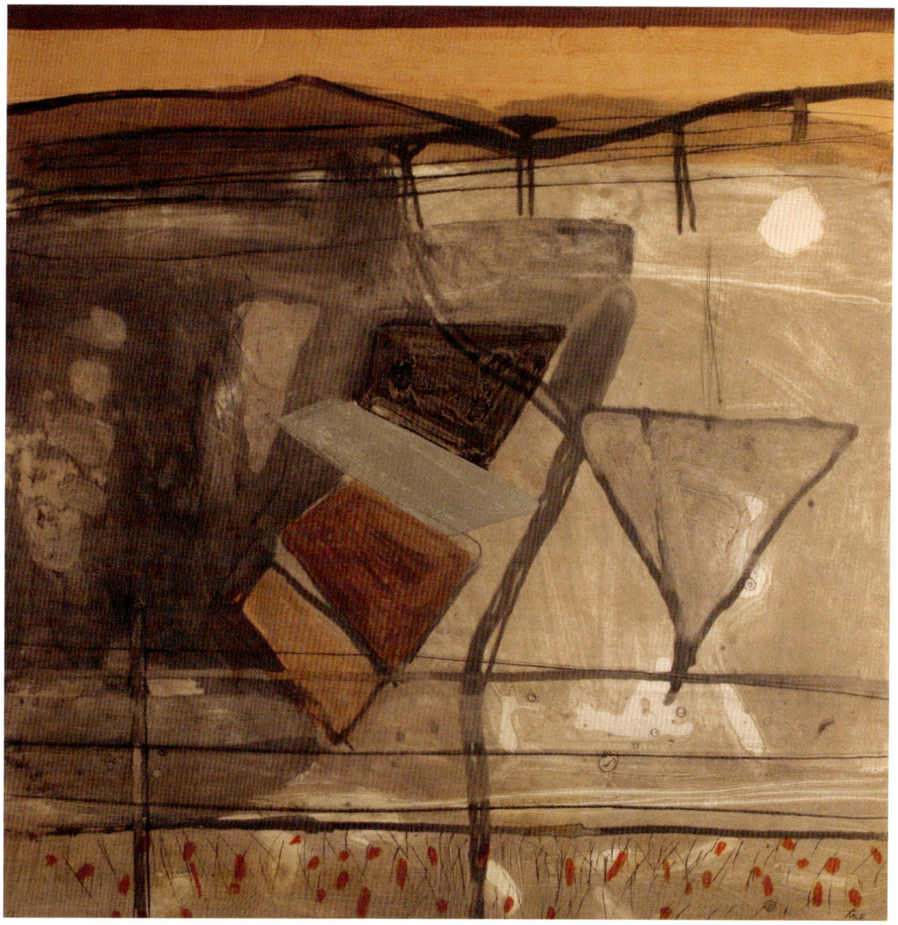

opposite Desirée Alvarez (US), *Bomber Birdcage*, installation, inkjet, drypoint, woodcut and sewing, printed by the artist at Lower East Side Printshop, Inc., New York, 305 x 91.5 x 91.5 cm (10 x 3 x 3 ft), 2000.

right Barbara Rae (UK), *Winter Light, Lammermoor*, collagraph, 83 x 83 cm (32¾ x 32¾ in.), co-published at Graphic Studio Dublin, 2000.

The origins of the Society of American Graphic Artists can be traced to 1915 and the idea of collaborative print projects based on the European model took hold in the United States. Important etchings were made by John Sloan, Hopper, Georgia O'Keeffe and the Expressionist John Marin. During the depression of the 1930s the US government funded the Works Progress Administration (WPA), which established shared printmaking facilities in many cities. Printmaking departments are now the norm in American universities and art colleges, and printshops and publishers have generated a wealth of innovative work by artists such as Philip Guston, Milton Avery, Willem De Kooning, Jackson Pollock, Claes Oldenburg, Josef Albers, Jim Dine, Sol LeWitt, Jasper Johns, Chuck Close, Louise Bourgeois, Robert Rauschenberg, John Cage and many others.

Two etchers who were influenced by Hayter became involved in important university workshops: Mauricio Lasansky set up an intaglio studio at Iowa University in 1945 and Gabor Peterdi became head of the graphic workshop at Yale University in 1952. The following year Peterdi began to use synthetic rubber casts, colour offsetting and cut-out plates in his intaglio practice. He also became interested in the concept of working with two opposing procedures – one being subtractive and the other additive – on a single plate. Peterdi's additive methods involved applying various plastics and glues (collagraphic elements) to etched metal or cardboard plates.

At about the same time Roland Ginzel started to make cardboard plates which he built up with lacquers and cut into to make marks. He scattered carborundum powder over the wet varnish. This was left to dry and when the plate was inked up the pigment was held between the carborundum particles, printing a tone similar to aquatint.

Glen Alps, a teacher at the University of Washington, created plates from pieces of wallboard which he sealed with varnish. He made an initial sketch on the plate with charcoal and then built up the image using clear lacquer, Liquitex acrylics, gesso, putty, plastic wood, modelling paste, car body-filler and Elmer's glue. He employed these materials to hold coarse wood shavings, pencil shavings, ground-up walnut shells, sawdust, string, brush bristles, cloth and textured papers. He would continue to work the plate, sanding elements and building up the layers until it was ready to proof. An embossed proof was taken and then the plate was inked up intaglio. The various materials would hold the ink in different quantities, resulting in a print with a range of tones. Alps named this plate-making process 'collagraphy' in 1956 and he exhibited his *Collagraph No. 12* at the Brooklyn National Print Exhibition in 1957.

In the 1960s John Ross and Clare Romano made cut-out cardboard plates to which they added acrylic gesso, fabric and sand. Ten years later, together with Tim Ross, they described how to make collagraphs in their book *The Complete Printmaker*. This influential publication spread knowledge of collagraphy across the world.

The collagraphic process, which involves adhering sand or carborundum to the plate to create tone, is sometimes confused with the different carborundum processes invented by Dox Thrash and Henri Goetz. Thrash's process involved using carborundum – an abrasive powder – to grain the copper plate, creating a textured ink-holding surface. As in mezzotinting, a burnisher was used to create pale tones and whites. This way of working can be seen clearly in Thrash's portrait *Charlot*.

In 1968 Goetz described his carborundum process in an article 'La Gravure au Carborundum' (Carborundum Engraving), which was published by Maeght with a foreword by Miró. It describes how the image was painted with oil or an acrylic medium on a duraluminium-plated plate. Carborundum was added to these media or sprinkled over the image. Any excess carborundum was shaken from the plate. The plate was then run through the press in contact with a stainless steel plate. The carborundum particles were forced through the duraluminium plating, exposing the metal. Etching tools could be used to draw lines in the layer. The plate was etched in hydrochloric acid (the duraluminium layer behaved as a resist). The resulting prints have a characteristic richness and Goetz taught the method to, amongst others, Miró, Max Papart, Antoni Clavé and James Coignard.

In the 1950s and 1960s artists including Andy Warhol, James Rosenquist, Rauschenberg, Johns and Edward Ruscha became interested in incorporating photographic elements into their work. A process camera could be used in combination with lith film (a transparent light-sensitive substrate) to create photo-positives. Photo-processes in lithography and screenprinting enabled them to achieve this; and when KPR (Kodak Photo Resist, which had been designed for the commercial market) was launched in 1953 it was soon adopted by artists for photo-etching. This new etching resist made photo-intaglio processes easier. The product was initially based on the photodimerization of cinnamic acid and its derivatives, which were incorporated in a resinous film. The liquid resist required the use of a thinner, a dye, a developer and a powerful remover, all of which are particularly toxic.

1970 TO TODAY

In the 1970s KPR liquid resist was superseded by DuPont's dry film photoresist, which was designed for the accurate, reliable and safer fabrication of circuit boards for the electronics industry. However, it was not until the 1990s that artists began to use dry film photoresists such as Riston, Photec, ImagOn and Puretch for photo-etching and in some cases for photo-collagraphy.

In 1972 Dan Welden, in North America, discovered that he could make successful intaglio and relief prints from light-sensitive flexographic printing plates which had been developed for the commercial printing industry by companies such as Toyobo. The plates are developed with water and can be purchased under Welden's nomenclature of 'solar plate'. In Denmark Eli Ponsaing made similar explorations, publishing these in 1989, describing the process as 'photopolymer gravure' and influencing European artists.

Prints made using flexographic plates and unetched dry film photoresists have been categorized as variously photo-polymer gravures, flexographs, photogravures, solar prints, non-etch prints, and varieties of intaglio-type. As these ways of working all involve the use of plates to which a layer of light-

Rossana Martinez (US), *Temple of the Sun,* collagraph, handmade paper and thread, 180 x 231 cm (71 x 91 in.), 1996. A range of collagraph techniques were used to create a group of richly textured plates. Martinez varied the inking technique and printed onto coloured handmade papers. The prints were then trimmed and some were coloured with gouache. The artist worked on a table, using a grid as reference when hand-sewing the prints together to form the piece.

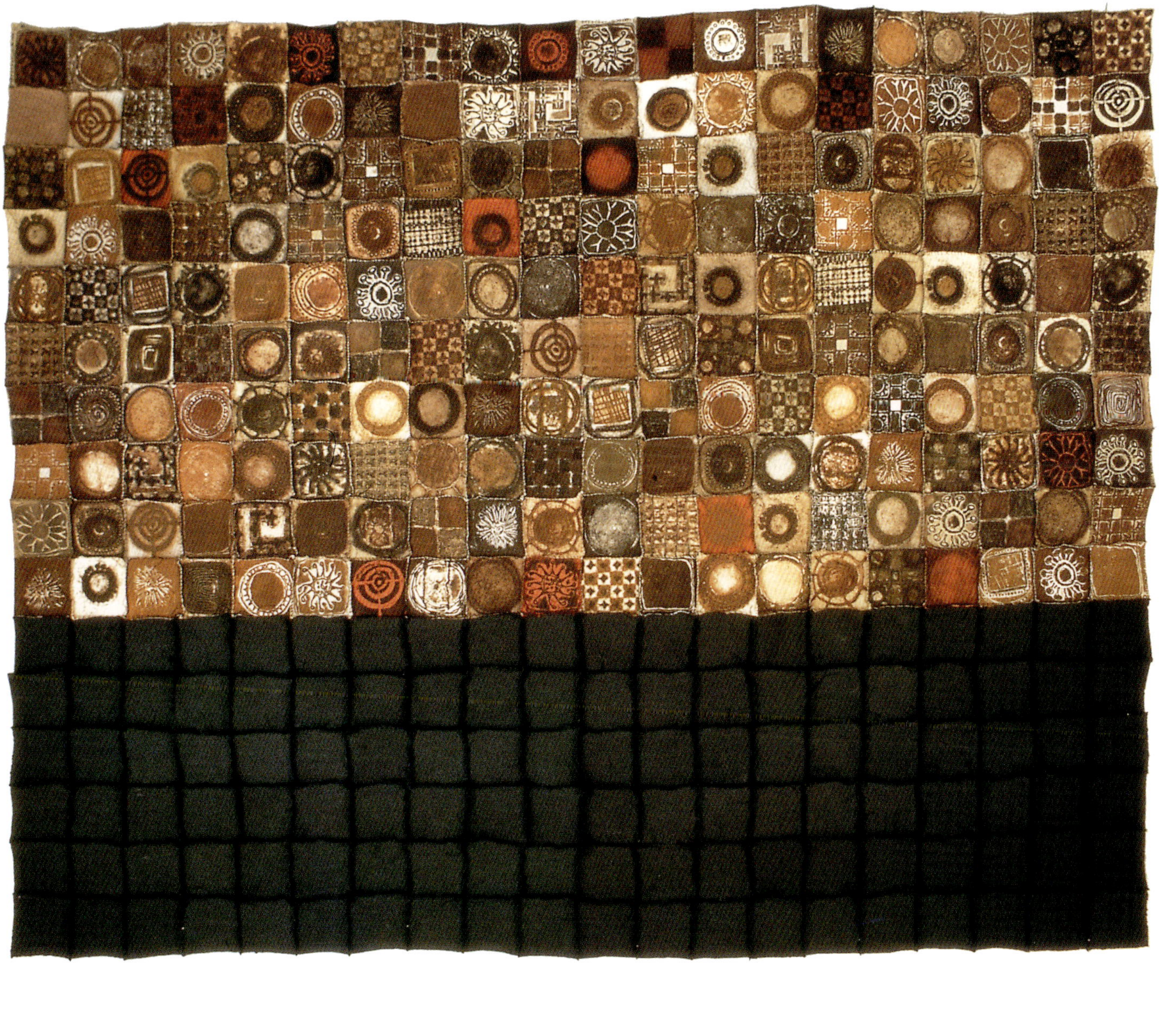

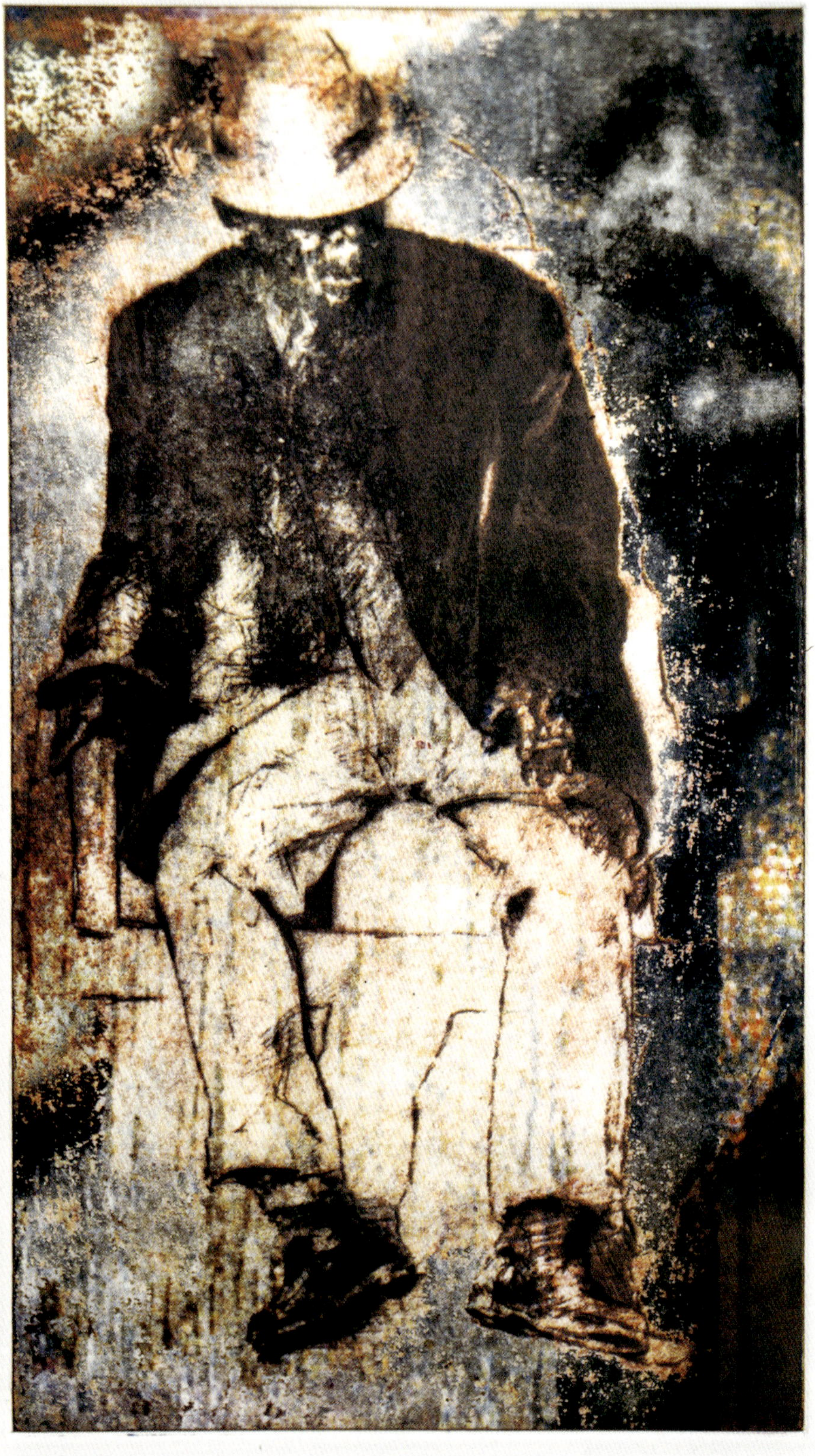

opposite Mark Zaffron (US), *2 Neighbors,* photocollagraph, 40.7 x 25.4 cm (16 x 10 in.), 2000. Four plates were laminated with Z*Acryl dry film photoresist and processed to create this edition of twelve prints (see p. 208).

sensitive film has been adhered, the method can be described as photocollagraphy and can be classified as within the family of collagraph processes.

This type of pre-prepared light-sensitive film-coated plate is placed in close contact with a positive, exposed to sunlight or ultraviolet light and developed in water. A halftone screen is first exposed to the plate if tone is required. The dry developed plate may then be inked up and printed in either the relief or intaglio manner. Some artists work into the film-coated plate using subtractive techniques such as drypoint, cutting or sanding or use additive methods such as painting on ink-holding or non-ink-holding media.

In the late 1970s printmakers found that they were able to make photopositives using a photocopier. Thin sheets of transparent acetate and PVC could also be used for making autographic positives and for assembling photographic elements or collages. In the following ten years home computers and programmes for digital image manipulation such as Adobe Photoshop became widely available. Digitally created images could be output on transparent film and used as photo positives. An early example of these new approaches was Joseph Albers's 1969 project 'Embossed Linear Constructions' at Gemini Graphics Editions Ltd. Albers and the master printer Kenneth Tyler hired an engineering programmer to translate Albers's ink drawings into digital tapes. These digital instructions were used to direct an automatic engraving mill to cut metal plates. Embossed prints were made from these shaped plates using a hydraulic forming machine.

In the 1980s information became increasingly available about the health and safety concerns related to traditional intaglio materials and working methods. Many of the materials were shown to be toxic to users and to the environment (see pp. 27–36). This had implications for the working practice of individual artists, educational establishments and fine art print studios, and in due course led to significant change.

In 1991 Nik Semenoff, working in Canada, encouraged artists to use the electro-etching process as a safer method of making intaglio plates. He also described the use of a range of mordants based on copper sulphate with different quantities of added salt (sodium chloride) and sodium bisulphate. He pointed out that by increasing the amount of salt in a recipe the etch would be more active and corrosive. Semenoff's key interest was to etch aluminium successfully as this is an inexpensive metal for students and artists to use.

In 1993–1994 Mark Zaffron, a printmaker and teacher in North America, first used DuPont's dry film photoresist Riston for fine art photo-etching. Zaffron introduced the film to Keith Howard and other printmakers as an acid resist. A number of manufacturers now produce ranges of dry film photo-resists, as well as associated laminating and developing machines.

Howard, working in Canada, discovered that the developed film on the plate could be inked up and printed without any etching taking place, and called this method 'non-etch intaglio-type'. The methodology (apart from the lamination) is similar to Dan Welden's solar plate technique.

At the same time artists were searching out non-toxic and non-flammable materials which would act as acid resists and replace traditional aquatint, stop-out, grounds and their solvents. They discovered that some household acrylic floor finishes could be flow-coated onto plates, dried and used as a hard ground. Graphic Chemical & Ink Company water-soluble block-printing inks rolled out on copper plates functioned as replacement soft ground or hard ground. Howard discovered that Speedball screenprinting filler could be used as an acid resist for stopping out on copper and also sprayed through a powered spray gun to create an aquatint. The diluted filler (with water 1:7) painted onto the plate could be dried and etched to generate unusual washes which resemble watercolour or lithographic effects.

Both Zaffron and Howard suggested that ferric chloride should be used in place of nitric acid, hydrochloric acid and Dutch mordant, and many studios have followed this lead. They also advocated the use of a vertical tank to hold the mordant. This way of etching allows the sediment to fall from the plate surface and is similar to an etching system used for circuit-board manufacture. Initially the printmakers involved in these techniques suggested removing the new resists with potassium hydroxide, caustic soda or a 50% solution of ammonia in water. Later these hazardous chemicals were replaced with the safer alternative of sodium carbonate (a mild alkali) diluted in water. Vegetable oils (rather than white spirit or turpentine) were used to remove traditional intaglio inks.

In 1995 Zaffron launched Z*Acryl products for safer intaglio printmaking on all metals. This is a coherent system of acid-resistant materials classified as safe to use. The resists may be removed from the plate with sodium carbonate diluted in water with no release of fumes. Zaffron has also developed vertical etching tanks, registration devices and other intaglio equipment.

Howard formed collaborations with a number of manufacturers, including DuPont, Golden Paints and the Badger Airbrush Company. He has also been involved in the production of equipment such as a portable UV exposure unit, an etching-press felt-protector and aquatint dot screens.

In 1996 Ad Stijnman, in the Netherlands, published his idea that the use of vegetable cleaning agent (VCA) would solve most of the problems of hazardous fumes in the etching studio. VCA refers to the chemical compounds – fatty acid esters – which are made from a vegetable oil and an alcohol. VCAs are almost non-volatile but gloves must be worn as they will defat the skin. They are replacing white spirit as industrial cleaners, and brand names include Avisol VCA, Bio-Solv, Rapid Wash E-404 and Vegeol. Some artists have started to use VCAs in their etching studios to remove traditional grounds, stop-outs and aquatints. However, the use of VCAs does not overcome the problem that these acid-resistant materials contain flammable and toxic ingredients. The processes of applying traditional resists to plates release fumes which require extraction.

In 1997 Friedhard Kiekeben published an article about Edinburgh Etch, the mordant he had developed at Edinburgh Printmakers Workshop in Scotland. This etchant consists of ferric chloride with the addition of a small proportion of citric acid. The citric in the solution acts in a similar way to the traditional addition of hydrochloric acid to ferric chloride, inhibiting the production of sediment and allowing copper plates to be etched face-up in a horizontal bath, but citric acid is a safer choice to work with than hydrochloric acid. In 2003 Kiekeben published information about his two new mordants for etching zinc and steel. The steel mordant, saline ferric etch, is formulated from ferric chloride solution with a small proportion of salt (sodium chloride). The zinc mordant, saline sulphate etch, consists of approximately equal quantities of copper sulphate and salt (75 gms of copper sulphate + 50–75 gms of sodium chloride) dissolved in one litre of water. For aluminium he recommended a saline sulphate etch consisting of 70 gms copper sulphate + 140 gms of sodium chloride.

In 1998 Cedric Green, based in France, published his methods of Galv-Etch (an electrolytic etching process). Later he developed his mordant Bordeaux Etch, which can be used to etch aluminium, zinc and steel. He recommended etching zinc in a concentrated solution of copper sulphate (250 gms to one litre of water). For etching steel and aluminium he recommended that salt (sodium chloride) should be mixed with the copper sulphate in equal measures (250 gms copper sulphate + 250 gms salt to one litre of water).

Green has also developed a system of resists which can be used in conjunction with VCA. He uses a linseed oil-based ink as a hard and soft ground and for tonal effects (in the form of 'fractals') in place of aquatint. He recommends that these resists are cleaned off with VCA or ethanol (95% ethyl alcohol) and advises printmakers to observe safe handling of these cleaning materials.

right Robert Adam (UK), *Thames*, etching, 56 x 76 cm (22 x 30 in.), 1986. A positive was painted and exposed to a screen, and this image was screenprinted onto an etching plate with sugar solution. The plate holding the sugar image was coated with an acid resist. Water was then used to dissolve and lift the screenprinted image. The exposed metal was aquatinted and the plate was etched.

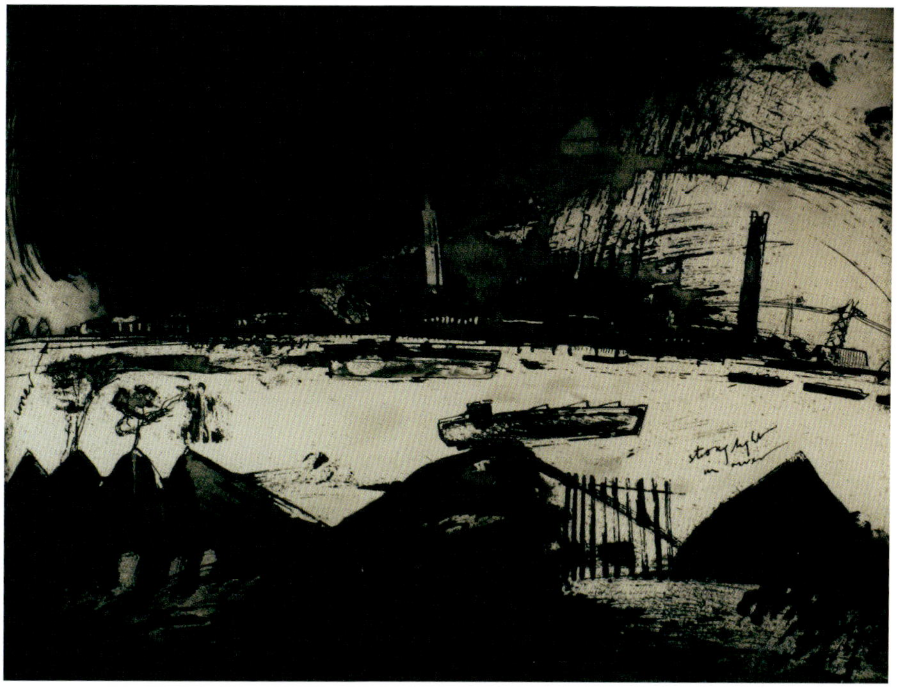

overleaf Werner Schmidt (Germany/Switzerland), *Rosy*, etching, 41.5 x 24 cm (16⅜ x 9½ in.), co-published at Graal Press, 2005. A collection of conté sketches were photocopied and arranged to create a positive. This was used to generate a photo-etching. Lascaux plate-backing, stop-out and aquatint resists were then employed. After the plate was stripped and polished it was printed with Akua inks.

Back in 1987 the present authors, Robert Adam and Carol Robertson, were seeking a means of avoiding the use of the toxic KPR and developed a method of photo-etching which involved screenprinting a positive image onto an etching plate. The printed sugar-lift image was then coated with a resist and later 'lifted'. They also employed the widely used technique of screenprinting a solvent-based resist onto an etching plate (this image was in a negative form). In 1990 they found that water-based acrylic screenprinting mixtures could be printed onto etching plates and used as effective acid resists. They employed this acrylic screenprinted resist when any photo-etching was required at Edinburgh Printmakers Workshop (EPW), where Adam had become director and Robertson was working in the studio. In 1994 Adam and Robertson, together with staff members and workshop artists Alfons Bytautas and Rebecca Mayo, were responsible for changing over the etching department to Howard's 'non-toxic' system, making the workshop the first major open-access and editioning studio to embrace these techniques.

The term 'non-toxic printmaking' was replaced with 'acrylic-resist etching' (ARE) because it was considered misleading to classify chemicals such as ferric chloride as non-toxic, and the main innovations concerned the replacement of solvent-based acid-resistant materials with acrylic or photopolymer acid-resistant materials. Furthermore it was recognized that the nomenclature of acid-resistant materials had evolved over the centuries and had a number of different roots, such as the description of materials (e.g. asphaltum, straw hat varnish), the appearance of a finished print (aquatint), the preparation of a base for oil or watercolour painting (ground) or a practical function of the process (e.g. stop-out varnish, rebiting varnish). The use of the term 'resist' (which has been standard terminology in the printed circuit-board industry worldwide since the 1970s) clearly describes the function of these materials and reveals their connection to each other (e.g. hard resist, stop-out resist, wash resist).

A series of ARE educational courses was initiated at EPW in March 1996 and led by Adam, Bytautas, Robertson, Karen

Guthrie and Kiekeben. These courses were attended by printmaking specialists from all over the world, including Henrik Bøegh, who later established the Grasfisk Eksperimentarium in Copenhagen, and Susan Groce, who introduced these methods to her department at the University of Maine.

In 1998 Adam and Robertson set up Graal Press and began a concentrated research programme into acrylic-resist etching, other intaglio processes and water-based screenprinting. A collaboration with the Swiss company Lascaux was initiated, and has resulted in the manufacture of a complete range of acrylic resists and a group of materials for generating marks on positives for light-sensitive printmaking processes.

The first commercially available water-based intaglio inks were formulated in North America by Susan Rostow and William Jung in the 1990s and are manufactured by their company Rostow & Jung Water-based Printshop and Inks Inc. These are sold as Akua-Intaglio and can be cleaned up with soapy water. In 2003 Caligo Safe Wash etching inks were launched in the UK. These are oil-based intaglio inks which do not contain any toxic driers. They are suitable for printing any type of plate and are also cleaned up with soapy water.

Intaglio methods in all their forms are used by artists around the world: as framed works, illustrations, book covers, ex libris plates, components in sculpture or painting, text pieces, ceramics, performances, installations, murals and site-specific works. There are many print studios, educational establishments, collections, societies, print galleries and specialist intaglio competitions, some of which are dedicated to particular media. Some artists choose a speciality, such as engraving, mezzotinting or collagraphy. Others make intaglio work as part of their general art practice and as a way of disseminating their ideas to a wider audience. Traditional and new materials are used for plates, resists and mordants; ancient and modern ink recipes are employed to print onto etching papers and other substrates such as tinfoil, fabric and plaster. The creative possibilities are endless and every effect can now be achieved in a way that is healthier, more environmentally friendly and safer for all.

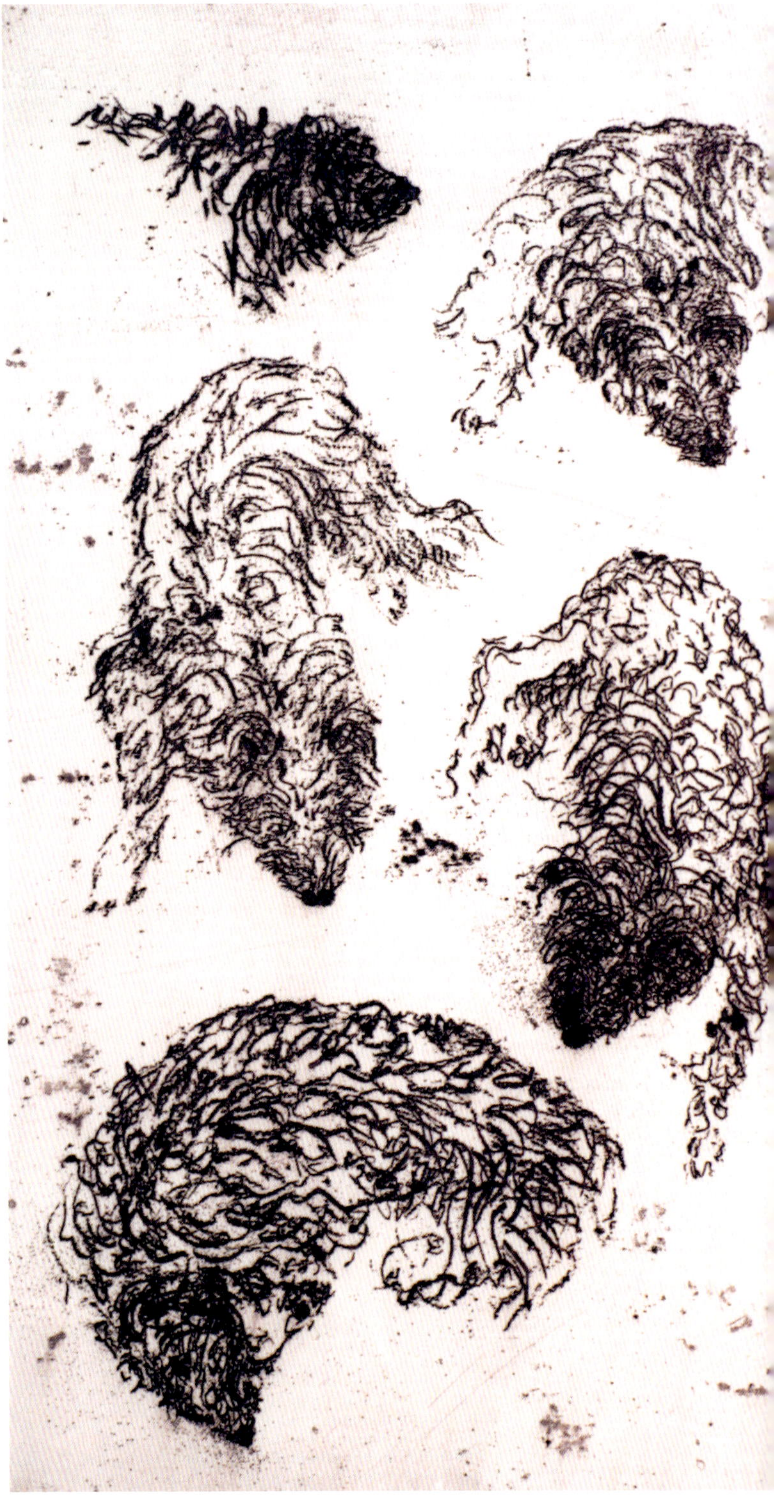

THE MOVE TOWARDS SAFER WORKING METHODS

TRADITIONAL INTAGLIO TECHNIQUES AND THEIR IMPLICATIONS FOR HEALTH, SAFETY AND THE ENVIRONMENT

PLATES AND TRADITIONAL PLATE PREPARATION METHODS

Steel, copper, brass and zinc are the traditional metals used for intaglio plates and these are still used today. Their characteristics and the preliminary processes of cutting, filing, cleaning, de-oxidizing, graining or polishing, together with associated hazards, have not changed a great deal and are described fully in 'Preparing the Plate' (pp. 66–80). The preparation and hazards of making plates from substrates such as wood, medium-density fibreboard (MDF), card, plastics and metals such as lead and aluminium are also described in the above chapter.

Traditionally toxic chemicals such as ammonia, hydrochloric acid, methylated spirits or acetic acid are used to degrease plates before the application of acid resists and prior to etching. Ammonia diluted in water (ammonium hydroxide or aqua ammonia), even in low concentrations, is corrosive and irritating to the skin, eyes and lungs, and can cause severe burns. The vapours are toxic so local ventilation must be used when ammonia is used to degrease plates: chronic irritation may result if ammonia is used regularly. If ammonia and bleach are mixed, a dangerous chloramine gas is released.

Copper is a very hydrophobic metal and is difficult to degrease with ammonia and whiting. Traditionally hydrochloric acid was mixed with salt (sodium chloride) and used as a degreaser for copper plates. Hydrochloric acid is an extremely dangerous and corrosive substance (see p. 153).

Methylated spirits is a toxic and highly flammable solvent: local extraction is necessary and waste must be disposed of according to local bye-laws. It contains a mixture of ethyl alcohol (95%), methyl alcohol (5%) and dye. It has a narcotic effect, can cause headaches, is an irritant and is easily absorbed through the skin. Methyl alcohol (methanol or wood spirit) is generated by the destructive distillation of wood, or by a synthetic process which involves reacting carbon monoxide with hydrogen gas. It is poisonous and is added to prevent methylated spirits being drunk as a cheap alcohol. Drinking methyl alcohol causes blindness, insanity and possible death.

Grease was also traditionally removed with a 30% aqueous solution of acetic acid from the lines drawn in waxy resists prior to etching. Synonyms for acetic acid are ethanoic acid, glacial acetic acid and 'vinegar'. Pure acetic acid is strongly corrosive and can cause serious burns. Full protective clothing, eye protection and an appropriate respirator must be worn when handling this. The Material Safety Data Sheet states that acetic acid should not be allowed to come into contact with strong oxidizers such as nitric acid. Household vinegar has also been used traditionally to remove grease and oxidization from plates and is a much safer alternative. It is manufactured from a dilution of acetic acid, from wine or from the fermentation of grains.

TRADITIONAL RESISTS, THEIR SOLVENTS AND ETCHING THE PLATE

In the early days of etching artists experimented with the materials around them in a search for acid-resistant substances. It was important that these would adhere well to the surface of the plate and could be drawn into accurately with etching tools. They found that a number of substances were

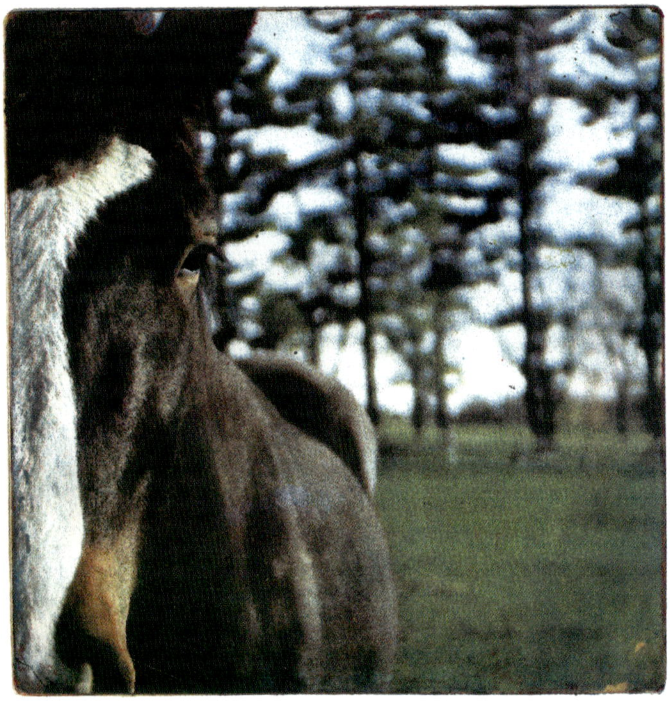

acid-resistant to varying degrees: bitumen for waterproofing boats; resins used for embalming, for incense or for caulking ships' decks; varnish for musical instruments; beeswax for candlemaking or casting; tallow for burning in lamps; Japan wax used as a pomade for sumo wrestlers; varnish for painters; linseed oil; olive oil; lard; and a shellac varnish used for sealing sailors' straw hats.

Over the years hard ground, soft ground, stop-out and alcohol varnish recipes were made from different combinations of these materials. Solvents such as chloroform, ether, benzene (benzol), benzine, naphtha, varnolene, toluene (toluol), petrol kerosene, turpentine, ketone thinners, turpentine substitute, methylated spirits, acetone or xylene were added to the recipes. Heat was used to combine the ingredients. These solvents were also needed to remove the resists from brushes, equipment and plates.

Bitumens are an important constituent of resists and are impure mixtures of hydrocarbons. They include naturally occurring asphaltum (carabe, bitumen of Judea, Gilsonite) which bubbles up through the earth and hardens; asphalt produced from the distillation of petroleum; and tars which are formed by the destructive distillation of organic matter such as pine trees or coal. Finely powdered bitumen can be used as an aquatint. Asphaltum and bitumens are soluble in turpentine and can be mixed with various gums to make grounds and stop-outs. Research has shown that thermal cracking of complex hydrocarbons produces polynuclear aromatic hydrocarbons, some of which are carcinogenic and mutagenic. Asphaltum is not classified as a carcinogen but there is evidence that at high temperatures its complex hydrocarbon structure may alter and produce carcinogenic substances.

Stop-out varnishes are liquid mixtures and are applied by brush. They generally contain combinations of some of the following ingredients: bitumens, rosin (colophony), powdered asphaltum, varnolene, turpentine, quick-drying petroleum, Japan wax, beeswax, burgundy pitch, ketone thinner and pitch resin. Straw hat varnish, plate-backing varnish and other alcohol varnishes often contain resins, shellac, black dyes and methylated spirits. Brunswick black or Japan lacquer contains bitumen, naphtha and other fast-drying solvents.

In due course the reliable recipes were manufactured commercially and these products are still available today. There are several traditional hard ground recipes: one consists of burgundy pitch, Japan wax, beeswax and bitumen. Another hard ground contains beeswax, powdered asphaltum, powdered rosin and xylene. Soft ground is a variant of these recipes with added tallow, vaseline or axle grease.

Another main source for acid-resistant materials was resin from trees and plants. Rubber solution (which is also gathered from trees) was sometimes included in recipes. Resins such as gum mastic, frankincense, myrrh, copal and rosin were used in recipes for grounds and stop-out varnishes. Rosin is used to create aquatints and is soluble in methylated spirits. It is a sensitizer which causes skin irritation (dermatitis) and has been linked to asthma. The powdered forms of these materials used for aquatint are particularly dangerous as the dust can be breathed into the lungs, and for this reason a particulate respirator must be worn. Local exhaust ventilation is often impractical as the air flow may displace the delicate layer of powder. Applying the resists inevitably results in the dispersal of loose powder around the immediate working area. Cleaning up this hazardous dust from studio surfaces, the floor, tools, aprons, clothing and gloves presents a health and safety problem. Sweeping agitates the dust; the use of a vacuum cleaner fitted with a special High Efficiency Particulate Air (HEPA) filter is often recommended but other safety advisors are concerned about risks of fire and dust explosion. This is because airborne rosin (or bitumen) dust is potentially explosive and the possibility of an accident in the studio is increased by the use of a naked flame to melt the rosin onto the plates. Aquatint boxes must be well maintained to avoid any risks of sparking from unlubricated bearings in the paddle mechanism or from static electricity.

During the heating process rosin, bitumen and plate-backing varnishes may release toxic vapours into the studio and may possibly ignite. Local exhaust ventilation is essential and personal respiratory protection should also be worn. (As an indication of the hazard associated with colophony fumes, in the electronics industry the use of traditional soldering flux has been linked to serious illness in the workforce. Consequently industrial working practice has changed and rosin-free flux is now used.)

When the resins are processed by distillation, turpentine and tars (burgundy pitch and black pitch) are produced. The addition of these pitches helps to make hard and soft grounds darker in colour but generally the addition of pigments or dyes tends to weaken resists, causing foul bite. In the 1800s a white lead coating was sometimes used by etchers to colour the hard ground. Shellac and methylated spirit varnishes (not designed for drawing through) were coloured with methyl violet dye.

In the twentieth century, in the search for durable, reliable and easily removed resists, artists replaced unreliable plate-backing varnishes with adhesive plastic films (see p. 101). They also painted and sprayed enamel and cellulose paints onto the plate to act as stop-out resist, plate-backing resist and aquatint. These resists require the use of acetone, cellulose thinners or powerful paint strippers to dilute and remove them. The fumes from the paints and their solvents are irritants and depress the central nervous system.

Methylated spirits (the hazards are described on p. 27) is sometimes mixed with rosin to make a liquid aquatint and is used to dissolve rosin from the plate before printing. Alcohol varnishes (shellac, straw hat) also contain the solvent and it is used to remove these resists from the plate.

Protective gloves are required when grounds and stop-outs are applied to the plate and when the coated plate is being worked on. These will guard against the sensitization and dermatitis which may result from repeated or prolonged skin contact. Some safety officials also state that eye protection should be worn.

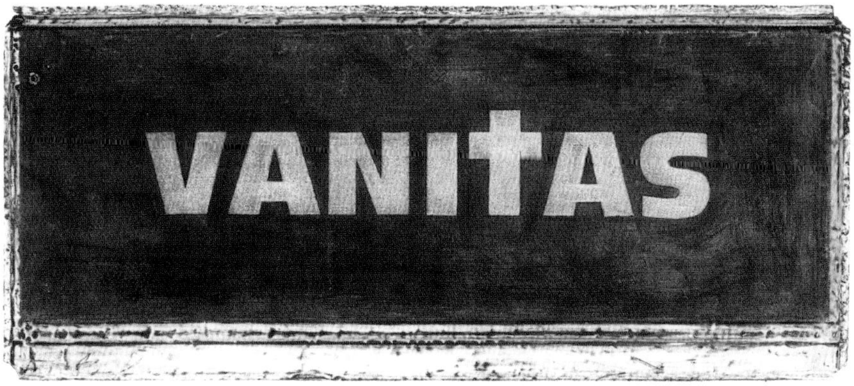

opposite The earliest light-sensitive plates were made using Bitumen of Judea. Ryan Laurey (US) employed the modern light-sensitive material ImagOn to create his four-colour intaglio print, *Horse*.

left Blazej Baláz (Slovakia) worked directly on tin with a burin and mezzotint rocker to create this image, *Tin Print*, 13.9 x 32.4 cm (5½ x 12⅝ in.), 1995.

The first light-sensitive resist consisted of a very thin coating of bitumen of Judea in a solution of anhydrous benzene and ether. The later process of photogravure involved the use of carbon tissue (paper, gelatin and pigment) and potassium bichromate. The more recent product KPR (Kodak Photo Resist) contains ethylene glycol monomethyl ether acetate and its developer consists of xylene ethylene glycol monomethyl ether acetate.

The process of photogravure requires the use of potassium bichromate (synonymous with potassium dichromate), which is a known carcinogen. Inhalation of this corrosive chemical is extremely destructive to tissues of the mucous membranes and upper respiratory tract. Typical symptoms are sore throat, coughing, shortness of breath and laboured breathing. Damage may include ulceration and perforation of the nasal septum. Skin contact is also dangerous and can cause irritation, sensitization, redness, pain and severe burns. Contact with broken skin may cause chrome sores and absorption, which may in turn result in systemic poisoning, affecting liver and kidney functions. Potassium bichromate is also extremely damaging to eyes and can cause blurred vision, redness, pain, severe tissue burns, corneal injury or blindness. Ammonium dichromate is sometimes used in photogravure and is considered to be even more toxic. They are both highly flammable and strong oxidizers.

KPR and its developer contain ethylene glycol monomethyl ether acetate which is highly toxic, mutagenic and easily absorbed through the skin. It is classified as a reproductive toxicant which means that exposure can cause alterations in male or female sexual behaviour, decreases in fertility or loss of the foetus during pregnancy. It is also categorized as a developmental toxicant: exposure can harm the developing child resulting in birth defects, low birth weight, biological dysfunctions or later psychological or behavioural problems.

Organic solvents used to make or dissolve grounds and many stop-out varnishes are distilled from bitumen or from petroleum (also a naturally occurring mineral). When petroleum is separated by distillation petrol, benzene, naphtha and kerosene are produced.

Benzene (benzol, benzin) is a known human carcinogen, causing leukaemia and damaging bone marrow. Exposure can lead to anaemia and can weaken the immune system. Primary symptoms include headaches, dizziness, rapid heart rate, drowsiness, tremors, confusion and – in women – irregular menstrual periods. Benzine is a different chemical: it is less toxic than benzene but is nevertheless an irritant and can damage the nervous system.

Toluene and xylene are similar to benzene but not so toxic. They are irritating to the skin, mucous membrane and respiratory tract, are absorbed through the skin and travel through the bloodstream to damage the kidney and liver. Xylene has anaesthetic properties and its vapours are highly explosive.

Turpentine (like rosin) is a product from the distillation of resin from pine trees. It is a volatile flammable mixture of hydrocarbon isomers and has a characteristic odour. Turpentine is an irritant of the skin, eyes, mucous membrane and upper respiratory tract. Exposure may cause shortness of breath, confusion, headaches, dizziness, nausea, dermatitis, eczema or sensitization of the skin. Inhalation of its vapour may also affect the central nervous system and the gastro-intestinal and urinary tracts. A principal component of turpentine is terpenes, and it is believed that exposure to this for longer than five years may increase the risk of developing lung cancer. When turpentine is heated it emits toxic fumes.

Acetone (ketone thinners) is highly inflammable and fume extraction is required. It can produce a narcotic effect and causes lightheadedness, headaches, increased pulse rate and irritation to skin, throat, lungs, nose and eyes.

Isopropyl alcohol is readily absorbed through the skin, and prolonged contact causes eczema and sensitivity. It is an irritant of the eyes and mucous membranes. The toxic solvent methylated spirits is discussed on p. 27.

Solvents that were used in the earliest resist recipes such as ether and chloroform are toxic. Chloroform becomes unstable when it is exposed to air, light or heat and breaks down to form hydrochloric acid, phosgene and chlorine.

The term naphtha (or naptha) is used to describe volatile distillates of petroleum or coal tar. Coal-tar naphtha may contain benzene and toluene. Solvent naphtha is made when benzene is removed from coal-tar naphtha by distillation and contains toluene and xylene. Petroleum naphtha is a grade of petroleum solvent, sometimes labelled turpentine substitute, white spirit, Stoddard solvent, varnolene or VM & P (Varnish Makers' and Painters') naphtha. These solvents are all flammable and can cause central nervous system symptoms such as fatigue, headache and dizziness. Their low viscosity and low surface tension mean that solvent-soaked rags and containers without lids allow large quantities of the solvent to evaporate into the studio atmosphere. Another concern is the generation of fumes from any heated printing ink, grounds or stop-out varnish left on the surface of the hotplates. Fumes are insidious in their nature and it is difficult for all studio users to protect themselves fully.

Working in these studio conditions for a day can lead to a sensation of 'drunkenness'. Tests on painters have shown that their balance, reaction time, perceptual speed and short-term memory can be affected. Epidemiological studies involving painters with long-term exposure to white spirit have shown an increased incidence of memory and concentration impairment, fatigue, irritability, dizziness, headache, anxiety and apathy. Evidence has also been found of increased lung and bladder cancer risks.

Solvent-induced brain damage is now recognized as an occupational disease and recent research concerning the use of solvents in the workplace and home is highlighting possible links with multiple sclerosis, dementia, Parkinson's disease, deafness and depression. Governments around the world are bringing in new legislation to reduce usage of harmful solvents.

The health, safety and environmental considerations concerning mordants are discussed in 'Etching the Plate' (pp. 151–161).

TRADITIONAL COLLAGRAPHIC PLATE-MAKING

Some of the materials which have been used to build up collagraph plates are toxic and some of the processes used are hazardous. Many of these materials have similar constituents and solvents to the traditional etching resists (see pp. 27–29).

Shellac flakes, though in themselves non-toxic, have to be dissolved in an alcohol such as methylated spirits to make a varnish. Lacquers used as sealants and their thinners often contain xylene, toluene or other solvents which should be avoided.

Epoxy resins and their amine hardeners are toxic, and techniques including melting materials or dissolving celluloid in acetone should be avoided.

Welding, soldering and brazing have been used to integrate metal elements onto plates. These processes have to be learned and safe metalworking practice should be followed.

TRADITIONAL INKS AND THEIR SOLVENTS

Traditional inks are still used in contemporary intaglio practice. There are hazards related to handling pigment powders and the absorption of toxic pigments from inks into the body through cuts and abrasions (see 'Inks and Additives', pp. 210–213).

Compounds of toxic metals such as lead, manganese and cobalt have been mixed with oils, resins and solvents to create siccatives or driers. These additives have been added to some oil-based inks to speed the drying time. Health studies suggest that driers containing cobalt, aluminium, petroleum distillates, 2-ethylhexanoic acid, 1,10-phenathroline and ethoxylated alcohols C12-C14 should be avoided.

Anti-skinning aerosols and sprays are used to prevent a skin forming in tins of oil-based intaglio inks. They often contain harmful solvents such as petroleum distillates, methyl ethyl ketoxime, hydroquinone and acetone oxime. These highly flammable substances are made even more dangerous as they are used in the form of a spray which can easily be inhaled.

Historically vegetable oils were used for cleaning up intaglio ink from plates (see pp. 215–216) but with the growth of the petroleum industry these were replaced by solvents.

SOURCING INFORMATION ABOUT CHEMICALS AND THEIR CORRECT USE

In most countries it is a legal requirement that manufacturers should provide product users with a Material Safety Data Sheet. An MSDS should be obtained and kept on file for each chemical used (or stored) in a studio so that any necessary precautionary or legal measures can be followed by the user. The MSDS provides important practical information about the chemical's routes of entry to the human body, necessary protective clothing and equipment, procedures for safe handling and storage, spillage control, fire-fighting and adverse chemical reactions. It will specify correct disposal methods, but local regulations must also be checked.

There are laws relating to the transportation, storage, handling and disposal of chemicals which are classed as hazardous. It is the responsibility of the person in charge of a workshop, studio or department to establish what the legal requirements concerning hazardous materials are, and to comply with them.

Health and safety officials and fire officers are often empowered to make random visits to workplaces. They will check machinery, storage of chemicals and other materials, safety equipment, fire extinguishers, signage and chemical labelling. Studio containers must be clearly labelled identifying their contents and indicating any hazards by showing a symbol or specifying whether a data sheet is necessary. Failing to comply with legislation can lead to accidents, heavy penalties and, increasingly, litigation.

In countries or states which operate a right-to-know policy, students, staff and neighbours of the organization (or premises) have to be provided with access to full information about any hazardous chemicals in use. In the UK it is a legal stipulation that MSDSs relating to hazardous substances are held for reference on the premises. The practical reason for this is that in the case of an accident, spillage or fire it is possible to refer rapidly to a data sheet for accurate guidance concerning the course of action. It is important to make sure the document is up to date, as ingredients and regulations change.

Sometimes this chemical health and safety information can be time-consuming and difficult to obtain. Companies are often happy to provide product literature but less than willing to provide an actual MSDS, and it has to be noted that product information sheets can on occasion masquerade as MSDSs but fail to provide crucial chemical information. Some MSDSs give the minimum information – or put a positive spin on the product information – but in these cases the chemical name, synonym or chemical number can be used to source the chemical's own MSDS from the internet. This MSDS may yield more objective information.

When searching for information on a specific chemical it is important to use the correct and complete chemical name, although typing in an accurate synonym or a brand name may provide results. It is easy, however, to make a mistake by typing in an inaccurate or incomplete synonym which can be misleading. For instance, 'magnesium' is explosive, whereas 'magnesium carbonate' is regularly used as an ink additive.

Useful guidance on reading and understanding MSDSs is available from government bodies. A wealth of up-to-date information about chemicals and health and safety issues can be obtained on the internet. Key words to use in a web search are 'etching', 'acids', 'colophony', 'organic solvent', 'cobalt driers', 'MSDS', 'printer health + safety', 'dust explosion', 'HSE' (Health and Safety Executive), 'GPMU' (Graphical, Paper and Media Union), 'COSHH' (Control of Substances Hazardous to Health) and 'environment + [name of chemical]'.

Government agencies and local authorities publish printed information concerning health and safety and environmental issues. For instance, booklets and courses are available, covering topics including risk assessment (this is a required procedure concerning any activity, whether teaching or non-teaching, which may expose employees, students or any other person to any substance that is hazardous to health). A directive from the European Community has also resulted in the emergence of the CHIP 2000 regulations – The Chemicals (Hazard Information and Packaging for Supply) [Amendment] Regulations 2000. This legislation aims to provide a high standard of protection for people and the environment from the harmful effects of chemicals.

HOW CHEMICALS ENTER THE BODY

The routes of entry by which chemicals find their way into the body are through ingestion, eye and skin contact, and inhalation. Brief exposure to toxic materials can be seriously harmful to high-risk groups (see below).

INGESTION

Ingestion is when chemicals enter the body by swallowing. Food should not be stored in the studio as it can absorb toxins from the air. Swallowing contaminated food will introduce these toxins to the digestive system and bloodstream. The same applies to beverages. Hand-washing before eating or smoking is important, as chemicals can be transferred to the lips by food or cigarettes. Studios and workshops should have a separate kitchen and eating and smoking area, and good hygiene is important. Substances can also enter the stomach through indirect means. For instance, coughing pushes material out of the lungs, allowing it to be swallowed and to come into contact with the stomach and other internal organs.

EYE AND SKIN CONTACT

Eye protection, gloves and protective clothing can guard the user from obvious physical contact with chemicals. Goggles or visors should be worn when working with corrosive or irritant substances (mordants, cleaning chemicals and degreasers) because of the risk of splashes. Solvent and corrosive vapours may produce eye irritation, which can lead to burning, painful and watering eyes. Contact lens wearers should take particular care.

Skin is absorbent: examples of its permeable nature are the use of essential oils in aromatherapy massage, and nicotine patches which act as a substitute for smoking. In the same way some harmful chemicals can pass through the skin into the body. Many chemicals will gain access to the bloodstream

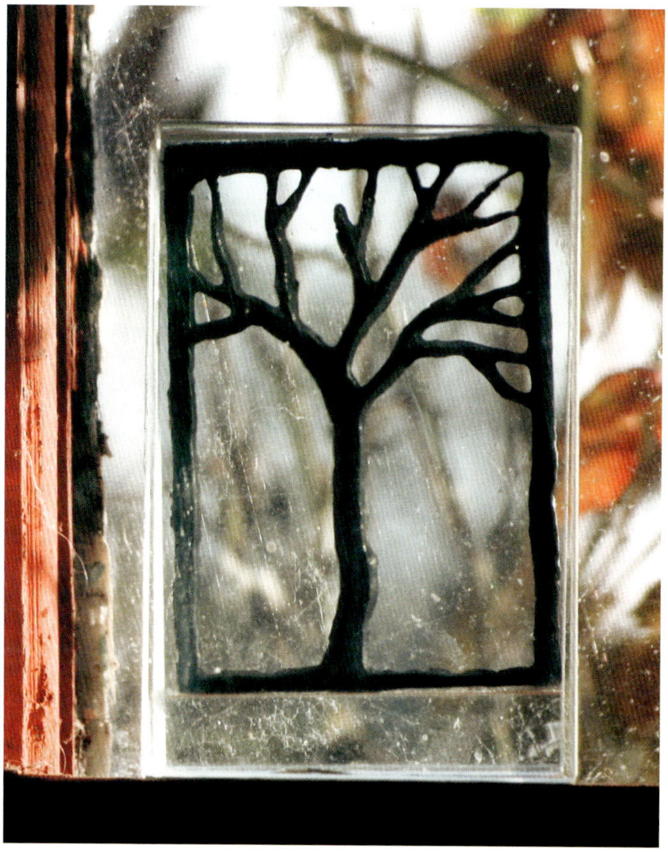

Carol Robertson (UK), *If the Ash is out before the Oak*, etched plate and glass, 9 x 6.4 cm (3½ x 2½ in.), 2006. Lascaux resists were used to protect this zinc plate when it was etched in a copper sulphate solution.

through broken skin, tiny cuts, scratches or rashes. Solvents can break down the skin's natural protective oils and fats, causing dermatitis and allowing toxins to be absorbed into the bloodstream. It is important to wear the appropriate type of glove as some are permeable to particular substances, and what may seem like perspiration can in fact be chemicals migrating through the material onto the skin. Nitrile gloves should be used when working with many solvents and chemicals. Barrier creams can be used on hands and arms to protect against the less dangerous materials such as printing inks.

INHALATION

Chemicals, traditional resists and solvents often release chemicals into the air which are toxic. Many of these chemicals are classified as volatile organic compounds (VOCs) and hazardous air pollutants (HAPs). The insidious nature of VOCs and HAPs makes their toxicity difficult to manage. A serious danger lies in inhaling fumes, and protective breathing equipment should be worn by all studio users when these fumes are present. However, the appropriate protective breathing masks have a limited life and are expensive, bulky and uncomfortable.

In an attempt to alleviate this problem, extraction systems are used to remove toxic fumes from print studios. The fumes are often heavier than air and the way they flow is affected by draughts, heating systems and the movement of people within the space. As a result, designing an efficient extraction system requires specialized knowledge, and the costs associated with installation and operation tend to be high. The use of limited-life filters on outlets is also expensive. These extraction systems may not comply with changing environmental legislation if they are merely redirecting the toxic fumes to another location where they may harm others who are not aware that they are being exposed to hazardous chemicals. Etchers often become unaware of the fumes in a studio, but visiting artists may notice them immediately and can be affected by a short visit.

HIGH-RISK GROUPS

- Pregnant and breastfeeding women are at particular risk as chemicals and other factors are able to cross the placental barrier and possibly cause damage and birth defects. The most sensitive time for chemical interference with normal development is from the eighteenth to the sixtieth day after conception. Hazardous chemicals include powdered cadmium and copper. Noise, vibration, strenuous activity and other stresses can be hazardous. The amount necessary to damage a foetus or embryo is much smaller than that which can injure an adult. Chemicals can also affect the respiratory and circulatory systems and some of these, especially heavy metals, can be found in a woman's milk several hours after exposure and can affect the infant.
- Children are more susceptible to the effects of hazardous chemicals than adults. They can work safely with acrylic resists, acrylic collagraphic media and water-based inks. Any etching, stripping and printing should be undertaken or supervised by an adult.
- Individuals on medications are also at a greater risk. Medical advice should be sought to ensure that any medication will not interact with materials used in intaglio processes to cause illness.
- The physically disabled, the elderly and those with allergies, sensitized conditions and illnesses are also within the high-risk group.
- Contact lens wearers should take particular care concerning eye protection.
- Smokers and heavy drinkers are at a higher risk than others of damage to their lungs and liver respectively. Nicotine and alcohol mixed with toxic chemicals in art materials can cause synergistic reactions.

A COMPLETE SAFER INTAGLIO SYSTEM

The system described in this book has a strong traditional basis and offers a wide range of approaches to intaglio image-making which can be explored freely. These ways of working are suitable for educational purposes, professional publishing and fine art practice. They are cost-effective, straightforward and logical to learn. Depending on the facilities available and the needs of individuals or groups, a choice may be made about whether to use direct, etching or collagraphic methods, or combinations of these.

In the various direct methods (see p. 81), the risks are related to handling the metal plates; the use of sharp tools such as drypoints and burins; the dust generated when working the plate; working with an abrasive spray gun within a special sandblasting unit; using a light-sensitive photopolymer mask; and inking up and the use of the etching press.

The etching process shares many of the same risks as the direct techniques. The materials used in the acrylic-resist etching process – from degreasing to cleaning up – are the safest and most environmentally friendly that are currently available. Plates are grained with pumice and degreased using a new generation of safer degreasers. Water-based acrylic resists can be used to explore a wide range of creative methods such as soft and hard drawn marks, textures, collage effects, lifted marks, expressive paint strokes, washes, aquatint and other tonal techniques. Digital, photographic, photocopied and autographic positives may be used in conjunction with modern light-sensitive polymer resists to bring an even greater range of marks to etching. Artist's painting and drawing materials or specially designed tusches can be used on different types of substrate or on existing positives. The light-sensitive coated plates (and the positive) are exposed to ultraviolet light in an enclosed UV exposure unit or to sunlight. The exposed plate is developed with a mild alkaline solution. The plates (with their resist) may be bitten in mordants which do not release toxic fumes and are the least hazardous etchants available. After the etching process, the resists are removed from the plate with cleaning solutions which are classified as safe to use in the home.

Collagraphy is considered to be the safest intaglio method, and can be used by high-risk groups and in studios where the use of corrosive substances is prohibited. Collagraphic materials and techniques may be used on any type of intaglio plate. Water-soluble collagraphic media include gesso, painting aids, painting mediums, texture gels, acrylic varnishes, some types of acrylic resist, screenfillers, polyfiller, acrylic floor sealants, PVA (polyvinyl adhesive) and some wood glues. Found materials or carborundum particles may be held in place on the plate with a water-based glue or medium. An acrylic layer may in some cases be painted over the finished plate to seal it. Photocollagraph plates in conjunction with positives bring an even greater range of marks to the medium and this process is comparable to the photo-etching method. Contact screens may be used to generate a tonal structure.

An artist can choose to etch into metal plates which have been worked with direct techniques, and etched plates may be developed further using engraving, drypointing, mezzotint, other direct methods and collagraphy.

The resulting intaglio plates may be inked up and printed, either with traditional inks made from linseed oil and pigments or with water-soluble materials. Traditional oil-based inks for intaglio or relief can be cleaned away safely and effectively with vegetable oil followed by soapy water. The newest generation of oil-based inks can be cleaned with soapy water. Water-soluble inks are water-washable.

Any known hazards to the user or the environment are discussed in each section, together with the appropriate working practice and any measures which can be taken to protect artists and studio users. Where a material is identified as hazardous, an MSDS should be obtained before it is used in a studio. Local legislation should also be taken into account and information sought from the relevant authority. The legislation concerning safety, the 'right to know', waste disposal and environmental issues varies from country to country and may change as environmental and health and safety laws tighten.

The ways in which chemicals can enter the body are described on p. 33, and a safe approach to working in the studio is outlined in 'Good Studio Practice' (pp. 56–58).

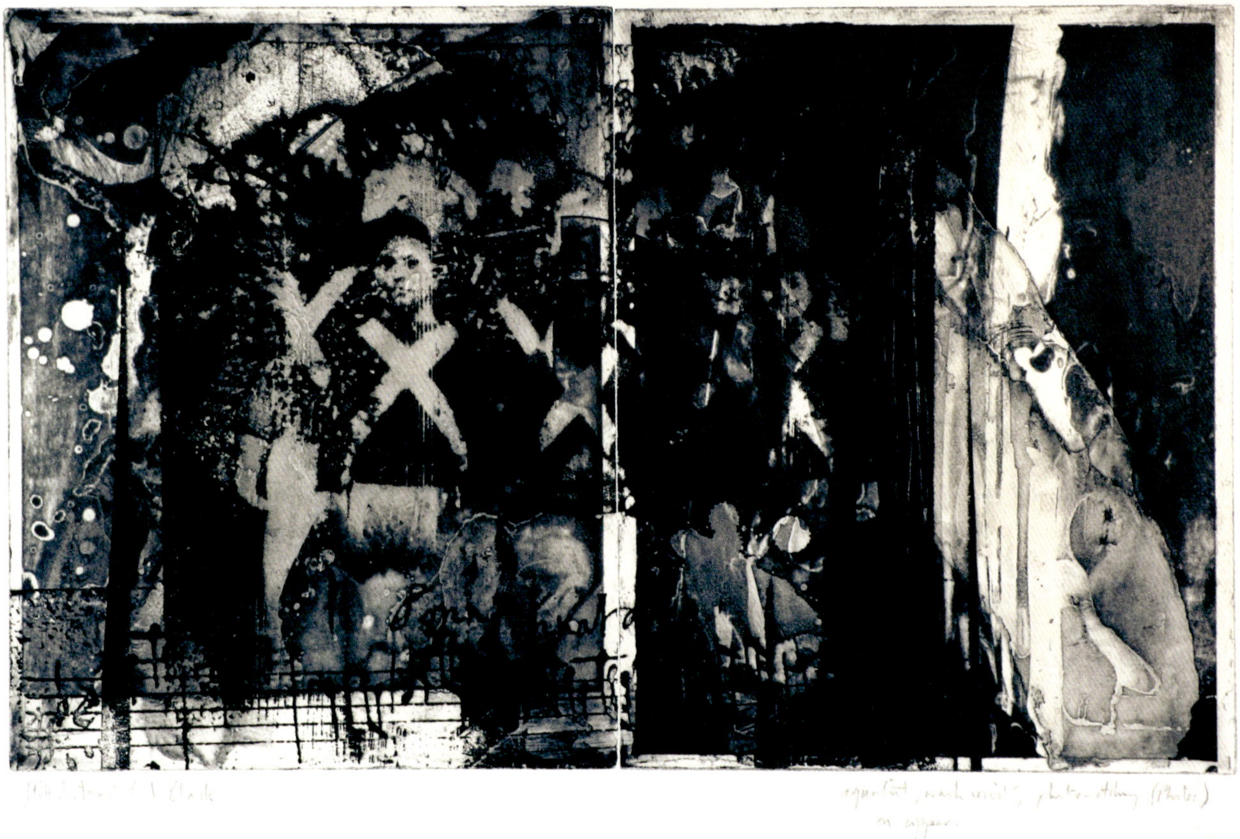

Robert Adam (UK), *The old song*, etching, diptych 30 x 49 cm (12 x 19¼ in.), 1999. Two plates were worked side by side with Lascaux wash and aquatint spray resists and etched in a series of stages. The etched plates were laminated with Photec and a composite positive exposed to them, again side by side. The stripped plates were polished before being printed as a diptych. This proof was one of a number evaluating different inks.

These intaglio methods allow artists greater freedom to work on their creative ideas, and artists who are new to intaglio printmaking quickly become self-sufficient. Teaching staff can focus on the artistic development of their students rather than being encumbered by safety concerns. Artists may choose to work with almost all the plate-making techniques in their personal studios, visiting the etching studio mainly for light-sensitive processes, the etching process and printing the plate.

PLANNING AND EQUIPPING A STUDIO FOR INTAGLIO PRINTMAKING

PLANNING THE STUDIO

A basic studio equipped with a press, some work surfaces, storage space and a sink with a water supply is adequate for printing intaglio plates and working with direct or collagraph methods.

If light-sensitive materials are being used, yellow blinds can be pulled down over the windows during the day to create 'safe light' working conditions. Light-sensitive plates can be exposed outside using sunlight or with a specialist ultraviolet unit which will allow consistent and reliable exposures to be made at any time. The developing area should be well ventilated.

The etching process requires a studio equipped with some specialist facilities. These include chemical storage, safety equipment, a ventilated airbrush workstation, UV exposure unit, ventilated developing area for light-sensitive resists, ventilated mordant area, rinsing and de-oxidizing sink, resist-removal sink and plate-drying workstations. Some legislation may require that a drenching shower is installed in case of spills or accidents involving mordants. Used mordants containing copper are toxic to the environment and must be disposed of by a specialist company.

DESIGNING THE LAYOUT

When identifying a potential studio, points to consider include access for large equipment and the possibility of future expansion. Consider the aesthetics of the space, noting sources of bright natural light, low levels of light, quiet areas, and nooks and crannies. Areas with good natural light should be used for creative plate-making and printing workstations. Small rooms and corners can be useful for storage, toilets and shower, as a clean paper-tearing or print-collating area, or for creating areas of low-level yellow light. An office with computer, telephone and filing cabinets is essential for most print studios and educational establishments. A quiet, private space is also useful for interviews, assessments and staff meetings. A kitchen with a microwave oven, refrigerator, kettle, table and chairs provides a place for artists to eat, drink and socialize. Books, journals and a noticeboard help to make this an area where studio users can relax and exchange information. Lockers are useful for aprons, brushes and tools, and clean storage space should be provided for coats and portfolios.

The architectural quality of indoor plants can be used to create a sense of private space. Scientific research has shown that spider plants, ivy and other plants actively detoxify the surrounding atmosphere and improve air quality.

In open-access and educational establishments the space should be designed with clear sight lines, especially to potentially hazardous workstations such as the guillotine and mordant area. This allows staff to monitor safe working practice in the studio and to act quickly in the case of an accident. If a workspace has to be separated within the main studio, the design should incorporate glass windows or clear plastic splashguards.

If large prints are planned, a clear decision concerning studio policy on the size of prints will have to be made at an early stage as all the equipment will have to accommodate the maximum size. This includes presses, guillotine, sheet-metal storage, plate storage, paper and print storage, plan chests, workbenches, plate-drying cabinets, UV unit, degreasing sink, mordant tanks, trays and sinks.

A fresh, light atmosphere can be created in a studio by equipping it with wipe-clean white benches. These surfaces remain white as studio users can easily see and clean away their

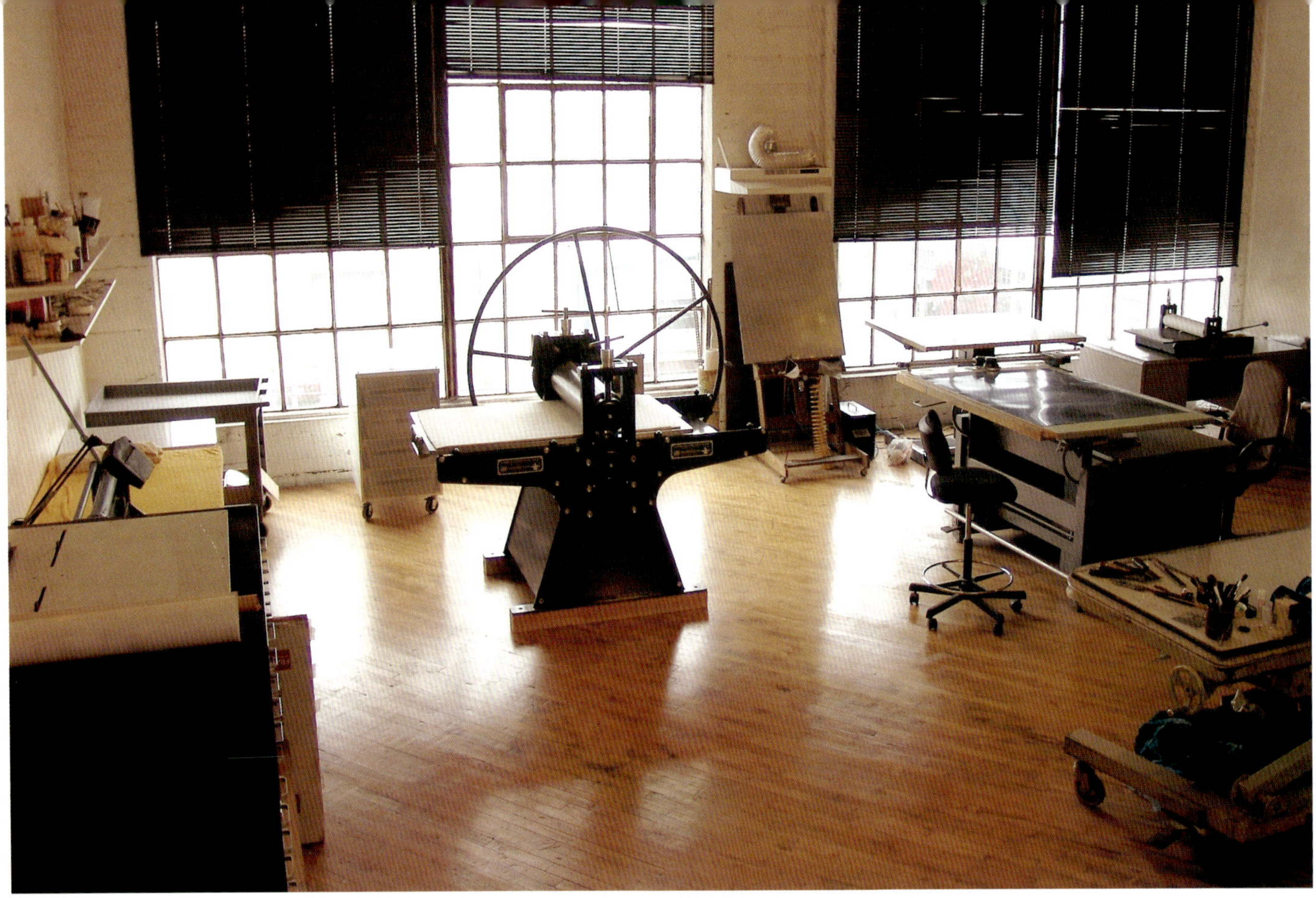

left-over ink or resist. Wipe-clean bench-tops are simple to make (see p. 40).

The CRATE etching studio in Oakland, California, is equipped with presses, spraying unit and clean white surfaces for inking and working.

WORKSTATIONS

In a busy studio the movement of artists working through the stages of the intaglio processes can be managed successfully with the use of well-designed workstations. The appropriate equipment for each process (including safety equipment) should be kept in a clearly marked location at the designated workstation. Containers holding materials and chemicals should be clearly labelled. A colour-coded system is helpful to guide artists to replace tools and materials after use. No alternative hooks or shelves should be made available so that equipment is always returned to the correct marked location ready for the next user. Appropriate safety and educational information should also be displayed. These visual aids can act as an important support for teaching and learning, and a shared studio structured in this way is user-friendly and any staff intervention can be managed sensitively. Artists unfamiliar with a particular intaglio process will rapidly gain confidence.

PLANNING THE SPACE

A practical way to plan the layout of a studio is to measure the room and draw it to scale on graph paper, creating a floor plan.

- Mark on this plan existing or new plumbing for hot and cold running water and drainage. Plumbing will be required in the mordant area, and for hand-washing, paper-soaking and degreasing sinks.

• Windows, doors (show direction of opening), ventilation and power points should also be indicated on the plan.
• Ensure that doorways and gangways are sufficiently wide to allow disabled access.
• Consult fire safety officers to locate fire exits and fire extinguishing equipment. The gangways should be planned to allow easy access to fire exits.
• Electricity will be required for extraction fans, airbrush compressors, lightbox, hands-free driers, drying cabinets, electric power tools, UV exposure unit, motorized presses and work lights.
• Workstations requiring extraction should be sited so that exterior venting is easily and inexpensively installed.
• Check with a plumber, electrician or architect that these plans are feasible and economic before starting work. When discussing the studio with building control and safety officials, make it clear that a safer intaglio system is being planned, in case it is assumed that it is necessary to enforce the stringent regulations applying to traditional etching (for instance the use of nitric acid).

POSITIONING EQUIPMENT

Moving studio equipment is awkward, so the planning process is easier using the scale drawing. Large items of equipment should be measured, allowing for operating space – for instance the movement of a press bed, the maximum size of sheet metal on a guillotine, or opening the drawers of a plan chest. Squares should then be drawn on a separate sheet of graph paper to represent these items, together with any space that may be needed around them. Each square should be clearly labelled and arrows included to show the direction of any moveable parts. When these paper shapes are cut out, they can be moved around on the scale drawing of the studio, bearing in mind that the passageways and space around the equipment should allow ease of movement. After the positioning of the equipment, plumbing and electrical wiring has been decided, the paper shapes can be glued to the scale drawing. Photocopies of the plan can then be made for reference and final adjustments of the positioning of new plumbing and electrical wiring.

SAFETY ISSUES

When planning a studio, the following safety issues should be considered:
• Fire doors may have to be installed, and fire exits must be kept clear at all times.
• Doors should have see-through panels made of safety glass.
• The design should take into account hazards such as awkward doors and stairs.
• Floors should ideally be level throughout the working space. If there are changes in level these will have to be accommodated in the design. Hard-surfaced floors are cold and tiring to stand on: non-slip rubber mats are useful for work areas.
• Mordant, degreasing and resist-removal areas should be equipped with non-slip plastic duck boarding and electrical power points should be the waterproof safety type.
• The layout should take into account the space needed to handle large plates safely and easily. Equipment should be sited so that no hazardous parts project into passageways; a band of fluorescent red acrylic painted on any protrusions or possible hazards will make them more visible.
• Earth leakage circuit breakers, residual current devices, isolating transformers or safety switches should be used.
• Hands-free dryers are safer than hand-held electrical equipment.
• Only short, heavy-duty extension cables should be used.
• To prevent accidents, electrical flexes should never be laid across passageways. Power points may need to be installed to avoid this.
• Storage shelves should be within easy reach.
• Safety and user information should be displayed clearly, but not intrusively. All containers must be labelled with their contents and any relevant safety symbol. MSDSs and full safety information should be available for reference.

EQUIPPING THE STUDIO

A well-equipped studio will require the following workstations and equipment (for detailed information about the equipment and materials see below):

- general studio facilities such as storage, hand washing, etc.
- an area for cutting and filing plates
- an area for preparing plates
- a plate-graining workstation
- a plate-polishing workstation
- a degreasing workstation
- plate-drying facilities
- a drawing and painting area designed for the intaglio method/s used in the studio; plate-making methods will require further specialist equipment (see below)
- a paper-tearing workstation
- a paper-soaking, draining and blotting workstation
- a printing workstation
- a print-drying workstation
- a print-collating area

Direct and collagraph methods will require:

- specialist materials and working tools

Etching methods will require:

- specialist materials and working tools
- a ventilated spraying workstation
- a mordant, rinsing and de-oxidizing workstation
- a resist-removal area

Light-sensitive processes will require:

- specialist materials and working tools
- a lightbox
- positive-making workstations or equipment (e.g. digital)
- a yellow safe-light room if light-sensitive materials are used
- specialist or simple exposure equipment
- a ventilated plate-developing workstation

GENERAL STUDIO FACILITIES AND EQUIPMENT

These include the following:

HAND-WASHING SINK, FIRST-AID AND EYE-WASH STATION

The hand-washing sink (with a warm water supply) should be easily accessible and only used for hand-washing. Barrier cream and hand-washing soaps should be provided in hygienic pump-type dispensers. Hand-washing preparations containing solvents or citric cleaners can be replaced with a more gentle classical solution of Marseilles soap and pumice powder: a little of this soap and some pumice powder applied to dry hands cleans off even oil-based intaglio inks. An eye-wash station and mirror should be sited in this area, which is also a good place to keep the studio first-aid kit.

COAT STAND, LOCKERS AND PORTFOLIO RACK

Coats and other clean clothing should be kept clear of soiled working overalls and aprons. Appropriate space and hangers should be provided for the number of artists or likely visitors to a studio. It is important that artists feel comfortable that their belongings and portfolios are in a clean and relatively safe place (see p. 37).

BLACKBOARD OR NOTICEBOARD

Shared studios benefit from good dissemination of information. A blackboard or noticeboard can be used for this purpose.

WIPE-CLEAN BENCH-TOPS

These are simple to make by fitting either hardened safety glass (with pre-sanded edges) or smooth gloss 300 gsm PVC sheet over existing benches or table-tops. White paper is laid between the bench and the glass (or PVC sheet) and the edges are parcel-taped to the edges of the bench. The paper can be used to ensure that the glass sheet is lying on a smooth even surface; PVC sheet should be used if the surface is uneven.

SAFETY EQUIPMENT

It is important that fire extinguishers are clearly visible and of the correct type for each possible hazard. This equipment has a limited lifespan and will need to be tested and replaced regularly. Fire officers will specify the number and type of extinguishers and other equipment required for a particular workspace. Premises may be inspected on a regular basis by fire safety officers who will monitor the systems which are in place.

STORAGE FOR GLOVES, VISORS AND USED APRONS

Safety equipment which is left lying on worktops tends not to be worn as it often becomes soiled. To avoid this, a set of hooks may be provided for aprons; gloves may be stored out of the way (plastic bulldog clips are available with a magnetic strip to hang them from); and visors can also be hung out of the way (with a loop of cord attached to the head-band).

REFILL, MAINTENANCE AND EQUIPMENT BAY

This should contain dishwashing basins of different sizes, plastic calibrated jugs, digital scales, plastic spoons and spatulas, dishwashing brushes, sponges, hand siphons, recycled clean containers, labels, a waterproof marker pen and clean dry rags.

STORAGE FOR PAPER AND PRINTS

A set of horizontal shelves or plan chests are needed for the safe storage of paper, registration sheets, PVC sheet and other transparent substrates, tissue paper, positives, dot screens, polythene storage bags, test strips, proofs and prints. One drawer can be set aside to store scrap acid-free paper for recycling and offcuts of card for inking up. Metal plan chests are long-lasting, intrinsically inert (i.e. not made from an acidic material) and maintenance-free. Wooden plan chests, although attractive, are more susceptible to damp, warping, wear and tear, and attack by insect pests and rodents. Plan chests with wipe-clean surfaces can be used to work on. Finished editions can be stored in clear polythene storage bags to protect against spills.

PLATE-STORAGE RACK

Plates should be cleaned and carefully prepared for storage as the plate surface can be damaged by corrosion caused by contact with salts, aggressive metal polishes, oils, waxes, some chemicals, water, mordants and moisture or gases in the air. Steel plates are particularly vulnerable to oxidization. Some printmakers apply a protective coating (such as Lascaux Hard Resist) to the edges and both sides of plates. Each prepared plate should be wrapped in acid-free tissue paper, as newsprint and cardboard are acidic and can damage the plate in a relatively short time. The wrapped plates can be stored in acid-free wrapping paper (or a disused proof), a tarnish-resistant cloth, boxes or polythene bags. A waterproof marker pen can be used to label each package with appropriate information (e.g. the date, title of work and name of artist).

The plates should ideally be stored in a unit made from an inert material such as metal, as many woods, MDF and plywood emit gases that cause corrosion. The plates should be stored vertically in a sturdy rack or slot in a dry area of the studio. Spaces of around 50 cm (20 in.) can be left between plan chests for this purpose. The base of the space or storage rack should hold the plates off the ground. Plan chests will be damaged if plates are stored in the drawers.

STORE ROOM

A well-maintained store room will improve the efficiency of the day-to-day running of the studio. A secure, well-ventilated room with a non-slip floor is ideal.

- The temperature should be cool but not drop below freezing as low temperatures can damage acrylics.
- An easy-to-manage stock control system should be established to keep track of degreasers, chemicals, mordants, resists, inks, sponges, rags, educational equipment and sundries. Most intaglio materials are purchased by mail order and may take some time to arrive: to avoid running out of any essential products, a back-up supply of materials should be held in the store room. At the point when the back-up

supply is required in the studio, replacements should be ordered.

- Safety information concerning storage of any hazardous chemicals should be clearly displayed. Recipes for mordants, photoresist developer and resist remover should be at hand in this area.
- The store room should be well organized and kept tidy. Sturdy shelves should be securely attached to the walls and the back of the shelves should be within easy reach. A step-ladder should be provided so that higher shelves can be reached safely. Rolls of bubblewrap packaging material, spare etching blankets or foam, and lightweight or rarely used articles can be kept on the higher shelves. Hazardous materials such as liquid ferric chloride must always be stored on the ground or on low shelves to reduce the risk of spills over the upper body.
- Areas for specific chemicals should be designated and clearly labelled: this is to separate incompatible chemicals (including janitorial cleaning chemicals) which could react dangerously with each other.
- Storage of chemicals and materials in recycled food containers can result in accidental ingestion.
- Chemicals which require dilution should be kept in the store room rather than the studio to avoid confusion. Funnels, calibrated containers and hand siphons for mixing and decanting chemicals make mixing up solutions simpler and safer. The solutions should be stored in clearly labelled unbreakable containers with lids. The store room should also contain spill-control equipment.
- Powders and crystals such as citric acid and sodium carbonate which are packaged in paper sacks can be kept dry by storing them in large plastic household waste containers (with lids) which are intended for outside use. The bins should only contain one type of material and must be clearly labelled.
- Photopolymers should be stored in a cool place and should be marked clearly as light-sensitive materials.

WASHING MACHINE

Press blankets can be washed easily on a wool setting.

WASTE PAPER BINS AND OUTSIDE STORAGE FOR EXCESS WASTE

Tall slim kitchen waste containers with swing lids are ideal for studios. They will last longer if disposable bin liners are used. To reduce the risk of fire (from soiled tissue papers and wipes), these containers should all be emptied into an outside waste container at the end of each day.

SUMP

The waste-water system in a studio should incorporate a sump which will collect any solid residues (e.g. degreasing powder and acrylic resists washed from plates). The sump should be emptied each week and the silt disposed of appropriately.

PLATE PREPARATION WORKSTATIONS

The area should be contained but easily accessible. The space should be well lit and fitted with non-slip safety flooring. Power points may be required, and power tools used for grinding and sanding should be used carefully and in accordance with the manufacturer's instructions. Electrical safety plugs should be used, and power tools and their flexes should be checked regularly for signs of wear and tear.

Sheet metals and plastics should be stored in a strong rack to guard against the danger of the metal falling. When metal plates are being prepared steel toe-caps, a thick apron and leather or suede gloves should be worn to guard against cuts and splinters. Eye protection and a dust mask should be worn as metal, wood or plastic filings and dust particles can damage the eyes and irritate the lungs. Contact lens wearers must be especially careful and should wear spectacles when preparing plates.

Cutting, filing, grinding and sanding plates generates noise and dust. Grit which has found its way into polishing rags or printing ink can cause scratches on the plate surface. Any metal, plastic and wood dust should be removed immediately with a vacuum cleaner. A waste bin and scrap metal bins should be provided for off-cuts.

WORKSTATION FOR CUTTING AND WORKING PLATES

A sturdy, powerful and sharp metal-cutting guillotine should be positioned with plenty of space around it. Relevant operating and safety information should be clearly displayed to remind artists that they should only use the machine after training. Powered guillotines must only be used by trained staff. Heat – or any tool which generates heat as it cuts – cannot be used if the plate is to be etched.

Storage should be provided for the following safety equipment and tools: ear defenders, eye protection, a dust mask, a thick apron, leather or suede gloves, a measuring rule and steel straight-edge, a pencil and a steel point, G-clamps, metal snips and a sharp Stanley knife.

A bay for a power sander and a stable workbench are useful for working with power tools such as an electric jigsaw (for wood and plastic plates). Power sanders should be fitted with a dust bag (plastic plates should not be dry sanded).

WORKSTATION FOR FILING PLATES

A sturdy bench is necessary, with storage for a couple of G-clamps, some files (coarse and fine for metal), a range of abrasive papers (for smoothing off the filed plate edges) and a disposable wiping cloth. A dust mask, eye protection, thick apron, leather gloves and steel toe-caps should be worn.

WORKSTATION FOR GRAINING PLATES

A wipe-clean working surface is required for this workstation. Large plates can be grained on the bench-top and smaller plates can be grained on wipe-clean workboards provided at the workstation. If a wipe-clean workboard for coarse graining materials and a workboard for fine graining materials is supplied, the risk of cross-contamination is reduced. A soft decorating brush (8 cm/3⅛ in. wide) should be provided for collecting the excess graining materials from these boards and the work surface. A range of colour-coded storage containers and bowls (clearly labelled with the particle size of the powders) should be stored on a shelf above the working surface. The bowls are used to store the different graining rolls to prevent the mixtures becoming contaminated. A jug of water and some disposable cloths should also be provided.

Process information and guidelines can be displayed at the back of the storage shelves (a reminder to grain the back of the plate is often helpful). Gloves, eye protection and an apron should be worn when graining plates, and a dust mask is required when making up the graining mixtures. Pumice powder and carborundum grits may be purchased from artists' and printmakers' suppliers.

WORKSTATION FOR POLISHING PLATES

Polishing is an important part of plate preparation but this process is also used throughout the working stages of the plate (see p. 75). The area for plate polishing must be separate from the plate-graining workstation as plates can be badly scratched by graining materials or metal particles which have found their way into polishing pads, rags or work surfaces.

The workstation can be based at a bench with a wipe-clean working surface. Storage space for the polishing materials (pumice, metal polishes, jeweller's rouge, etc.) and a selection of polishing rolls should be provided (see p. 74). If an electric polishing pad is to be used, a power point and relevant safety signage will be required.

DEGREASING WORKSTATION

This frequently used and important area should be well lit and fitted with non-slip flooring and electrical safety switches for lighting and extraction. A polypropylene sink (the size depends on studio use and plate dimensions) with drainage and a hot and cold water supply is ideal for degreasing plates. Polypropylene sinks are not intrinsically strong and will require some support from a stand made from wood or metal. Sinks and their stands can be purchased from specialist suppliers or made to a particular specification by a plastics fabricator and a carpenter or metal worker. Flexible hoses should be attached to the taps to enable the artist to rinse all of the plate with ease.

A storage shelf is required for a bottle of dishwashing liquid (with a bowl and soft application brush), a storage container of ready-to-use degreaser (with a bowl and soft application brush) and a squeezy-type container of neutralizing solution. These materials and their designated brushes and bowls should be colour-coded to prevent contamination. A draining container (kitchen-type) is useful for the storage of some wet-and-dry abrasive paper. Clean and dry storage for gloves and a visor should be provided. Safety and procedural information should be clearly displayed.

Power tools such as electric sanders should not be used in this wet area. In small etching studios the degreasing sink may be shared with the etching or resist-removal sink if there is a sound understanding that any resist remover contaminating the plate surface during the degreasing process (for instance from cleaning brushes or duck boards) will destabilize resists and cause foul bite.

PLATE-DRYING FACILITIES

Copper, brass, zinc and aluminium plates can be dried either naturally or with plate-drying equipment but mild steel plates will rust rapidly unless a dryer is used. Plates which are wet from rinsing after degreasing, etching or stripping can be dried with a hands-free dryer or in a vertical drying cabinet. Plates which are coated in resists or collagraph media may be dried in a horizontal drying cabinet. In a small or cleverly designed studio, a single combined drying cabinet is all that is required. Larger studios will benefit from having several drying cabinets. Hairdryers and electric fan heaters should not be used in wet areas because of the risk of electric shock.

HANDS-FREE DRYER

A wall-mounted hands-free warm-air dryer, activated by a photo-electric cell, is inexpensive, as these machines are mass-manufactured for washrooms. They are effective, economic to use, hard-wearing and safer than using a hand-held dryer.

A fixed warm-air fan is an alternative but for safety reasons must be wall-mounted and controlled by a cord pull-switch and connected to the power supply through a circuit breaker. The main disadvantage in a busy studio is that the dryer will inevitably be left switched on for periods of time, contributing to electricity costs, noise levels and heat.

VERTICAL FAST-DRYING CABINET

Wet plates can be placed vertically on a rack or shelf in a fast-drying cabinet where they will dry quickly, protected from dust and out of harm's way. A narrow wooden cabinet will take up little space in the studio and can be part of a larger drying unit.

DRYING CABINET WITH HORIZONTAL SHELVES

Acrylic materials dry naturally at room temperature but the use of a cabinet will speed the drying process up. A number of plates can be dried horizontally in a cabinet where they are protected from dust and accidental damage.

The cabinet consists of an enclosed wooden box containing pull-out shelves, stretched with mesh, through which warm air can circulate. An electric fan heater positioned at the base of the unit is used to generate a current of warm air. The lowest shelf should be used for plates holding wash resists, in case these run and drip. An extractor fan may also be fitted if required.

The cabinet should not be used to dry wet plates as the water may drip onto plates coated in resist and damage them. The cabinet would also become humid which would adversely affect the resists on plates.

opposite A horizontal drying cabinet with etching and collagraph plates on its pull-out shelf. The top surface is used as a workbench.

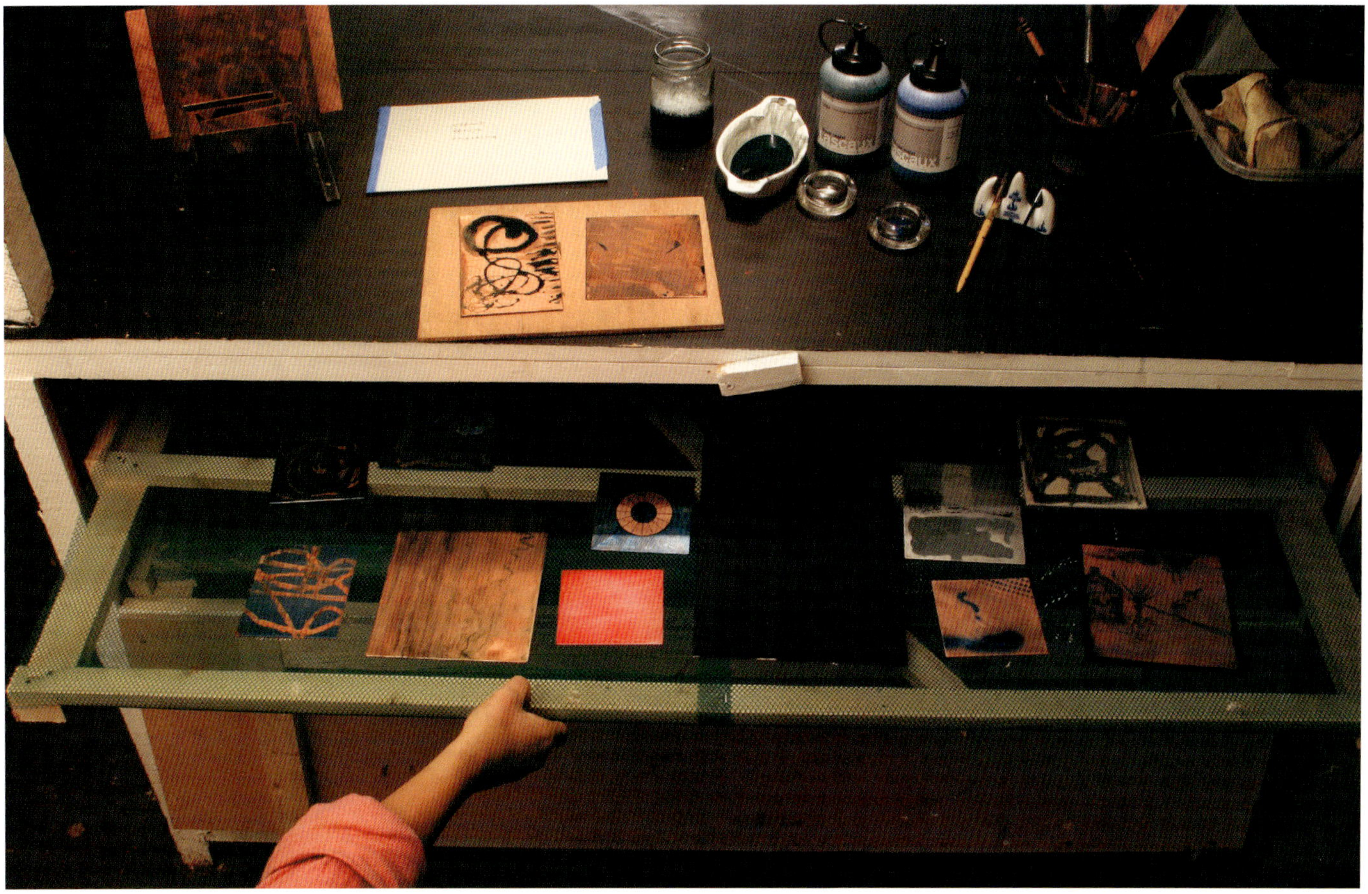

DRAWING AND PAINTING AREA

An appropriately sized, well-lit, attractive space is useful for a variety of purposes, including direct methods, working with resists or collagraph media, painting or drawing on positives, assembling photopositives, sketching and developing ideas on proofs, making registration sheets and writing up process notes.

The area should be within easy reach of the drying cabinet and a sink. A work surface can be centrally positioned to accommodate groups of individuals and larger-scale projects, and can also be used as a teaching and demonstrating area. Chairs which can be stacked add to the flexibility of the space. Adjustable desk lights and table-top magnifying glasses are helpful for artists who are drawing fine detail or checking etched lines. A range of colour-coded workboards (such as cutting boards, painting workboards and wipe-clean workboards) should be provided as these help prevent the work surface being cut or damaged. The workboards (holding plates or positives) are easily lifted to the drying cabinet or out of the way of another artist. Prints in progress can be displayed against a white wall using clean spring clips. If the working surface is cleared at the end of each day, the area will remain clean, tidy and accessible to all studio users.

Workstations for acrylic resists, collagraph media or autographic positive media can be positioned within this area (see below). The different workstations and their related products and materials should be clearly labelled, or colour-coded, or positioned separately from one another to prevent confusion arising between the different systems and materials.

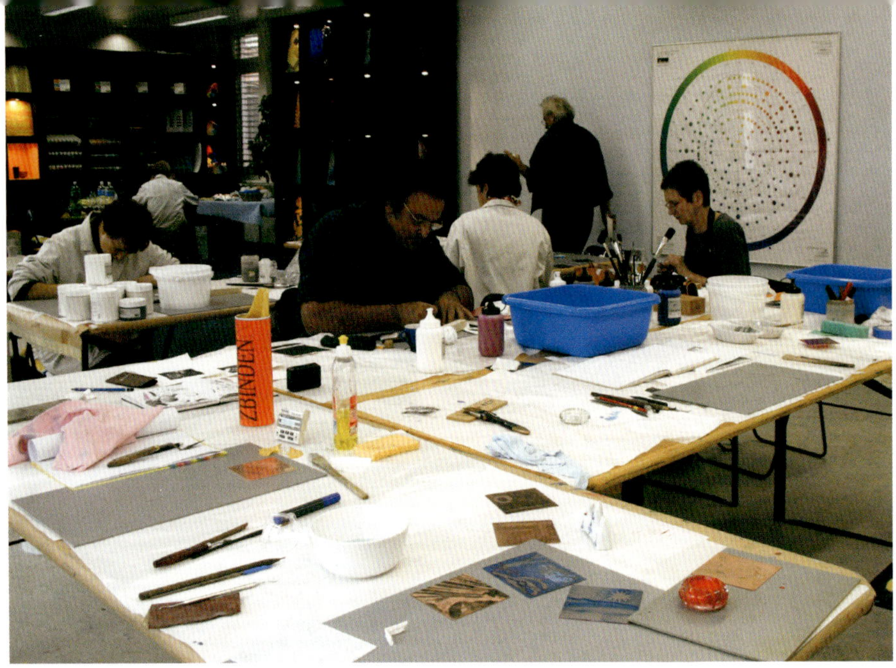

Acrylic resists used in an art room. Note the grey workboards and basins of water.

VISUAL AID FOLDERS

A shelf for visual aid folders, printmaking books and other educational material is useful. Visual aid folders can be made, and added to, so that they form a reference library of test strips, types of positive, exposure times, resist recipes, collagraph materials, printed effects, magazine articles and internet documents.

A4 ring-bound folders with plastic envelope sleeves are suitable for holding the material. Sections of proofs and prints can be trimmed to fit the envelopes. Once a folder is set up, artists working in the studio can add to this realia to create an evolving compendium of marks which is invaluable for anyone using the studio.

PAPER-TEARING AND PRINT-COLLATING WORKSTATION

A wipe-clean bench area is used for preparing editioning paper or collating finished prints. Tools and useful equipment such as a T-square, a metal straight-edge, a metre stick, a graphics rule, PVC templates for commonly used paper sizes, scissors, a cutting mat, pencils and a waterproof pen can be hung on a wall. A set of wooden registration jigs, masking tape, erasers, scalpels, a printer's chop and some glass cleaner with a cloth may be stored on a shelf. The locations of the equipment can be marked by drawing their silhouettes in waterproof pen. In large workshops prints are often collated and signed in the gallery space.

EQUIPMENT AND WORKSTATION FOR DIRECT INTAGLIO METHODS

A sturdy workbench and chair are required for drypointing or engraving. An area for mezzotinting should be equipped with a mezzotint rocker and arm.

Electric sockets will be necessary if a powered engraving tool or other electrical equipment is to be used. An abrasive gun should be operated within an enclosed sandblasting unit that has extraction. The equipment required for making positives and the lamination and exposure of photomasks is described on pp. 50 and 51. Relevant safety and operating information related to the use of power tools should be clearly displayed.

Adjustable spotlights, a mirror and a stand-alone magnifying glass are useful. Storage boxes for drawing tools, sharpening stones and other materials, and a shelf for books and visual aid folders, may be provided. A waste disposal bin and dustpan and brush will be needed for cleaning up metal particles.

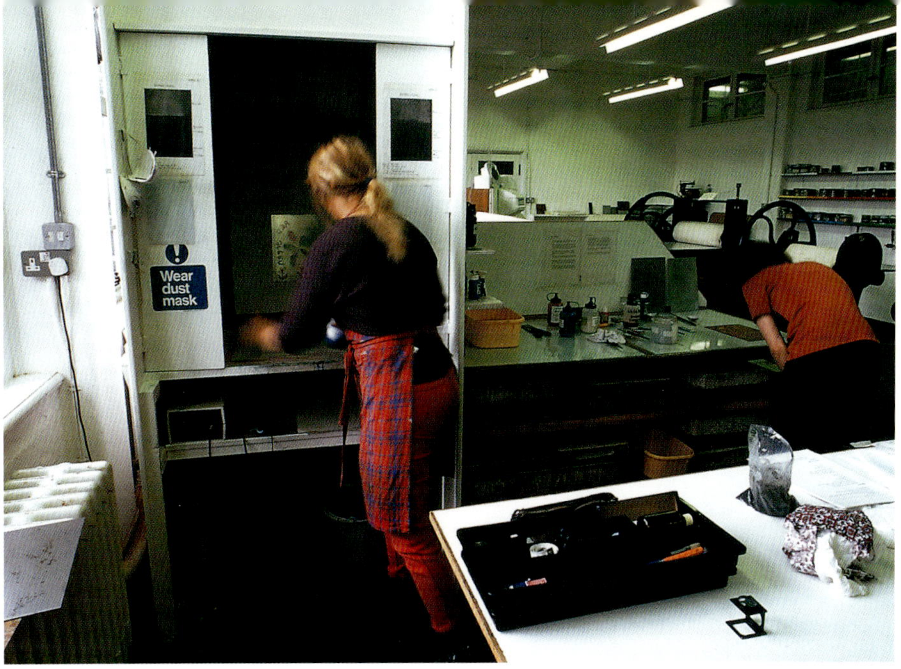

A ventilated workstation for spraying plates. The two side panels can be opened to accommodate large plates. The glass-coated bench to the right is used for the application of acrylic resists.

EQUIPMENT AND WORKSTATIONS FOR ACRYLIC-RESIST ETCHING METHODS

WORKSTATION FOR APPLYING ACRYLIC RESISTS

A wipe-clean working surface will be required together with some storage shelves for the resists and tools. A colour-coded system with process information will help etchers become familiar with the different resists. The containers of resist can have a coloured stripe added to them or a label written with waterproof marker pen. Only one container of each resist should be on the shelf at any time (if studio users are asked to place any empty containers on the work surface the staff can quickly see which materials need replacing). Lift media should be stored on a separate shelf or in a clearly defined area away from the resists. China or glass palettes (with flat bases and sufficiently wide for the broadest brush) can be stacked on the shelf. Brushes for paint-on resists should be hung on the wall of the workstation. Heavy containers such as clay flower pots are useful for storing brushes and crayons. A nitrile roller may be required for some application methods: information should be provided concerning the correct care of the roller. Clean plastic trays and funnels are required for pour-on resists and these will need their own space on a shelf. The resist-coated plates can be dried in a horizontal drying cabinet, which ideally will be below the work surface.

WORKSTATION FOR SPRAYING

The spray gun or airbrush should be used in a spray booth which has an extractor fan to draw away excess vapour and acrylic spray. The unit should preferably be positioned near a horizontal drying cabinet so that the sprayed plates can be dried quickly. Storage should be provided nearby (or as part of the unit) for an air compressor, visual aid folder, spray gun or airbrush, box of spare parts, tools, extra bottles, dishwashing liquid, resist, cleaning wire, cleaning bottle, a pack of newsprint, a bucket of water, a bucket for dirty water, a plastic jug, a magnifying glass and some masks for aqueous mists.

Ventilated spray booths are made for the graphics industry and can be purchased from a specialist supplier. Wooden fold-away or permanent home-made units can be constructed fairly easily and an extractor fan may be fitted (in the centre, directly behind where the plate is sprayed).

- Sprayguns and airbrushes: the choice of set depends on the needs of the user, the type of studio and on the viscosity of the material being sprayed. Useful information about brushes and spraying tips can be found on the internet or in specialist

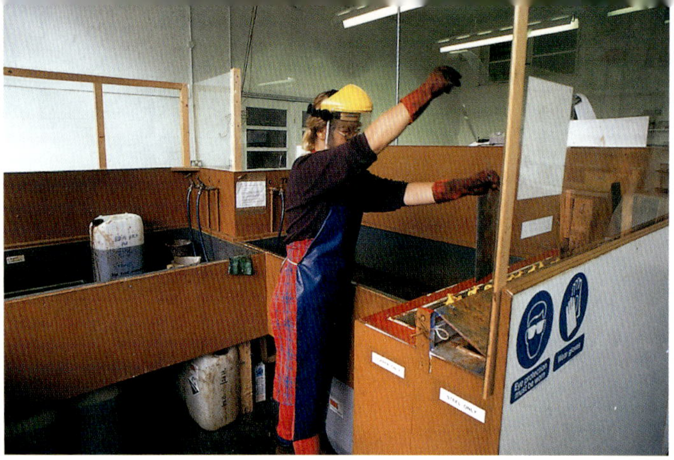

A plate is lowered into an etching dip tank. Clear splash guards can be seen around this airy etching workstation which is designed for the use of ferric chloride and copper sulphate.

books. A double-action, internal-mix, bottom (siphon) feed airbrush such as the Vega 2000 is ideal for busy studios as air can be directed through the nozzle to blow out clogs and to clean the brush (between each use). The trigger on these dual-action brushes is pressed down to activate the air flow and pulled back to determine the amount of fluid released. Paasche, Iwata and Badger brushes of this type are cleaned with water at the end of each working day.

The single-action, internal-mix, bottom-feed Badger 200 NH or the basic single-action, external-mix, bottom-feed spray gun such as a Badger 250-4 may be used but these brushes require cleaning after each use.

Spare parts can be purchased from suppliers. The use and cleaning instructions provided by the manufacturers should be followed.

- Powering the spray gun or airbrush: the spray gun or airbrush is powered by either a disposable canister of air propellant or by a portable or stationary oil-free compressor. Compact, lightweight, quiet compressors are designed to run for short periods only and should be set for automatic shut-off (e.g. SILAIR 15 auto, TC2000 Auto Stop or Medea Great White Shark). Compressors made for DIY and car maintenance have a storage tank for the compressed air which makes the machine bulkier (e.g. Thorite SP3050, Clarke Ranger, Sealey 50ltr Direct Drive 2.0hp). Once these types of machine have filled their tank with compressed air, the engine shuts off automatically. The set-up and user instructions provided by the manufacturers should be followed. PTFE plumbers' tape should be used on all connections to maximize the air flow.

WORKSTATION FOR ETCHING, RINSING AND DE-OXIDIZING

This area should be warm, ventilated and well lit, with sinks fitted with drainage, a supply of hot and cold water, and flexible hoses for the taps. The plumbing should be of a plastic material and a sump should be fitted. The sinks should be large enough for cleaning, de-oxidizing and rinsing plates as well as accommodating trays of mordant. Vertical etching tanks for ferric chloride should be positioned on the floor and must be supported by a strong external framework of metal or wood (due to the weight of the mordant). They should be sited next to the sinks so that the etched plate can be lifted directly from the mordant into the sink for rinsing.

The workstation should be fitted with non-slip flooring, and lighting, bubblers and extraction should be operated by electrical safety switches. A colour-coded and labelled shelf can hold squeezy-type containers of de-oxidizing solution and dishwashing liquid, PVC strips, plastic clothes pegs and a roll of parcel tape (for attaching the hanging strip to plates). A waterproof pen can be hung in the area so that each artist can write the time and his or her name on the hanging strap.

A safe, dry and well-labelled storage space is required for supplies of mordants and other chemicals. It is important that the correct equipment is used when making up mordants and filling or emptying trays (or tanks). For this reason a plastic storage trunk should be kept nearby for digital scales, a hand siphon, a plastic calibrated jug, a plastic bucket, an acid-pump and a home-made ladle for emptying dip-tanks.

Safety and procedural information must be clearly displayed and an eye-wash station with a mirror placed within the area. Acid-resistant aprons, protective gloves, arm-length gauntlets, particulate respirators, goggles and visors should be stored in a clean, dry, accessible place. The correct fire extinguishers and suitable absorbent material (in case of spills or leaks of mordants) should be positioned nearby.

- Flat trays, rinsing trays and vertical tanks for mordants: flat trays have been used traditionally to hold the mordant while the plate is etched. Specialist trays can be purchased from printmaking or photographic suppliers. These trays are strong and usually have a pouring lip. Inexpensive trays designed for gardening, storage or leisure purposes are often used by etchers but these may crack or break if lifted (when full). Even professional trays should not be lifted and it is a dangerous practice to move a tray full of mordant to another area. Mordant trays should be used in flat sinks with drainage and a water supply. They should be emptied carefully using a siphon or a jug. Flexible hoses should be attached to the taps to enable the artist to rinse all of the plate and soiled sink with ease. Safety legislation in some countries or states will specify that a rinsing tray (a flat tray full of clean water) should be provided for plates lifted from the mordant.

Vertical dip tanks are used for etching with ferric chloride by the circuit-board industry. These tanks have mechanisms which spray the ferric onto the plate that is to be etched and this method of etching prevents a build-up of sediment and provides a clean bite. A much simpler vertical tank which employs air bubbles to aerate and agitate the ferric chloride can be used by artists. The plates are held on plastic straps as they etch in the tank and a number of plates may be bitten at one time. The slim vertical tanks are space-saving and make using ferric chloride a cleaner and easier process. These dip-tanks are made from welded polypropylene (or moulded polyethylene) and can be purchased from specialist manufacturers or made up to a design by a local fabricator. Air bubbles can be generated by a circuit-board industry bubbler or an aquarium air pump (kept on a shelf near the mordant tank) attached to a length of plastic tubing. The tubing is secured at one end of the dip tank so that the bubbles rise and create a current in the mordant.

DRENCHING SHOWER

This room should be functional at all times and studio users and staff should be aware that the facility exists.

WORKSTATION FOR REMOVING RESIST

This area should be ventilated, well lit and fitted with a large sink equipped with drainage, a sump and a water supply. Flexible hoses should be attached to the taps to enable the artist to rinse the plate with ease. The workstation should have non-slip flooring and electrical safety switches for lighting and extraction. Similar trays to those used for etching (see above) are suitable for holding resist removers such as sodium carbonate. A lid should be used to reduce the smell of detergent in the

This dip tank and sink is for stripping large plates. The plastic containers hold materials such as carborundum, resists, collagraph media and tusches, as well as files, palettes, sponges and other tools.

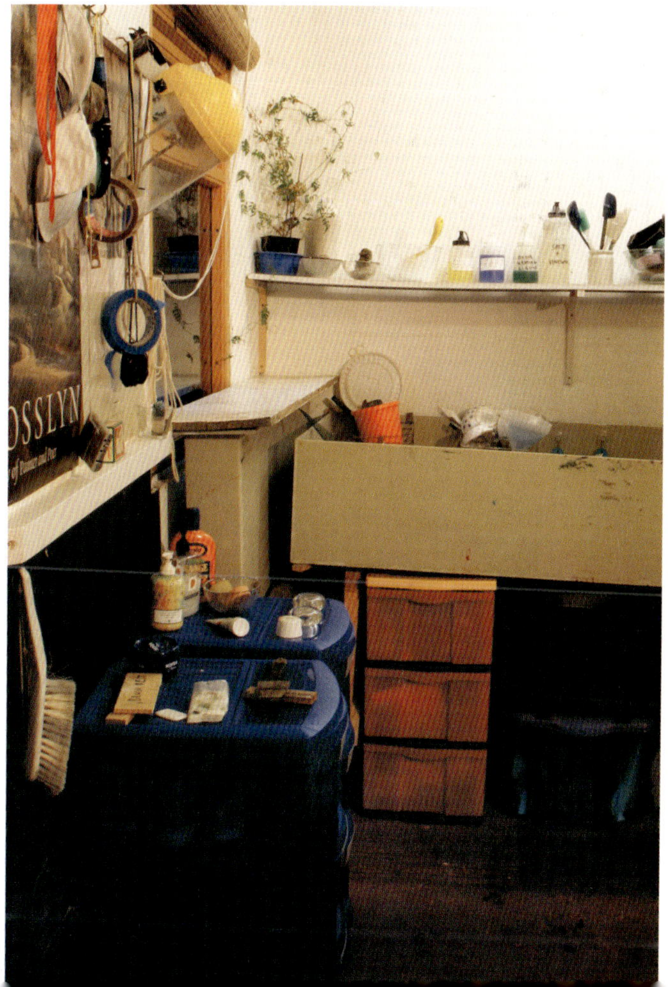

studio and to reduce evaporation (a lid can be made from a piece of Perspex or Plexiglas cut to size). A space-saving vertical tank can be used to hold Mystrol or Lascaux resist remover. The plates may be held in a home-made bag of synthetic garden netting, which is lowered into the stripping solution.

It is important that safety and procedural information is clearly displayed and that waterproof aprons, gloves and visors are provided. An eye-wash station with a mirror should be sited in this workstation.

EQUIPMENT AND WORKSTATION FOR COLLAGRAPH METHODS

Collagraphs can be made on a well-lit, wipe-clean workbench. Some storage shelves should be provided for the different acrylic media used. A colour-coded system with some process information will help intaglio printmakers become familiar with the materials. Heavy containers such as clay flower pots are useful for storing brushes, paint shapers and palette knives. A range of china or glass palettes can be stacked on the shelf. A drawer or box is useful for storing collage materials.

The equipment required for making photocollagraph plates and positives is described below and on pp. 51–52.

EQUIPMENT AND FACILITIES FOR LIGHT-SENSITIVE INTAGLIO METHODS

YELLOW SAFE-LIGHT ROOM

A darkroom equipped with yellow or red safe lights can be used. Yellow safe-light working conditions may also be provided in other ways: yellow cotton blinds can be pulled down over the windows; lights can be covered with yellow filters which may be purchased from photographic suppliers; a semi-permanent yellow-light room can be created by painting windows or clear light covers with a yellow water-soluble paint such as Lascaux Gouache. Dry film photoresist and photomask are very sensitive to dust so this workspace must be clean.

FACILITIES FOR LAMINATION

A drying cabinet may be used to warm the coated plate prior to lamination. An etching press set at normal printing pressure may be used to laminate the dry film photoresist or photomask onto the plate. A clothes iron is also effective. In the circuit-board industry a ventilated laminating machine which has a heated roller is used.

FACILITIES FOR UV EXPOSURE

A self-contained UV exposure unit with a powerful single UV light source (a point source) with special safety glass, reflective panels, safe lights, light integrator, powerful vacuum lid and external controls is well worth the expense. These machines make detailed, accurate plates very quickly, are safe to operate and save space in the studio. The UV light source used in these units is quartz halide and exposures are rapid (usually less than thirty seconds). The integrator measures the precise amount of light emitted in light units, allowing fine control and accommodating any variation in the strength of the bulb. As a result exposures can be repeated with complete consistency. The least powerful quartz halide bulb is the most suitable for intaglio printmakers as it offers the widest latitude of exposure times. More powerful machines sometimes require a three-phase electric power supply, which is costly to install. Suitable machines can be purchased through printmaking materials suppliers, directly from manufacturers or second-hand.

Before self-contained UV exposure units were available, a room had to be made light-safe. The UV light source was mounted on the wall and operated from outside the room. A vacuum clamp-down unit held the positive and the plate together, and when the air was extracted these were held firmly in place between the glass and the flexible rubber of the lid. The unit was then swivelled round so that the screen was vertical and could be moved towards the light source. The floor was marked out with lines to indicate different exposure possibilities. The UV lights were turned on and an integrator or minute timer was used to measure the length of the exposure.

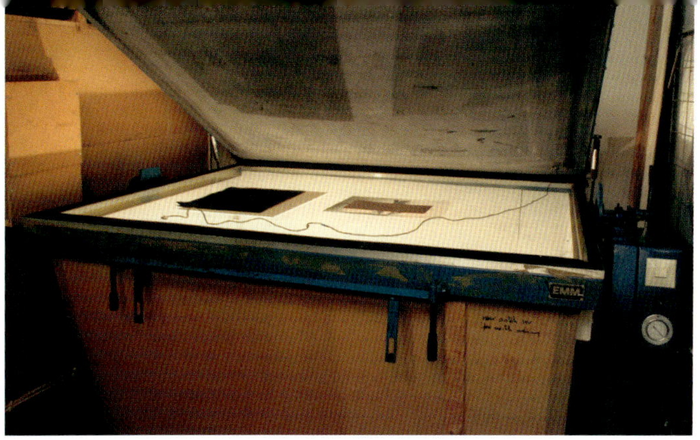

A tracing-paper photocopy positive and a plate can be seen on the glass of this self-contained UV exposure unit.

This type of system takes up a lot of space, and is less safe than an enclosed unit as there is a possibility of the user or another artist becoming exposed to hazardous UV rays. However, these swivel units can be adapted to create the basis of a home-made, enclosed, self-contained unit. Simple UV bulbs or a quartz halide light source can be used. A light integrator may be installed as part of the system, or exposure times can be measured in minutes and seconds. This kind of exposure unit is generally considered to be less effective but some of the prints illustrated in this book were made with such a system.

Great care has to be taken to avoid scratching the glass and some printmakers lay a clear gloss sheet of PVC over the glass for the plate to lie on during exposure. Glass cleaner and a duster should be stored nearby so that the glass surface can be kept free of dust and grease. The UV lightbulb of the exposure lamp will need to be replaced occasionally.

FACILITY FOR SUNLIGHT EXPOSURE

A simple sunlight exposure frame can be made to hold the positive in close contact with the light-sensitive plate. The frame consists of a heavy, unscratched piece of tempered glass with taped edges and a wooden board – such as a drawing board – covered with a soft foam sheet (the foam will sink down when the light-sensitive plate and the glass are laid on it). An opaque quilt can be used to cover the assembly to block out the light before and after exposure (usually between 12 and 17 seconds). The plate can be placed in the frame (under safe-light conditions) and carried into the sunlight. A trolley may be used to transport a large frame.

WORKSTATION FOR DEVELOPING PHOTORESIST AND PHOTOCOLLAGRAPH PLATES

This area should be set up according to the light-sensitive materials which are being used. It should be well ventilated and lit, and fitted with non-slip flooring and electrical safety switches. Dry and clean storage for safety clothing should be provided and any safety and procedural information shown on the relevant MSDS should be clearly displayed. A sink with flexible hoses attached to the taps, developing trays, drainage and a hot and cold water supply is ideal for developing and rinsing plates.

Digital scales and plastic calibrated jugs and containers are required for making up some developing solutions. In busy studios a 20-litre (5-gallon) plastic barrel with a dispensing tap (available from home-brewing suppliers) should be provided to store a quantity of developing solution, as this should always be fresh for each photoresist-coated plate.

FACILITIES FOR DRYING AND CURING

After developing, the plate should be dried (follow product instructions) and cured by further exposure to ultraviolet light (either sunlight or from a UV exposure unit).

PLATE STORAGE

Photocollagraph plates made with dry film resists may be cleaned, wrapped in tissue and stored vertically. It is recommended that Solarplate, Toray, Torelief, Printight and Toyobo plates should not be stored in the studio as they emit an unpleasant odour.

WORKSTATIONS FOR MAKING POSITIVES

LIGHTBOX

A lightbox makes working on positives much easier. One can be purchased from specialist art suppliers or may be available second-hand. A lightbox is an enclosed unit with a glass top and a fluorescent light source underneath. A simple home-built lightbox can be constructed from a heavy, tempered, ground-glass table-top, supported on trestle legs. Fluorescent light units with diffusers can be installed beneath. This type of glass top and trestle can be purchased in IKEA shops and fluorescent light units are available in home improvement stores.

WORKSTATION FOR MAKING POSITIVES WITH AUTOGRAPHIC MEDIA

This workstation is used when making autographic positives, and when altering, splicing or editing photocopied, photographic or digital positives. A wipe-clean working surface and some shelves should be provided for storing the different tusches, diluting liquids and china or glass palettes in a range of sizes. A set of heavy pots such as clay flower pots is useful for storing brushes, pencils, conté crayons, pigment sticks, paint shapers and ink pens. A drawer or box is needed for storing frottage and texturing materials. A colour-coded storage system with some process information will help intaglio printmakers become familiar with the process and the materials. A plan chest nearby may be used to store transparent substrates, finished positives, work in progress, dot screens and an exposure calculator.

FACILITIES FOR MAKING PHOTOCOPY POSITIVES

A standard photocopier can be used to magnify, reduce, reverse or alter the contrast or tone of an image and to create a positive. More complex machines available through reprographic companies offer other special effects. Colour photocopiers can be used to make basic colour separations.

FACILITIES FOR MAKING DIGITAL POSITIVES

A digital studio should be equipped with an up-to-date computer connected to the internet, with suitable software such as Adobe Photoshop. A printer, DVD or CD writer, a scanner, a Wacom Tablet and digital still and video cameras are also useful. Community digital resources such as open-access studios often run educational courses and equipment-hiring facilities.

FACILITIES FOR MAKING PHOTOGRAPHIC POSITIVES

Photographic processes use toxic chemicals to develop and fix films, so safety clothing should be worn and the darkroom should be equipped with good extraction and ventilation equipment. Suppliers of lith films and related chemicals offer up-to-date health and safety advice. The darkroom should be fitted with non-slip flooring and good lighting (normal, yellow and red). It should be equipped with large wipe-clean work surfaces, sinks with drainage and water supply, enlarger or process camera, trays (for the developing and fixing chemicals), dot screens, lith film, chemicals, digital scales, exposure calculator, specialist chemical storage unit, and electrical safety switches for lighting and extraction. The plumbing should be made from plastic materials and a chemical sump should be fitted. It is important that safety and procedural information is clearly displayed and that clean and dry storage for waterproof aprons, gloves and visors is provided. An eye-wash station with a mirror should be provided, as should the correct fire extinguishers and suitable absorbent material (in case of spills or leaks of mordants). Process cameras, enlargers and other photographic equipment and materials can be purchased second-hand or from specialist suppliers.

EQUIPMENT AND FACILITIES FOR PRINTING

The printing area must be well lit and have a strong weight-bearing floor with a non-slip surface. For maintenance and safety reasons free-standing presses should be positioned centrally in the space to allow easy access to all sides at any time. Adequate space must be allowed for the printer and for any moving parts of the press (e.g. the roller, the wheel handle or the bed). A rectangle of the floor around the press can be colourfully and attractively painted to help draw attention to the area that the machine requires when moving. Relevant operating and safety information should be clearly displayed and should remind artists that loose clothing can become caught in machinery (as can long hair, jewelry and headphone flexes), and that they should only use or adjust the press after training. This area should not be used as a thoroughfare as the moving machinery can cause injuries to bystanders.

Storage should be provided for registration blocks. Workstations for inking up plates and soaking and blotting paper should be sited within easy reach of the press.

PRESSES FOR INTAGLIO PRINTMAKING

Any type of intaglio plate may be printed on an etching press. These are sometimes known as rolling or copper-plate presses and have operated on the same basic principle for centuries. The press consists of a frame which supports two heavy rollers and a solid steel plate, called the bed. The plate, dampened printing paper and soft blankets are laid on the flat horizontal bed which is driven under pressure between the two rollers.

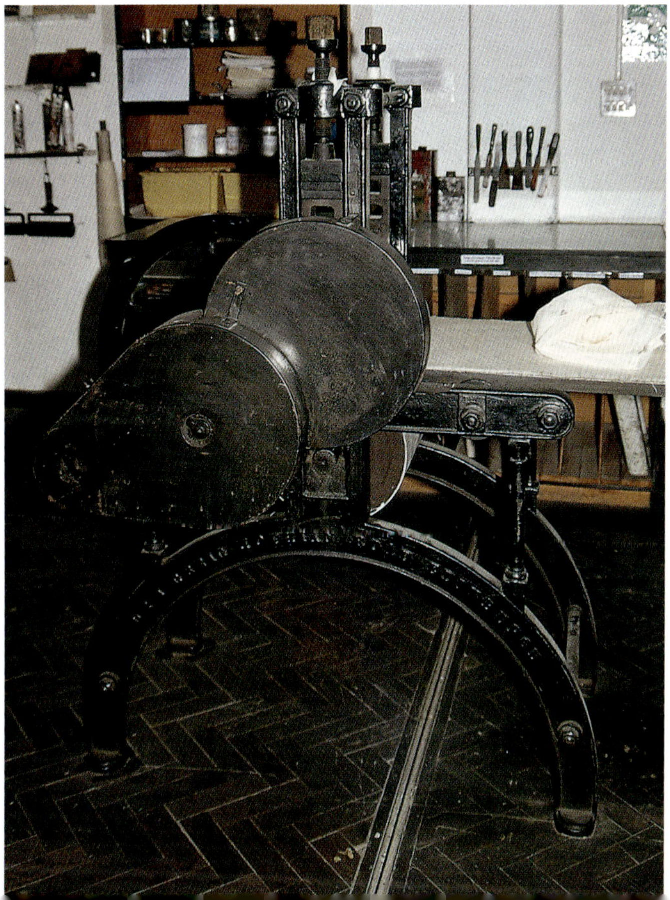

Star-wheeled presses are hand-driven by pulling the long spokes which are attached to the spindle of the upper roller. Most modern machines have a geared system and are driven by a hand-operated flywheel. Presses can also be motorized and some have pressure gauges. The pressure exerted on the plate and paper is controlled by a screw mechanism on both sides of the top roller. After passing through the rollers, the blankets are lifted and the paper peeled from the surface of the plate. The ink is transferred from the plate into the fibres of the paper by the even and steady pressure exerted by the motion and the rollers.

The first printing machines were constructed from strong woods, such as elm or lignum vitae for the rollers and oak for the frame. In the 1830s iron replaced the wood and all modern presses are made from metal. Etching presses have long lives and it is usually possible to buy a second-hand machine.

New etching presses are available from manufacturers and printmaking suppliers such as Rochat, Takach, Griffin, Polymetaal and Intaglio Printmaker. The sizes range from small bench-top models to large free-standing machines. Manufacturers' addresses are given in the section listing suppliers (pp. 231–233) and an internet search may provide other information. Some printmakers make their own presses and offer information about their construction methods on their websites.

Specialist help will be needed to install large machines and presses should undergo regular safety checks by an engineer. Local safety officers may require that the press roller, gears or chain are fitted with guards, or that the printing wheel is fitted with a shield to prevent limbs or clothing being caught in the spokes. Machines should be routinely oiled and greased and checked by studio staff for any signs of damage or general wear and tear. New presses are generally supplied with a tool box for maintenance.

A printing workstation, equipped with a historic press and a glass-topped inking bench.

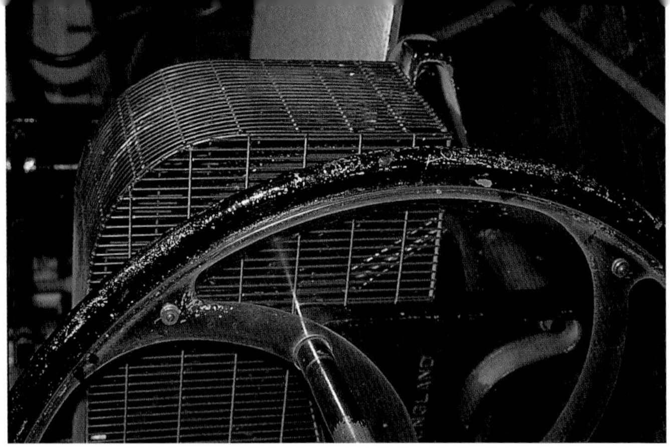

The mechanism of this hand-operated press is fitted with a guard and a sturdy clear plastic sheet has been attached to the wheel for safety purposes.

The presses should be used according to the manufacturers' instructions and the bed should not be run through at an excessive speed. It is possible for the safety stops (which are usually located on the underside of the ends of the press bed) to be sheared off: when a safety stop has been damaged in this way the machine should not be operated as the entire heavy press bed can roll out and fall on the floor, possibly injuring somebody.

BLANKETS FOR INTAGLIO PRESSES

Tightly woven traditional woollen blankets or felts are used on the press. Three slightly different blankets are laid over the plate and paper in a stepped sequence. The blanket closest to the dampened paper is used to absorb most of the water and size which is squeezed from the paper during the printing process. This thin blanket has a fine woven structure and is known as the 'sizing catcher'. The size taken up by the blanket eventually stiffens the fabric, which affects the printing quality. It can be removed by hand-washing or by machine-washing on a wool programme. A specialist washing liquid for woollens is used, as ordinary powders would be too harsh. Ideally the blanket should be dried flat and a spare sizing-catcher blanket should be used while the other is drying.

The middle blanket is thicker and is known as 'fronting' or the 'forming blanket'. This soft pliable blanket helps to press the softened paper into all the indentations on the plate surface.

The third blanket, next to the top roller, has a soft nap and is known as the 'swanskin' or 'pusher blanket'. These blankets should be allowed to air after printing but will rarely need to be washed if acid-free tissue is used and the sizing catcher is well maintained.

Traditional printing blankets can be purchased from specialist intaglio suppliers and press manufacturers. The blankets are expensive and, as they are spoilt if they become inky, printers should only ever handle them and operate the press with clean hands. Blankets can also be destroyed if they are cut or crushed. This can happen if plates with unbevelled edges are run through the press or if bulky, sharp items are impressed into soft ground. Objects that have been accidentally left on the press bed (e.g. scalpels, pens and keys) can easily damage blankets and possibly the roller of the press. After printing is finished for the day the blankets should be released from the roller to prevent the fibres being crushed.

Foam blankets and pressure-sensitive foam sheeting (5–10 mm/¼–½ in. thick) can be used as an inexpensive alternative to traditional felt blankets. The cellular structure of these materials moulds easily to the form of the plate and excellent prints can be pulled. This type of blanket is particularly suitable for processes which can easily result in damage to blankets (soft resists, deeply bitten plates, monotyping, etc.) but the most delicate aquatint will also print well. These blankets tend not to become as damp as felts, but the size from the paper should be rinsed from the foam occasionally. Fabric interfacing (available from haberdashery stores) can be used as an inexpensive sizing catcher.

A number of manufacturers sell registration sheets, and home-made devices can also be made. The registration sheet should wipe clean easily or be covered with acid-free tissue paper or a clear PVC sheet.

PAPER-SOAKING WORKSTATION

A large sink with drainage and a cold water supply is required for soaking paper. The paper may be drained on a vertical

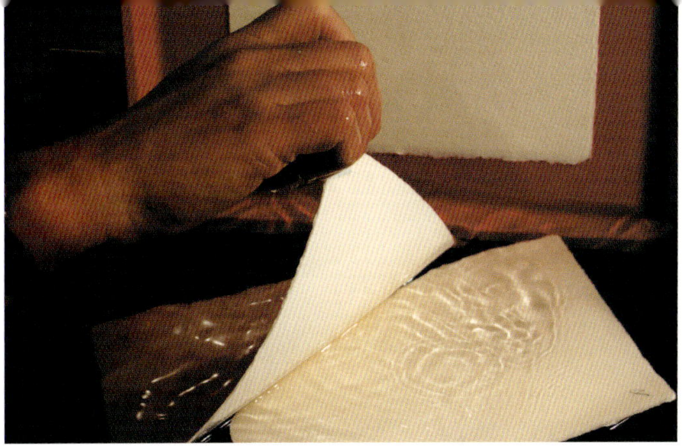

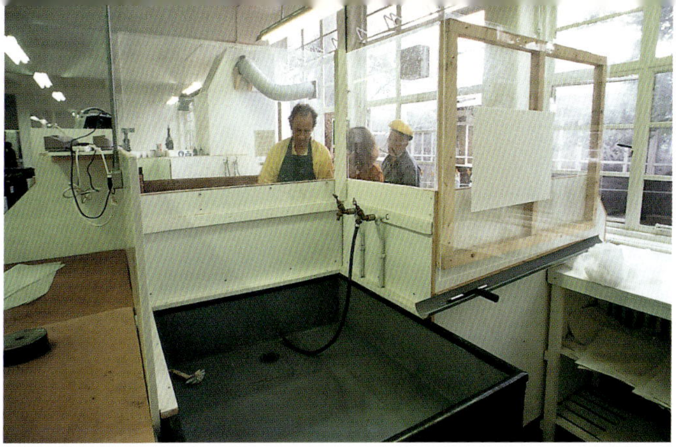

above left A simple paper-soaking sink consisting of two trays purchased from a supermarket.

above right A purpose-built paper preparation workstation. The dampened and drained paper is blotted on the bench on the right.

screen positioned above the sink. This can be made from a sheet of Plexiglas (Perspex) or a rigid gauze stretched over a wooden frame. A plastic gutter fitted below the screen will catch the water as it drains from the paper.

Next to the sink a sturdy workbench with a wipe-clean surface can be used for blotting the paper. A ball of acid-free tissue is useful for removing flecks of dust from dampened paper. A spray bottle for water should be provided for papers which cannot be soaked. Used blotting paper can be dried at the end of the day. Some studios use cotton towels instead of blotting paper. A clean empty shelf should be available for printmakers who use the method of soaking all of their editioning paper and wrapping it in plastic before use.

INKING-UP WORKSTATIONS

WORKSTATION FOR INKING UP OR MONOTYPING WITH WATER-BASED INKS

The bench should be positioned so that an artist inking up plates is well clear of any moving machinery. A glass work surface should be provided, together with a shelf for storing a range of water-based printing inks, soft scrim, pieces of card, tissue squares, surgical gloves, plastic palette knives, basins, sponges and drying rags.

WORKSTATION FOR INKING UP OR MONOTYPING WITH OIL-BASED INKS

The bench should be positioned so that an artist inking up plates is well clear of any moving machinery. Hotplates are not necessary in a modern warm studio and the intaglio plates can be inked up and cleaned directly on the glass or PVC wipe-clean surfaces. This practice cuts down on the amount of ink-soaked newspaper in the studio waste container, which in turn reduces the fire risk. Easily accessible shelving should be provided for cut card, tissue squares, inks that are in use, Easy Wipe compound, copper-plate oils, an ink dabber or ink roller, whiting powder, a paintbrush, cleaning oil and containers of a soapy solution (water with a drop of dish-washing detergent). A magnet strip (from kitchen stores) can be attached to the back of the unit or wall to hold a number of flat-ended ink spatulas. A storage system will be required for clean rags, re-usable rags and dirty rags. If intaglio inks are used in cartridge form with an applicator, a holding stand will have to be created to accommodate them. To reduce fumes in the studio, oil-based inks containing driers can be kept in closed plastic storage containers. A storage container will be required for clean scrim and a neat pull-out rack which fits discreetly under the bench surface can be made for drying used scrim. A set of spring clips attached to the wall may be used to hold and store oily inking-up gloves. These oily gloves should not be used elsewhere in the studio as the grease from them could contaminate other acrylic-resist or degreasing processes.

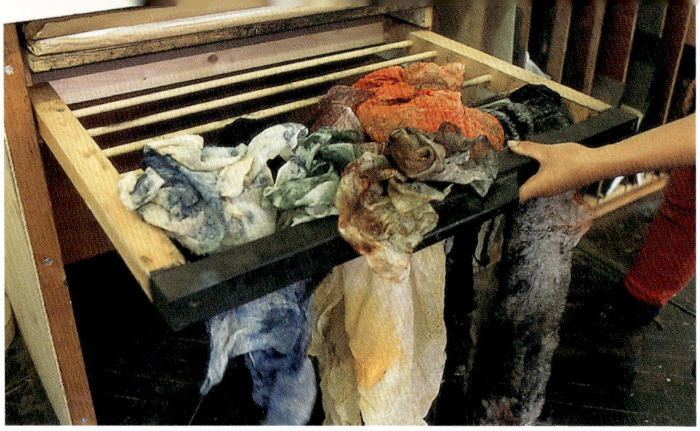

This scrim-drying and storage rack can be slid back under the bench.

WORKSTATION FOR MAKING WATER-BASED PRINTING INKS FROM PAINTS AND ACRYLIC MEDIA

This should consist of a glass work surface and some storage for plastic palette knives, digital scales, some storage containers, a range of water-based paints and a range of acrylic binders.

WORKSTATION FOR MAKING OIL-BASED OR WATER-BASED PRINTING INKS FROM PIGMENTS

A glass work surface, a glass muller, plastic palette knives, digital scales, a particulate respirator, a hand liquidizer (for water-based inks), powder pigments and a range of binders will be required for making inks. The powder pigments should be stored in clearly labelled glass jars with tightly fitting lids. A waterproof marker pen is ideal for labelling the jars as paper labels become very soiled and difficult to read. These finely divided substances are hazardous as they can be inhaled easily. The purchase of flammable and potentially explosive materials such as zinc powder or toxic pigments (for example lead, cadmium and manganese) should be avoided. Previously purchased pigments should be identified and labelled. A particulate respirator should be stored in its own closed container and used when working with powder pigments.

PRINT-DRYING AND FLATTENING WORKSTATION

There are several different ways of drying prints. An effective and traditional method is to place the print between two absorbent pin boards (the boards are usually slightly larger than the press bed). The print is laid between sheets of tissue paper to speed up the drying process, to protect the print from acid in the boards and also to protect the boards from the wet ink. The boards (containing the prints) are built up in a stack on a bench and weighted. The prints will dry fully in around two or three days depending on the temperature and humidity of the studio. A modern version of this system which will dry the prints more quickly is to build the stack inside a drying cabinet (see p. 44).

Monotypes and intaglio prints with heavy ink deposits should be dried on a horizontal metal rack (as used for drying screenprints) or a ballrack (a wooden rack with marbles which can be rolled to hold the paper in position). Once the ink is dry the back of the prints may be sprayed lightly with water and flattened between pin boards.

A shelf for spare blotting paper, tissue paper and some narrow paper strips (used for identifying and locating prints in the stack) is useful.

GOOD STUDIO PRACTICE

It is essential to make safety information available to students, employees and studio users, as the processes and equipment in print studios are potentially hazardous. Well-organized studio systems will reduce the risk of accidents or injury, increase efficiency and help to avoid problems in the general running of the studio and in individual processes. The following is a suggested model for studio information relating to the fine art intaglio system described in this book:

- All studio users must act professionally and show consideration and respect for their colleagues.
- Familiarize yourself with the location of fire exits, fire-extinguishing equipment, eye-wash stations and first-aid equipment in the studio.
- Immediately report to a member of staff any accident, near miss, faulty equipment, hazard or hazardous practice. These

incidents should be recorded and dated in an 'incident book' maintained in the studio. One of the reasons for this is to allow speedy action to be taken to prevent further incidents.

- Never use an electric tool or touch an electrical socket or unprotected switch when the floor or your hands are wet.
- No smoking in the studio.
- When working in the studio wear strong, non-slip shoes and close-fitting clothing. Tie back long or loose hair to eliminate any risk of entanglement in machinery or tools. Jewelry and flexes (of personal stereo headsets or audio equipment) can also be caught.
- Remove rings, necklaces, earrings and bangles, as paints, inks and chemicals can be trapped next to the skin and etching chemicals will react with the metals.
- Wear steel-toe-capped footwear when working with metal sheets, plates, guillotines or presses. Wear leather gloves when filing plates.
- For etching, wear a waterproof apron, eye protection, appropriate gloves and stout, non-slip footwear with steel toe-caps .
- A particulate respirator is necessary when working with powders, dusts or pigments.
- A face mask for aqueous mists is required for the airbrushing process.

WORKING WITH EQUIPMENT AND MACHINERY

- Do not miss out procedures which could compromise safety.
- Be constantly aware of other studio users in the vicinity and do not obstruct clearways.
- Workstations should be used only for their intended purposes, and displayed information should be heeded.
- Do not operate any equipment until you have been thoroughly instructed in its safe use.
- Take full responsibility for being in control of any tool or machinery; moving parts can injure a bystander. Do not distract other studio users, or allow yourself to be distracted when operating machinery or equipment.
- Only use equipment in its designated space. No equipment should be altered or modified.
- Obtain assistance from a staff member if you need to adjust the pressure on the press.

MAINTAINING TOOLS

Specialist intaglio tools which are mainly or historically used for a specific process are described within that section.

- It is important to learn how to sharpen tools as this is part of everyday practice. Tools are sharpened to prevent 'over blunting' and to keep the tip or blade in good condition. Intaglio printmaking tools such as needles, steelpoints, burins, stippling tools, scrapers and mezzotint rockers normally require sharpening when they are first purchased.
- Sharpening equipment and stones can be purchased from tool suppliers. The all-purpose 'Crocker Sharpener' can be used to hold a burin at the correct pitch and angle while it is honed on an oil stone. Burin sharpeners have two angled openings in which the burin is placed when being sharpened.
- Slip stones are made from a medium grit and are suitable for general sharpening, including curved gouges. India stones are made from a tough aluminium oxide abrasive which provides a smooth cut, and the useful India combination stone has a fine grit on one side and a coarse grit on the other side. Hard Arkansas stones are highly favoured and this natural stone is used for honing and polishing a finishing edge. The Norton

A sharpening stone, oil and tools.

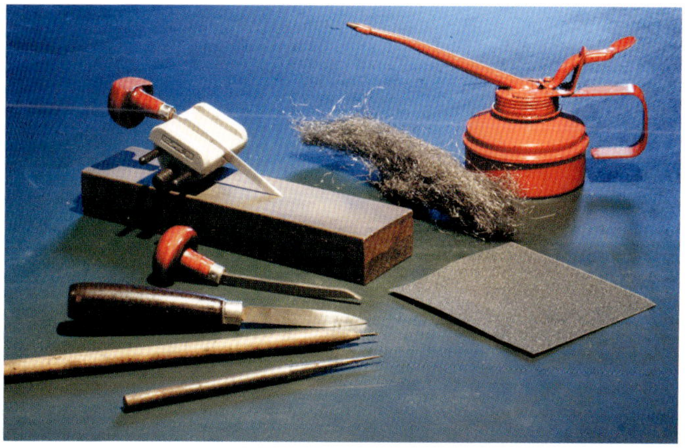

Lily White Washita stone is a special, fast-cutting, natural stone that produces a very fine edge.

- Either water or oil can be used as a lubricant when sharpening tools on stones. This information is usually provided when the stone is purchased.
- Tools should be used for their own specific task. After work on the plate is finished the tools should be cleaned, sharpened and then polished with a leather cloth before being stored in a dry place (corks can be placed on their sharp tips). Scrapers, steelpoints and roulette wheels benefit from being oiled after use.

CARING FOR THE STUDIO

- It is good practice to allow time to tidy up at the end of each work session.
- The floor should be vacuum-cleaned rather than swept to reduce dust.
- Remove dust periodically from inside drying cabinets with a vacuum cleaner.
- Benches and workstations should be left clear and clean, with all tools returned to their storage locations.
- Debris should be removed from the sinks, and these should be rinsed free of any chemicals.
- Waste containers should be emptied daily into an external waste receptacle.
- Presses need to be checked and greased regularly.
- Studio containers for graining paste, degreaser, neutralizing solution, de-oxidizing solution and cleaning oil may need to be refilled.
- Card can be cut for inking plates.
- Empty paint containers can be soaked in water overnight prior to cleaning and recycling.
- The glass on the lightbox and the UV exposure unit should be cleaned regularly.
- Pot plants should be watered regularly.

PERSONAL EQUIPMENT

Some suggested tools, materials and consumables for full-time intaglio printmakers:

- eye protection, apron or overalls, and a range of appropriate gloves
- graphics ruler, T-square and metal straight-edge
- plate materials
- pencils, erasers, pens and a waterproof marker pen
- a portfolio
- a sketchbook
- scissors, scalpels or knives
- a range of resists or collagraph media
- some good quality paintbrushes
- intaglio drawing tools for direct methods, working into resists or collagraphy
- parcel tape, masking tape and clear adhesive tape
- PVC sheet, tracing paper and grained transparent substrates
- tusches and materials for making positives and a translucent blue highlighter pen
- positive-making equipment (e.g. digital)
- a hardboard folder and red cartridge paper
- proofing, editioning paper and tissue paper
- polythene envelopes for storing paper and prints
- a camera for documentation
- a notebook or a computer for documenting edition details
- a personal embossing stamp (printing chop).

THE PRINCIPLES OF INTAGLIO PRINTMAKING

There are three main activities involved in contemporary intaglio printmaking: the artist's concept, the creation of an intaglio plate and printing from the plate.

THE ARTIST'S CONCEPT

There can be many different starting points, such as a desire to utilize found materials, draw delicately, document a series of events, paint expressively, clad a sculpture, work from dark to light, form delicate white lines, explore intaglio printmaking methods in order to find a new expressive language, allow a mechanical process to generate marks, draw *en plein air*, or employ text, photographs or digitally created material.

Once a concept has been arrived at, it can be realized by selecting the most suitable method from the wide range of

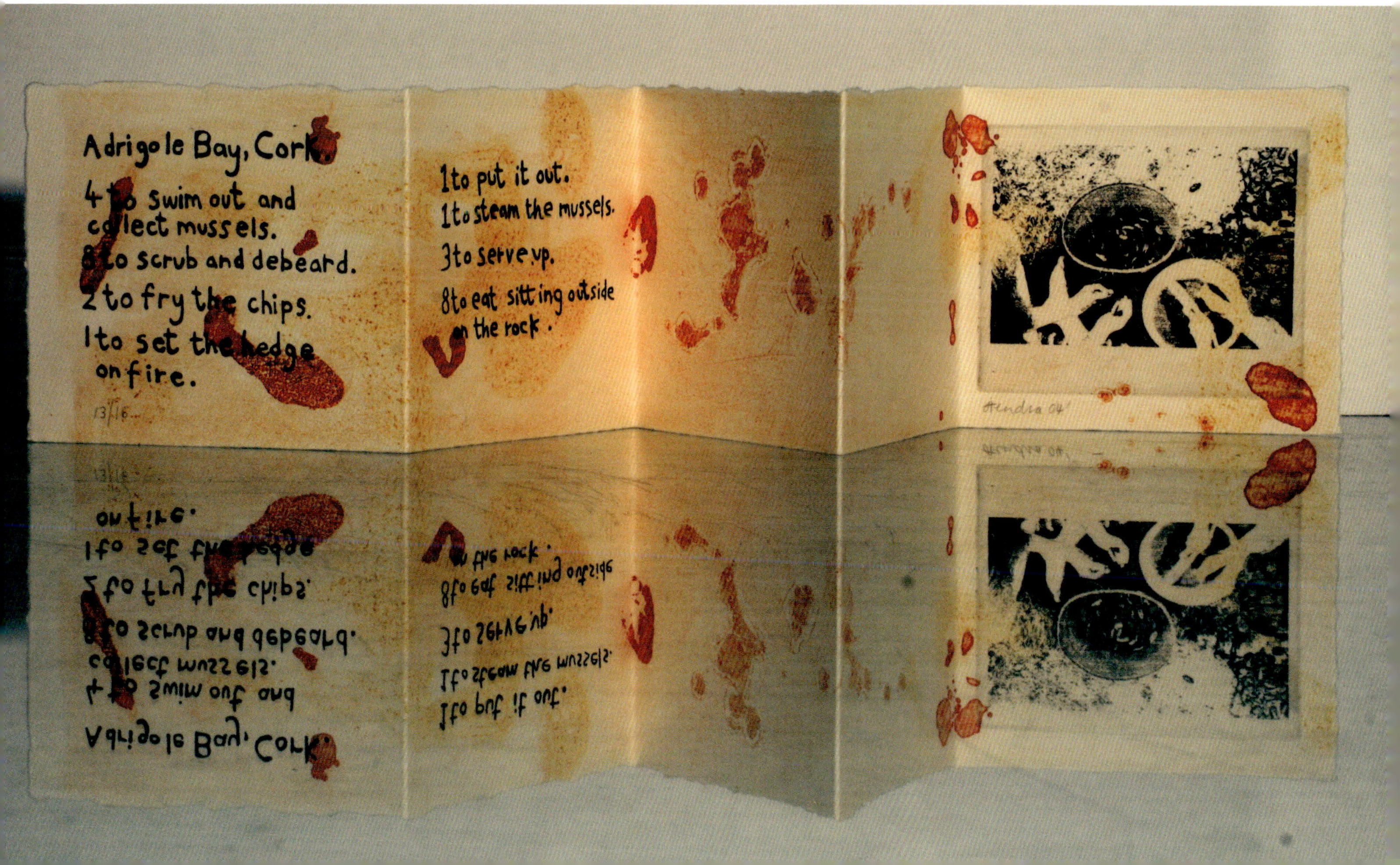

Jenny Hendra (UK), *Dinner at Adrigole Bay*, etching, 23.5 x 41.5 cm (9¼ x 16⅜ in.), 2004. The artist required an edition of prints that would fit the box size of an art vending machine (see www.hayvend.com). A drawn paper prototype and a map were made to test, plan and make the five etched plates for this complex image. Two spit-bitten zinc plates were printed intaglio with orange and red gouache. Two deeply bitten text plates (see p. 120) were inked up in relief with an oil-based ink and printed. The photo-etched plate (see p. 123) was inked up with an oil-based intaglio ink and printed onto the paper which had been dampened on the back. Each dried print was folded into a zigzag book and placed in the vending machine box.

intaglio processes. For instance an artist interested in gestural painting techniques can choose to paint with gesso in the collagraphic process, experiment with lift techniques used within the etching process or make autographic positives for light-sensitive methods. Each of these approaches has particular characteristics which may appeal to the artist for different reasons.

Other factors also influence the choice of process: the tools and media used, the image size, the potential for colour, the required equipment, safety issues, cost, speed of execution and the durability of the plate. Another important issue is how the piece is to be presented: it may take the form of a framed work, a varied folio or a book, or it may be part of an installation, sculpture or performance.

MAKING AN INTAGLIO PLATE

Intaglio printmaking can be considered a bridge between sculpture and drawing or painting in that it involves shaping a plate surface from which an image is printed or cast. It also shares with sculpture the idea that processes are followed to realize the concept.

Traditionally students were taught to make drypoints or engravings as an introduction to plate-making, but artists may start by using the intaglio materials and methods most suited to their concept. They can go on to study other techniques within the medium. Experienced intaglio printmakers can choose to work on plates with methods dating from previous centuries, or can explore new materials and technologies, or can invent their own intaglio techniques.

Intaglio plates can be made from sheets of metal, plastic, thin wood or thick card. They seldom measure more than 5 mm (¼ in.) thick and are usually around 1.5 mm (1/16 in.). Plates are generally rectangular or square but may be any shape that the artist requires. After any sharp edges are removed and the plates have been cleaned, a range of intaglio techniques can be used to create drawn, painted, photographic, digital or action marks on the surface. These methods and the resulting intaglio plates can be broadly classified as being either subtractive or additive. These simple and descriptive categories were first used in the 1950s.

SUBTRACTIVE METHODS

Subtractive methods involve removing or displacing parts of the plate surface to create ink-holding indentations or smooth (non-ink-holding) hollows. All the direct methods and etching techniques can be classed as subtractive.

Direct methods involve removing material from the plate by physical force and include scraping, engraving, polishing, drypoint, mezzotint, burnishing and the action of some power tools.

A more complex subtractive method is to use a mordant or electrolysis to create ink-holding indentations in a metal plate surface. Decaying, dissolving or corroding lines and marks in these ways is known as etching. All of the etching methods such as aquatint and photo-etching can be classified as subtractive.

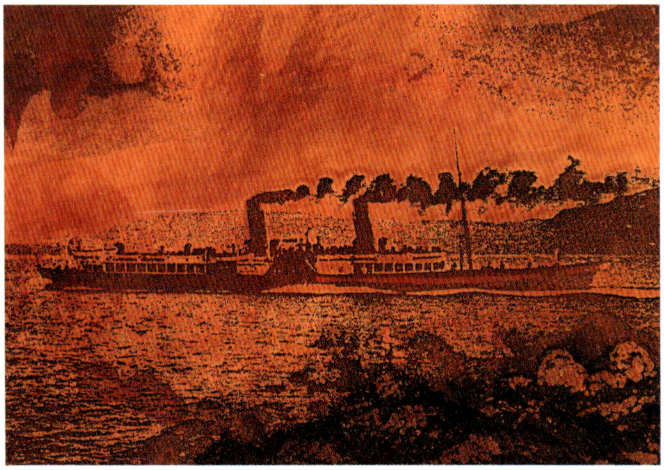

A detail of an etching plate that was made with photoresist together with Lascaux aquatint spray, plate-backing and stop-out resists. The darker tones are the areas that have been etched (see magnified detail on p. 64).

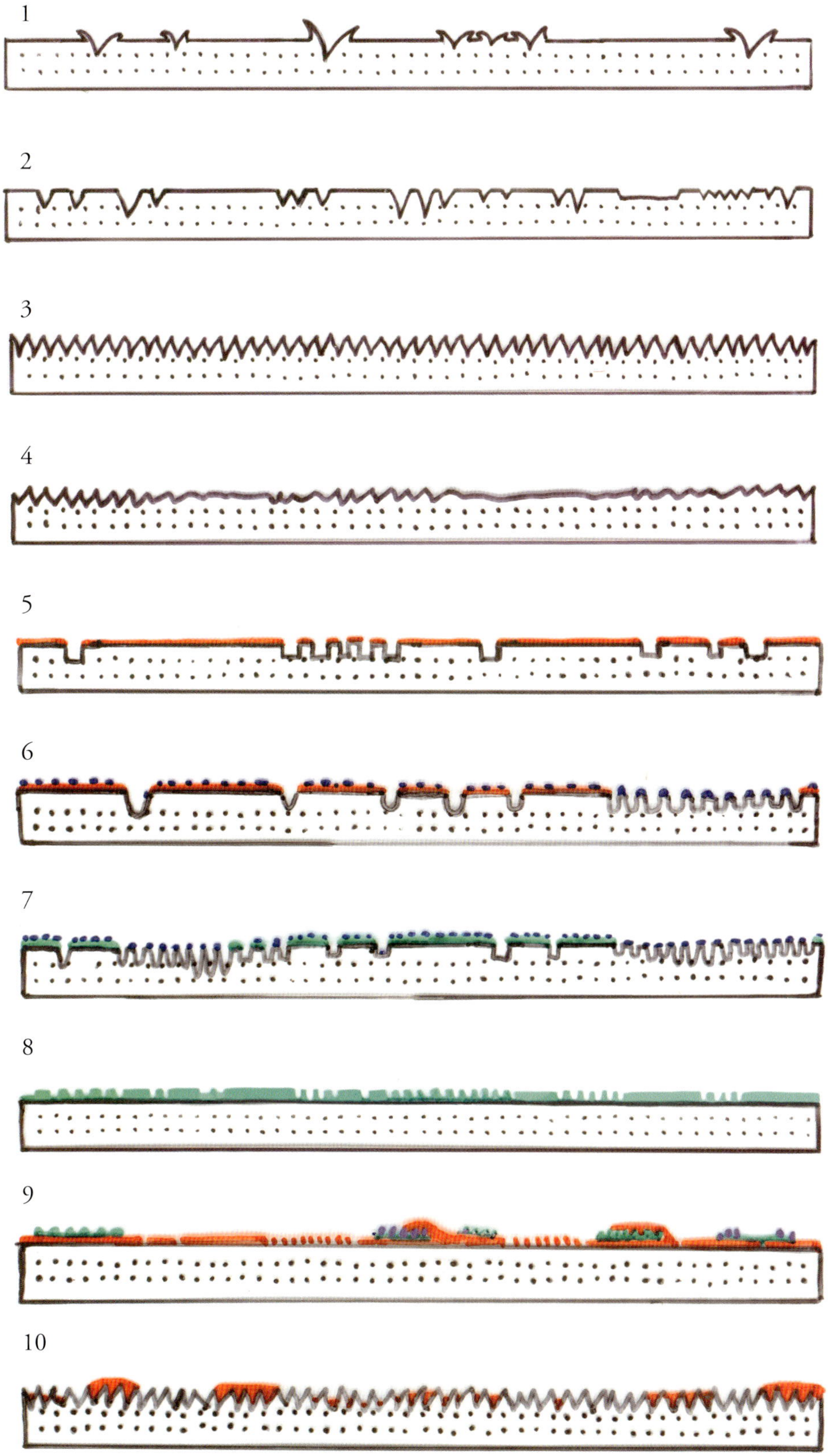

Diagrammatic sections of intaglio plates
1. A drypoint showing indentations and burr.
2. An engraving with any burr removed.
3. A rocked mezzotint plate.
4. The mezzotint plate after burnishing.
5. Hard or soft resist that has been worked into and etched.
6. Hard or soft resist that has been worked into, aquatinted (with sprayed dots of resist) and then etched.
7. A photo-etching showing photoresist that has been aquatinted (with sprayed dots of resist) and then etched.
8. A photocollagraph showing the layer of dry film photoresist: this has been exposed to a dot screen and a positive holding an image, developed, cured, dried and is now ready to print (the plate itself is unchanged).
9. A collagraph showing worked non-ink-holding media, ink-holding media and dry film photoresist (the plate itself is unchanged).
10. A mezzotint plate with added non-ink-holding collagraphic media that is ready to print.

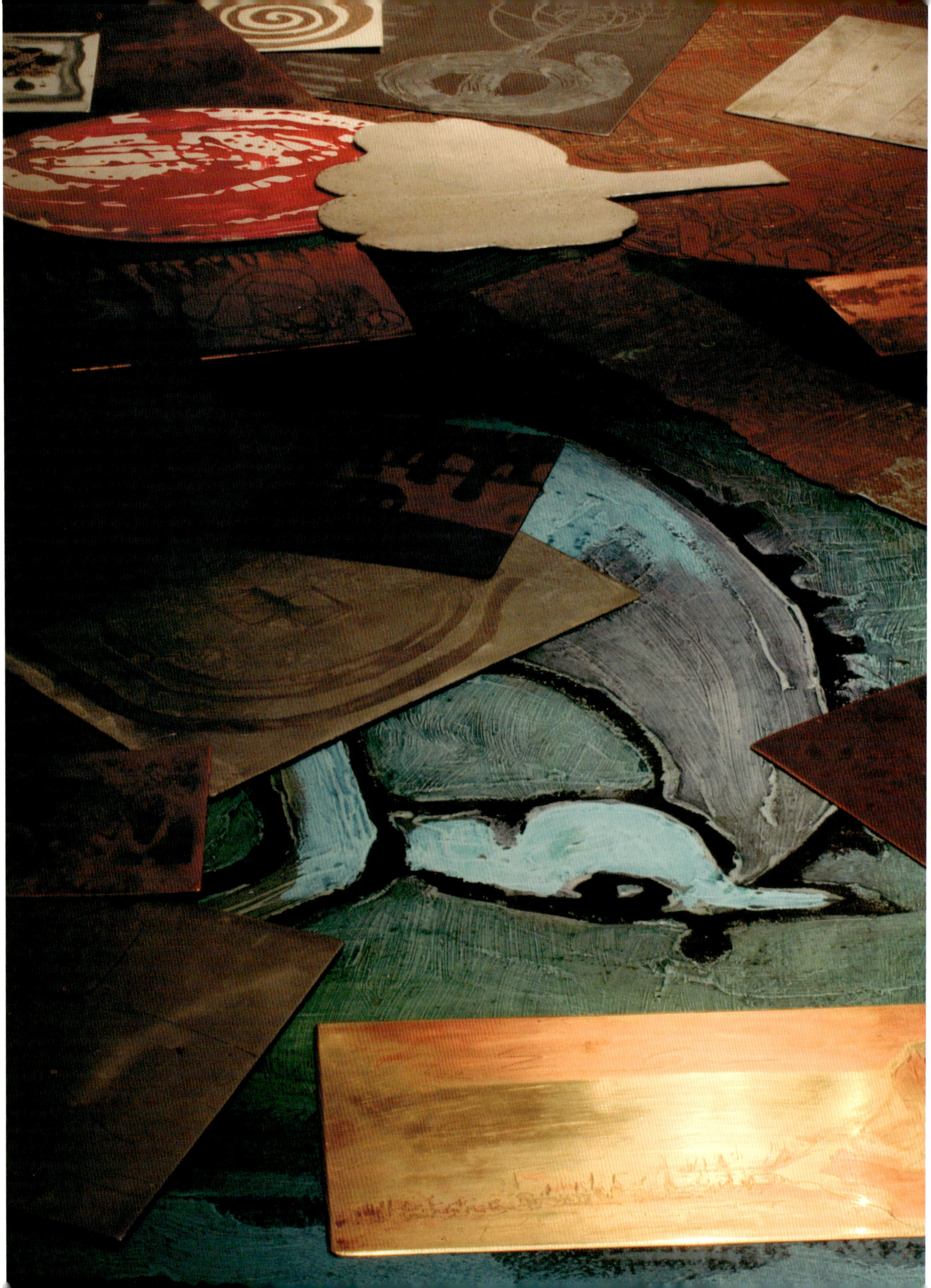

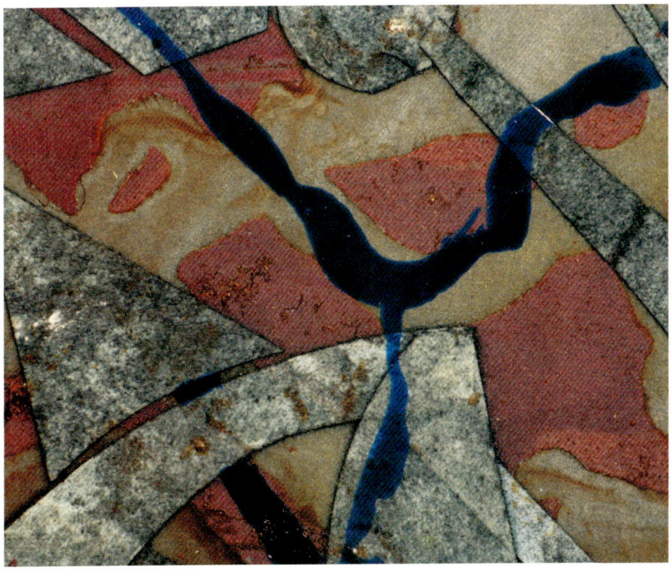

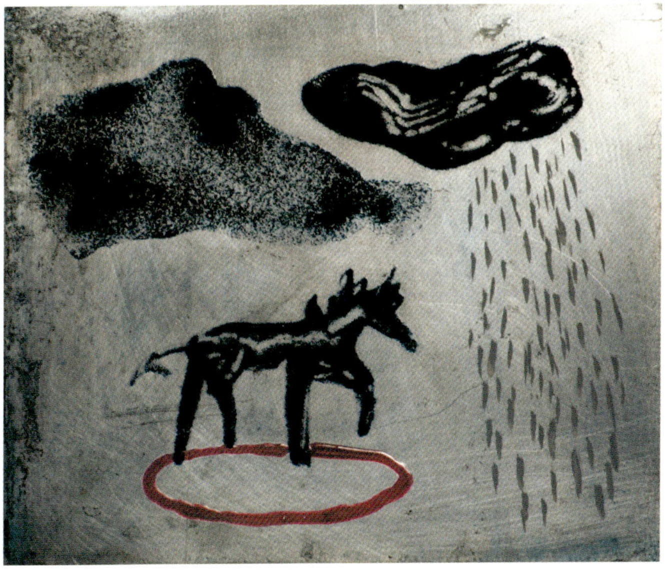

opposite A range of collagraph and etching plates made from brass, copper, aluminium, steel, card and plastic. Carborundum and sand sheets used for the puncture process can also be seen.

above left Thin newsprint and Lascaux resists have been applied to this steel collagraph plate, which is showing signs of corrosion.

above right Lascaux Hard Resist was used to adhere the carborundum to this sealed aluminium plate. Lascaux Gesso and Lascaux Plate-Backing Resist have also been added to the plate.

ADDITIVE METHODS

In these methods a material or medium is added to the plate surface. The added media may be ink-holding, non-ink-holding or both. Parts of this added layer may then be dissolved, removed or displaced to alter its ink-holding properties. In additive processes (unlike subtractive processes) the original supporting plate surface remains intact and the image is formed from the additive material on the plate. Collagraphy and photocollagraphy can be classified as additive methods.

COMBINED INTAGLIO METHODS

The artist can choose to make radical or fine changes to the plate after any process has been used. For example an etched plate with deeply roughened areas can be smoothed flat by scraping and burnishing, or it may be smoothed by filling the indentations with a collagraphic medium which will dry to a smooth surface. In other cases smooth areas can be textured and new images may be superimposed. This approach of combining intaglio methods can be used to create a plate surface which is richly worked and displays subtle complexities. The stages of building the surface may even be planned so that the plate can be polished to reveal earlier etched elements.

PRINTING FROM THE PLATE

Whichever method is chosen, the basis of successful intaglio printmaking lies in gaining an understanding of how the surface of the plate will hold the printing ink and of how the inking-up and printing process relates to this.

The traditional process of inking up begins with the artist applying a stiff ink to the entire plate surface. The plate is then

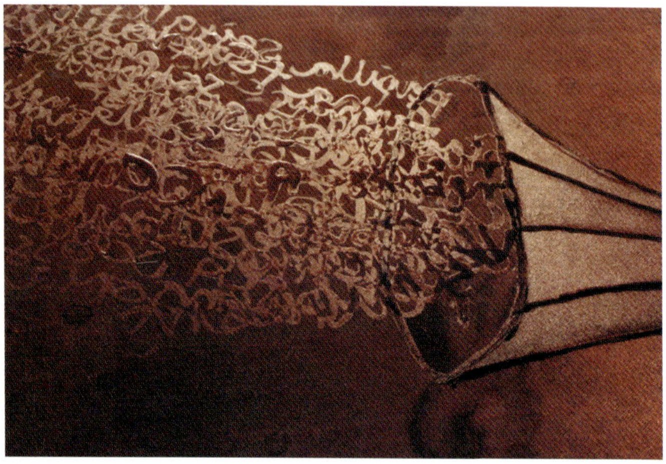

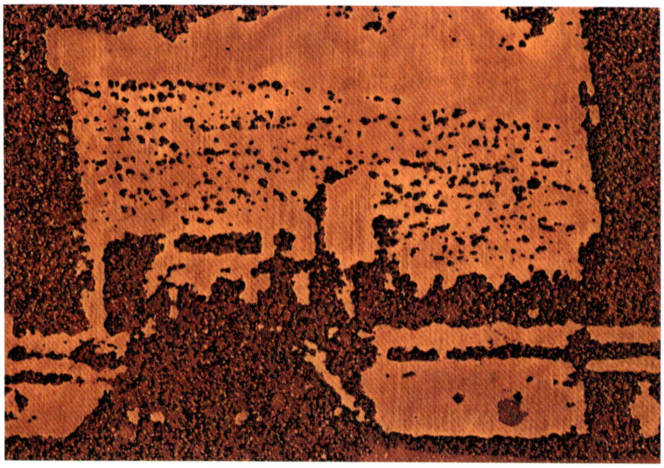

top Different dilutions of Lascaux Hard Resist filled the indentations on this pre-rocked mezzotint plate (see a detail of the print from this plate as the frontispiece and on p. 175).

above A magnified detail (between the ship funnels) of the plate illustrated on p. 60 showing the use of photoresist and Lascaux Aquatint Spray Resist. The etched reticulated areas are darker than the unetched copper.

wiped so that the ink remains in the indentations and the smooth areas of the plate become clean (the inking-up and printing processes are described in detail on pp. 193–213).

The inked-up plate is laid on the bed of an etching press, covered by a sheet of dampened printing paper and then run through the machine. The enormous pressure applied by the press rollers forces the ink from the plate into the fibres of the paper, creating characteristic prominent inky lines and rich velvety tones. The printing process embosses the textured plate into the softened paper and the printed marks will be a mirror image of the marks on the plate. The artist repeats the inking-up and printing process for each proof or print that is required.

As certain features on intaglio plates will hold the ink in characteristic ways, it is possible to analyze plate surfaces and make accurate predictions about how they will print. This skill can be developed by comparing a range of plate surfaces with their related prints. The lines and marks on the plate and print surface may be examined through a magnifying glass. When making this comparison, it can be helpful to imagine the topography of the plate as a landscape with craters, river beds, mountains, escarpments and plateaux. Magnified images of plate surfaces and prints can also be created using a digital scanner. The resulting computer images or printouts are a useful educational support and can be used to illustrate the different types of surface, some of which are described below.

- Lines and pits which are deep, small or narrow will hold the ink easily and print strongly.
- Shallow indentations will hold less ink and print as a lighter tone.
- Lines and pits which are very deep may hold excessive amounts of ink, causing smudging, bleeding or blurring on the print.
- Areas which look like wide river channels with flat smooth beds will retain the printing ink only along their inside edges, printing as two related contour lines. This characteristic effect is known as 'open bite'.

Alison Bracey (UK), *A Place to Dream*, installation, 2003.
Inspired by a visit to Iceland, the artist used etching, collagraphy, screenprinting and photography to create this installation.

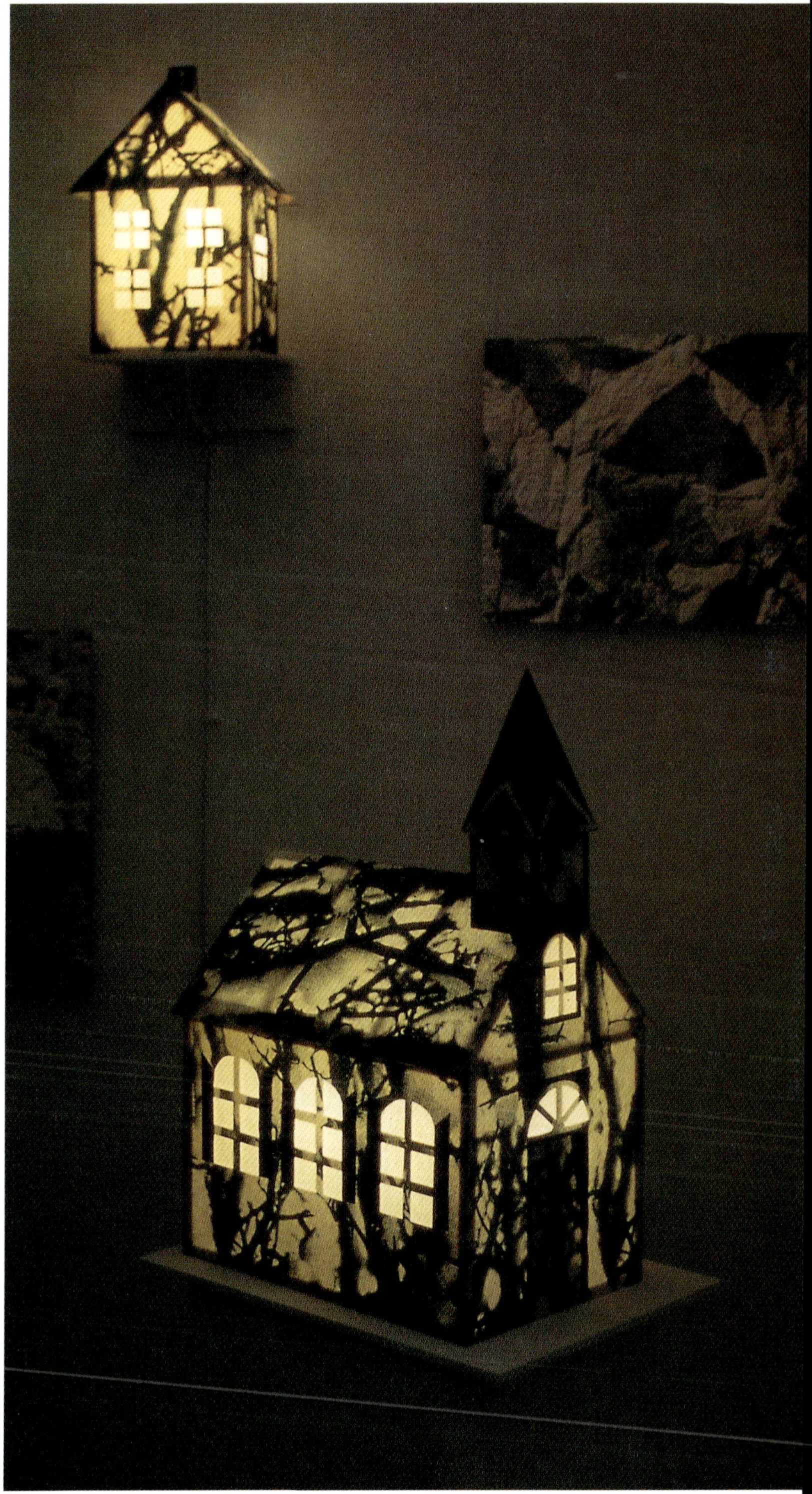

• High smooth areas (plateaux) on a collagraph plate will only retain ink around their contours (outside edges), resulting in a similar printed effect to open bite.

• Densely concentrated groups of tiny indentations will hold the ink as a series of dots and print as a tonal effect. This type of scrobiculated surface can be seen on plates which have been stippled, or where a roulette or the 'carborundum etching' technique have been used.

• Fine reticulated indentations will hold the ink and print as a tonal effect. These networks can be seen on etched plates where an aquatint resist has been used. The network is created when the metal surrounding each dot of resist is etched away. The printed effect is known as 'aquatint'. A reticulated ink-holding surface can also be generated by adhering carborundum particles to a collagraph plate.

• Lines on a directly worked plate which look like a ploughed furrow and show a burr of displaced metal have been made by drypointing. The groove and the burr will both hold ink and the resulting printed line will have a soft, velvety appearance. After a number of prints have been taken the ridge-like burr gradually wears down and the richness of the print will diminish.

• Surface stains may look striking but generally will not print.

PREPARING THE PLATE

SELECTING PLATE MATERIALS

A variety of sheet materials may be used for making intaglio plates and each has its own characteristics. Experienced printmakers select a substrate which is suitable for their chosen intaglio technique and subsequent printing method. Artists who are new to printmaking can experiment with different types of substrate.

The most commonly used metals for etching are copper, brass, zinc and mild steel. Aluminium has become popular in some countries in recent years as it is an inexpensive metal. However, it is dangerously reactive to some mordants and chemicals and for that reason its use is forbidden in most traditional studios. Lead has also been used as a plate material by some printmakers in the past but it is heavy and toxic to handle.

Plates made from plastic, Plexiglas, Lucite, PVC, celluloid, laminates, vinyl tiles, discarded lithographic plates, thin wooden board, Masonite, thick sturdy card, foil-coated card, found materials and metals including tin may be used for other intaglio printmaking methods such as direct or collagraph techniques.

Plate materials can be purchased from metal suppliers, building merchants, printmaking suppliers or art stores. Found materials are also sometimes used. Plates for intaglio printmaking should be strong, flat and malleable so that any sharp edges which would damage the press blankets may be filed and smoothed down. Severely blemished or corroded sheets are generally unsuitable but minor scratches and marks on the surface can be removed.

The thickness of an intaglio plate should be between 0.8 mm and 1.5 mm (around 1⁄16 in.). This corresponds approximately to the traditional measures of 20 gauge to 16 gauge (note that in the gauge scale, the higher the number the thinner the plate). This thickness allows the surface to be worked deeply, sculpturally and vigorously, and will print with a pronounced emboss. Lightly etched plates can be reworked or grained smooth and used for a fresh image. Thinner plates can generally only be used once, are more awkward to wipe and handle, and are less pleasant to work with. In some printing processes, such as multicolour prints and multiple plates, the emboss made by the plate will be flattened by subsequent printings so a thinner plate may be cost-effective to use. If the plates used in a studio are of different thicknesses the printing pressure must be altered for each plate. All the different plate materials must be correctly prepared before any of the intaglio methods can be started.

COPPER

This warm-coloured metal is a satisfying material to work with and has been used for decorative purposes for centuries. It is the classical choice of fine art printmakers for engraving, drypoint, mezzotint and etching. It may be etched reliably without generating noxious fumes and the most delicate washes, lines and marks can be printed. Mordants which have been used to etch copper must be disposed of according to local legislation as copper is harmful to the environment.

Copper fluctuates in price and is generally more expensive than zinc or steel. Unpolished sheets of half-hard copper may be purchased from metal merchants. Smaller-sized copper plates with a polished or mezzotinted (see below) surface are available from printmaking suppliers.

Copper is a harder metal than zinc but more malleable than steel, allowing editions of up to 20 or 30 before any noticeable deterioration. The number of good quality printings from a plate will depend on the delicacy and type of marks, the care taken in inking and wiping, and the printing pressure. Coloured inks may be affected by the copper and will not print true. All of these difficulties can be overcome if the finished plate is steel-faced.

STEEL-FACING COPPER

The process of steel-facing copper plates by electroplating is also known as 'acierage'. It was invented in the 1850s by two Frenchmen named Garnier and Salmon. The protective coating is actually iron, and it does not alter the fine detail on the plate as it is so thin. Many prints may be taken, and coloured inks will print faithfully as the steel facing will not interact chemically with the ink pigments. The facing will eventually wear down but it can be removed carefully and replaced with another layer. Specialist steel-facing services are often advertised in artists' professional journals.

PRE-MEZZOTINTED COPPER

Pre-mezzotinted copper plates are available from printmaking suppliers. These can be burnished in the traditional manner or painted on with collagraph materials.

ZINC

Zinc is a softer metal than copper or steel and is often used for direct intaglio techniques such as drypoint and mezzotint. However, zinc plates will wear down more quickly than a harder metal and zinc cannot be steel-faced to prolong its printing capacity. Very fine aquatints or mezzotints will deteriorate after about 20 prints.

Zinc is more reactive than copper or steel. Some home-made types of resist will interact with the metal, resulting in failure of the resist and foul bite. This metal also reacts violently to some mordants and requires special etching arrangements (see pp. 155 and 159–161). Zinc will also interact with pigments in some inks, such as yellows, altering their colour and affecting their brightness.

Zinc sheet is extensively used in the building trade as a roofing material and generally costs less than copper though more than steel. Large unpolished sheets can be purchased from building merchants. Small plates with a polished finish are available from specialist printmaking suppliers. Zinc plates are sometimes available with an acid-resistant coating on the back. This coating is difficult to remove from the plate.

BRASS

This golden yellow metal is an alloy of copper and zinc with trace elements of iron and silicon. Brass has similar working characteristics to copper but is more resilient.

STEEL

Cold-rolled mild steel is the specific grade used for etching. The manufacturing process of cold-rolling involves the sheet metal being compressed and squeezed between rollers without the application of heat. The amount of pressure applied to the sheet determines the hardness and other properties of the finished metal product. The different treatments result in sheets described as skin-rolled, quarter-hard, half-hard or full-hard depending on how much cold work has been performed. Each of these specifications will etch differently, and if consistency is important it is worth making a note of exactly which type of steel is being used in the studio. Steel which has been heat-treated at any stage of manufacture will etch erratically. Sheet steel for etching should always be cut with a guillotine as cutting methods which involve heat will affect the etch.

Unlike copper, zinc and aluminium, steel has an intrinsic granular structure which will hold the ink, printing as a characteristic plate tone. It is a hard metal, slower to etch and less easy to work on directly than zinc or copper. However, after the plate has been etched, light tones may easily be introduced to the plate using acrylic collagraphic techniques. Steel is ideal for colour work as it does not interact with ink pigments, printing them faithfully. Because of its elemental quality, steel seems particularly suited to vigorous tactile work. Oil-based monotypes also work well as the texture of the plate holds the painted mark quite accurately.

A steel plate will rust rapidly in contact with water (e.g. after etching and stripping). Rust marks will print, so it is important to avoid unwanted corrosion when the plate is being worked. This can be achieved if the plate is dried rapidly in a drying cupboard. Steel plates used for collagraph methods may be painted on both sides with Lascaux Hard Resist to reduce the risk of rusting. Plates should be stored in a dry place after being lightly oiled to prevent rust.

Steel is generally only available in large sheets and a sturdy, powerful and sharp guillotine is required to cut it. It is used in the fabricating industry and so is widely available and inexpensive. The metal generally arrives from the manufacturer coated in a greasy film which must be thoroughly removed by repeated degreasing.

ALUMINIUM

This silver-coloured metal is commonly used in the fabricating industry and is usually cheaper than steel. Aluminium is not generally recommended for printmaking due to its reactive nature. In a shared studio, where a range of mordants and metals are being used, there is a real risk that an aluminium plate could be placed mistakenly in a mordant for copper or for steel, resulting in a violent and dangerous reaction such as the generation of hydrogen gas and heat.

However, some printmakers favour aluminium and etch it with copper sulphate. It is lighter in weight and colour than zinc and – as it is a soft metal – only short editions are possible. Aluminium may be sealed with a layer of Lascaux Hard Resist and used for collagraphs.

TIN

One of the earliest known metals, tin is silvery-white in colour and corrosion-resistant. It has a low melting point and an affinity for adhering to other metals. It is occasionally used to make collagraph plates.

PLASTIC, PLEXIGLAS, LUCITE AND PVC SHEET

These materials are used by printmakers for monotyping, engraving, drypoint and collagraph techniques. Celluloid (cellulose nitrate plastic) was developed and marketed by John Wesley Hyatt in 1870 and used for drypoints by artists such as Picasso. This material was soon replaced by other plastics, such as Lucite (methyl methacrylate polymer), which was invented in the 1930s and was one of the first plastics derived from petrochemicals. Plexiglas was manufactured by another company around the same time and this brand name became more associated with the clear plastic sheet. PVC (polyvinyl chloride) was developed in 1912.

Small particles of many types of plastic or PVC sheet are toxic so these materials should not be sanded. The more flexible types should be chosen as more brittle sheets may splinter under the great pressure exerted by the press. Clear sheets are particularly useful as a map may be drawn on the back and used as a guide when image-making.

WOOD, MDF, LAMINATES AND HARDBOARD

Thin sheets of plywood, MDF (medium density fibreboard), laminated board and hardboard (Masonite) are often used as collagraph plate substrates. Dust particles of MDF and many types of natural wood are toxic and care must be taken when cutting or drypointing these materials. A particulate respirator should be worn and dust should be vacuumed up to protect other studio users. The sheet may be sealed with an acrylic varnish on both sides to reduce further dust and to prevent warping. Photopolymer films will also bond strongly to the surface of wood, sealed with an acrylic layer.

LINOLEUM AND VINYL

These materials may be worked into with engraving or linocut tools and may then be inked up in the intaglio manner. The plate can be printed onto heavyweight paper or a cotton linter.

The press will have to be adjusted to accommodate this thicker material and a foam blanket should be used. Alternatively a plastercast may be made of the inked-up plate.

CARDBOARD AND FOIL-COATED CARD

Thick, sturdy cardboard may be used for collagraph techniques but as plates tend to become damaged easily this material is less suitable for large editions. Tinfoil glued to card or foil-coated card from disposable food storage carton lids can be used successfully: marks and lines made using ballpoint pens and large blunt nails will print quite well. These materials are easily cut to different shapes and sizes.

FOUND MATERIALS

Intaglio plates have been made from found objects such as sheets of corroded metal, cogs, gaskets, card, doilies, origami and delicate wire. Artists sometimes arrange these directly on the press bed or on a thin, protective, smooth PVC sheet. The objects may be cleaned and used to create an emboss or in some cases may be inked up. These materials must be thin with no sharp edges which might damage the press or cut the blankets. A foam printing blanket should be used for all deeply textured plate surfaces.

CUTTING AND FILING PLATES

CUTTING PLATES

The decision about the maximum size of a plate is determined by the image, press-bed dimensions, the size of the mordant tanks, and standard paper and plate sizes. Pre-cut plates can be purchased in a range of sizes from intaglio suppliers but it is more cost-effective to purchase sheet metal and cut this to size on a metal-cutting guillotine. Plates in any case may sometimes need to be reduced in size or an image may benefit from being trimmed.

• The plates are worked on in the plate preparation area. Eye protection and a dust mask should be worn as metal, wood or plastic filings and dust particles can damage the eyes and irritate the lungs. When preparing plates, contact lens wearers must be especially careful and should wear spectacles instead. Safety footwear with steel toe-caps will offer some protection if a plate is dropped, and a thick apron and leather or suede gloves will help guard against cuts and splinters.

• Metal plates may be cut to size with metal snips or on a metal-cutting guillotine. The plates may be measured up, marked with a waterproof marker pen or a steel point and then cut accurately to size.

• Plastic sheets may be measured up and the 'cutting line' drawn with a waterproof marker pen. Strips of masking tape (firmly stuck down on the line on both sides of the sheet) will reduce the risk of cracking during the cutting process. The sheet should be laid on a cutting board on a stable bench and a steel straight-edge positioned along the drawn line. A sharp Stanley knife should be used to score the plastic repeatedly, cutting deeper each time. Some artists use an electric jigsaw to cut plastic, Perspex or PVC sheets but this method creates quantities of hazardous dust.

• Wood can be sawed.

• Card and linoleum can be cut with scissors or a knife.

• Plates used for multicolour printing should be G-clamped together and filed to ensure that they are exactly the same size as each other.

BEVELLING PLATE EDGES

It is important to file the plate edges to a 45° bevel as these may otherwise cut the printing paper or the felt blankets of the etching press. The bevelled edges should then be smoothed down with fine abrasive paper to remove sharp splinters and fragments of metal which can injure hands and damage resists.

Equipment and materials required

Work in the plate preparation area at the workstation for filing plates (see p. 43).

• safety clothing

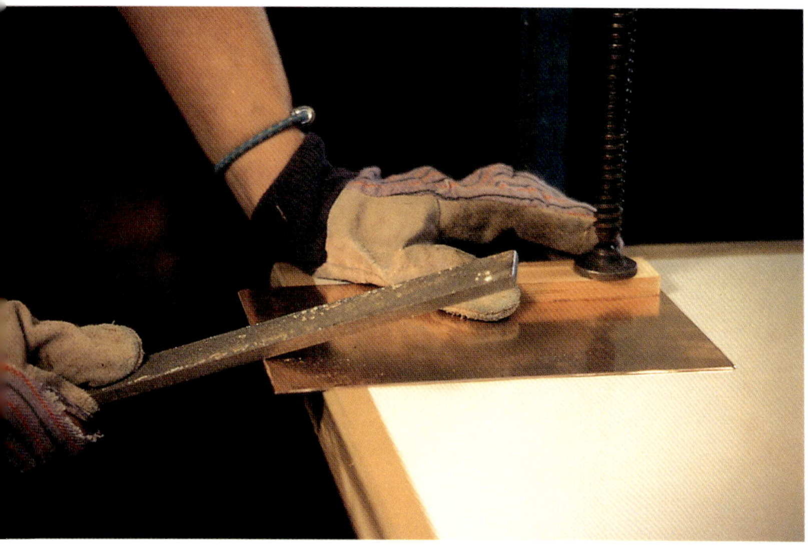

A copper plate being bevelled.

- two G-clamps
- a coarse and fine file for metal
- a range of abrasive papers
- a disposable wiping cloth

Working method

Flat and straight coarse and fine files with wooden or plastic handles may be purchased from tool suppliers. Files should be kept for the different metals and never used on other materials. When files used for copper and brass become clogged and less effective, buy new files and use the old ones for steel plates.

- Safety clothing and protection should be worn as when cutting plates (see above).
- Secure the plate to the bench with G-clamps.
- Take up a comfortable position and hold the file against the edge of the plate. Without applying too much pressure move the file rhythmically at an angle along the sharp edges of the plate to smooth them down to a 45° bevel. Round off each corner of the plate.
- To gain control of the file and its effects notice how the teeth on the file cut the metal and how the different filing movements attack it.
- For perfect filing, the teeth can be wiped with a leather pad after every third stroke. This removes filings from the teeth and helps prevent gouges in the plate. Soapstone or chalk can also be rubbed on the file to minimize clogging.
- The filed edge should have a regular fine bevel. Use a sheet of fine abrasive paper to smooth away any remaining splinters that can be felt on the edges or corners. When the filed edges feel smooth, the plate is ready to be prepared for the next process.
- The workstation should be tidied up and the metal dust removed with a vacuum cleaner.

CLEANING AND DE-OXIDIZING PLATES

Successful platemaking and printing depend on correct preliminary cleaning, as the presence of unwanted materials such as dried ink, paint, resists, oxidization, alkaline residues or grease can cause a range of technical problems. These substances will create a surface which is too powdery and unstable for resists or collagraph materials to adhere to firmly, or else the action of the mordant may be blocked, preventing any etching taking place. Some materials cannot be drawn through easily, or they may interact with resists, collagraph materials or printing inks, causing foul bite or discolouration.

For these reasons the plate must be thoroughly cleaned, deoxidized, degreased and correctly rinsed before the application of any resist or collagraph material, and prior to drypointing, mezzotinting or monotyping. In most cases the graining, polishing or degreasing processes which are described on the following pages will clean the plate. Soiled plates can be cleaned and de-oxidized with a range of professional or household materials. The correct safety clothing should be worn for each method even when the cleaning materials are classified as safe for ordinary household use.

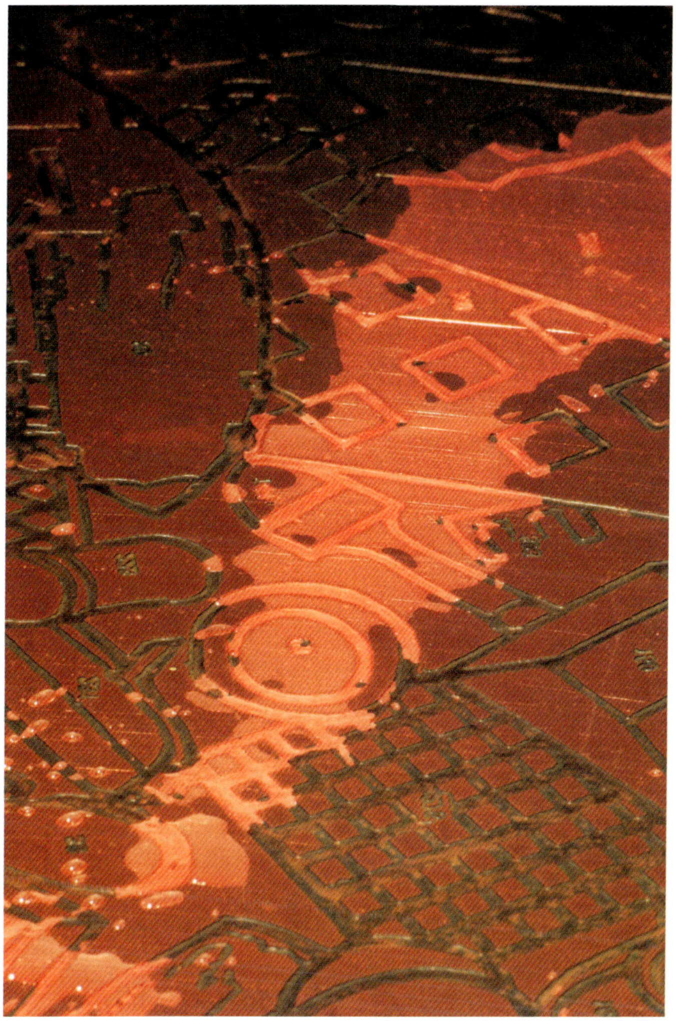

A splash of de-oxidizing solution on a copper plate (see plate on p. 12 and print on p. 199).

• Metal plates which are coated in solvent-based paints or resists can be stripped in a low-toxicity paint stripper (follow product safety instructions).

• A solution of Marseilles soap left on a plate overnight will break up most varnishes and paints.

• Resists should be identified and removed with the appropriate resist remover.

• Metal-cleaning preparations can be used if the plate is very soiled or is a found object.

• A mild detergent such as household dishwashing liquid and water can be used to clean dirt and oil from the plate. This will remove a certain amount of oxidization from zinc and aluminium.

• Oxidization caused by contact from mordants, moisture, chlorides and pollutants in the air can be removed from copper and brass with salt dissolved in household vinegar, or lemon juice. Oxidization on steel plates may have to be scrubbed with steel wool. Plates may also be polished clean with fine whiting (precipitated chalk) or a paste of rottenstone and mineral oil.

• Lime deposits on metal may be removed using laundry water softener.

GRAINING THE PLATE SURFACE

This preparatory process involves working the entire surface of the plate with an abrasive paper or a grainy paste to generate a fine tooth. The grained plate feels even with a satin finish and but when it is examined with a magnifying glass the toothed surface has a serrated or jagged appearance. These tiny hooks and barbs provide an ideal surface onto which resists and collagraphic media can grip.

Toothing the plate by hand with a water based graining paste is quiet and inexpensive. This method relates directly to classical intaglio plate preparation, to the graining process used in stone lithography and to the process of pre-polishing. A small quantity of metal is removed during the process and oxidization marks, irregularities or imperfections on the plate surface are ground away. A very fine tooth is suitable for all standard etching bites, photoresists, fine layers of resist and photocollagraphs. A coarser tooth may occasionally be required for some types of collagraph and very long etching bites.

A non-scratch fabric graining roll is used to rub the paste in a circular motion against the plate surface and this action causes the particles in the paste to create numerous tiny scratches. The size and characteristics of each scratch are determined by the type, shape and size of the particles in the graining paste as well as the directional movement and pressure of the graining roll. The printmaker abrades the plate in this way until the entire surface of the plate is evenly scored and has the texture of a grained lithographic stone or a fine drafting film. After the plate has been worked and inked up, the tooth will hold a small quantity of ink which will print as a light plate tone. If a white or very pale tone is required, the toothed surface may be polished smooth to prevent it holding any ink.

Silica sand, aluminium oxide, carborundum grains and pumice powder are the most commonly used abrasive materials. Silica sand is a component of abrasive papers for sanding wood (but is sometimes used by printmakers). Its use is considered to be hazardous as it contains free silica which can cause silicosis, a form of lung cancer. Aluminium oxide is widely used for abrasive paper and is considered safer to use than sand. If plates are sanded with an abrasive paper rather than grained, 'wet and dry' paper should be used with water. Aluminium oxide is also available as an abrasive grit in the following grit sizes: 36, 46, 60, 80, 100, 120, 150, 180, 240 and the very fine 320. Carborundum (silicon carbide) is a synthetic abrasive which was first made in 1890 by the inventor Edward Goodrich Acheson. Carborundum grains are available in a range of sizes (coarse: 36–80 grit; medium: 120–180 grit; fine: 220–400 grit) and can be used for several intaglio printmaking processes. Carborundum is an excellent abrasive material without any of the disadvantages of silica sand or aluminium oxide. It can be purchased from printmaking suppliers and jewelers' suppliers. Pumice stone is a volcanic ash that is formed by the solidification of lava permeated with gas bubbles. This natural mineral is sold as a powder and is available in a range of different sizes (very fine, fine, medium and coarse). It is considered to be one of the most gentle media for graining and polishing. Pumice is available from artists' suppliers, soapmaking suppliers and printmaking suppliers. Household cream cleaners (such as Cif) make an effective tooth on plate surfaces and will also act as an alkaline degreaser.

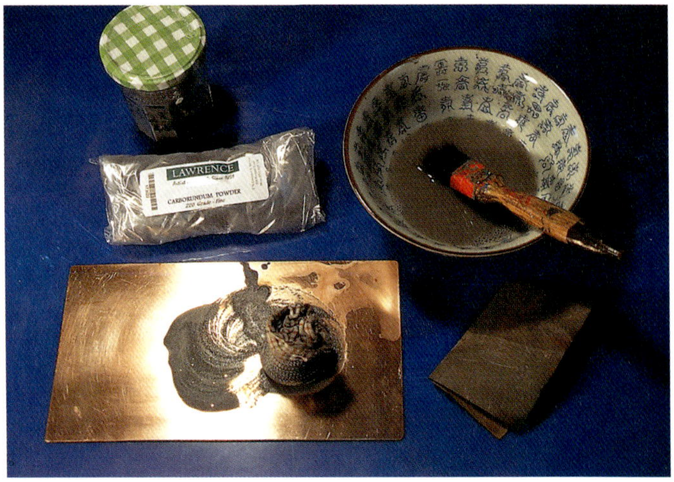

Tools and materials for graining a plate.

MAKING A GRAINING PASTE

Equipment and materials required

Work in the plate preparation area at the workstation for graining plates (see p. 43).

- storage containers of pumice powder (fine, medium or coarse)
- storage containers of carborundum (180 and 220 grit)
- some squat, sturdy plastic containers with lids
- a plastic tablespoon
- some water in a jug
- a waterproof marker pen
- a bowl and a graining roll for each graining paste

Working method

- Wear a dust mask and gloves when making up the paste.
- Spoon four tablespoons of water into the container and then add six tablespoons of the selected abrasive. Mix into a thick paste, adding another tablespoon of water if required. Once

the excess dry abrasives have been returned to their storage containers the dust mask may be removed safely.

• Label the container 'graining paste' and write the size or type of powder added. If several different types of graining paste are being used in the studio there is a risk that larger particles can become mixed up in the fine graining mixtures: this contamination will result in large unwanted scratches on plates which are being finely grained. To avoid this, each mixture should have its own designated storage container and graining pad. The graining roll should also have its own clearly labelled plastic storage bowl.

• Store each paste (with the lid on to reduce evaporation) and stir in a little water from time to time to prevent it drying out and becoming powdery.

TECHNIQUES FOR GRAINING PLATES

Equipment and materials required

Work at the workstation for graining plates (see p. 43) and wear neoprene gloves, eye protection, footwear with steel toecaps and an apron.

- the graining paste in a sturdy plastic container with a lid
- a waterproof wipe-clean workboard
- the filed metal or plastic plate
- a bowl and a graining roll (see p. 74)
- a soft decorating brush (8 cm/3⅛ in. wide)
- some disposable wiping cloths

Working method for graining plates by hand

Plates for etching and collagraph methods are finely grained as a preparatory stage. Steel plates have a natural grain and do not need to be toothed. Gesso can be painted on card and MDF plates to create a strong surface with a tooth. Plates used for monotyping techniques will print differently if they are grained as the toothed surface will hold the inks more firmly and the ink is less likely to bleed off the edges of the plate.

• Lay the plate in the middle of the waterproof wipe-clean workboard. Study its surface, checking for scratches and rust. The process of scraping and burnishing may be used to remove scratches and marks (see pp. 93–94). Etching plates should be grained on both sides as a tooth will also be needed for the plate-backing resist. Soft metals such as aluminium will be easier to grain than harder metals. If the plate is very dirty it should be cleaned before graining.

• Select an appropriate graining paste. Dip the graining roll in this and apply the abrasive to the plate surface. Rub steadily in small circles, pressing down firmly on the roll. Minor scratches and oxidization marks are removed when the plate is grained. The plate becomes matt-looking and the aim is to make the entire surface evenly toothed.

• Watch out for larger abrasive particles which will describe unwanted deeper circular scratches on the plate. This can be prevented by removing any large unwanted particle (from the base of the graining roll) and continuing rubbing until any unwanted scratches or scores are softened and evened out.

Working method for graining plates using power tools

Metal plates can be toothed using an electric or pneumatic power tool. Drills, grinders or sanders can be fitted with equipment such as sanding pads or wheels which can be used to create a tooth on the plate. The kits, relevant adaptors and user information are available from the suppliers.

Working with power tools is hazardous and the equipment must be correctly set up in a dry area. The tools, flexes, circuit breakers and plugs must be well maintained and used safely. Sanders create noise and dust, and must be fitted with a dust bag or local extraction system. Electric machines must never be used in damp areas or for wet sanding because of the risk of electrocution. Pneumatic tools can also be hazardous and the operator must wear full face protection. Angle grinders are considered to be one of the most dangerous power hand-tools to use and need to be equipped with safety guards as they may throw off flying fragments. The operator should never stand directly in front of the wheel when it is started up due to the possibility of a graining wheel disintegrating. It is very important that machines are set to rotate at the correct speed and the manufacturer's instructions should be followed carefully.

If a decision is made to use power tools the safety guidelines provided by departments such as the US Department of Labor, Occupational Safety & Health Administration (OSHA) should be downloaded from the relevant website and followed. Training should be given to students, and safety clothing suitable for metalworking should be provided and worn. The process will generate heat and the operator must wear well-fitting leather metalworking gloves which allow a good grip of the machine. Plates must be firmly attached to the bench with G-clamps and artists should be aware that accidents are often caused by bangles, scarves, necklaces, long hair, wristbands, rings, objects on the workbench and the electrical flex becoming caught up in the machine.

Working method for cleaning up

Graining paste will dry out as it is used, and after graining is complete any uncontaminated paste can be scooped up and brushed back into the storage container. The surface of the plate and the waterproof workboard should be wiped with a soft disposable cloth. If the paste is full of grit and metal particles it should be wrapped in the cloth and disposed of with the studio waste; pastes which have been used on copper plates will contain copper particles which have to be disposed of in accordance with local legislation. The paste should not be washed down the sink in case it blocks the plumbing or contains copper particles. The graining roll should be stored in a dedicated labelled storage container. The workstation should be tidied up and wiped clean. The plate is now ready to be degreased. Soiled hands or skin can be cleaned with soap and pumice and then rinsed with water.

MAKING A GRAINING OR POLISHING ROLL

A tightly rolled and bound cloth can be used for graining or polishing. A separate roll is made for each process to prevent contamination resulting in unwanted scratches. A plastic bowl can be used to store each polishing roll separately.

Equipment and materials required

- a ruler
- a piece of cotton fabric
- string
- scissors
- a plastic bowl

Working method

Work on a clean bench.

A range of roll sizes can be useful, the following measurements are for a standard- to large-sized roll (5 cm/2 in. diameter base measurement and 3 cm/1⅛ in. diameter handle when finished).

- Choose a cloth with no seams or thicker areas (an old dish-drying towel). Measure and cut the cloth to approximately 40 x 50 cm (16 x 20 in.).
- Lay the cloth flat so that the long sides are to the left and right. Fold the cloth in half so that the two short edges meet at the top. The folded cloth now measures 40 x 25 cm (16 x 10 in.).
- Take the top edge and fold it down so that its edge lies 5 cm (2 in.) from the bottom edge. Smooth the rectangle down so that it lies flat. The folded rectangle now measures 40 x 15 cm (16 x 6 in.). Take the bottom edge and fold it up so that it lies 5 cm (2 in.) from the top.
- Take the right-hand end of the now 40 x 10 cm (16 x 4 in.) rectangle of cloth and fold it over so that its edge lies 6 cm (2½ in.) away from the left-hand end of the rectangle (after this fold the dimensions are 23 x 5 cm/9 x 2 in.).
- Turn the cloth around so that the fold is at the top. Start rolling at the bottom end and roll up the cloth as tightly as possible.
- Hold the cloth in your hand, with the broader end as the base, and check that it would be easy to work with. If the roll feels too large, too small or too tall, unwind the cloth and refold it in a different way until it feels comfortable. When the

roll feels satisfactory it can be bound tightly with string so that it holds its shape. Tuck in the ends of the knot.

POLISHING THE PLATE SURFACE

The process of polishing involves smoothing down any errors, irregularities, unwanted grained areas or imperfections on the plate surface. A small quantity of metal is removed so that the final polished surface is smooth, shiny and non-ink-holding. These smoothed areas will print as whites or very pale tones.

Various techniques and materials can be used to create a fine or mirror polished surface. The polishing process involves using polishing materials to make a series of increasingly fine scratches on the surface. The size and characteristics of each scratch are determined by the type, shape and grade of the particles in the polishing compound. The scratched lines should intersect at 90° to form a complex network. Each time the direction is changed the polishing action cuts across the earlier lines and reduces their depth.

Traditional and modern polishing materials are used by jewelers, antique restorers, housekeepers, modelmakers and metalworkers. Liquid and paste polishes, compound bars made with very fine abrasives (chrome oxide or white aluminium oxide), flexible abrasive blocks, charcoal blocks, fine steel wool, fine bronze wool, very fine emery cloth (Crocus cloth), jeweler's rouge (a reddish powder mainly composed of ferric oxide), rottenstone, Vonax (for plastics) and Satene abrasive compounds (greaseless, air-drying, abrasive compositions for coating mops or scurfs) are available from specialist suppliers. The polishes may contain acids, anti-oxidants, ammonia, anhydrous chemicals, inhibitors, slip agents, grime removers, enhancers or organic solvents. The particles in these preparations may be zirconium silicate, aluminium silicate carbides, diamonds, jeweler's rouge, garnets, chromium oxide, plastics, pumice or whiting (precipitated chalk). Very fine abrasive powders or grains (see p. 72) can be purchased and mixed up into home-made polishing pastes. Light oils or tallow-based lubricants (Bobbing grease, Albo or J grease) or water can be added to the powders to create a polish.

Polishes are applied or removed from the plate with non-scratching lint-free cloths, mops, microfibre polishing cloths, felts, scurfs or bobs. Each cloth should only be used with one type of polish. Cloths which are impregnated with polishing materials are also available.

MAKING WATER-BASED POLISHING PASTES

Equipment and materials required

Work in the plate preparation area at the workstation for polishing plates (see p. 43).

- storage containers of pumice powder (fine, very fine)
- storage container of jeweler's rouge or whiting (for a highly polished finish)
- some squat, sturdy plastic containers with lids
- a plastic tablespoon
- some water in a jug
- a waterproof marker pen
- a bowl and polishing pad for each polishing paste

Working method

- Wear a dust mask and gloves when making up the paste. Spoon four tablespoons of water into the container and then add six tablespoons of pumice (or rouge). Mix the two together into a thick paste; another tablespoon of water may be added if required. After any loose abrasives have been returned carefully to their storage containers the dust mask can be safely removed.
- Label the container 'Polishing paste' and write the size or type of powder added. If several different types of polishing paste are being used in the studio there is a risk that larger particles can become mixed up in the fine polishing mixtures. This contamination will result in unwanted deeper scratches on plates which are being finely polished. To avoid this, each

mixture should have its own designated storage container and polishing pad, felts and cloths. The cloths should also have their own clearly labelled plastic storage containers.

• Store each paste (with the lid on to reduce evaporation) and stir in a little water from time to time to prevent it drying out and becoming powdery.

TECHNIQUES FOR POLISHING PLATES

Polishing is used as a preparatory process for drypoint plates when the artist requires a pale (or white) imperfection-free background for an image. Some types of photoresist and acrylic resist can be applied to polished plates. Polishing is also used as a finishing or working method in the etching process and this often reveals the complexity of the surface, particularly when an image contains a range of subtle tonalities and reticulations. Grained etching plates may be smoothed down to remove unwanted plate tone or to enhance the contrast. Errors may be polished smooth and the area reworked.

Equipment and materials required

Work at a well-ventilated workstation for polishing plates (see p. 43) and wear gloves, eye protection, safety footwear with steel toe-caps and an apron.

• selected polishing materials
• a waterproof wipe-clean workboard
• the intaglio plate to be polished
• a bowl and polishing roll (see p. 74)
• some disposable wiping cloths

Working method

• Wear the correct safety clothing to avoid particulate absorption of metals through the skin and lungs.

• Lay the plate centrally on the waterproof wipe-clean workboard. Study the plate surface, check for scratches and rust, and make a decision about which polishing procedure to use (see below). Remember that any polish or abrasive is only as fine as its coarsest particle.

• If the plate is very dirty it should be cleaned before being polished.

• The process of scraping and burnishing may be used to remove scratches and marks (see pp. 93–94).

• Wipe the plate clean with a soft cloth after every polishing stage to remove the dirt and residue from the plate. The final polish should follow the direction of the grain of the metal.

• Marks made by the buff, and polish lodged in indentations, can be removed with sodium bicarbonate or flour.

A SIMPLE TECHNIQUE USING A WATER-BASED POLISHING PASTE

• Dip the polishing roll in the selected polishing paste and distribute the very fine abrasive to the plate surface. Rub steadily in small circles, or work across the plate, making sure to change direction. Minor scratches and oxidization marks are removed when the plate is polished. The plate becomes satin-looking and then shiny. A soft lint-free cloth can be used to buff the surface until it shines.

• Watch out for larger abrasive particles which will describe unwanted deeper circular scratches on the plate. This can be prevented by removing the large unwanted particle (from the base of the polishing roll) and continuing rubbing until any unwanted scratches or scores are softened and evened out.

• The paste dries when it is used and after polishing is complete any uncontaminated paste can be scooped and brushed back into the storage container. The surface of the plate and the waterproof workboard may then be wiped with a soft disposable cloth. If the paste is full of grit it should be wrapped in the cloth and disposed of with the studio waste; pastes used on copper plates will contain copper particles which may have to be disposed of in accordance with local legislation. The paste should not be washed down the sink in case it blocks the plumbing or contains copper particles. The workstation should be tidied up and wiped clean. The plate is now ready to be degreased.

PROFESSIONAL TECHNIQUES FOR A MIRROR FINISH

Professional metal polishers break the process up into several stages. They call the first stage 'abrasive finishing': a polishing pad and very fine abrasive powders (very fine pumice powder or 240 or 320 carborundum grit) are used as in the polishing process described opposite. The marks created from this process are removed with a hard sisal mop and an aluminium oxide compound: this secondary stage is known as 'pre-polishing' and a satin finish is achieved. In the third stage ('bright finishing') a fine aluminium oxide polish is used in conjunction with softer polishing mops to produce a smooth reflective surface. The final process uses soft loose-leaf calico mops and a white or blue aluminium oxide to generate a mirror finish.

THE STEEL WOOL METHOD

Extra fine steel wool is used and the plate is polished in different directions. When the plate becomes shiny, a soft dry rag is used to buff the surface. With this method some care must be taken not to polish out the indentations on the plate which hold the image. It is a useful creative method for altering worked plates of all types.

BLOCK AND BAR METHODS

A block of charcoal or a bar of rouge or chrome oxide can be purchased from intaglio suppliers for polishing plates. The block is dampened and rubbed over the high surfaces, leaving the indented lines intact.

BRAND TECHNIQUES

Some retailers sell a product or a set of products and cloths with their own polishing information and tips. This can be a good approach but it is worth avoiding products that contain organic solvents, ammonia, anhydrous chemicals or acids.

TRADITIONAL RECIPES

One of the most ancient polishing materials is marestail (*Equisetum arvensae*). This primitive plant has a high silica content in its stems. It was used by the Europeans for polishing metals, and dried plants can be purchased from specialist art suppliers.

A brass polish which successfully removes oxidization can be made by mixing one tablespoon of salt with 200 ml of white vinegar in a bowl. Add small quantities of baking flour, and stir to make a paste. Apply the polish to the metal and leave for 30 minutes before rubbing the mixture away with a soft cloth.

Lemon juice and salt can be mixed together to make a useful polish for copper and brass. Another recipe, which can also be used on zinc and aluminium, involves combining whiting (precipitated chalk) with a little water. The instructions and health and safety advice for making a paste should be followed.

POLISHING PLATES USING POWER TOOLS

Polishing metals with a powered hand-held machine is called power buffing. The power source is usually electric or pneumatic. The polishing compound or abrasive powder is applied using the powered tool. Drills, grinders or sanders can be fitted with polishing equipment such as buffs or polishing wheels, felts, mops, lambswool bonnets or polishing pads. The kits, relevant adaptors, and user and safety information are available from the suppliers. Working with powered tools is hazardous and the equipment must be correctly used (as when graining plates: see pp. 73–74).

The best polishing results are achieved by applying a light, slow and steady pressure on the buff. This makes it easier to control the tool and fewer unwanted marks will result. This gentle way of working will generate less heat and the particles in the polish will rapidly smooth the surface.

CLEANING UP

After the plate has been polished, the workboard should be wiped with a disposable cloth. The polishing paste should not be washed down the sink in case it blocks the plumbing or

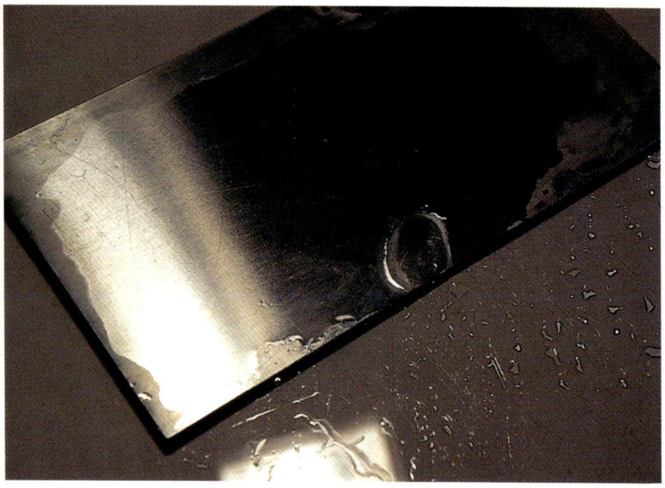

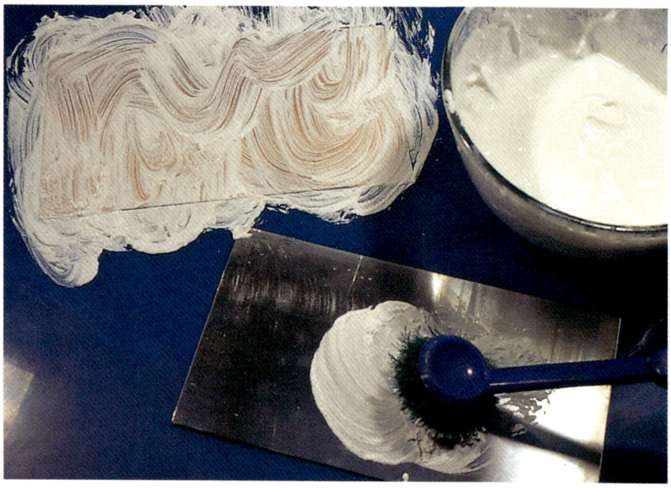

contains copper particles. The workstation should be tidied up and wiped clean.

DEGREASING AND RINSING PLATES

An intaglio plate will become greasy as a result of handling when measuring, filing and cutting, and from airborne contaminants in the studio. Manufacturers also often coat steel sheets with a greasy layer to protect the metal from oxidization. Greasy residues are not usually visible on a dry plate but if the plate is rinsed with water these areas will repel the water, revealing their presence on the surface.

Greasy areas on a plate will prevent a strong bond forming between the plate surface and guide drawing materials, resists or collagraphic materials. In the etching process, oily residues can also shield the plate from the action of the mordant and prevent etching taking place.

The group of cleaners which have been designed to remove grease from surfaces are known as 'degreasers'. When they are applied to the plate surface, any grease is soon removed and the surface is described as having been degreased. When the plate is correctly degreased, water will flow evenly over the surface of the intaglio plate.

A powerful degreaser will be required to remove all the grease but degreasers which contain ammonia, chlorine, phosphorous or benzalkonium chloride should not be purchased. Most powerful commercial degreasers and household cleaners are alkaline. Many of these products appear to rinse away easily from the degreased plate but when the plate dries a fine film of white powder is left on the surface. If the resist or collagraph material were to be applied to this surface the alkaline residue remaining on the plate would prevent a firm bond being made and would interact with the acrylic material, weakening it and causing it to fail. For this reason the alkaline residue should be removed with a neutralizing solution which will alter the pH of any residue left on the plate.

CPS manufacture a degreaser made for screenprinting which may be diluted with water and used as a neutralizing solution. This product can also be used as a degreaser and has the advantage that it does not harm acrylic resists or collagraph materials. Some lemon juice in water also makes a good homemade neutralizing solution.

Equipment and materials required

Work at the degreasing workstation sink (see pp. 43–44) and wear gloves, eye protection, safety footwear with steel toe-caps and an apron.

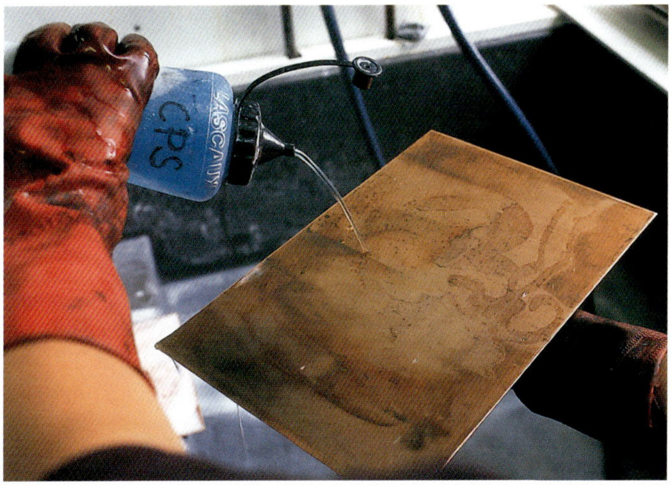

1. Grease repels water from the edges of a zinc plate. The grease resulting from touching the surface is clearly visible.
2. Alkaline degreaser is applied to break up and remove any grease.
3. A neutralizing solution is used on the degreased and rinsed copper plate to remove any alkaline deposits from the degreaser. The plate is then rinsed with water and dried.

- a metal or plastic plate
- a sink with warm water
- a waterproof workboard
- an alkaline degreaser
- neutralizing solution
- a bowl and plastic dishwashing brush

Working method for degreasing

- Wear the correct safety clothing
- Lay the plate in the centre of the waterproof workboard in the plate preparation sink. Trickle some water over the plate and observe both the surfaces to see which areas are greasy.
- Mix the alkaline degreaser with water in the bowl to form a thick white paste. Use the scrubbing brush to distribute the paste to both sides of the plate. Leave the degreaser to work for 5 minutes, scrubbing occasionally and turning the plate over. If the degreaser is being repelled the plate is very greasy.
- Put the waterproof workboard to one side and rinse the degreaser from the plate and the gloves. When all the degreaser has been washed away, trickle water over the plate surface and observe its behaviour. The water should flow evenly over the plate surface. If the water is repelled the plate is still greasy and the degreasing process should be repeated until water can run effortlessly over the entire surface of both sides of the plate.
- When water runs freely over the plate surface, degreasing is complete.

Working method for rinsing

- Rinse gloves and plate thoroughly and balance the plate on the fingertips of one hand. Pour the neutralizing solution onto the plate until the surface is entirely covered. Tilt the plate gently in a circular motion for 2 minutes to allow the solution to neutralize any alkaline traces.
- Rinse thoroughly with water and, taking care not to touch the flat surfaces, dry the plate using a hands-free drier or drying cabinet, or by allowing to dry naturally.
- The dry plate, degreased and free of alkaline residues, is now ready to have a resist or collagraphic material applied to its surface.

DEGREASING BETWEEN ETCHES

Some etching techniques introduce grease to the plate; for instance if an oil-bar stencil has been used the oil bar and the cleaning process will have made the surface greasy. This grease will resist the action of the mordant and prevent biting, so the plate must be degreased before further etching. An alkaline degreaser may damage some types of acrylic resist so an acidic degreaser or household dishwashing liquid should be used.

Equipment and materials required

Work at the plate preparation workstation and wear gloves, eye protection, safety footwear with steel toe-caps and an apron.

- a metal etching plate
- vegetable oil
- a soft, clean rag

Steel plates are often coated with a greasy layer to protect the metal from unwanted corrosion. For *Grey 63*, 105 x 150 cm (41½ x 59 in.), printed at Wildwood Press, 2003, Jerald Eans (US) made drawings of the forms of two shaped steel plates. The images were converted using Cad-Key software at L. E. Sauer Machine Co. in St Louis. They were then sent to a laser-cutting machine in the plant and 16 eighteen-gauge plates were created. These were inked up and used interchangeably to produce 17 unique diptychs.

- a waterproof workboard
- household dishwashing liquid
- neutralizing solution

Working method

- Apply some vegetable oil to remove the greasy material and then wipe the plate using a soft, clean rag.
- Coat the back and front of the plate with a thick layer of dishwashing liquid and leave it face-up on the waterproof workboard for 5 minutes.
- Rinse away the dishwashing liquid with warm water in the degreasing sink, taking care not to touch the plate surface. The plate may then be etched or, if another resist is to be applied, flooded with neutralizing solution, rinsed with water and dried.

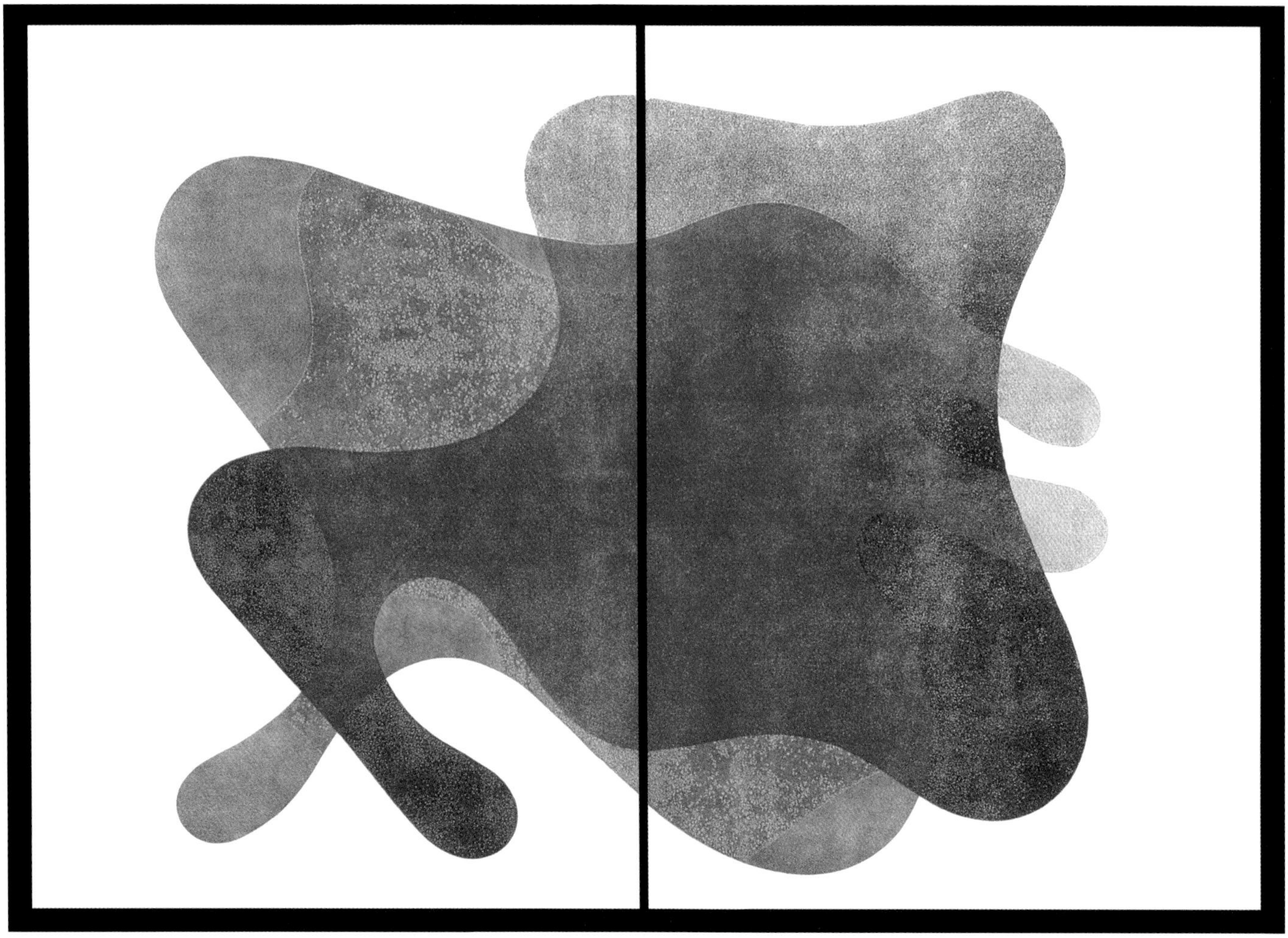

DIRECT INTAGLIO METHODS

The term 'direct methods' can be used to classify the group of techniques which involve working the surface of the plate using direct physical force. These include drypoint, criblé, engraving, stippling, mezzotint, roulette work, burnishing and scraping, abrading and polishing, and the use of power tools. Parts of the plate surface are removed or displaced during this subtractive working process. For example, the action of a scraper physically removes some of the metal, whereas drypointing, stippling and burnishing tools displace the metal.

Each technique has its own history, characteristic handling qualities and printed effects. The artist can choose to work the plate solely with one technique or can employ a combination of methods.

Direct methods may also be used on plates which have already been etched. For example, etched lines may be drawn into with engraving or drypointing tools to alter the quality of the line; a roulette or mezzotint rocker may be used to darken a tonal area; and errors may be corrected by using the scraping and burnishing process. Some types of collagraphic media can also be worked into using these techniques.

PREPARING PLATES FOR DIRECT METHODS

New plates are cut to shape, their sharp corners and edges bevelled and their surfaces cleaned and prepared. Rough or deeply scratched plates may be smoothed down by graining and polishing to prevent the tools catching and snagging on the uneven surface. Drypointing and engraving tools may also be prone to slip or skip on a highly polished surface and the glare from a reflective plate can make it difficult to see the image when the drawing is being made. Refer to the chapter on plate preparation for further information about cutting, bevelling, graining and polishing (see pp. 66–80).

The plate surface may also be prepared with either of the following traditional techniques. If direct methods are being used in a studio equipped with etching materials, the plate can be dipped in a mordant for a few seconds: this process is known as flash biting (see p. 157). The polished metal will change colour over its entire surface and the resulting dulled surface will provide a gentle tooth for the drawing tool. After the plate has been prepared it should be cleaned, de-oxidized if necessary and degreased before work begins. A polished plate surface can also be dulled by rolling a ball of Plasticine over it.

MAKING A GUIDE DRAWING FOR DIRECT METHODS

Before working into a plate with tools, a practice or guide drawing may be made on the surface. This drawing will not print and can be considered as a map which describes the position of a mark or textured area rather than being an aesthetically pleasing image. The guide drawing can be checked in a mirror for compositional and textual errors before the lines and indentations which will hold ink are made in the surface of the plate. There are several different approaches to making a guide drawing.

- A chinagraph pencil, oil, litho or wax crayon can be used to draw directly onto the surface, or carbon paper can be used to transfer a drawing to the plate. The intaglio tool can then be used through the drawn or offset lines.
- If direct methods are being used in a studio equipped with etching materials, a plate holding a guide drawing made with an oily crayon can be lightly etched. During the etching process the greasy drawing material resists the action of the mordant, protecting the metal below, whereas the exposed metal is etched shallowly and darkens. This traditional method

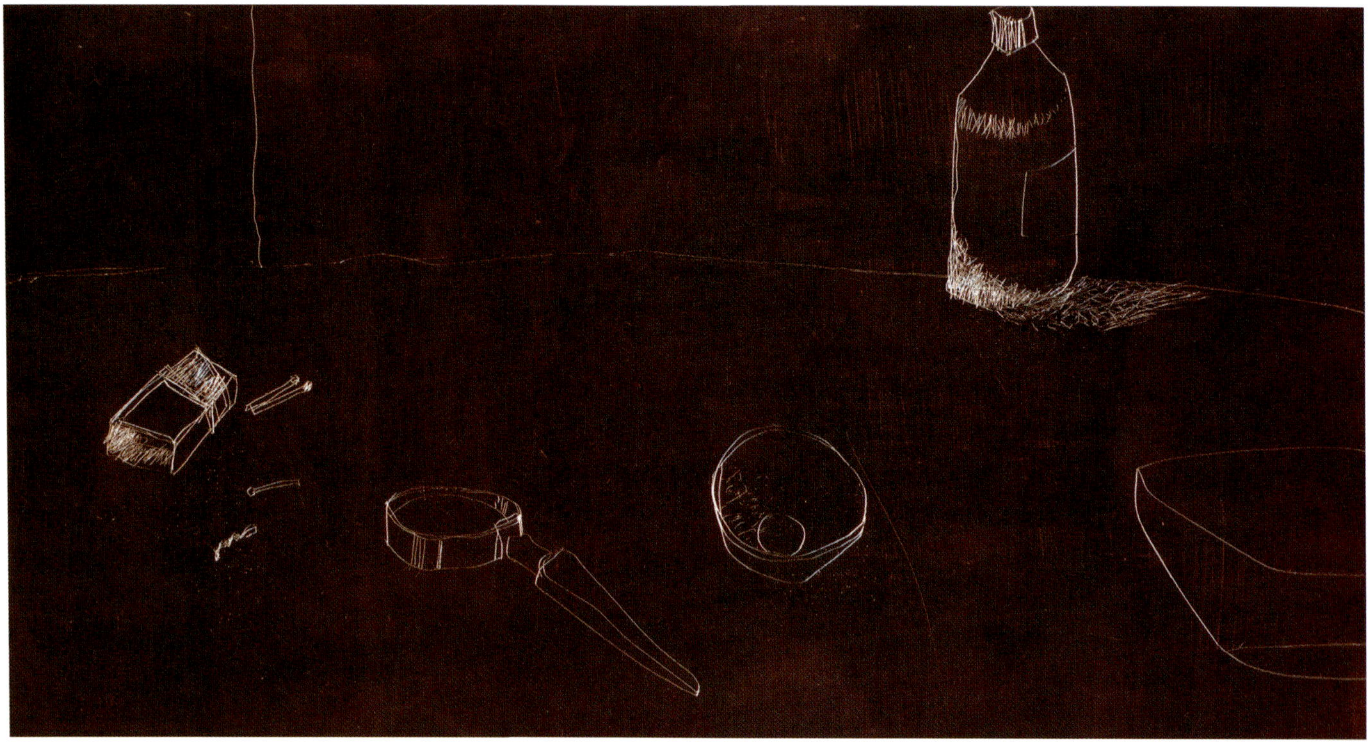

Before using a drypoint needle a simple pencil guide drawing was made on this zinc plate, which had been painted with Lascaux Dark Coating.

was used so that if the greasy guide drawing was smudged during the working process the bright unetched metal lines could be followed.

• An engraving technique involves applying a thin layer of gum arabic to the plate (acrylic hard resist could be used). When this is dry, a soft pencil is used to draw onto the coating, then a sharp point is used to follow the drawing and break through the gum. The resulting shallow indentations are filled with etching ink and the engraving tools are then used on the plate. After the engraving is finished, the fine scratches made for the guide drawing are removed by polishing with some Crocus cloth wrapped around a wooden block.

• A new approach which is suitable for drypoint or engraving involves colouring the entire plate surface with black or white Lascaux coloured coating for hard resist (see p. 108 for application method). When the matt coloured coating has dried, a graphite pencil or crayon can be used to make a guide drawing. Tracing, carbon or transfer paper may also be used on this surface. The coating is designed for etching needles to pass through, so offers no resistance to a point. When the drypoint is complete, the coloured coating is washed away with water before inking up the plate.

• Plastic, wood and card plates can be drawn on with waterproof marker pens. On a transparent plastic plate, the guide drawing can be made on the back so that when the plate is turned over the image is reversed.

ENGRAVING

Goldsmiths originally invented and developed the art of engraving and, like the intaglio printmakers and wood engravers who adopted the method, they use the traditional tools and techniques to this day. The only change to the practice is that electrical and air-powered engraving tools are now available and some goldsmiths use microscopes when working with fine detail.

The main method that is used to engrave plates is known as 'line engraving' and involves cutting into the plate surface with an engraving tool (burin or graver) to create lines. The engraver uses a gentle pushing movement rather than a drawing action to generate characteristic crisp lines that can be made to swell or taper, rotating the plate to engrave curved lines. The deeper indentations will hold more ink than the shallow troughs and the printed tone will be darker and richer. Drypointed and etched lines are sometimes reworked with a burin to alter and increase their character. Any burr that is generated during the engraving process is continually scraped and polished from the plate.

Robert Adam (UK), *Towards Burano*, engraving, 13.5 x 29 cm (5¼ x 11⅜ in.), 2003. Akua inks were used to print an edition of 25.

Dotting methods such as criblé, 'engraving in the dotted manner', stipple engraving and the related etching crayon (or chalk) method are used to create tonal images. They involve the careful placing of tiny indentations and the printed effect is similar to the modern system of halftone. The printed tone is darker in areas where the dots are placed very closely together and becomes lighter as the distance between the dots increases. The burr that is forced out when the metal is punched or spiked is usually scraped away (unless the plate is to be printed as a drypoint). For the method of criblé or engraving in the dotted manner, punches, a steel awl or a dotting mallet with a sharp steel point are used to punch numerous small round indentations into the surface of a polished plate. Stipple engravings are made by making tiny dots in the plate surface with a needle point, roulette wheel, drypoint, multiple point, drum roulettes or stippling tool. The dots are created in the crayon (or chalk) method by working into a layer of hard resist with stippling tools. The dots and flecks are then etched and sometimes the marks are reinforced

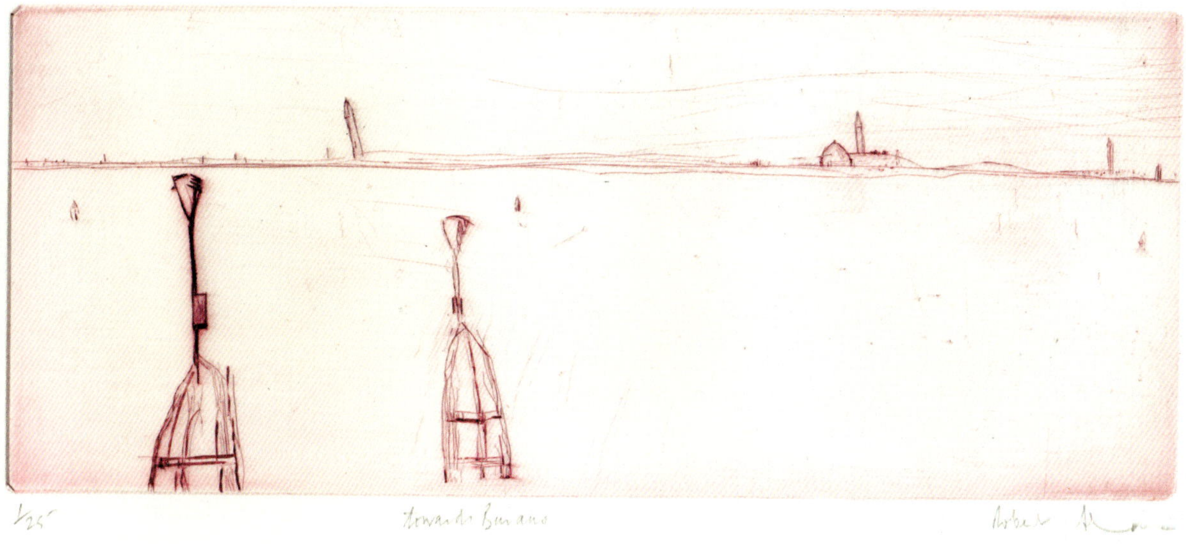

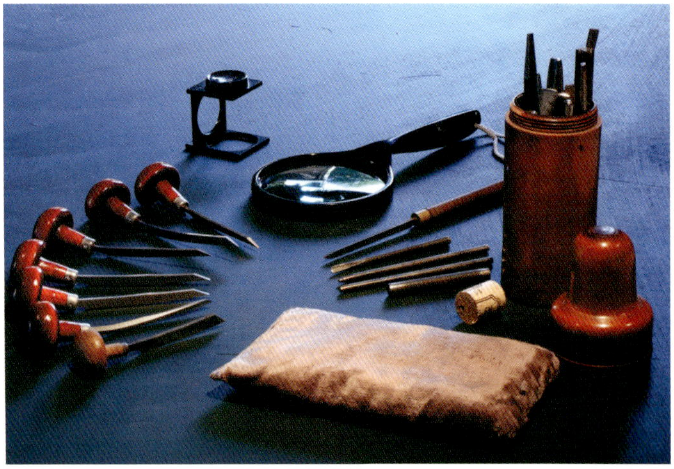

right Clockwise from bottom left: a range of engraving burins, a folding linen tester (8x magnification), a magnifying glass (5x magnification), a scraper and its protective cork, a collection of punches with their container, and a sandbag.

opposite left An electric engraving tool with assorted attachments.

opposite right Engraving a plate with a hand tool (note the shallow angle).

with an engraving tool. In this way this method combines etching with engraving.

PLATE MATERIALS

Copper is considered to be the ideal metal as it is soft to engrave and has the advantage that it may be steel-faced to allow a larger edition. Brass or zinc is favoured by some artists. Mild steel is a more difficult metal to work due to its hardness, although interestingly in the 1800s these plates were tempered after engraving to make them even more durable.

ENGRAVING TOOLS

Manual and powered tools can be purchased from specialist intaglio and modelmakers' suppliers.

Traditional burins have a wooden handle which is shaped like a mushroom cut in half. The curved side is designed to fit snugly into the palm of the hand and the flat side faces the plate. The handle supports a tempered steel rod of around 8 cm (3 in.), with a sharpened flat tip. The rod is usually shaped to curve up into the handle so that the tool can be kept close to the surface of the plate as cuts are made. The burins that are chosen should be in proportion to the size of the artist's hand (less than 2 cm/¾ in. of the rod should extend beyond the hand).

Burins of different widths and with different shaped tips are used to generate a range of marks and types of line. Lozenge-shaped burins are normally used for wood engraving but can be used to create deep fine lines. Round and flat scorpers (gravers or scaupers) are gouges rather than gravers and are used to cut away broad lines. Elliptical tint tools are available in different sizes and generate a range of deep lines. The multiple-tint tool has a number of tiny cutting points on its tip (from 25 to 200 lines to the inch) and is used to produce closely spaced parallel lines for cross-hatching. Burins must be kept sharp and well maintained.

Powered tools are sometimes shaped like traditional burins such as the specialist Lindsay chaser tools but are more usually pen-shaped. The lightweight and inexpensive Dremel electric engraver has a powerful motor. It uses solid carbide engraving points and other tools can be fitted. Rotacraft manufacture a range of cordless engraving tools (powered by battery) which can be used to engrave non-ferrous metals. These tools have a rotary action for effective engraving and a single speed of 12,000 rpm. They can be fitted with a range of points (10 diamond engraving bits and 5 grinding stones). The specialist Turbo Carver is powered by an air compressor and operates at an extremely high rotational speed and with very little torque. This tool weighs about the same as a pencil and uses cutting bits called friction grip dental burrs, which

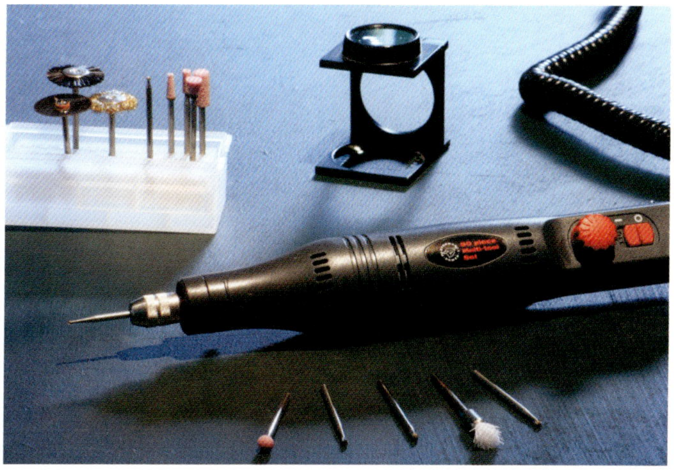

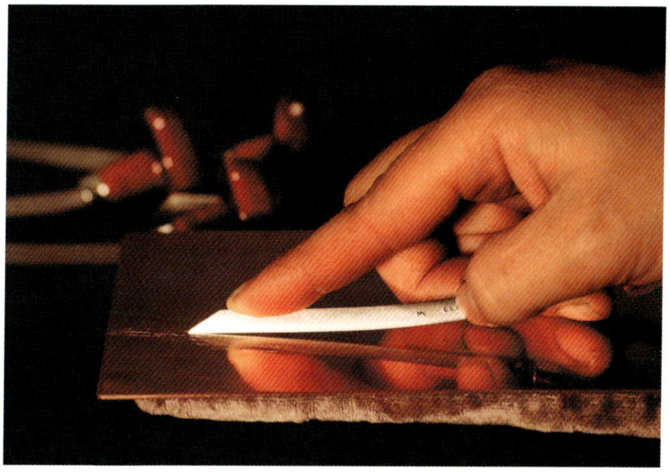

are available in carbide, diamond, stone and rubber. The very fine carbide needle point has a 0.07 mm (0.003 in.) tip, which can be used for ultra-fine detailing. The Lindsay Ultimate AirGraver has beautifully made traditional-looking burins although the tool is air-powered. These specialist tools are used by craftsmen to engrave very fine detail on metals, glass and scrimshaw.

Scrapers, burnishers and polishing materials are used to remove any burr and fragments of metal from the plate surface as well as making corrections (see p. 93).

A smooth-surfaced sandbag, leather pad, engraving vice or other raised flat support is used below the plate so that it can be rotated easily during the engraving process.

Metal punches with different shaped tips (stars, circles and squares) can be used to create indentations in the plate. Steel awls and dotting mallets for engraving in the dotted manner are no longer manufactured but it may be possible to buy antique tools. The awl had a flexible handle and a hammer-like head with a sharp steel point and a round top which was used for repoussage (see p. 94). Roulettes, stippling tools and drypointing tools are readily available (see pp. 88–89).

WORKING METHODS

Small test plates can be made to try out different types of substrate, plate preparation methods, tools, and engraving and printing techniques. An image can be created using one or all of the engraving techniques. Work in a drawing area which is set up for direct methods (see p. 46) and gather together the following materials:

- a clean and prepared plate (see p. 81)
- chosen materials for guide drawing (see pp. 81–82)
- engraving tools, scraper and burnisher, polishing materials
- a sandbag
- a little light oil

Principle: the engraved lines hold the ink (any burr is removed).

Once the engraving tools have been sharpened and the plate surfaces have been prepared with any guide drawings, drawing into the test plates can begin.

For line engraving techniques the artist normally works in a sitting position at a workbench with a range of engraving tools close at hand. It is important to be able to lean over the plate without any tension in the back and neck as the body must be relaxed to engrave successfully. Both arms need to be able to move freely as one hand is used to guide and cut with the burin while the other revolves the plate on the sandbag. These movements are powered by controlled energy from the shoulder, arm and palm.

The burin is held in a comfortable way and the artist can rest an elbow on the workbench. The handle of the burin is secured by the little finger and held stable by the thumb and two bent middle fingers and the forefinger. The hand that manipulates the plate should always be behind the cutting tool in case it should slip.

Test plates can be used to practise engraving expressive lines, squares, intersecting lines, spirals, serpentines, different line endings, dots and crosshatching. Any burrs or fragments of metal can be removed intermittently with a scraper or a snakestone and water if necessary.

The burin will cut into the metal smoothly if gentle but steady pressure is exerted on the tool. Much less pressure than expected is needed to engrave a line which will print; in some cases simply gliding the burin across the plate surface is sufficient. Dark lines are built up by repeatedly working the line rather than trying to cut a deep channel in a single stroke. This type of unnecessary force makes it difficult to control the tool and can break the burin's shaped tip (facet). Lines which are too deeply engraved will hold an excessive quantity of ink, which will print as a smudged bleeding line.

The angle, speed, pressure and any variation while creating the cut will affect how the burin behaves and the resulting engraved line or mark. The tool should be held at a low angle to the surface, and after the tip has been driven into the metal the angle can be lowered further to avoid digging too deep. The burin should be kept almost parallel to the plate. Experimentation and practice will show that the burin will slip if the cutting angle is too shallow, whereas if the angle is too extreme the tip will jam and create juddering lines. Any unsteadiness or hesitation will show in the character of the printed line.

Spirals and serpentines can be made by rotating the plate as the burin is used. The lines can be made to end abruptly or fade smoothly by stopping in the cut channel or by continuing while gradually releasing the pressure.

Tone can be created by crosshatching or by making groups of short strokes or dotted areas. A burin can be used to make triangular dots or the plate may be moved to generate round shapes. Stippling tools, punches, needles and a range of roulettes can be used directly on the plate surface to generate soft tonal effects.

DRYPOINT

This sensitive and immediate intaglio technique is used to create a wide range of expressive lines, dots and textured marks. An image may be drawn on a new plate or the technique can be used to add or rework lines and marks on engraved, etched or collagraph plates.

For linear work a drypointing tool (point) is used to work directly into the plate surface. During the drawing action the

below left Rosemarie Fiore (US), *MTA Redbird Series, Picture Windows #33 Train,* drypoint and collage, 98 x 245 cm (38½ x 96½ in.), 2003, published by the Lower East Side Printshop Inc. Fiore created an installation by acquiring the graffiti-scratched windows from the Redbird #33 subway train, intaglio inking these and printing them onto handmade abaca paper. The printed elements were then cut and collaged in the correct configuration onto Somerset Velvet Radiant white paper.

below right A detail from David DuBose's drypointed aluminium plate (see print overleaf).

opposite Mikael Kihlman (Sweden), *Old Lady in Samokov,* drypoint, 69.5 x 46.5 cm (27⅜ x 18¼ in.), 2001.

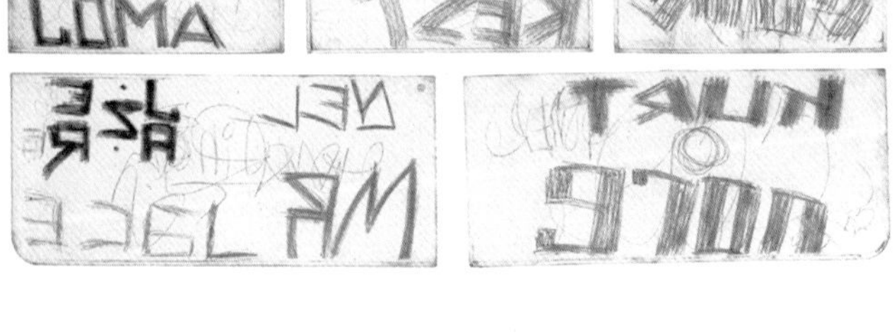

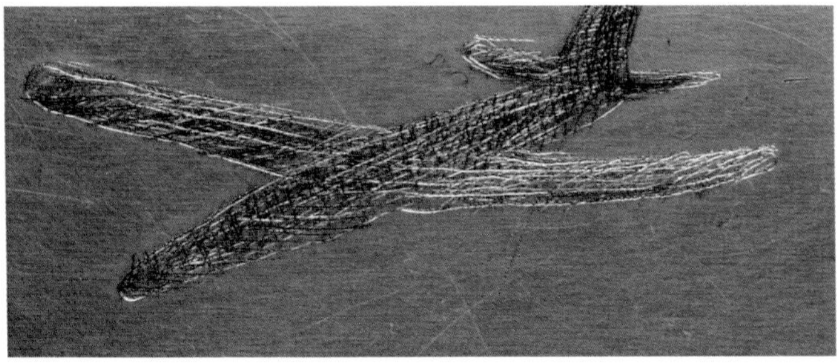

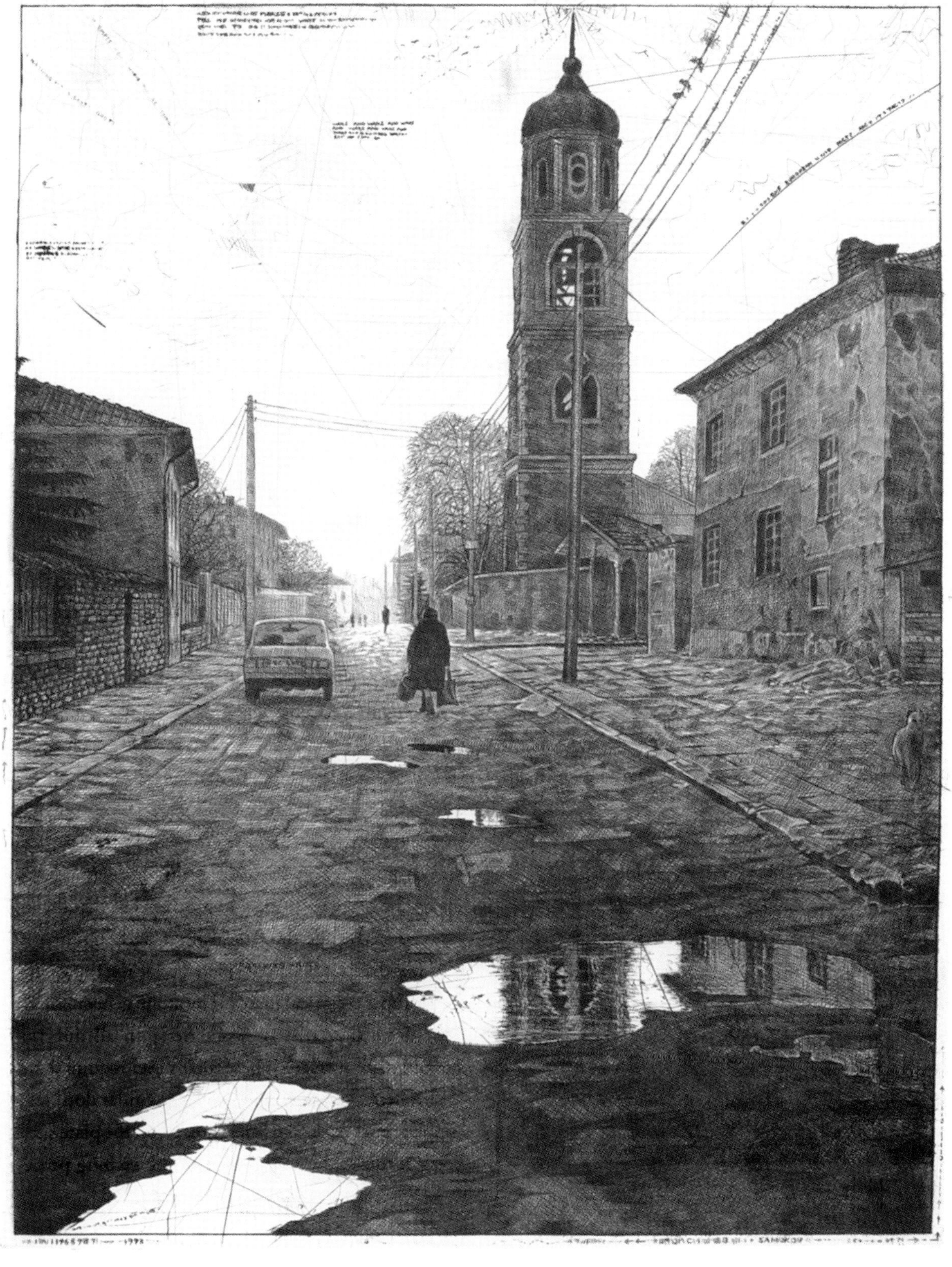

displaced metal forms a raised burr on the surface along the length of the lines or marks. The printing ink will be held both in the incised line and the ragged burr and will print with a rich velvety quality. Other types of tool such as roulettes, wire brushes, engraving tools, awls, files and power tools can also be employed to mark the surface and any burr that is generated is left on the plate. Plates worked in this way and their characteristic prints are referred to as drypoints. Unlike many other intaglio methods, drypointed plates cannot be used for relief printing techniques due to the raised ridges of metal and the shallowness of the cuts.

The inking-up process and the pressure exerted by the press soon wears down the burr on the surface of the plate and, as the remaining indented lines are often very shallow and unable to contain much ink, the prints gradually lose their richness and clarity. For this reason editions of drypoints are usually under thirty and some plates provide as few as six good prints. Larger editions can be printed if a copper plate is drypointed and then steel-faced.

David DuBose (US), *Lament*, drypoint, 10 x 12 cm (4 x 4¾ in.), 2005

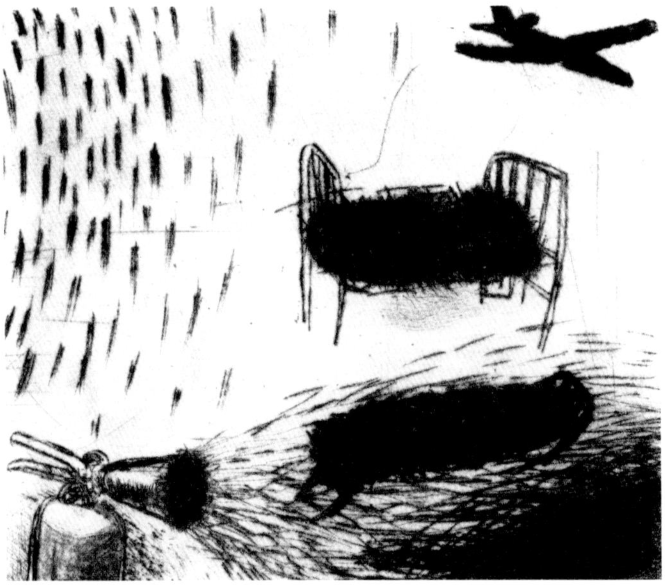

Some artists such as Picasso have treated the method in a different manner, known as drypoint engraving. In this technique the artist scrapes and polishes the burr from the surface as in engraving. The depth of tone is created by repeatedly drawing into the surface to increase the depth of the drypointed mark.

PLATE MATERIALS

Drypointed plates cannot be polished after the image is made as this will remove the burr so it is important to choose or prepare a plate bearing in mind how its surface will print. Polished or smooth plates will wipe clean and print as a white or pale tone, whereas textured surfaces such as steel, scratched, worked or grained plates will hold the ink and print. A variety of substrates, including previously engraved or etched plates, may be used (see pp. 66–77 for detailed information about plate materials and preparation).

DRYPOINT TOOLS

A range of drypointing tools are available from intaglio suppliers.

Steel points are made of hard tempered steel with a drawing tip that is sharp and round without any irregularities. These are available in different weights, from the heavier Haden point to the lighter Whistler point. If the tip of the tool is damaged, worn or ragged it will be difficult to draw with and it may remove rather than displace the metal. This can be avoided by correct care of the steel point and by regularly sharpening its tip on an oilstone.

Diamond points have a precious gem mounted on a steel shaft. The stone is obtuse and protrudes so that the tool can be easily angled while drawing. Rubies and sapphires have been used but diamonds are considered to be the finest drawing tool for working on metal plates. The stone generates a strong line and allows the artist to work freely in all directions (on a smooth plate surface). These tools never require sharpening.

Roulettes can be used to create irregular dots, regular dots, stipples, lines or dotted lines directly on the plate surface (or to break through the resists used in the etching process). They

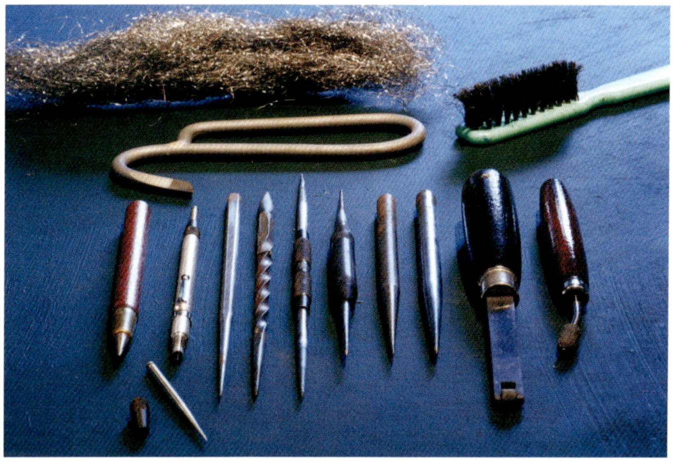

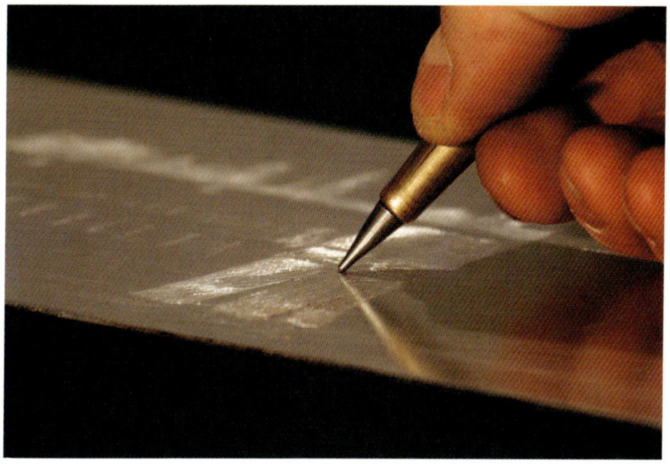

above left Tools for drypointing.

above right Using a diamond point on a zinc plate.

have a curved or straight wooden handle which holds either a spiked wheel, double wheels or a textured drum which can be rotated freely. When this metal wheel or drum is run firmly into the plate surface, incisions and burrs are generated. A wide range of drum roulettes (American) are available with different patterns (stipple and parallel line) and different gauge sizes (coarse 45 per inch; medium 65–85 per inch; fine 100–150 per inch). A random pattern roulette (irregular-, egg- or cone-shaped) can be used to produce a pebble-like effect on the plate. Wheel roulettes (single-row toothed) are also available in different sizes (from 8 mm wide by 8 mm diameter to 5 mm wide by 5 mm diameter/$\frac{5}{16}$ x $\frac{5}{16}$ in. to $\frac{3}{16}$ x $\frac{3}{16}$ in.) which can be used to generate tonal effects.

Textures can be generated with wire brushes, wire wool and files. Engraving tools such as burins, stippling tools, punches and awls may also be used to mark the surface, but the burr is left on the plate (see pp. 84–85).

Power tools fitted with different points, bits or burrs can also be used to generate marks and lines on metal and other types of plate. The power tools which are designed for engraving can also be used to make drypoints.

Other tools such as engineers' scribers, dentists' tools and heavy steel nails can be used instead of the specially designed points. The tips can be modified for drypointing by grinding and sharpening. Some artists have used ballpoint pens on foil-coated card to create a type of drypoint effect.

WORKING METHODS

Small test plates can be made to try out different types of substrate, plate preparation methods and tools, and to gain dexterity. Work in a drawing area which is set up for direct methods (see p. 46) and gather together the following materials:

- a clean and prepared plate (see pp. 81 and 66–77)
- chosen materials for guide drawing (see pp. 81–82)
- drypoint or drypoint engraving tools

Principle: drypointed marks and lines hold the printing ink in both the indentation and the burr.

Once the test plate surfaces have been prepared and any guide drawings have been made, drawing into the plate surfaces with points can begin.

The point is held in the same way as a drawing pencil, and the different angles and pressure will provide a variety of controllable effects. When the point is held in a vertical position, the burr will gather on each side of the indented line. If the tool is angled the burr will run along one side of the line. An acute angle will generate a large and ragged burr (but if the angle is less than 30° from the plate surface the burr will be too fragile). Changes and corrections may be made to the image by scraping and burnishing or by localized abrading and polishing. The different lines and burrs may be examined with a magnifying glass before printing.

Artists who specialize in drypoints examine the image (before steel-facing or printing the plate) by filling the marks and lines with a soft mixture of pigmented Vaseline rather than proofing to prevent unnecessary wear on the plate. When the plates are ready to be printed they are inked up gently with a fine ink made especially for printing drypoints, as a coarse ink will abrade the burr and surface excessively. The press is set up with care as too much pressure will flatten the burr, spoiling the plate. The best results will be achieved when an appropriate intaglio paper is selected and prepared carefully (see p. 217).

After the test plates have been printed, the prints and plates can be examined and compared. Decisions may then be made about the type of plate material, preparation method, guide drawing and point which will be most suitable for a particular concept. These notes, plates and prints can be kept in a visual aid folder for future reference.

Drypoint engraving tools and working method:

- a steel point or diamond point
- a scraper and burnisher (see p. 93)
- plate polishing materials (see p. 75)

Principle: drypointed plates which have had the burr removed will hold printing ink in the indentations.

The working method is the same as for drypointing but the burr is removed by gentle scraping and polishing. The technique described for removing the burr in engraving may also be used on a drypoint engraving but extra care is required as the drypointed lines are often very shallow (see p. 85).

MEZZOTINT

This tonal technique involves working from dark to light and is sometimes called *la manière noire* ('the dark manner'). The word mezzotint can be interpreted as meaning halftone, as it has its roots in the Italian words *mezzo* ('half') and *tinta* ('tone'). The characteristic prints are also known as mezzotints and they have rich deep tones, a complex range of mid-tones and glowing highlights.

The first stage of this direct method involves creating a uniform regular tooth on the plate surface. A mezzotint rocker is used in carefully planned criss-cross directions and the teeth of the tool creates both indentations in the metal and a burr on the surface. Usually the entire plate is roughened in this way and the resulting burr of innumerable copper spurs resembles a velvet pile: it is this which holds the ink and prints as a deep tone.

After the plate has been rocked the artist can begin to create the image by carefully scraping away and burnishing down areas of the textured plate where pale tones or whites are required (the reduced burr will hold less ink, printing as a lighter tone, and a completely smoothed area will hold no ink, printing as a white). When the finished plate is examined the remaining burr (which will hold the ink and generate velvety blacks) stands up the highest on the plate surface, the grey tones (the slightly scraped-down surface areas) will be a little lower and the lowest smooth indentations will print as whites. Further indented marks which will print as dark tones can be added to the mezzotinted surface with rockers and roulettes. Rocked plates can also be worked on using collagraphic techniques to create a controllable range of tones and whites (see pp. 173–175 and illustrations on pp. 2 and 64).

opposite Judith Rothchild (US/France), *Artichoke*, mezzotint, 18 x 13 cm (7 7/16 x 5 1/8 in.), 1998. The plate was hand-rocked with a four-inch 100-line rocker and drawn onto directly from life using a small burnisher. A scraper was not used. Charbonnel black ink mixed with some burnt umber and burnt sienna was used to print the plate in an edition of 100 on 300g Hahnemühle paper.

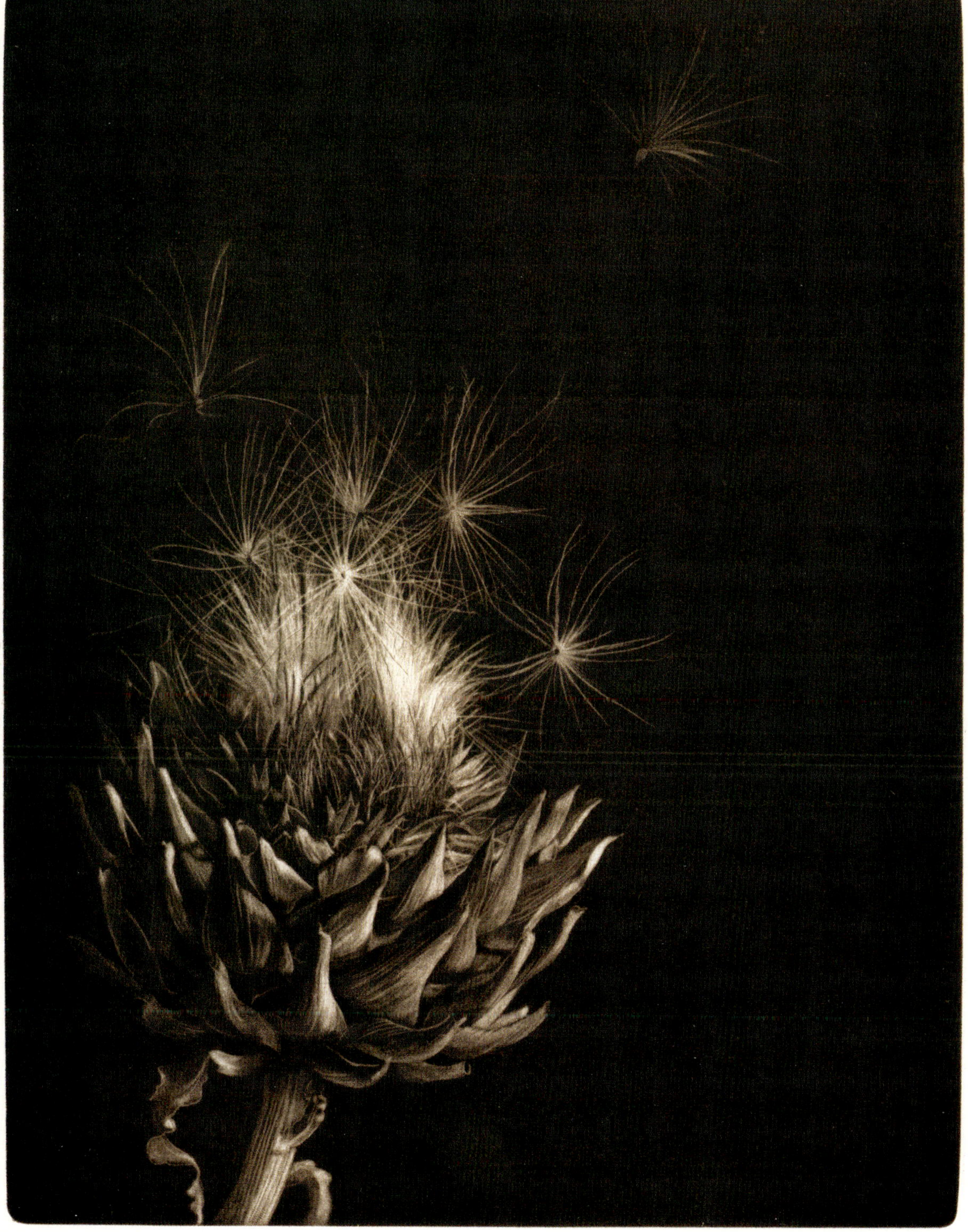

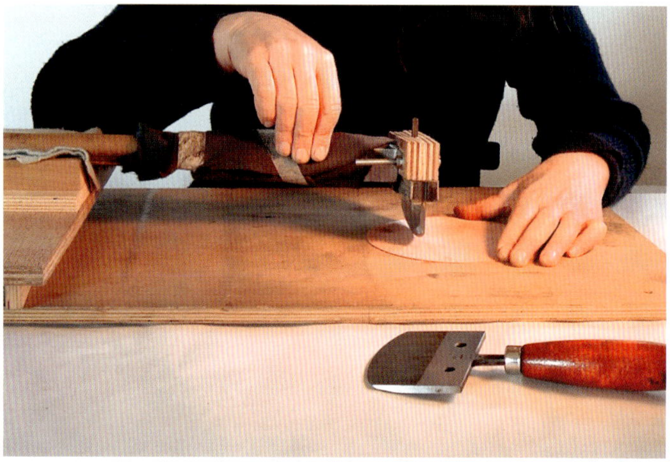

Judith Rothchild using a rocking pole to guide the rocker over the surface of a circular copper plate. A large mezzotint rocker is lying on the bench.

Other ways of working from dark to light are sometimes employed by artists. The plate can be textured by hand or by air-abrading with abrasives to generate a pitted and scored surface. Alternatively, the etching process can be used to create an ink-holding surface which is lined or pitted (see pp. 124–128).

PLATE MATERIALS

Rocking the plate is a laborious process and so copper is an ideal choice as it may be steel-faced (see p. 67). Pre-prepared plates with a finely and uniformly rocked surface can be purchased from specialist printmaking suppliers. Steel plates have been used in the past but, as the ink does not cling as well to the steel burr, the printed effect was considered to be colder and less interesting-looking than mezzotints taken from copper plates.

MEZZOTINT TOOLS

Mezzotint rockers are robust and heavy tools with a wooden handle and a curved blade which is shaped like a wide chisel. The underside of the blade has a serrated cutting edge and the number of teeth is classified by gauge. Rockers are available in standard imperial widths from ½ to 6 in. wide and the gauge sizes may be coarse (45 lines per inch) and throw up a large burr, medium (65 or 85 lines per inch), or fine (100 lines per inch), which is more suitable for delicate shading. Special steel weights can be attached to make rocking the plate easier. The rocker may also be held in a special apparatus consisting of a rigid lightweight rocking pole, protractor square and folding stand with a spherical pivot. This assembly partially mechanizes the rocking of the plate, offering greater control of the process by assisting in the tracking of the rocker across the plate surface.

Different types of roulettes, scrapers and burnishers and their related working methods are described opposite and on pp. 88–89.

WORKING METHOD

The plate is filed, cleaned and degreased before it is rocked or textured. Finer gauges are more effective if the tool is held in the rocking apparatus, whereas a coarser gauge will provide good results if the plate is hand-rocked. The plate is laid on a workboard on the bench and the mezzotint rocker is held firmly, with the serrated side of the blade facing away from the body. The tool is rocked from side to side and gradually walked across the plate until the entire surface is covered in horizontal parallel lines. The plate is then rotated through 90° and the rocking process is repeated. The process continues in this way by rotating the plate sequentially through the following angles: 45°, 90°, 22.5°, 45°, 45° and finally 45°. This results in eight sets of lines separated by segments of 22.5°. The scraper and burnisher is used in the normal way (see opposite). Small errors can be reworked with a smaller rocker or roulette.

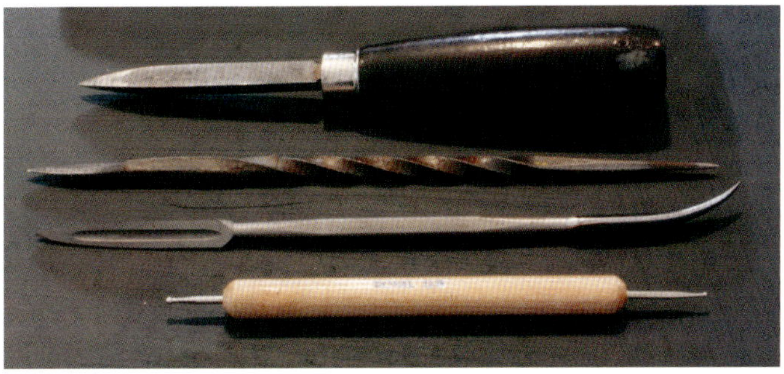

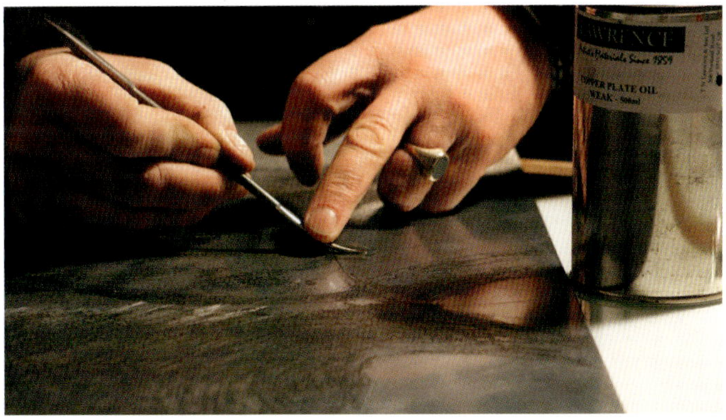

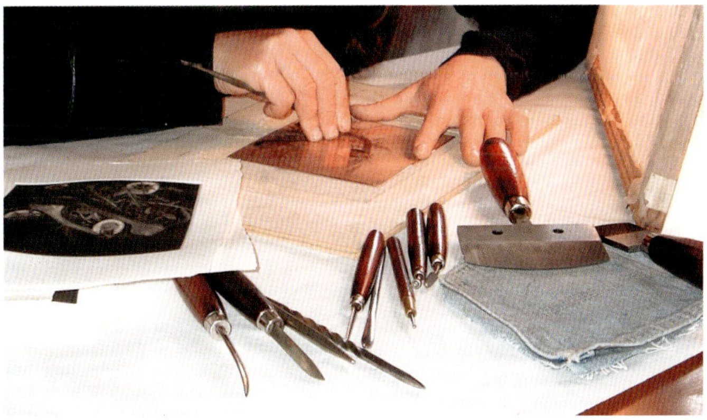

top Scraping and burnishing tools

centre The error on this zinc plate has been scraped down (see illustration overleaf). The artist is burnishing the area smooth, using some copperplate oil as a lubricant.

bottom Judith Rothchild burnishing a copper mezzotint plate.

SCRAPING AND BURNISHING

These direct techniques are used to create mid-tones and whites on plates which have a tonal structure on the surface (e.g. mezzotint, aquatint, etched structures or gesso) and to remove imperfections, irregularities, rough plate edges, unwanted burr, foul bite and errors on all types of intaglio plate.

SCRAPING AND BURNISHING TOOLS

Scrapers have wooden handles which hold a hardened three-sided steel shaft which has a pointed tip. As each edge of the shaft is sharp it is common practice to wrap some masking tape around the blade (extending the handle by 4 cm/1½ in.) so that the tool is more comfortable and safer to manipulate. New tools have rough edges and should be finely sharpened on a stone.

Burnishers are made from hardened steel and have a straight or curved shaft. The tip is smooth and is usually curved, allowing the artist to press down on the tool. Ball burnishers are used to create highlights and have a small smooth ball on the tip.

A scraper burnisher is a combination tool which has a scraper tip at one end and a burnishing tip at the other.

WORKING METHODS

The side and tip of the tool are used in a repetitive scraping motion to shave away the unwanted plate material (a damp cloth should be used to lift away the shavings) and care should be taken to work in a direction away from the body. When large areas of the plate are scraped, a dust mask should be worn to provide some protection from the particles. In some cases a G-clamp (with a soft protective pad) should be used to hold the plate firmly while the surface is worked on.

Mezzotinted plates are scraped carefully, as even a small reduction of the burr will print as a paler tone as less ink is held. Faulty or inaccurate engraved or etched lines may be corrected by scraping down the metal on each side of the indented

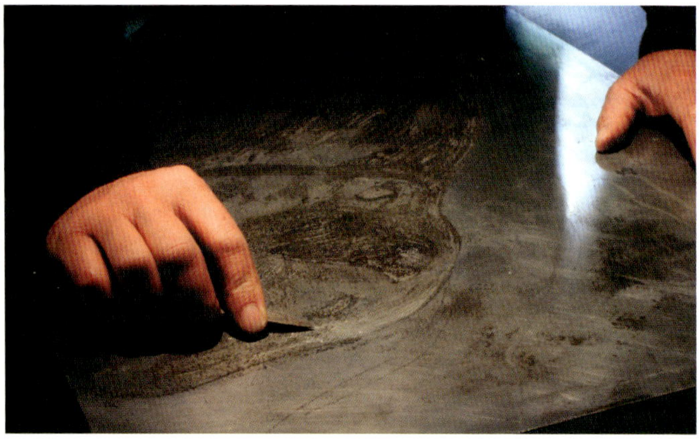

An artist using a scraper to alter an image on an etched zinc plate before burnishing. The image was created with Lascaux Soft Resist.

line to form a shallow 'basin'. If the plate was inked up, this basin would print as a variable pale tone (the slightly rough metal will hold a certain amount of ink), so if whites are required the basin is burnished smooth (the smooth basin will not hold any ink). If the basin is very deep the repoussage method is used to correct the plate.

The burnisher is used with a flowing or sometimes circular movement, and a little light copperplate or vegetable oil will lubricate the burnishing action, making the process easier. The pressure exerted by the artist on the burnisher displaces the metal and smoothes the surface out (the smoothness can be tested with a finger). Some types of collagraph surface such as gesso and photocollagraph plates can also be burnished. A magnifying glass may be useful when making detailed adjustments or corrections. Surfaces which have been scraped or burnished can be worked further using any of the direct, etching or collagraph techniques.

REPOUSSAGE

This metalworking technique originated in the Bronze Age and is used by intaglio printmakers to correct errors on the plate. For example, an area on a plate which has been scraped back and then reworked can sometimes print incorrectly if the hollow (or basin) is deep.

To correct this the plate is turned over and a mark made on the spot which requires repair. The plate is placed face-down on a soft clean cloth laid over a solid flat steel surface. The rounded end of a 'chasing' (*repoussé*) hammer is then used to beat the back of the plate carefully until the hollow basin becomes level with the surface of the face of the plate. If the hammer is used too vigorously, blisters or swellings may appear on the front. These may be tapped down gently on the face of the plate, using the flat side of the hammer head (a soft cloth should be placed between the hammer and the metal).

Another means of raising a hollow area is to attach some small, shaped pieces of blotting paper to the underside of the plate (in the exact area of the hollow). The plate is then laid on the etching press bed, covered in a softened sheet of paper and run through the press. The depressed areas are raised up to become level with the front plate surface.

AIR-ABRADING TECHNIQUES, INCLUDING THE USE OF LIGHT-SENSITIVE AND OTHER MASKS

Fine abrasive powders can be sprayed onto an intaglio plate to create a very finely scrobiculated surface. These abraded areas are generally shallow and the plate will soon wear down. The image can only just hold a stiff fine ink and will print as a pale modulated tone.

The image can be formed by freehand work or in conjunction with a mask which will protect the metal that is not to be abraded. Lascaux Hard Resist can be applied as a mask and drawn into to create linear images, and painted marks can be made using Lascaux Stop-Out Resist. Both of these materials are able to withstand blasting for some time: thinner layers will break down more quickly than thicker layers.

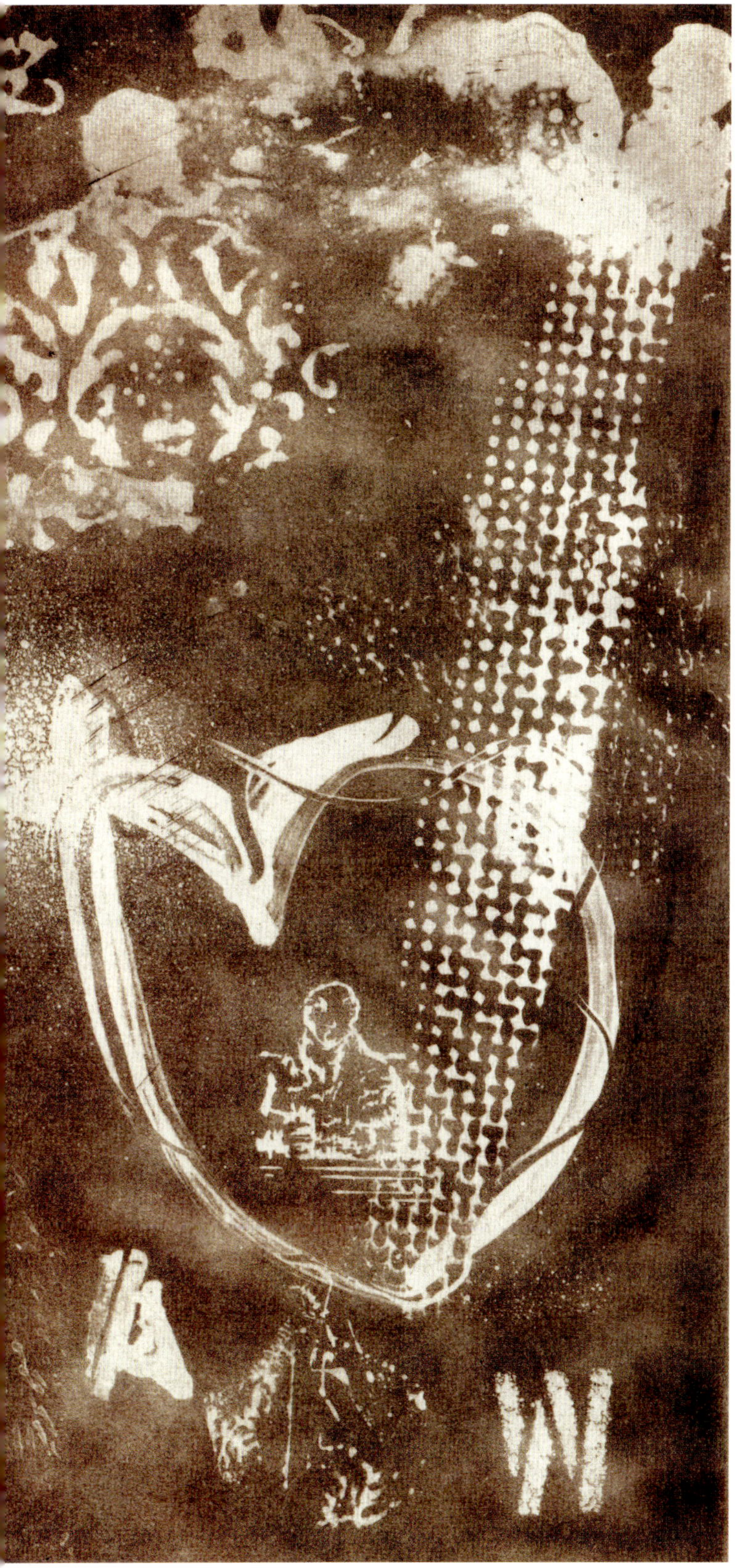

Lascaux Stop-Out Resist was painted, splattered and offset onto an aluminium plate. When the resist was dry, the plate was air-abraded with fine aluminium oxide using a hobby spray gun, generating a variable shallow pitted surface. After spraying, the resist was removed and the abraded plate inked up and printed.

The use of a light-sensitive mask (photomask) allows autographic, digital, photographic and photocopied marks and images to be abraded onto the plate surface. RapidMask (made by DuPont) is specially designed for this purpose, and some types of photoresist may also be used as simple masks. The photomask is applied, laminated and exposed to a negative or a positive in a similar way to the dry film photoresists which are used for etching (see pp. 140–148). However, after exposure the coated plate is blasted and the exposed areas of the RapidMask become blue and begin to disintegrate. The artist continues spraying until the exposed metal (in the form of the image) has been abraded to the correct depth. The remaining photomask is removed with water.

Fine dusts (180 or 220 grit) of aluminium oxide or silicon carbide and the particles which have been abraded from the plate are hazardous. For this reason this process should only be carried out within a special blasting unit such as the 'Minicarver'. This enclosed tabletop unit has a surge-free spray gun and a siphon system, together with efficient abrasive powder extraction and a recycling system. An air compressor is required to power the spray gun. Sandblasting or air-abrading equipment is used by hobbyists, fossil collectors, glass engravers and for the removal of paint from metal. Suppliers and further information can be sourced on the internet.

ETCHING

THE ETCHING PROCESS AND THE USE OF RESISTS

In this subtractive method a corrosive substance or electrolysis is used to attack the surface of a metal plate to create ink-holding crevices, channels and pits. When an etched plate is examined with a magnifying glass, the lines and marks look clean and have no burr. The word 'etch' derives from the German word *ätzen* ('to eat with acid'), which is from the same root as the German word *essen* ('to eat').

Metals can be corroded by a number of chemicals, including pollutants in the air, resulting in a change in the colour of the metal and later by a roughened or pitted surface. Some contemporary artists have left intaglio plates outside to corrode and have then inked up and printed from the eroded surface. Traditionally a corrosive powder (flour of sulphur) was sprinkled onto the surface of a polished and oiled copper plate to create delicate pitted areas. The resulting surface can be inked up and prints as a soft tone. Another etching method, spit biting, involves painting a liquid etchant onto a polished plate to create slightly corroded areas.

In order to generate precise deeper lines and darker tonal effects, etchers searched for directing the mordant. They developed recipes for acid-resistant materials and coated their plates with these protective media. By drawing through the coating, the metal was revealed. The plate was then immersed in a bath of corrosive solution so that only the exposed lines were etched. After etching the plate was rinsed and the protective coating removed from the back, sides and front of the plate. The corroded marks and lines would hold the ink.

below left A photoresist and Lascaux Aquatint Spray Resist were applied (for the text) and the plate was etched in a tray of mordant. The plate was stripped and Lascaux Aquatint Spray Resist was applied to the entire plate, which was then spit-bitten with ferric chloride (see the print on p. 157 and p. 226).

below right As a teaching exercise this copper plate has been etched right through to the Lascaux Plate-Backing Resist (magenta) which was protecting the back of the plate. The blue stop-out and clear hard resist protecting the front of the plate in the form of the spiral have remained intact.

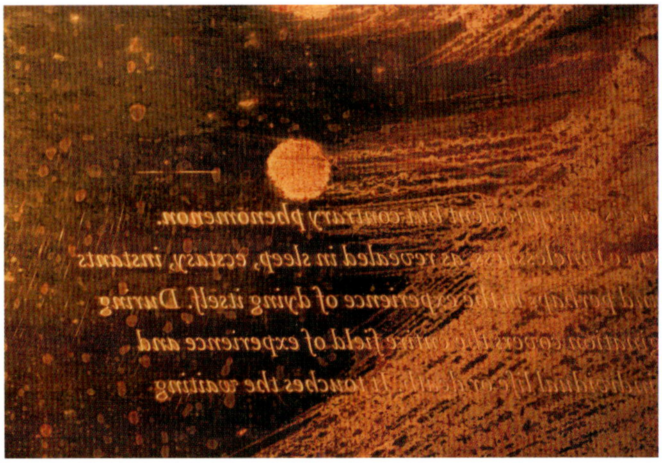

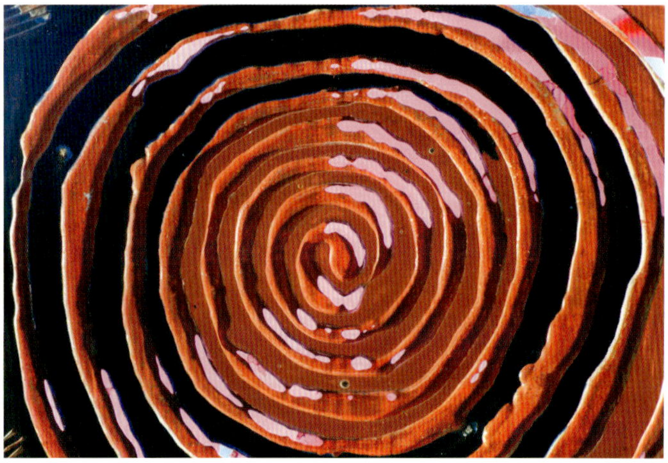

These acid-resistant compounds and their modern equivalents are classified as resists. The word 'resist' is derived from the Latin *resistere* ('to make a stand') and has come to mean 'a coating applied as a protection against chemical action'. Sometimes the word 'ground' is used instead of resist (although this term can cause confusion as 'ground' can also describe the surface of a plate which has been worked with a mezzotint rocker).

Unlike the physical activity required by the direct methods, the depth of the etched line is controlled by the length of time the plate is left in the corrosive solution. A shallow etch holds less ink and prints as a paler tone than a more deeply etched line. By applying resists in different ways or by breaking through the layer of resist many different types of lines and marks can be generated.

When a broad line or large dot is bitten and then examined under a magnifying glass, the etched forms resemble a channel, basin or pool of which the base is usually quite smooth and will not hold ink. The ink is caught on the edges of the form and it is only this ink that prints. This distinctive effect is known as 'open bite'.

When printmakers require broad tonal lines or areas, they have to direct the mordant to bite many tiny ink-holding pits or channels within the mark. The closeness and depth of these pits or channels provides a range of tonal effects. A number of techniques will create these textures: these include puncturing resists with sand or sandpaper, applying resists in tiny dots to the surface of the plate as in the aquatint process or using a dotted positive in conjunction with a photoresist.

The knowledge that all resists will behave in the same logical way (i.e. will prevent etching from taking place) and that the exposed areas of metal will etch either as open bite, small pits, narrow lines or fine networks makes it simpler to understand the platemaking process. Using a magnifying glass to examine the plate frequently enables the artist to check that the resists are still intact and that the plate is etching normally. The depth of the bite can be felt with an etching needle.

Understanding these basic principles helps an artist to gain control of the etching process. It becomes clear that an image can be generated with any combination of intaglio techniques and the artist is freed from the common belief that processes and materials must be used in a fixed order.

below left A print showing open bitten pencil lines around thumbprints made in soft resist (see p. 117).

below right An aluminium plate was coated in hard resist and dried. The resist layer was then punctured using a sheet of coarse sandpaper cut into the shape of a star. The plate was etched in a copper sulphate solution.

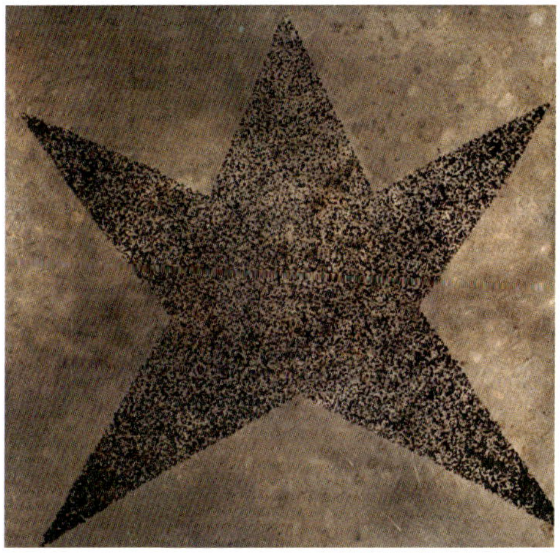

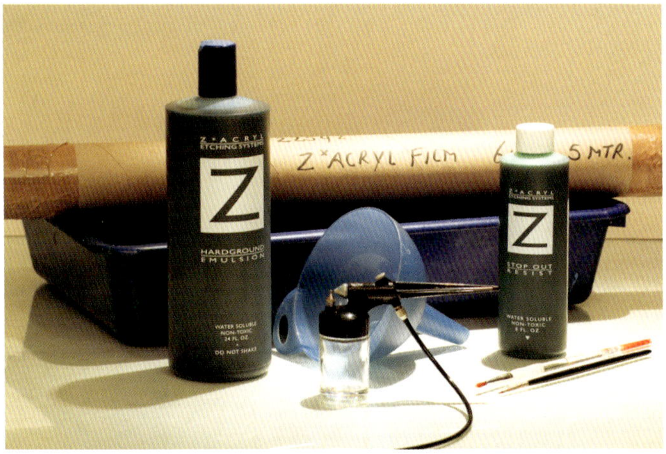

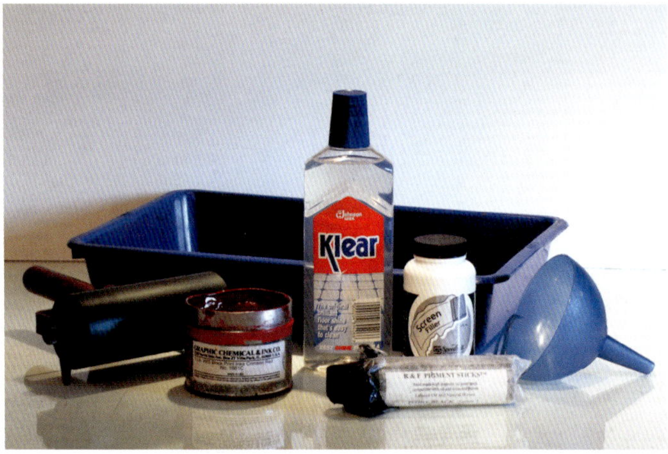

The wide variety of modern resists are made from a new generation of materials such as water-based acrylics and photo-polymers. These resists are easy and pleasant to use, reliable, environmentally friendly, and much safer to work with and to remove from the plate. They can be applied to the plate in a number of different ways, including pouring, offsetting, rolling, spraying, airbrushing, laminating, screenprinting and with a range of painting methods. Many creative working methods including stencil and lift techniques can be explored.

ETCHING WORKING PRACTICE CHECKLIST

STARTING POINTS

Consider concept, types of mark, press size, plate size, paper size and edition size, work out tonal structure, write down approximate sequence of resists and bites.

PREPARING THE PLATE

Cut metal to size, bevel and smooth edges and round corners, clean, grain or polish, de-oxidize, degrease, neutralize, dry, wipe with tissue, apply plate backing and edge protection.

CREATE AN IMAGE USING RESISTS

Follow the application and working method for the selected marks and effects (assuming printing with black ink on white paper).

- dark clean lines and detailed drawn marks – select a hard resist (with or without dark coating)
- dark collage-type impressions, soft drawn effects or bold drawings – select a soft resist
- dark marks – select a hard resist and remove areas or paint with stop-out resist, then aquatint
- contour marks – paint with stop-out resist and etch deeply
- a black ink-holding grid to create a mezzotint-like surface – select a soft resist and impress scrim
- pale brush strokes, splatters and offset marks and dark drawn lines – select a stop-out resist
- dark bold shapes and painted marks – select stencils and lifts and use with a spray resist
- scrobiculated tonal effects – use the hard resist and puncture method or a soft resist and sugar
- reticulated tonal effects (uniform or modulated) – select a spray resist
- tonal changes to lines and areas – select a stop-out resist and use the stage-biting method
- editing, altering and repairing – select a stop-out resist and redraw
- complex wash effects and tonal marks – select a wash resist and use with a tonal process, e.g. uniform aquatint

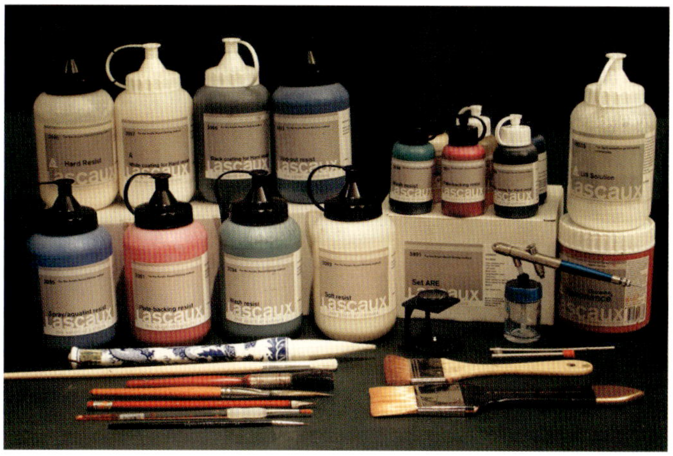

Materials for resisting the action of the mordant and their application equipment:
opposite left The Z*Acryl range.
opposite right Household and art materials.
left The Lascaux range of resists and lift solution.

- pale 'crayon' lines – draw with an oily resist and apply with a spray aquatint
- dark monotype-like lines – roll on a layer of oily resist and draw into
- any type of effect – select a photoresist and use with a positive.

PREPARE FOR ETCHING

Dry the resist (except for oily resists), plan any stage biting that is to take place, check the resist, repair if necessary, attach an etching handling strap.

ETCHING TECHNIQUES

- wear protective gear and follow safe practice
- flash bite to ascertain which areas are etching (except for wash resist)
- etch the plate, time the etch, remove from mordant, rinse thoroughly, monitor the depth of corrosion (using a magnifying glass), check for foul bite, de-oxidize if necessary, rinse, bite further if necessary.

AFTER ETCHING

Remove from mordant, rinse thoroughly, remove strap, rinse thoroughly, de-oxidize, rinse thoroughly, tidy tape and plastic from mordant sink, wash sink and gloves, dry plate.

FURTHER OPTIONS

Make alterations to the resist, or apply a new resist; remove the resist; use any of the direct methods on the metal; make corrections and lighten areas by scraping and burnishing; enhance the contrast by polishing the metal; add collagraphic elements or media to the plate to create further light or dark marks; proof the plate.

PRINTING THE PLATE

Dry plate, soak printing paper, set up press, position registration sheet, cover with a sheet of tissue, put on gloves and prepare ink, ink up plate, lay plate on tissue, remove gloves, position plate in register, blot printing paper, position paper, cover with tissue, cover with blankets, operate press safely, lift blankets, tissue and print, examine print, dry print between boards.

FINISHING UP FOR THE DAY

Clean plate, tidy studio, store plate, dry prints may be collated and signed.

PLATE-BACKING RESISTS

Before the image is created on the front face of an etching plate a resist is applied to the back and sides of the plate. This resist will protect the metal and will prevent any etching taking place in these areas.

Plate-backing resists should be durable and difficult to scratch or chip. The back of a plate which has been protected with a plate-backing resist may generally be re-used. Some types of pre-backed intaglio plate are available. These are coated on one side with a tough resist which cannot normally be removed from the plate.

If the back of the plate is not protected it will be bitten irregularly and its edges may become ragged. The plate will be awkward to ink up and the image on the front may print inaccurately due to the irregular thickness of the plate. In addition this unnecessary etching of the back of the plate diminishes the potential life of the mordant and some acids may react in a hazardous way when etching a large area.

TYPES OF PLATE-BACKING RESIST AND THEIR APPLICATION METHODS

LASCAUX PLATE-BACKING RESIST

Lascaux manufacture a quick-drying plate-backing resist which can be painted onto the sides and back of the plate. The translucent coloured acrylic resist is reliable, tough and difficult to scratch. The mordant cannot creep under this resist and it is easy to remove from the plate after etching (see p. 215).

Equipment and materials required

Work on a clean workboard in the drawing area.

- a clean, prepared, grained, degreased etching plate
- Lascaux Plate-Backing Resist
- a clean, wide, square-ended, flat, soft, fine-haired brush such as a 5 cm (2 in.) Prolene brush made by ProArte
- a clean china or glass palette
- basin of warm soapy water, sponges and clean drying cloths
- a brush rest
- clean newsprint

Principle: a specially designed coloured resist is painted over the entire surface of the back and sides of the plate to protect the metal from the action of the mordant.

Applying Lascaux Plate-Backing Resist with a soft brush.

Working method

- Copper, brass, zinc, steel or aluminium may be used with this resist. New plates should be prepared (see pp. 66–80). Previously etched plates should be clean and degreased.
- Lay out the materials and make sure that the working area is clean and not dusty. Set out a basin of warm soapy water, some sponges and clean drying cloths so that it is easy to clean the brushes and other tools intermittently in soapy water. This practice will prevent the acrylic resist drying on the tools. When working with water-soluble resists and dishwashing liquid, it is good practice to wear gloves and an apron.
- Raise the plate up from the working surface by laying it on top of a slightly dampened 'S' sponge. Squeeze a small quantity of Lascaux Plate-Backing Resist into the palette. Apply the resist thinly to the plate in even strokes with the brush. Work steadily from one side of the plate to the other, repeat and stop. The resist is self-levelling and dries rapidly (if brushing continues the resist will start to lift off the surface of the plate and catch on the brush). Use a small, soft, fine brush to paint the edges of the plate. Dry the plate in the drying cabinet.
- Examine the dry plate and check that it is entirely covered in a translucent layer of resist. A second coat may be applied if the coating looks streaky, the plate is steel or it is to be etched deeply. This second coat should paint easily over the first coat, deepening its colour and strengthening it.

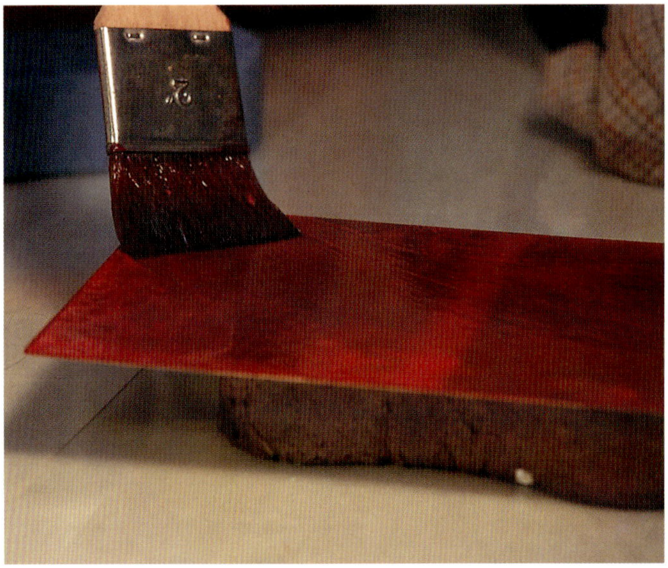

• Dry the plate thoroughly in a horizontal position.
• The resist should be cleaned from the brushes and palette with warm soapy water immediately after the plates are coated. Excess resist may be kept in a 'left-over resists' bottle. Tidy the work area, wash and rinse the palette and brush thoroughly. The soft bristles of the brush should be smoothed out and the brush laid on a rest to dry.
• Check the front of the dry plate for unwanted dribbles of resist. These can be scratched off with a scraper.
• Normally the resist is removed from the plate after the etching process is complete (see p. 215).

ADHESIVE PLASTIC FILM AND PLASTIC PARCEL TAPE

Adhesive plastic film and parcel tape are readily available from office suppliers and have often been used by printmakers as resists. However, there are a number of disadvantages associated with their use.
• The bevelled sides of the plate will need to be protected with stop-out resist.
• During etching the mordant often seeps under the film or the tape and will etch the back of the plate, which can affect the final print.
• When the film is peeled from the plate surface after etching, any trapped corrosive solution may splash up, causing injury to the artist or someone working nearby.
• Some types of film and parcel tape can be particularly awkward to remove from the plate and a residue of glue is often left on the surface.

Because of these difficulties artists are tempted to ink up and print with the backing still on the plate. Unfortunately any trapped mordant is squeezed out by the pressure of the rollers onto the blankets, damaging them. If the plate is printed with parcel tape still attached, the pressure may also emboss the 'bands' where the tape overlaps on the plate back, creating ridges on the plate surface.

Equipment and materials required
Work on a clean workboard in the drawing area.
• a clean, prepared, grained, degreased etching plate
• a sheet of adhesive plastic film or a roll of plastic parcel tape
• a sharp scalpel or craft knife

Principle: adhesive plastic film or parcel tape is used as a resist and applied to cover the back of the plate.

Working method
• Paint the edges and a 2 cm (1 in.) wide band of stop-out resist or plate-backing resist around the perimeter of the back of the plate, and dry this for 10 minutes in the drying cabinet before applying the adhesive film or strips of tape.
• Place the plate face down on a clean cutting board. If adhesive plastic film is being used, cut a piece slightly larger (1 cm/ ½ in. all round) than the plate. Peel off the film's backing sheet and lower the sticky film onto the back of the plate and smoothe it down from the centre. Cut the excess film from around the plate edges. Press down the film firmly to ensure good adhesion.
• If plastic parcel tape is being used, work methodically and carefully from the top of the plate and position each strip so that it overlaps the previous one. Press down the edges firmly to ensure good adhesion and to prevent the mordant 'creeping' under the tape. Cut the excess tape away from around the plate edges.
• After etching submerge the plate in a basin of warm water and remove the film or tape.
• An abrasive household cleaner such as Vim can be used to remove any leftover traces of glue.

PHOTORESIST USED AS PLATE-BACKING RESIST

A sheet of dry film photoresist may be laminated and processed to act as a plate-backing resist. Follow the laminating and exposure instructions but expose the coated plate for

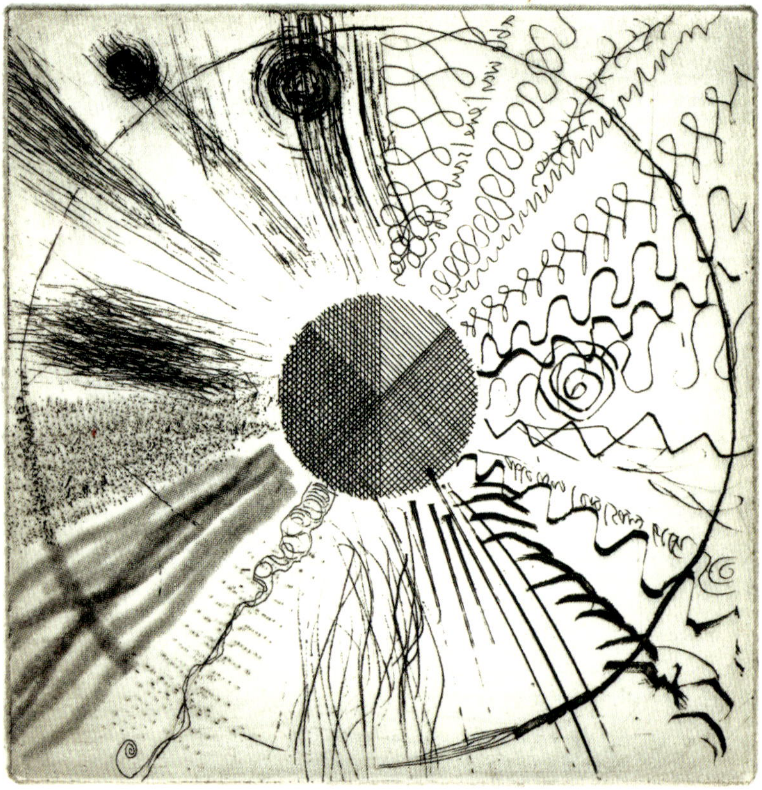

right A range of tools (including roulettes, scrapers, wire wool and needles) were used to draw into Lascaux Hard Resist to create a print (actual size) which demonstrates the different qualities of each tool. The cross-hatching in the centre demonstrates how cleanly and accurately this resist etches.

opposite Roulettes, etching needles, a traditional échoppe point and three large modern échoppes, needles and holders, a wire brush, wire wool, abrading paper and a folding magnifying lens.

double the normal exposure without a positive (see pp. 140–146). Take care that there is no dust, dirt, hair or fluff on the glass, as this could block the light and cause pinholes, lines and open areas in the resist. After the plate has been exposed, follow the developing, curing and drying instructions given on pp. 146–148. The sides of the plate are not protected by the layer of photoresist and will need to be stopped out. After etching, the photoresist and stop-out resist can be removed (see pp. 214–215).

HARD RESISTS

Hard resists are used when precise marks, clear sharp lines or delicate drawings are required. This type of resist is applied in a thin and even layer and generally covers the entire plate surface. The various types of acrylic hard resist are applied to the plate using different techniques (including painting, pouring and rolling).

When the coating is dry, etching needles, roulettes and scrapers can be used to make precise marks and clear sharp lines in the resist. These tools only need slight pressure to cut through the resist to reveal the metal. Crosshatching and stippling can be used to create tonal effects. Broader marks can be made in the resist by scraping away or by painting on a resist remover. If tone is required, an aquatint or other tonal structure may be applied to these open areas. Hard resists will not smudge during drawing and the layer of resist is strong, allowing the artist to work outside the etching studio. They are highly effective acid resists and foul bite is unlikely. This means that the printed image looks cleaner and clearer than with traditional resists as there is less 'noise' (as in digital imaging, this term describes marks which look like spots and flecks of dust and grime). If this effect is wanted, dust and hair can be deliberately dropped into the wet resist, or the plate can be scuffed and scraped by rubbing a little gritty sand over the surface after the drawing is made.

The various image-making methods and the different types of hard resist (together with their characters and their application methods) are described below.

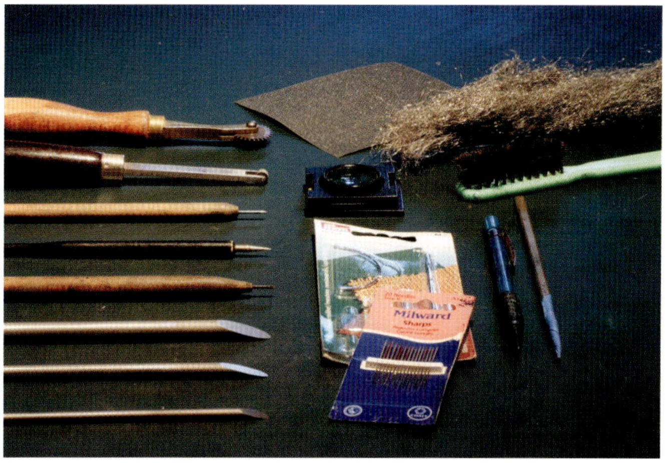

MAKING A GUIDE DRAWING

After the selected hard resist has been applied to the plate and dried, it can either be worked into to reveal the metal or a guide drawing can be made. The guide drawing will not break through the resist and will not be etched: it can be considered to be more like a map in that it describes the position of lines, marks and textured areas. The finished sketch may be looked at in a mirror to see how well the image is working when reversed. There are several different approaches to making a guide drawing.

- Carbon paper can be used to transfer a drawing to the dry resist-coated plate.
- A soft pencil or graphite crayon (3B to 7B) can be used to draw directly onto a hard resist coloured with Lascaux coloured coating. Soft coloured chalks such as conté and tracing paper, carbon or transfer paper may also be used on this surface.
- Some types of waterproof marker pens may be used successfully on the resist.

DRAWING INTO THE RESIST

A range of tools can be used to work into the hard resist. Etching needles are designed for this type of drawing and can be purchased from intaglio suppliers. The tips are generally slightly rounded as this shape glides more easily over the plate surface without snagging or catching. The échoppe point is specially shaped to produce lines which swell and thin. Small chisel-shaped tools can be used to create calligraphic lines. A range of simpler needles are also available. Sewing or darning needles attached firmly to a wooden paintbrush handle can also be drawn with effectively.

Scrapers, roulettes, steel wool, coarse sandpaper and wire brushes (see pp. 88–89 and 93) can be used to make a variety of different marks. Needles are useful for crosshatching and sharp points are effective for stippled effects.

Part of the image-making process is controlling the tone of the lines and marks. The classical method is to draw the complete image and etch it lightly. The lightest lines and areas are then stopped out (see p. 122). The plate is then etched again and the lines successively stopped out. This process generates a series of different depths of bite which print with different tonal values. A test strip can be made so that the biting times and their related tones can be determined.

Equipment and materials required

Work on a clean board in the drawing area.

- a plate coated with a clear or coloured hard-resist layer which has been thoroughly dried
- etching needles, échoppe points, scrapers, roulettes, wire wool, coarse sandpaper and wire brushes
- magnifying glass or linen tester

Principle: scratched-away lines and marks will etch; wider areas will etch as open bite unless an aquatint has been applied.

Working methods

- Follow the application and preparation instructions for the hard resist which has been selected (see opposite).
- Draw into the hard resist with the etching needles or other tools. The layer of resist should be thin and completely dry, allowing the needle to glide through its surface in any chosen direction. The exposed metal should look bright and clean, and the excess resist can be brushed from the plate without smearing.
- When the drawing process is complete, any corrections are made (see p. 108 for procedure for colour-coated plates).
- Drawing corrections may be stopped out, the stop-out resist is dried thoroughly and the area is redrawn if necessary (see pp. 121–123).
- The dry plate may then be etched (see pp. 151–161).
- After etching, the plate is examined and a decision made about the next stage, e.g. continue etching, continue drawing, stop out, apply aquatint or strip off the resist.

WORKING INTO THE RESIST TO CREATE BROAD OPEN AREAS

Broader areas or marks may be opened by painting resist remover onto the layer of dry resist. When the weakened areas of resist have been removed from the plate, the exposed metal may be processed further (e.g. an aquatint, wash resist or photopolymer may be applied) or the plate can be etched as an open bite.

Equipment and materials required

Work on a waterproof workboard and wear eye protection, gloves and an apron (see pp. 214–215).

- a plate with a thin even layer of resist (colour-coated resists work particularly well)
- some resist remover
- Lascaux Screenprinting Paste
- some paintbrushes
- a china or glass palette for the resist remover
- a waterproof permanent marker pen
- a basin of soapy water and some disposable rags
- soft tissue or cotton wool
- a sink and low pressure hose

Principle: broad painted areas of dry acrylic resist are removed from the plate surface.

Working method

- Follow the application and preparation instructions for the hard resist which has been selected (see opposite).
- Lay the dry hard resist-coated plate on the waterproof workboard. Hard resists which have been coloured with Lascaux coloured coating work particularly well as the absorbent nature of the coating holds the remover in place.
- Squeeze a small amount of resist remover into the palette kept for this purpose.
- Draw the desired shape with the marker pen on the area of resist to be removed. Some types of marker pen can resist the action of the mordant so care should be taken not to draw on the exposed plate surface unless non-etching lines are wanted.
- Paint the selected resist remover within the drawn image and leave for 5 minutes (the resist remover may dissolve the pen lines). The plate must be dry or the resist remover will spread over the entire surface, weakening all of the resist. A little Lascaux Screenprinting Paste may be added to the resist remover and this thicker mixture is more suitable for creating painting marks.
- After 5 minutes fold a soft tissue into a small pad and carefully absorb any excess resist remover without spreading the liquid over the plate. The remover will not have dissolved the resist visibly but it will have weakened it.
- Rinse the plate with plenty of water (using a soft hose) to wash away any residues of resist remover (any coloured coating

will wash away). The resist in the form of the painted shape should break away and lift off cleanly.

- Softly rub any remaining areas of weakened resist with a hog's hair brush. If the layers of resist (or coloured coating) are thick, the process will need to be repeated until the surface of the plate is reached.
- After rinsing, the plate should be degreased with an acidic degreaser and dried before any other resists are applied. This type of broad mark will etch as open bite unless an aquatint or tonal method is applied to the plate. Any final corrections are made with stop-out resist.
- Clean the brushes and tools in soapy water and rinse these well to prevent any contamination if the brush is used to apply a resist in the future.
- The dry plate may then be etched (see pp. 150–161).
- After etching, the plate is examined and a decision made about the next stage, e.g. continue etching, open further areas, make drawn marks, employ a lift, apply aquatint or strip off the resist.

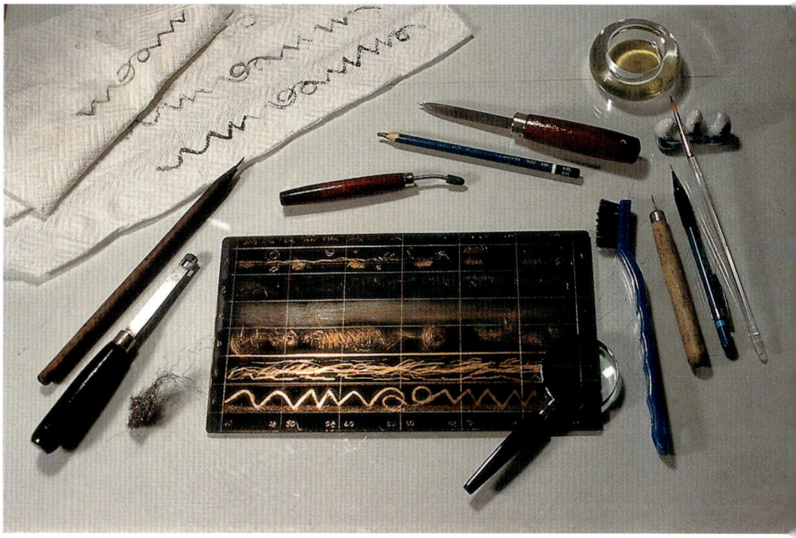

A plate coated in Lascaux Hard Resist (coloured with Lascaux Black Coating) has been drawn into, and broad open areas are now being created with resist remover. The offset marks from this process can be seen on the absorbent tissue (top left).

TYPES OF HARD RESIST AND THEIR APPLICATION METHODS

Different types of hard resist may be applied to the plate by brush, by airbrush, with a soft roller or by flow coating. Each method requires some practice to develop skill at applying a thin and even layer to the plate.

LASCAUX HARD RESIST

This is a clear, waxy, fast-drying, self-levelling, reliable resist which may be applied to any etching metal. It is water-soluble and dries to become water- and acid-resistant, withstanding long bites. The resist may be used at any stage of the plate's development and is compatible with all the Lascaux acrylic resists and many photoresists. A thin layer can be painted on finely grained or deeply bitten plates and this brushing action ensures that the resist protects the deepest etched lines. This resist may also be diluted with water and applied to the plate by flow coating (see pp. 108–110). The dry layer of hard resist is quite robust so the plate may be drawn on elsewhere and transported to the etching studio. Etching needles will glide through the waxy layer without cracking or crazing and any excess resist can be brushed away without smudging. After etching the resist is easily removed from the plate or may be left on the plate and printed as a collagraph material (see pp. 162–175).

APPLICATION METHODS

The plate surface, the type and condition of paintbrush and the painting technique are all factors which will affect the quality of the layer of resist. Experiment with different painting techniques and types of paintbrush on test plates to gain familiarity with the application process. Once some ideal brushes have been found keep them for applying resists. The process of applying the resist and care of the brush should be demonstrated carefully to students.

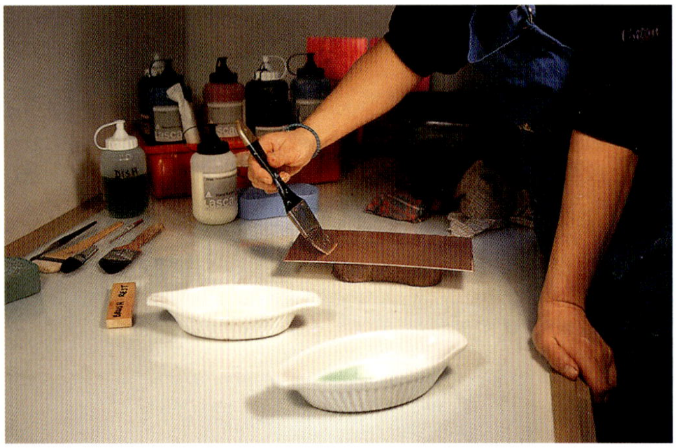

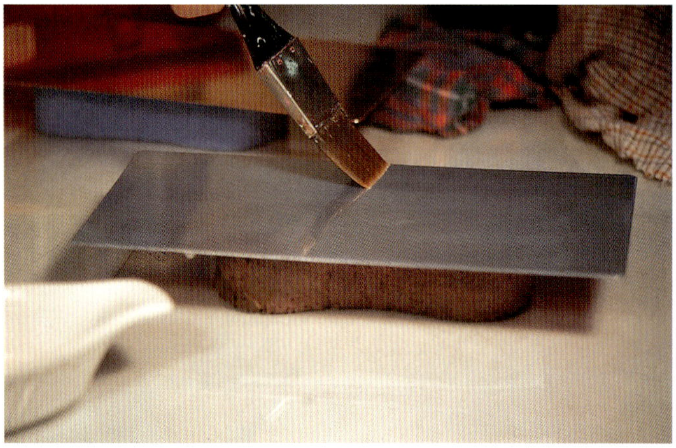

above left Applying a Lascaux Hard Resist with a soft brush. Note the china palettes, basins of water and brush rests.

above right The brush strokes can extend off the plate if a sponge is placed underneath.

Equipment and materials required

Work in the workstation for applying acrylic resist.

- a clean, prepared, degreased etching plate
- a clean, damp sponge which is smaller than the plate
- a clean, wide, square-ended, flat, soft, fine-haired brush such as a sable or watercolour brush or a 5 cm (2 in.) Prolene brush made by ProArte
- Lascaux Hard Resist
- a china or glass palette
- a basin of warm soapy water, sponges and clean drying cloths
- a waterproof permanent marker pen
- household dishwashing detergent
- a brush rest

Principle: a layer of hard resist is painted on the plate surface so that it is suitable for working into and will protect the metal from the action of the mordant.

Working method for brush application

- Copper, brass, zinc, steel or aluminium may be used and must be prepared correctly. New plates should be bevelled, cleaned, finely and evenly grained, degreased and backed. Previously etched plates should be clean, degreased and backed. Write the name of the plate or artist and 'HR' (abbreviation of hard resist) on the back of the plate with the waterproof permanent marker pen. This note can be useful to identify the plate and to confirm that the plate has been coated.
- Lay out the materials and make sure that the working area is clean and not dusty. Set out a basin of warm soapy water, some sponges and clean drying cloths so that it is easy to clean the brushes and other tools intermittently in soapy water. This practice will prevent the acrylic resist drying on the tools. When working with water-soluble resists or dishwashing liquid, it is good practice to wear gloves and an apron.
- Raise the plate up from the working surface by laying it on top of a slightly dampened 'S' sponge. Plates which are hot from the drying cabinet should be allowed to cool to room temperature before application as the hard resist will dry too rapidly on a warm plate.
- Shake the container of resist thoroughly to distribute the wax and then squeeze a small amount into a clean dry palette.
- Apply the resist thinly to the plate in even strokes with a soft brush. The type of brush is important as a coarse brush will lay down a ridged layer or a layer with gaps. Before working on the plate, paint a brush stroke onto a clean sheet of paper to check

that the brush is clean. This resist is designed to be quick-drying so the painting process should only take a few minutes.

- Work steadily from one side of the plate to the other and allow the brush strokes to extend off the plate to avoid unwanted pools of resist forming at the edges. Rotate the plate through 90° and, without reloading the brush with resist, brush the entire plate surface again. The objective is to produce a thin, even coating on the plate without any ridges or missing areas. To avoid painting with an overloaded brush the excess can be wiped away on the edge of the palette.
- Small particles of dust or hairs on the plate are usually held in the resist and will not cause foul biting. If excessive quantities are in the resist the brush, palette, plate and working area should be cleaned and the application process started afresh.
- When the plate has been coated with a thin and even layer of hard resist, lift it from the sponge-rest and allow it to dry thoroughly in a horizontal position. Plates may be left unattended in a horizontal drying cabinet where they will dry faster and are protected from accidental damage and dust.
- The resist should be cleaned from brushes and the palette with warm soapy water immediately after the plates are coated. Excess resist should be stored in a container for 'recycled resists' (for use as a plate-backing resist or a collagraph medium). The workstation can then be tidied up.
- When the plate is dry, it can be examined for flaws. Any previously etched areas of the plate are easy to see through the clear layer of resist. Printmakers new to the resist may initially find it hard to see or feel the layer of resist, and may find it helpful to flash bite their plates to check that they have coated the entire surface correctly. Some deeply bitten plates and steel plates may require two coats of hard resist.
- When the resist is dry, it may be coloured (see overleaf) or worked into (see pp. 103–105).

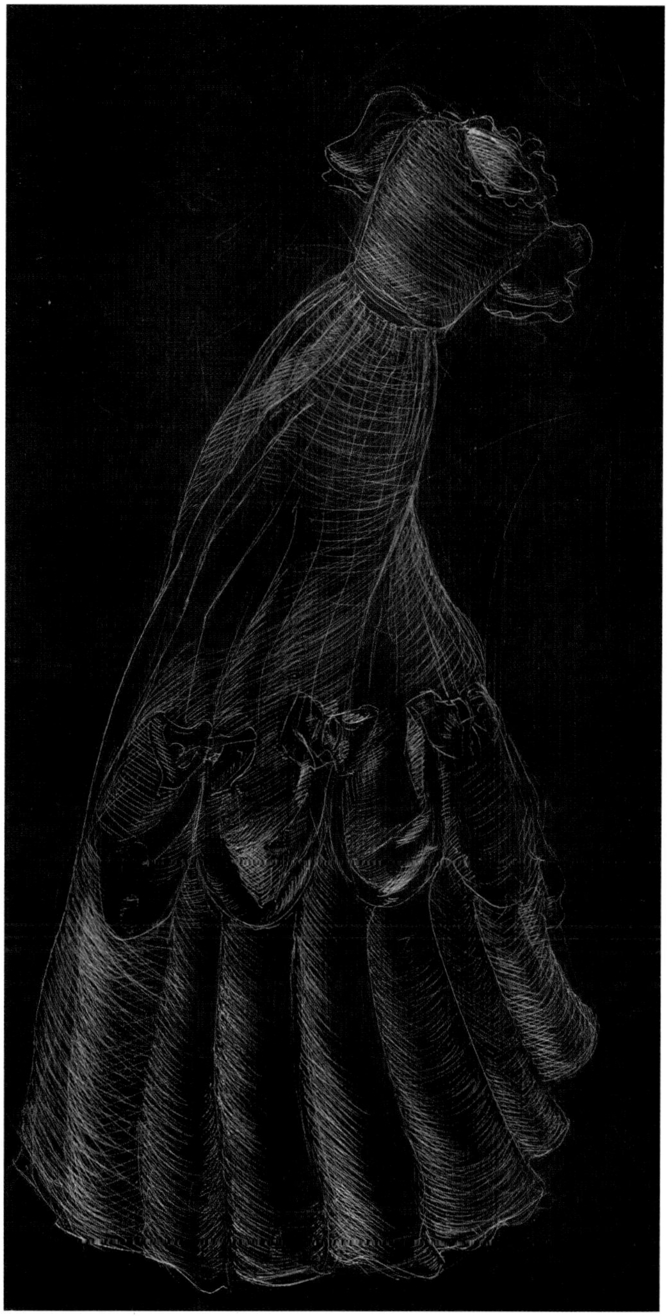

Duncan Robertson (UK), *Wedding Dress*, 14 x 27 cm (5½ x 10⅝ in.), 2003. A zinc plate was coated in Lascaux Hard Resist (coloured with Lascaux Black Coating). After a guide drawing had been made in pencil, the resist was drawn into with etching tools.

Working method for airbrush application

An airbrush may also be used to apply a thin, even coating of slightly diluted Lascaux Hard Resist to the plate (see

p. 130). The multitude of tiny spots of hard resist can be felt when a drawing is made and the resulting line may look jagged on close examination.

COLOURING LASCAUX HARD RESIST

The dry layer of resist may be coloured to black or white. This is particularly helpful for the initial drawing on a plate as the scratched-away lines and marks can be seen clearly. The image will appear in the form of bright lines on a dark-coloured ground and dark lines on a white-coated ground. The water-soluble coloured coating is removed after the drawing is complete.

This practice is analogous to the tradition of smoking the plate and to the technique of applying a white lead coating. As with solvent-based resists, the addition of dyes and colours to resists generally makes the layer less acid-resistant and less sensitive to draw through. It is for these reasons that the coloured layer is applied separately to the dry hard resist.

Equipment and materials required

Work in the workstation for applying acrylic resist.

- an etching plate coated in a layer of hard resist which is thoroughly dry
- a clean, damp sponge which is smaller than the plate
- Lascaux Black Coating or Lascaux White Coating
- the resist brush
- a china or glass palette
- a basin of warm soapy water, sponge and clean drying cloths
- a drying cabinet

Principle: the dry hard-resist coating is coloured to make the drawing more visible.

Working method

- Lay out the materials and make sure that the working area is clean and not dusty. Set out a basin of warm soapy water, some sponges and clean drying cloths so that it is easy to clean the brushes and other tools intermittently in soapy water. When working with water-soluble art materials or dish-washing liquid, it is good practice to wear gloves and an apron.
- Raise the dry, resist-coated plate by laying it on top of a slightly dampened sponge (if the plate is large, several sponge supports will be required).
- Shake the container thoroughly and squeeze a small amount of the Lascaux coloured coating into a palette. It will take several layers to achieve a good coating. The coloured coating is slower drying than the resists and painting on plates that are warm from the drying cabinet helps create a thin, even covering.
- Apply the coloured coating thinly to the plate in even strokes with the brush. Work steadily from one side of the plate to the other. The first coating will normally look patchy and streaky but should be dried, as these initial brush strokes provide the base for subsequent layers.
- When the plate is dry but still warm, repeat the painting process at right angles to the previous strokes. The second coating will adhere to the first streaky layer and will be even and smooth.
- Dry the plate horizontally before starting to draw.
- Clean the brushes thoroughly with warm soapy water and rinse well and at the end of the session tidy the workstation.

Z*ACRYL HARDGROUND EMULSION

This resist is an acrylic polymer solution and is applied to the etching plate by flow coating. Flow coating is the name given to the process of pouring a fluid liquid resist down the face of an etching plate to create a thin coating over the entire surface. This resist is lightly tinted and compatible with the other Z*Acryl etching products which have been specially designed for etching copper in ferric chloride. A range of other metals and etchants may also be used. The resist is self-levelling and dries to a thin film in minutes. It may also be sprayed with an airbrush to create an aquatint. The water-soluble resist dries to become water- and acid-resistant. It can be removed easily from the plate at any point in the process (see p. 214).

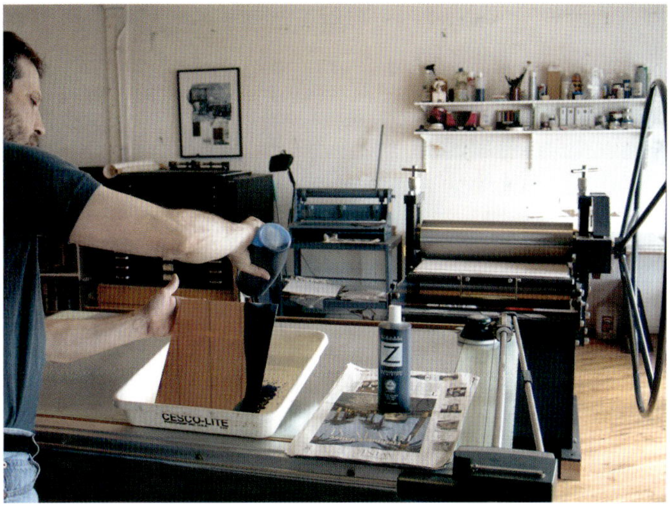

left Z*Acryl Hardground Emulsion is poured onto the front surface of the copper plate.

below left The plate after being flow-coated.

below right The coated plate is 'stepped' several times on clean newsprint and dried in a vertical position.

Equipment and materials required

Work in the workstation for applying acrylic resist.

- a bevelled, clean, finely grained, degreased, neutralized, rinsed and dried etching plate
- Z*Acryl Hardground Emulsion
- several sheets of newsprint
- a very clean, dry, plastic tray (ideally with a pouring corner), which is slightly larger than the width of the plate
- a very clean funnel
- a plastic tea strainer
- a recycled container used for storing excess resist
- a basin of warm soapy water, sponges and clean drying cloths
- a waterproof permanent marker pen

Principle: a layer of resist is flow-coated on the plate surface so that it is suitable for working into and will protect the metal from the action of the mordant.

Working method

- New plates should be bevelled, cleaned, finely and evenly grained or polished, degreased and backed. Previously etched plates should be clean and degreased. Several layers of resist will be required for deeply bitten plates. Each layer should be dried between each coating.

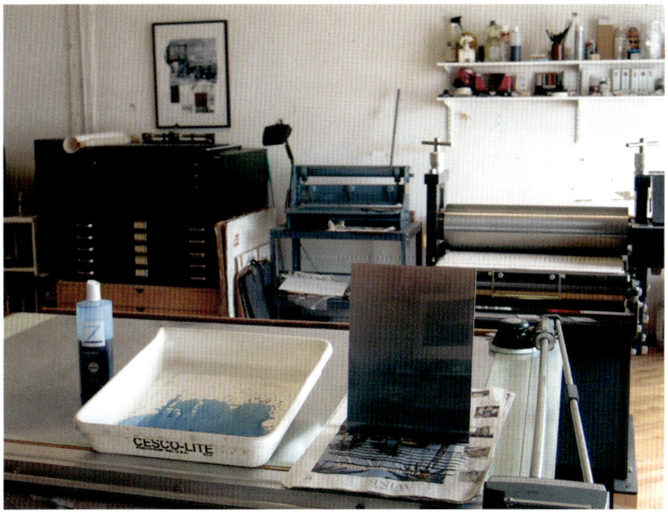

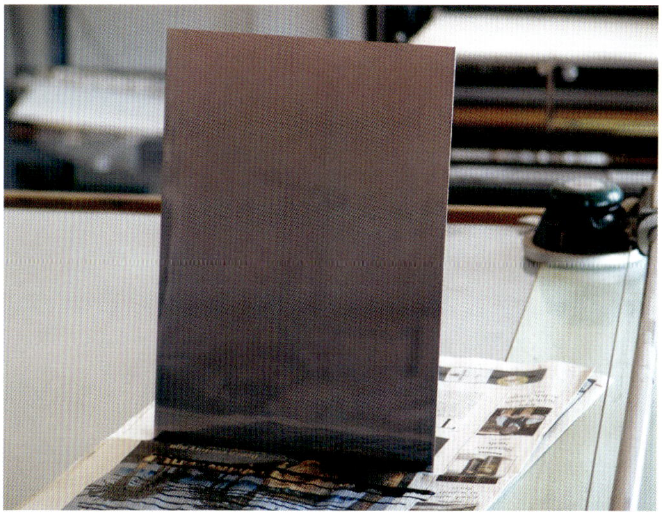

• Write the name of the plate or artist and 'HGE' (abbreviation of hardground emulsion) on the back of the plate with the waterproof permanent marker pen. This note can be useful to identify the plate and to confirm that the plate has been coated.
• Lay out the materials and make sure that the tray is very clean and not dusty. Set out a basin of warm soapy water, some sponges and clean drying cloths so that it is easy to clean the tools intermittently in soapy water. When working with water-soluble resists or dishwashing liquid, it is good practice to wear gloves and an apron.
• Avoid working near fans or near dusty areas such as open windows or doors. Lay the folded newsprint flat under a support against which the plate can be positioned after it has been coated. Do not shake the resist container as this may result in bubbles in the layer of resist.
• Stand the cool, dry plate upright in the tray. With one hand support the plate from behind in a nearly vertical position. Turn the bottle upside-down and squeeze a generous quantity of the fluid resist over the front surface of the plate. It should flow easily over the entire surface to create a thin and even layer. Any greasy areas will cause it to flow erratically. As soon as the surface is covered lift the plate from the tray and stand it upright on the folded newsprint, leaning against a support.
• The plate should be left to dry vertically on a pad of clean newsprint. Lift the plate several times at the beginning of the drying period to prevent the plate sticking to the paper and to guard against a ridge of resist forming at the bottom of the plate. It may take 30 minutes to dry thoroughly, depending on the thickness of the layer and the humidity levels in the studio.
• The coated plate should be examined carefully. Any small particles of dust or hairs on the plate will be held in the resist and generally will not cause foul biting. If excessive quantities are in the resist the plate should be cleaned off and the working area sponged down to remove dust and the application process started afresh.
• Excess resist may be poured through a funnel and strained into the product container.
• Clean the tray and tools thoroughly at the end of the session and tidy the work area.
• The dry plate can be drawn into with etching tools (see p. 103).

HOUSEHOLD AND ART MATERIALS USED AS HARD RESISTS

Some clear household acrylic floor finishes may be used as hard resists (Future, Klear, Carefree and some other types). These materials are manufactured by companies such as SC Johnstone and Johnsondiversey. The ingredients in these household or commercial janitorial products may alter, and often vary from country to country, which directly affects their performance as resists. These resists work best on finely grained copper plates. They are often too brittle to bridge deeply bitten areas and may fracture as they dry. Test plates should be made to assess the mordant resistance and brittleness of the different products. The application and drawing methods for the Z*Acryl hardground emulsion can be followed. Some types of acrylic floor finish are incompatible with other resists and photopolymers, causing them to break up and resulting in foul bite. Tests can be made to check for any adverse effects of this kind.

A layer of dry Graphic Chemical & Ink Company Water-Washable Block Printing Ink may be used as a hard resist on copper (see p. 117). When working with water-soluble art materials or dishwashing liquid, it is good practice to wear gloves and an apron.

SOFT RESISTS

Soft resists are used to generate etched effects which resemble collages, monotypes or drawings made with crayons or soft pencils. The various types of soft resist are applied to all or parts of the plate using different techniques (including drawing, painting and rolling). The capacity of the resist to offset from the plate surface allows the artist to create a broad

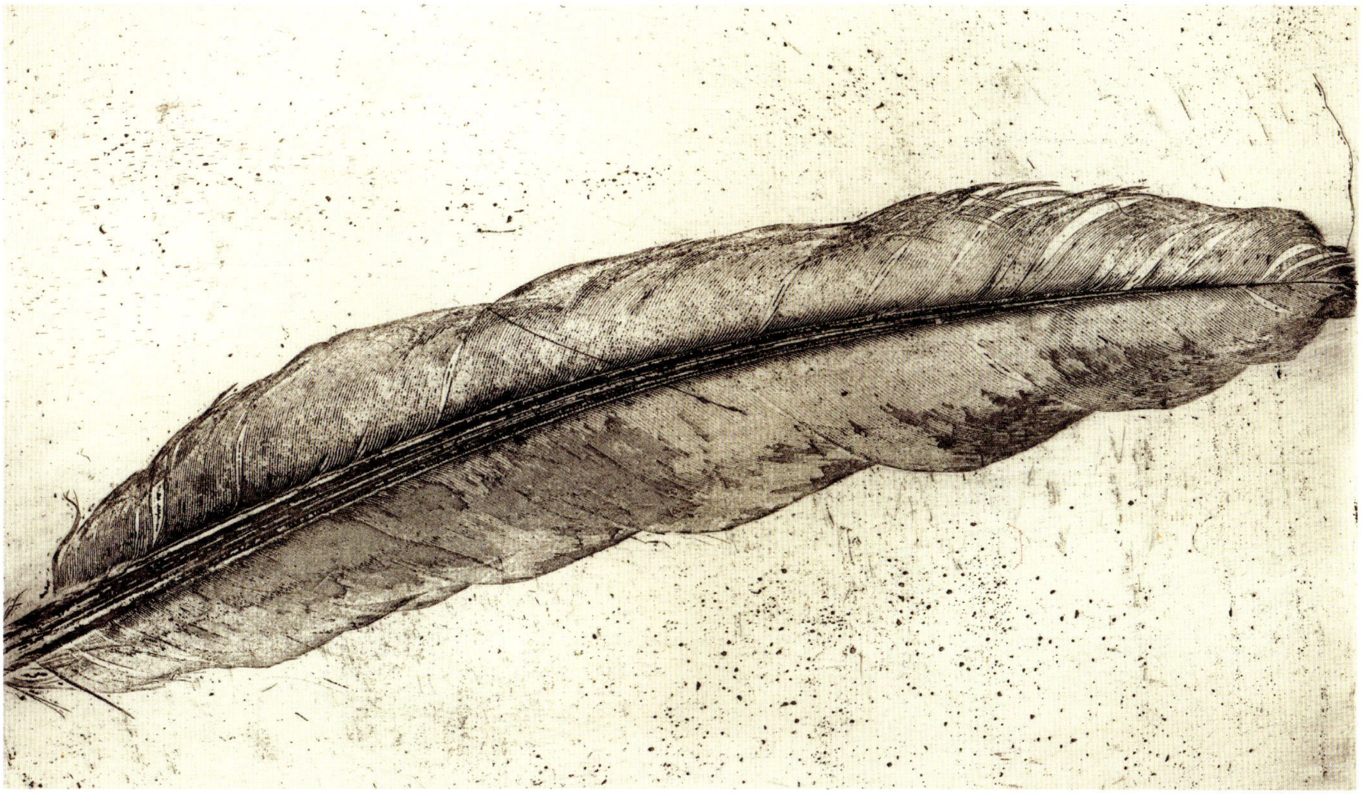

Barbara Diethelm (Switzerland), *Feather*, etching, 2003 (detail). Lascaux Soft Resist was painted onto a copper plate and after 15 minutes a feather and many tiny flower seedheads were impressed into the resist (using a press). Lascaux Aquatint Spray Resist was applied and the plate was etched in ferric chloride.

range of textures. The resist can also be drawn into directly to generate bold, lively lines and marks. Oily soft resists remain soft and fragile, whereas acrylic soft resists dry to become hard and durable and can be worked further.

Other processes can be used which either share the methodology of working with soft resists or generate plates and prints which resemble the characteristic soft resist.

The various image-making methods and the different types of soft resist (together with their characters and their application methods) are described below.

CREATING COLLAGE-TYPE IMPRESSIONS

Collage materials can be pressed into a layer of soft resist to create interesting textured images. An etching press is used to push the collage into the resist and the sharpness and quality of the image will vary depending on the type and moistness of the resist and on the pressure exerted by the press. The results are often sharper if the pressure is decreased by altering the settings or by removing a blanket. Test plates can be made to discover the optimum setting and to experiment with the different types of resist.

Equipment and materials required
Work in the printing room.

- a plate with a moist layer of soft resist
- a timer
- textured low-profile elements (feathers, netting, fabrics such

as lace, thread, string, leaves, origami shapes, paper shapes, doilies, wrinkled tissue paper, embossed paper)

- a sheet of smooth clear PVC (300 gsm)
- tissue paper

Working method

- Follow the application and drying instructions for the type of resist which has been selected (see pp. 115–119).
- Use the period that the drying resist is being timed to plan the collage. Roughly arrange the collage materials on a piece of card the same size as the plate. Avoid using wire, coins, keys or other hard objects that will cause damage to the blankets or press.
- Position the plate (face up) on a sheet of clean tissue paper on the etching press bed.
- Carry the collage in a simple folder over to the press and position the card with the collage elements next to the plate.
- Move the collage elements into place on top of the resist.
- Lay a sheet of PVC on top of the collage, followed by some clean sheets of tissue (to protect the blankets) and the blankets of the etching press.
- Roll the resist-coated plate, the collage, the PVC sheet, the tissue and the blankets through the etching press.
- After they have passed through the press, the blankets, tissue paper and PVC sheet are lifted away. The collage will be embedded in the soft resist. To avoid damaging or marking the coating use an etching needle to lift each item from the plate.

This copper plate was coated with Lascaux Soft Resist and after 12 minutes paper stencils and string were impressed into this. The resist was then worked into with some Lascaux Wash Resist and water to create a further range of marks. Lascaux Aquatint Spray Resist was applied and the copper plate was etched in ferric chloride.

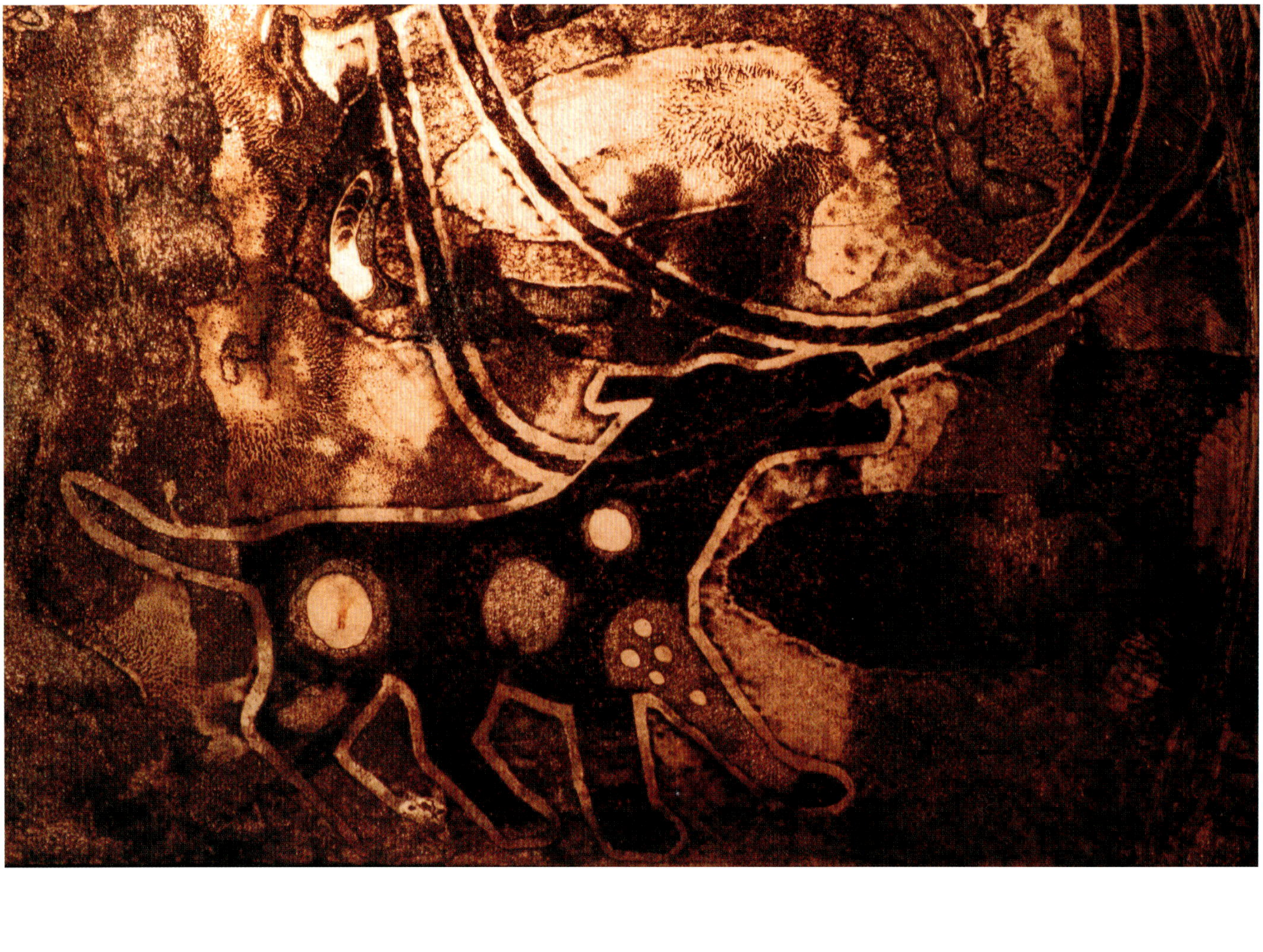

• Lift the plate (by manipulating the sheet of tissue on which it is lying) and examine it in good light. (Artists new to this resist may wish to dry and flash bite the plate: the darkened image can be clearly seen and assessed.)

• While the resist remains soft, lines and marks can be added to the image with etching tools or stiff bristled brushes.

• Acrylic resists can be worked into with water or wash resists to create reticulated effects. When the acrylic soft resist dries, the plate may be drawn into as though it were a hard resist (see p. 102), an aquatint may be applied or it may be edited with a stop-out resist. After flash biting, examine the plate in good light. If the image looks fine the plate can be etched to the required depth. The normal stopping-out method can be used to control the tone of the lines and marks (see p. 122).

• Oily soft resists are more difficult to stop out and monitor than acrylic resists (see p. 118). Flash biting is generally ineffective, as residual grease in the drawn lines and marks can initially slow down the etching process.

• After etching, the plate is examined and a decision made about the next stage, e.g. continue etching, stop out, apply aquatint or strip off the resist.

THE CLASSICAL OFFSETTING DRAWING METHOD

Drawings made with this method resemble monotypes or drawings made with crayons or soft pencils.

Equipment and materials required

Work on a clean workboard in the drawing area.

• a plate with a moist layer of soft resist
• a timer
• 3 rectangles of cut card (each 2.5 x 5 cm/1 x 2 in.)
• a sheet of tissue paper cut to the size of the plate
• a rough textured paper cut to the size of the plate
• a pencil, crayon, round-tipped stick or brush handle

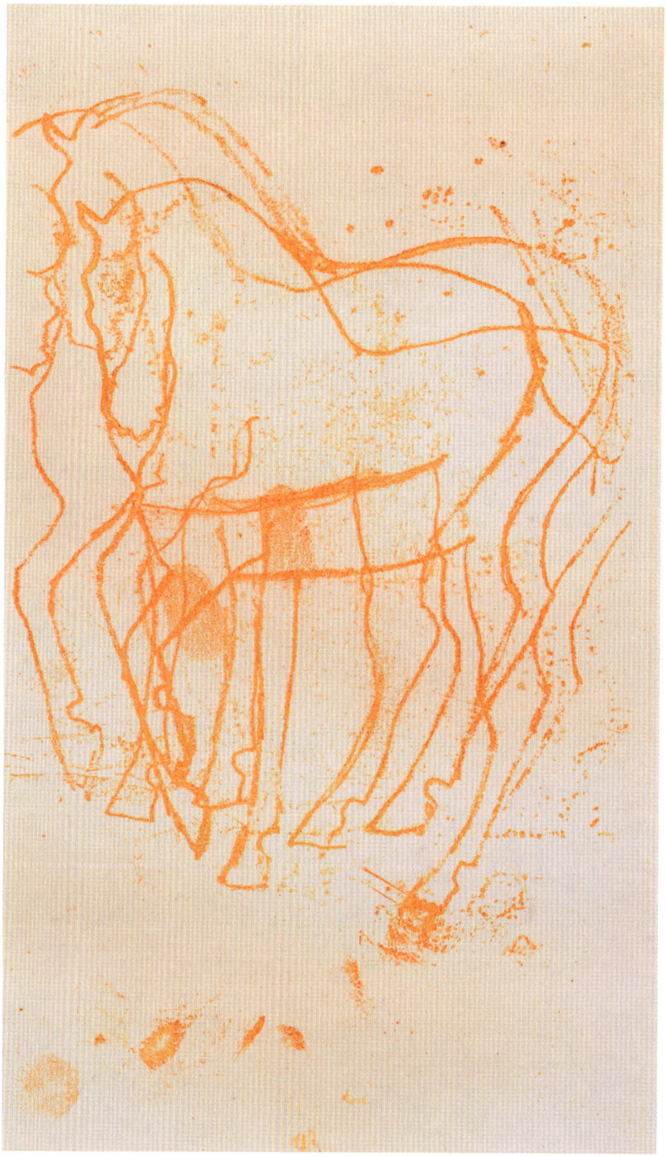

This drawing was generated on a steel plate coated with Lascaux Soft Resist using the classical offsetting drawing method. After applying Lascaux Aquatint Spray Resist the plate was bitten in a copper sulphate solution.

Working method

- Follow the application instructions for the type of soft resist which has been selected (see opposite).
- Lay the coated plate on the clean workboard in a good position for drawing. To secure the plate and prevent it from slipping, position two rectangles of cut card against the lower edge of the plate and one against its left side. Masking-tape these cards to the workboard.
- Lay the cut sheet of tissue paper on the plate and lightly masking-tape its corners to the workboard to hold it securely.
- Position the map, key drawing or textured paper on top and hinge the top edge to the workboard with a strip of masking tape. The paper's surface will determine the type of mark.
- Draw on the paper, remembering that the image will be reversed. The pressure of the pencil or crayon on the paper causes the tissue to absorb the soft resist, revealing the metal plate surface in those areas. Artists often use a drawing support (a wooden device which spans the plate like a bridge) to guard against leaning on or touching the plate while drawing.

below Jenny Hendra (UK), *Lilac,* etching, 14 x 26 cm (5½ x 10¼ in.), 2004. The steel plate was inked up with Lascaux Gouache and printed on Arches paper.

opposite Detail of the *Lilac* steel plate. The artist drew directly in Lascaux Soft Resist with soft pencils and conté crayons. Initially the plate was open-bitten, then Lascaux Aquatint Spray Resist was applied and the plate was etched further.

- When the image is complete, hinge up the drawing paper. Then peel the tissue paper slowly and carefully from the resist. The drawing will have offset onto the tissue paper where it is clearly visible but the image will be very difficult to see on the plate. If the tissue paper image looks fine the next stage of the process can be started. The tissue paper should be kept as an aid when stopping-out and for general reference. It is also interesting to compare it with the final print.
- Follow the instructions for working the resist further, drying and etching the plate which are described under 'Creating Collage-Type Impressions' (p. 111–113).

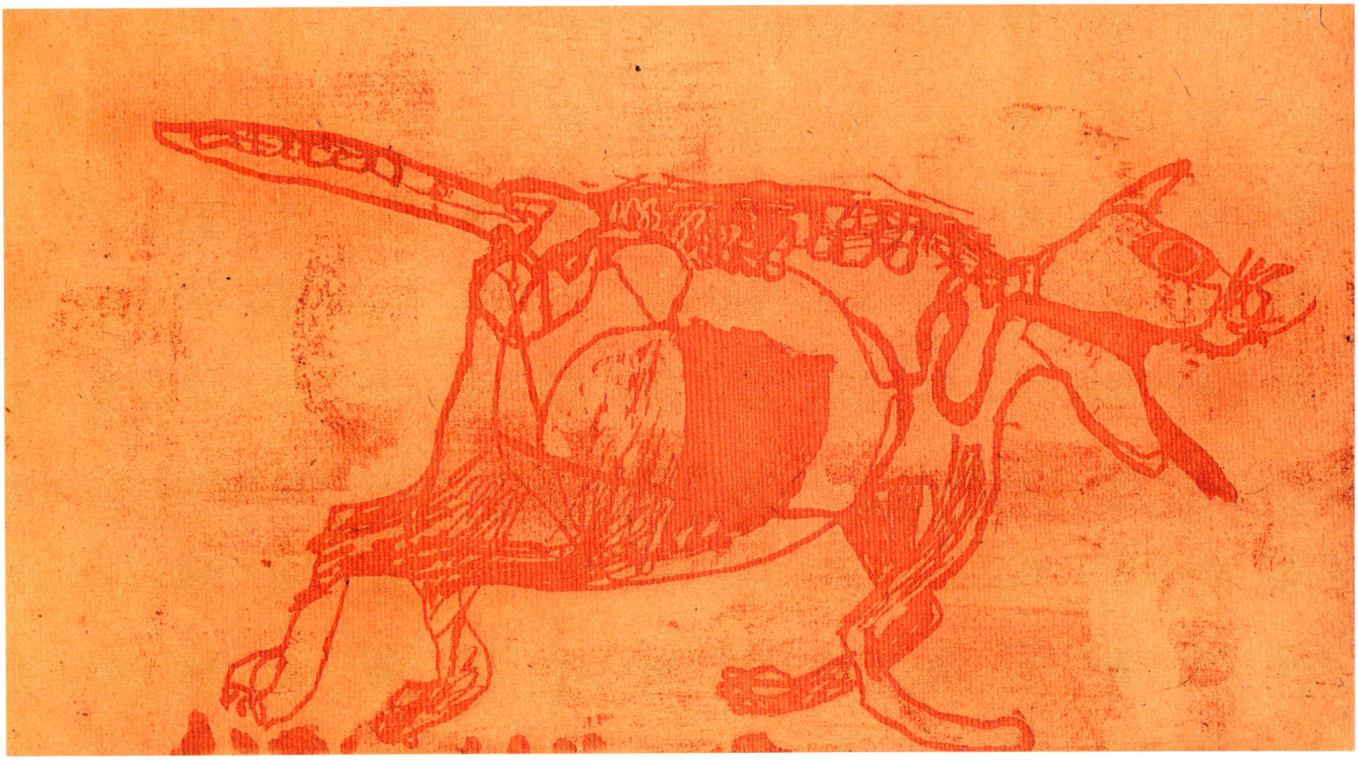

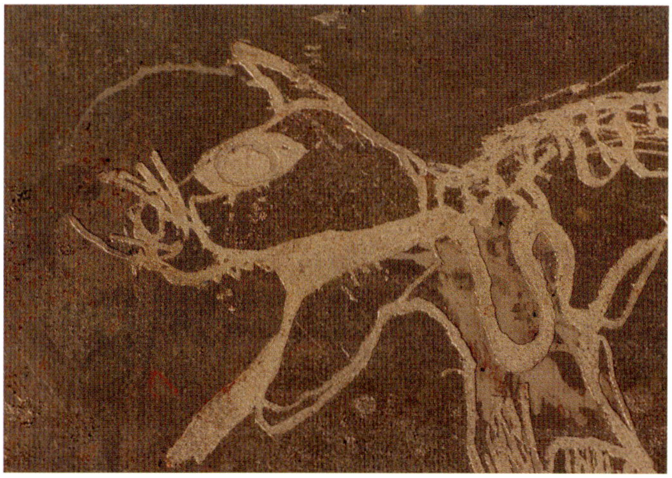

DRAWING DIRECTLY INTO THE SOFT RESIST

Soft pencils and water-soluble crayons can be used to draw directly into the moist layer of soft resist on the plate to generate bold and vigorous lines and marks.

Equipment and materials required

Work on a clean workboard in the drawing area.

- a plate with a moist layer of soft resist
- a timer
- soft pencils and water-soluble crayons

Working method

- Drawing can begin a few minutes after application of the resist. Soft pencils and water-soluble crayons grip onto the finely grained surface of the plate, leaving a deposit. This technique works in different ways with the various resists.
- Soft lines and marks with a lot of noise can be made using oily resists which never dry.
- If more accurate drawings are required, a slow- or a fast-drying acrylic soft resist can be selected. As the resist dries the quality of the drawing changes. Graphic Chemical & Ink Company Water-Washable Block Printing Ink has a very slow drying time. Lascaux Soft Resist can be drawn into for up to one hour. There is a natural point at which the drawing process is arrested, as the Lascaux resist becomes quite dry and the drawing tools snag and rip the layer. If the artist wishes to continue drawing after one hour, the initial drawing should be etched, the plate stripped and re-coated with soft resist, and the drawing continued.
- After drawing, the acrylic soft resist is dried thoroughly. The dried acrylic resist can then be drawn into with etching needles and tools (see p. 103). Graphite or crayon residues can sometimes act as acid resists and so should be washed away with warm water before etching. The image may be edited with stop-out resist.
- Follow the instructions for working the resist further, drying and etching the plate which are described under 'Creating Collage-Type Impressions' (pp. 111–113).

TYPES OF SOFT RESIST AND THEIR APPLICATION METHODS

Different types of soft resist may be applied to the plate by brush, with a soft roller or by drawing. Each method requires some practice to develop skill at applying a thin and even layer to the plate.

LASCAUX SOFT RESIST

This new generation of soft resist has been specially designed for artist printmakers. A range of techniques may be explored, as this resist is able to pick up fine textures accurately and holds detail well. Clear contrasts and sharp definition are possible.

This self-levelling, reliable soft resist is compatible with all the Lascaux acrylic resists and many photoresists. It can be painted on a range of etching metals and is effective on deeply bitten or finely grained plates, which means it can be employed at any stage of the plate's development. The entire surface or localized parts of the plate may be covered with a thin layer which dries to become transparent. To become familiar with the resist make some test plates, notes of results, times, warmth and humidity of the studio, and keep the proofs in a visual aid folder.

Equipment and materials required

Work at the workstation for applying acrylic resist.

- a clean workboard
- a bevelled, cleaned, grained or bitten, degreased, neutralized and rinsed etching plate
- a clean, wide, square-ended, flat, soft, fine-haired brush such as a sable or watercolour brush or a 5 cm (2 in.) Prolene brush made by ProArte
- Lascaux Soft Resist
- a china or glass palette
- a basin of warm soapy water, sponges and clean drying cloths
- a waterproof permanent marker pen
- a timer

Principle: a thin layer of soft resist is painted onto the plate and dried for a specific period so that the creative techniques special to this medium can be used.

Working method

- Choose the image-making method and prepare any collages or preliminary drawings before coating the plate.
- Follow the instructions given for applying Lascaux Hard Resist (see pp. 105–108). The plate should not be placed in a drying cabinet.
- When the soft resist has been painted on the plate, it should be allowed to dry (at room temperature) for a specific period

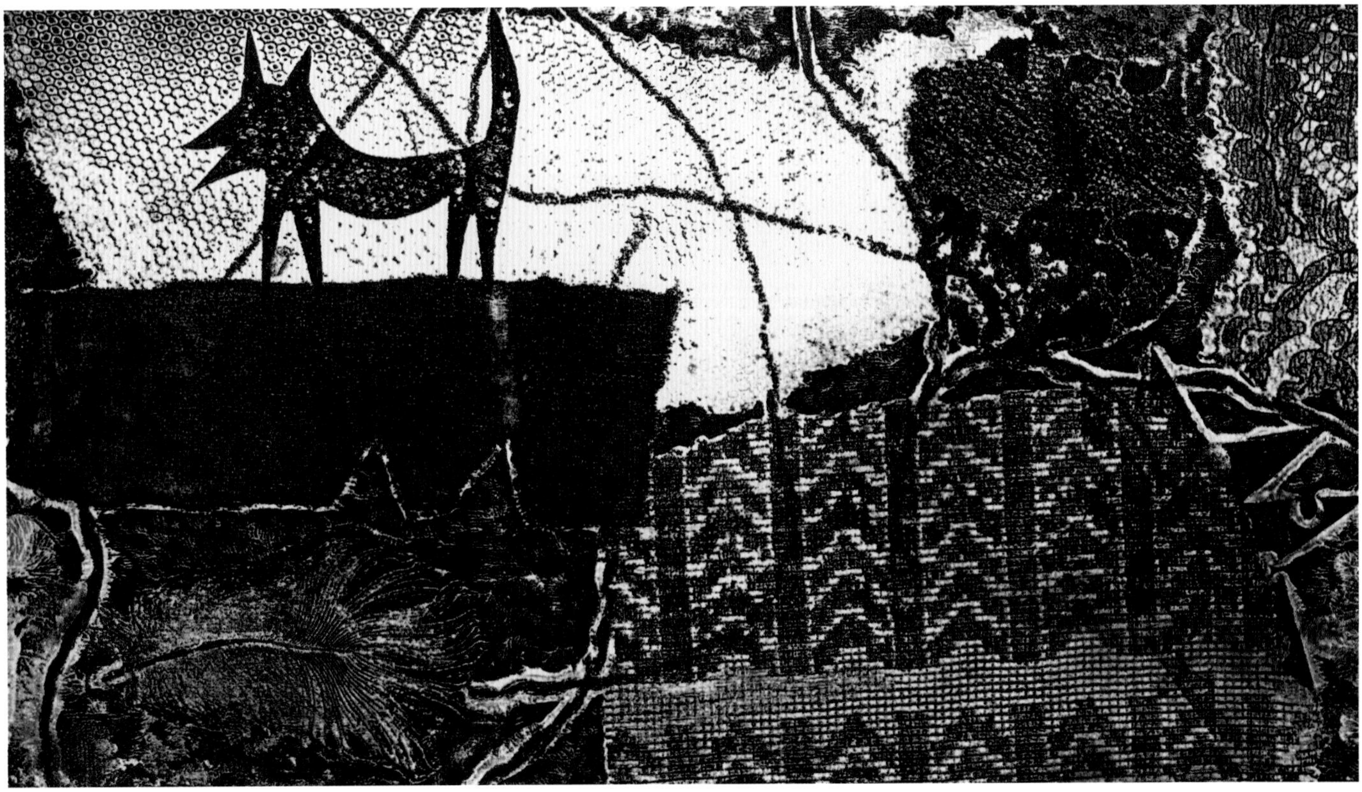

A print from a zinc plate made by impressing paper stencils, netting, lace and threads into Lascaux Soft Resist. Lascaux Stop-Out and Aquatint Spray Resist were also used.

depending on the particular creative process which is to be used.

• If a direct drawing is made immediately in the resist, the fluid resist will fall back into the lines, closing them. If the resist is allowed to dry for a few minutes it will become firmer and will hold its shape when drawn into. As the drying process continues the character of the drawn mark will alter. When the resist becomes too dry, it will begin to snag and rip during drawing.

• Coatings for collage and offset drawing methods are normally dried for around 10 to 15 minutes before the processes are started. This is to avoid the paper or PVC sheet adhering to the resist. The crispness, contrast, delicacy and quality of the image can be controlled by making a judgment about the dryness of the resist. A method of learning how to achieve the best results is to apply an even layer of the soft resist to a test plate. Immediately set a timer and then, at repeated 2-minute intervals, press a finger into the coating and draw a square round the fingerprint with two different types of soft pencil. The resulting print from this test plate can be used to determine optimum timings (see p. 97).

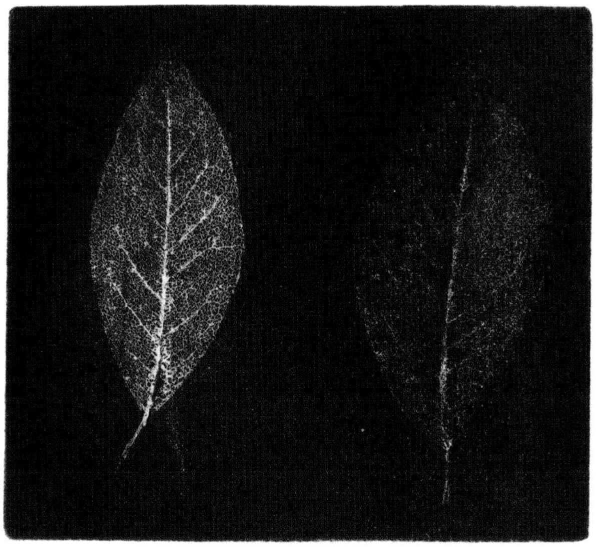

Leslie Boyd, *Leave,* etching, 19 x 22 cm (7½ x 8⅝ in.), 2004. To create these pale leaf skeletons the artist painted actual leaves with Lascaux Stop-Out Resist and offset them onto the plate (see p. 120). She then applied Lascaux Aquatint Spray Resist over the whole plate and etched it. Several applications of aquatint built up the tonal complexity of the background.

WATER-WASHABLE ART MATERIALS USED AS SOFT RESISTS

Graphic Chemical & Ink Company Water-Washable Block Printing Ink may be applied to the plate with a soft roller and used as a soft resist. This relief printing ink is available in a range of different colours which all behave in slightly different ways when used as resists. The black has a large pigment size and does not function well for this purpose. The peacock blue and the crimson red inks are suitable for use on copper plates. These printing inks make fragile resists and are slow drying, taking up to 10 hours to dry thoroughly. This will suit artists who want to draw for long periods but is less ideal for short class times. As this resist is applied by roller, deeply bitten plates are difficult to coat evenly.

A fast-drying, strong, mordant-resistant material such as Lascaux Hard Resist may be added to the relief ink to quicken the drying time, to strengthen it and to make it suitable for use on other metals such as zinc. This mixture generally does not store well and should be used immediately. When working with water-soluble resists or dishwashing liquid, it is good practice to wear gloves and an apron.

Equipment and materials required

Work on an inking-up surface in the drawing area.

• a bevelled, cleaned, grained, degreased, neutralized and rinsed etching plate
• Graphic Chemical & Ink Company Water-Washable Block Printing Ink
• a clean, unscratched glass or stone inking surface
• a clean nitrile roller (a little wider than the plate)
• a plastic palette knife

• a basin of warm soapy water, sponges and clean drying cloths
• a waterproof permanent marker pen

Principle: a coloured printing ink is rolled over the entire plate and used as a soft resist so that the creative techniques special to this medium can be used.

Working method
• Plates should be bevelled, cleaned, finely and evenly grained, degreased and backed.
• Lay out the materials and make sure that the surface and roller are clean and not dusty. Avoid working near fans or near dusty areas such as open windows or doors. Set out a basin of warm soapy water, some sponges and clean drying cloths so that it is easy to clean the rollers and other tools intermittently in soapy water. This practice will prevent the resist drying on the tools. When working with water-soluble resists or dish-washing liquid, it is good practice to wear gloves and an apron.
• If you are working with copper the ink can be used as it is. If you are etching another type of metal, thoroughly mix up a few drops of Lascaux Hard Resist (or other durable resist) with the relief printing ink using a palette knife. If you wish to be very accurate use digital scales to make up a range of mixtures and experiment with these on some test plates. Note the results and keep the proofs and notes in a visual aid folder.
• Use a palette knife to position a reservoir of the resist at the back of the inking slab and then lay out a strip of the mixture. Spread this out thinly with a spatula to the length of the roller. Use the roller to distribute the resist in a neat even square on the slab. If too much is applied remove a little and then use the roller to smooth out the resist. While rolling up the slab, feel how the roller can be handled either to lift up or distribute the resist more heavily. Lines will appear in the square of resist if the roller is not lifted and spun a little.
• Roll the plate up and remember that the resist must cover the entire plate surface evenly. The rolling technique, the type of roller used and the condition of the roller are all factors which will affect the quality of the rolled-on layer. The process of rolling on the resist and care of the roller should be demonstrated carefully to students.
• If excessive quantities of dust and fluff are caught up in the resist the roller, plate and working area should be cleaned and the application process started afresh.
• The plate may be worked into a few minutes after application. The mixture should be cleaned from rollers, spatulas and the inking surface with warm soapy water immediately after the plates are coated. The mixture does not store well so should be wiped up with a disposable cloth and put in the studio waste container.

OILY ART MATERIALS USED AS SOFT RESISTS

R & F Pigment Sticks (an oil paint in stick form) can be used as a soft resist on all metals. This oily material does not dry on the plate and if the plate is warmed the layer will soften further and the open lines will close up. Any greasy residue in the lines and marks will inhibit biting. After making the image any repairs to the resist are difficult to manage: one technique is to paint on a small amount of the resist with a soft brush. The fragile layer can easily be scuffed, allowing foul bite and unwanted etching to take place. (See illustrations in 'Oily Resists', pp. 148–49.)

Some etchers have used other oily materials such as lipstick, etching ink and oil paints.

Equipment and materials required
Work on an inking-up surface in the printing area.
• a bevelled, clean, finely grained etching plate
• a black R & F Pigment Stick
• a clean nitrile roller (a little wider than the plate)
• some cleaning oil and dry rags
• a waterproof permanent marker pen

Principle: an oily drawing material is rolled over the entire plate and used as a soft resist.

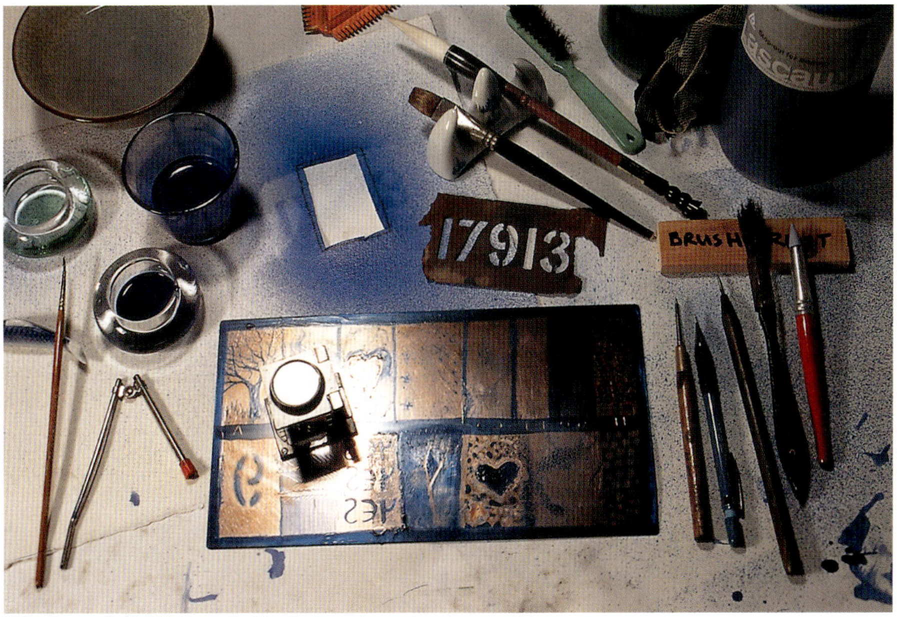

Making a teaching plate to demonstrate a range of techniques for Lascaux Stop-Out Resist. Painting, stencilling, squeegeeing, offsetting, lifting, impressing, splattering and spraying methods were used in the different panels as well as working and drawing into wet and dry panels of resist. Lascaux Aquatint Spray Resist was also applied (see print on p. 121).

Working method

- Plates should be bevelled, cleaned, finely grained, degreased and backed. Previously etched plates should be clean, degreased and backed. It is very important that the plate backing is applied before an oily soft resist is used on the front of the plate. The resist may not be easily rolled into previously bitten lines and marks.
- Lay out the materials and make sure that the surface and roller are clean and not wet or dusty. When working with art materials containing pigment, it is good practice to wear gloves and an apron.
- Draw a serpentine shape with the soft pigment stick on the plate. Then use the roller to distribute the resist evenly across the plate. Note how lines and thin stripes can be made in the layer of resist if the roller is not lifted and spun a little (these areas may begin to etch). The rolling technique, the type of roller used and the condition of the roller are all factors which will affect the quality of the layer. The process and care of the roller should be demonstrated carefully to students.
- When the plate surface is evenly coated with soft resist, any of the three creative methods may be used.
- The rollers, spatulas and the inking surface can be cleaned with cleaning oil. The oily residue should be removed carefully with dishwashing liquid to prevent any remaining grease affecting the application of acrylic resists.

STOP-OUT RESIST AND CONTROLLING TONE

This type of resist is named after the classical process of stopping-out. Stop-out resist is used for creating, editing or correcting images on the plate as well as being a vital part of the stage-biting process. The different brands are generally coloured so that they are easy to see on the plate. They may be painted, splattered, sprayed or offset onto the plate surface to create a wide range of marks. Stencilling methods can also be employed. When the marks are dry, the stop-out resist may be drawn into with etching needles or worked back into to generate broad open marks. The different creative techniques (including the stage-biting process) and types of stop-out resist are described below.

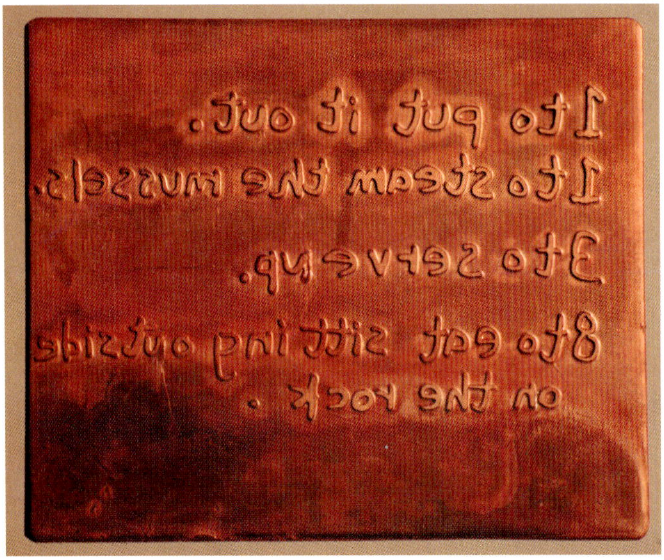

The text was written with a quill pen loaded with diluted Lascaux Stop-Out Resist and the copper plate was then deeply bitten. The artist applied the ink by roller to the areas of high relief and printed it using an etching press (see pp. 59 and 157).

PAINTING METHODS

Painting, offsetting, stencilling and splattering techniques can be used to apply stop-out resist to the plate to create non-etching areas and textures. These techniques can also be used to close bitten areas during the stage-biting process. Some types of stop-out may be diluted in water to create a further range of effects (see 'Wash Resists' p. 138).

Equipment and materials required

Work in the drawing area or at the workstation for applying acrylic resist.

- a prepared etching plate
- the selected stop-out resist or diluted mixture
- a china or glass palette
- a clean workboard
- a basin of warm soapy water, sponges and clean drying cloths
- a range of brushes and colour shapers
- embossed wallpaper, sponges, netting, fabrics, feathers, leaves
- a toothbrush, coarse brush, spray diffuser and a small palette knife
- stencils made from waxed card, plastic, metal or paper
- a jug of clean water

Principle: a coloured resist is applied to the plate surface to protect the metal from the action (or any further action) of the mordant. The unpainted areas will etch as open bite unless an aquatint or other tonal effect has been applied.

Working method

- Plates should be bevelled, grained, degreased and backed. Previously etched plates should be rinsed, de-oxidized, degreased, backed and dry.
- Lay out the materials and make sure that the working area and board are clean and not dusty. Set out a basin of warm soapy water, sponges and clean drying cloths so that the brushes, diffusers and other tools can be cleaned immediately after use. This practice will prevent the resist drying on the tools and, as the resist will wash from the bristles easily, delicate Chinese and sable brushes may be used. When working with water-soluble resists or dishwashing liquid, it is good practice to wear gloves and an apron.
- Select a creative technique and squeeze a small amount of resist into a palette. It is worth noting that a common error when using stop-out resists (especially diluted mixtures) is to start to perceive the image as a tonal painting and to forget that it is the exposed metal that will etch and form the image. The process of flash biting can be used to assess how the plate will etch.
- Dry or wet brush marks can be made or the resist may be poured or spattered onto the surface.
- Patterns, textures and repeating motifs or shapes can be generated by stencilling or by painting stop-out onto found materials, such as embossed wallpaper, leaves and feathers, and then offsetting the resist onto the plate surface.
- Soft marks may be created by diluting the stop-out resist with a few drops of water. As the dilution increases, the

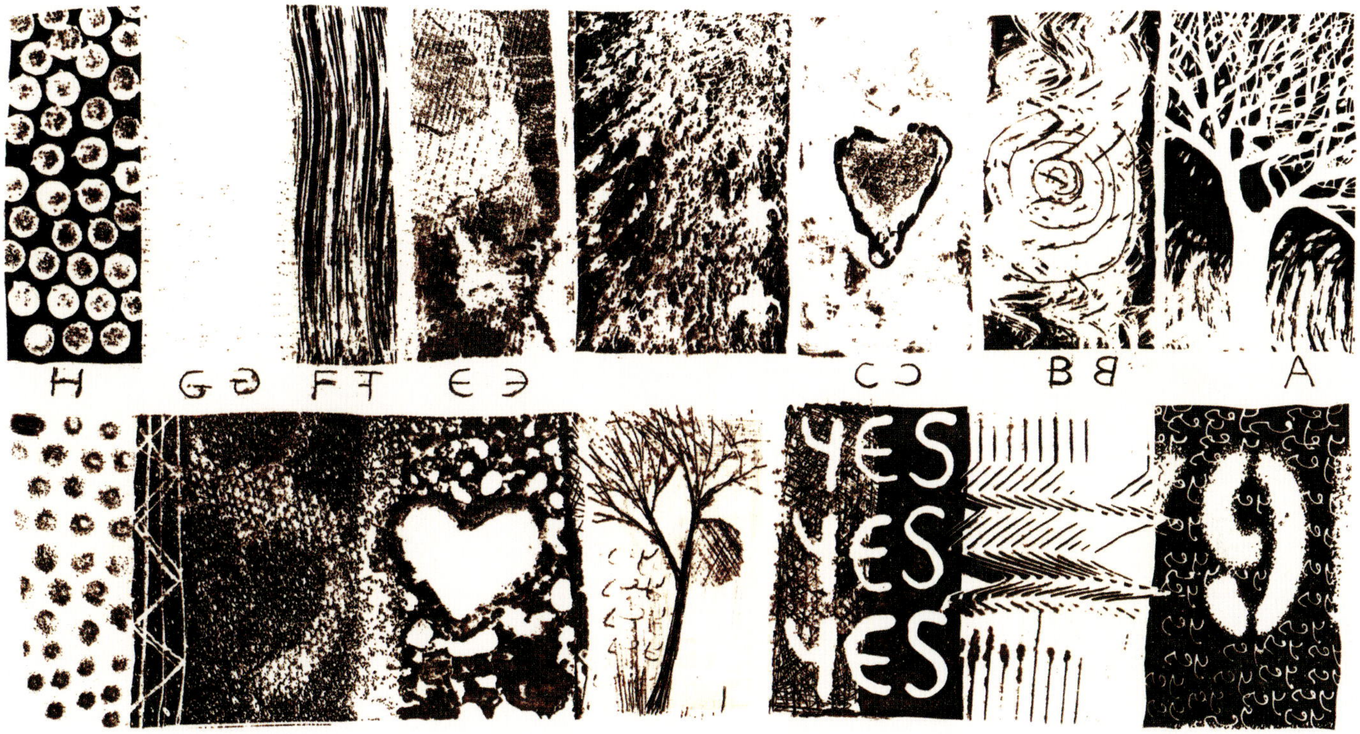

A print from the plate seen on p. 119. Lascaux Stop-Out Resist and Aquatint Spray Resist were used to create this range of effects.

mixture will begin to behave like a wash resist and its mordant-resistant properties will also change.

- Tiny dots of stop-out resist (or diluted resist) can be applied by flicking the loaded bristles of a toothbrush or coarse paint-brush with a small palette knife. Simple tonal effects (see p. 128) can be made using a diffuser.
- When applying the resist for stage biting, check with a magnifying glass that the selected areas are adequately protected from any further etching.
- After the image has been made the resist should be dried thoroughly. Clean the brushes and other tools at the end of the session and tidy the work area.

DRAWING INTO THE STOP-OUT RESIST

When the resist has dried completely, it may be drawn into with a range of etching tools to create lines and marks. Broader marks can be made by dissolving the resist to reveal the metal. These image-making methods are described in the section on hard resists (see pp. 103–105).

CORRECTING OR EDITING AN IMAGE

When an image made from other resists (for example, soft resist or photoresist) requires editing or altering, stop-out resist is applied to the plate to cover small scratches, fish eyes, unwanted marks and drawing errors. This classical process is referred to as stopping-out. If necessary, drawing techniques can then be used to re-establish the stopped-out parts of the image.

When the area is large or the marks are special to a particular technique, the original type of resist and working method may be used in place of the stop-out resist.

Equipment and materials required

Work in the drawing area or at the workstation for applying acrylic resist.

- the etching plate that requires stopping-out, editing or altering
- a scraper burnisher
- some small soft brushes
- the selected resist (stop-out or other)
- a china or glass palette
- basin of warm soapy water, sponges and clean drying cloths
- a range of etching tools, steel wool, wire brush

Principle: images on plates may be corrected before etching using stopping-out techniques.

Working method

- If the original resist is unstable or a large area needs to be re-established, remove the resist (with a scraper) from around the part of the image that requires alteration.
- Lay out the materials and make sure that the working area is clean and not dusty. When working with water-soluble resists or dishwashing liquid, it is good practice to wear gloves and an apron. Use a soft brush to apply a thin layer of resist to the exposed metal. Tools should be cleaned immediately after application and the plate worked into or left to dry.
- When the stop-out resist is thoroughly dry, etching needles and tools can be used to make a corrective drawing. If a soft resist is used for the repair, follow the relevant working method.
- The corrected plate may now be processed further (e.g. the application of an aquatint) or etched.

STOPPING-OUT AND THE STAGE-BITING PROCESS

The terms stage biting or step biting are used to describe the process of deliberately biting the plate in a series of steps so that the image is etched to different depths. This process is used to generate a range of tones or to build up the subtlety

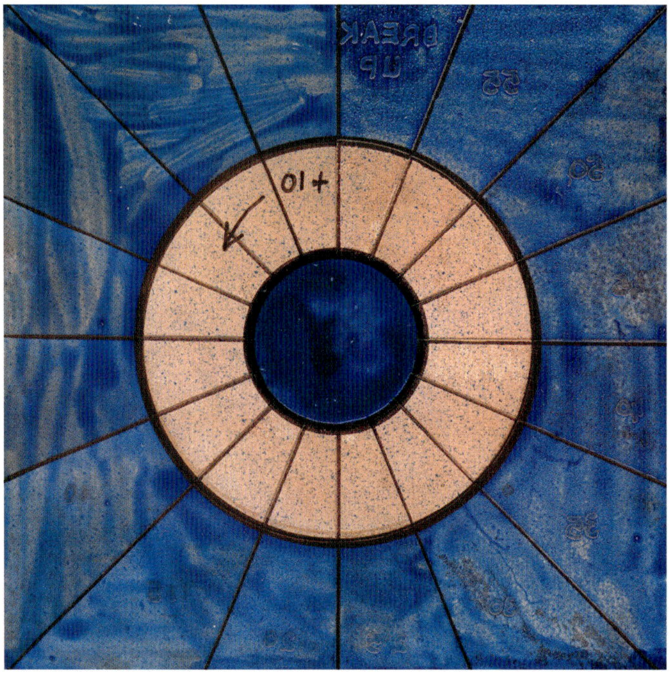

and complexity of an image. A test plate may be made and printed so that the artist can choose the correct length of time to etch the plate. The test plate is made in the following way.

A long narrow plate (e.g. 5 x 40 cm/2 x 16 in.) is backed and the face coated in a uniform aquatint or a resist holding a linear image or textures. The length of each test panel (e.g. 2.5 cm/1 in.) and the duration of each etching period (e.g. 2 to 3 minutes) is decided. The first panel is stopped out (and dried) before the etching process to provide a printed example of the unbitten metal (this will print white or as plate tone).

The test plate is then etched for the first timed interval, creating a shallow bite which will hold little ink and print as the palest etched tone. The plate is removed from the mordant, rinsed, de-oxidized, rinsed again, dried and a second panel is then stopped out and dried.

The plate is etched once more for the timed interval to create slightly deeper indentations. The plate is again removed from the mordant, rinsed, de-oxidized, rinsed, dried and the third panel is stopped out and dried. This will print as a slightly darker tone.

This stopping-out process is repeated until the plate has only one panel left uncovered with resist. After etching this, the resist is removed from the test plate and a print is taken.

The print shows the tones and effects which have occurred after each specific period of etching. It may sometimes reveal the point at which the result becomes poor, e.g. tiny dots of resist may be undercut and become detached from the metal (resulting in open bite) or a line may be bitten too deeply (resulting in a smudged print). The artist writes the cumulative length of each bite under each tonal section of the printed strip, e.g. a plate with one unbitten panel and 15 sections each bitten at 2 minutes will show a range of bites from 2 minutes, then 4 minutes, then 6 minutes up to 30 minutes (see illustration on p. 130).

TYPES OF STOP-OUT RESIST

Different types of stop-out resist vary in their effectiveness as acid resists, their compatibility with photoresists and their ability to be drawn into. It is important to use a reliable resist for stopping out.

LASCAUX STOP-OUT RESIST

This coloured stop-out has excellent handling qualities and may be diluted with water, allowing the exploration of all of the creative techniques described above. The blue marks are easy to see, hold their shape accurately, dry quickly on the plate, and may be drawn and worked into. The resist may be applied to deeply bitten or finely grained plates made from any type of metal.

Lascaux Stop-Out Resist may be employed at any stage of the plate's development and is compatible with all the Lascaux acrylic resists and many photoresists. It is powerful and reliable, and long bites can be undertaken with very accurate results.

Normally the resist is removed from the plate before printing unless additive marks are required. This resist is also a useful collagraphic material (see pp. 162, 166 and 174).

Z*ACRYL STOP-OUT RESIST

This acrylic resist may be employed at any stage of the plate's development and is compatible with all the other Z*Acryl acrylic resists and Z*Acryl photopolymer.

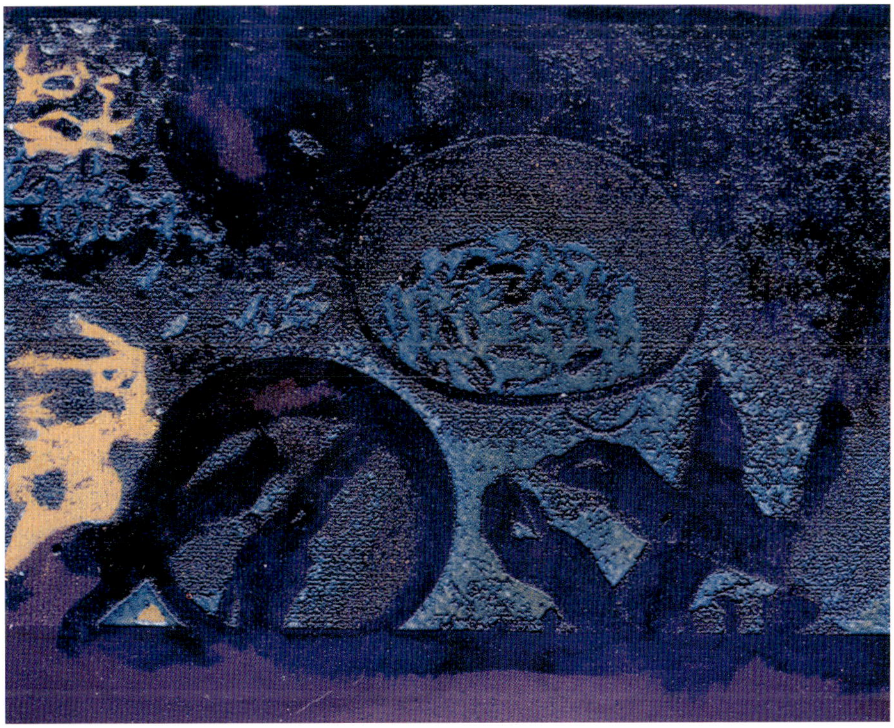

opposite The last stage of stopping-out on this aquatint etching time test plate (see print on p. 130). The inner ring was etched for a further 10 minutes.

left Lascaux Stop-Out Resist (blue coloured) has been applied to protect perfectly etched areas from further biting. The violet areas are photoresist; the exposed areas of copper are aquatinted (Lascaux Aquatint Spray Resist) and ready to be etched again (see photoresist on p. 148 and print on p. 59).

The manufacturer recommends using a soft, rounded brush or foam brush to apply the resist to copper and other metal plates and warns against bubbles in the coating. For this reason the container should not be shaken. After the first layer of resist has been dried the manufacturer suggests rubbing it with a soft, clean cloth to see if any resist breaks free from the surface of the plate. This may occur as residual oxidization on the plate can cause the resist to fail so it is important that the plate is deoxidized and speedily dried before the first application. This layer should be dried thoroughly before the second coat is applied. The tinted resist has enough body to prevent it spreading or running. Any bubbles, brush strokes or other flaws can be repaired by painting on some more stop-out. The brushes and other tools can be cleaned easily with warm soapy water.

The dry Z*Acryl Stop-Out Resist should be removed from the plate as soon after etching as possible (see p. 214). If the resist is left on the plate for a long time it becomes stronger and a solution made of 50% household ammonia and 50% water will be required to remove it. There are a number of health and safety concerns related to the use of ammonia (see p. 27).

OTHER STOP-OUT RESISTS AND ARTISTS' MATERIALS USED AS RESISTS

Not all acrylic stop-out resists contain the safest possible ingredients. Golden Artist Colors, Inc. manufacture Golden Stop-Out Varnish for intaglio printmaking. The health and safety information for this resist provided by the company states 'Warning: This product contains a chemical(s) known to the State of California to cause cancer. Always protect yourself against known and potentially unknown chronic hazards of this and other chemical products by keeping them out of your body. Do this by avoiding ingestion, excessive skin contact, and inhalation of spraying mists, sanding dusts and concentrated vapours.'

If the dry Golden Stop-Out Varnish is left on the plate for more than a few days it becomes stronger and a solution made of 10% household ammonia in cold water will be required to remove it (see p. 27 for health and safety concerns related to the use of ammonia).

Some printmakers use acrylic paints, acrylic mediums, acrylic varnishes or fillers for water-based screenprinting as stop-out resists. Make careful notes and test plates to determine which metals the product can be used on; how visible it is on the metal; whether it works well as a resist, is compatible with photoresists and with other acrylic resists; whether it can be drawn through and worked into successfully; and if it can be removed safely from the plate when it is dry. Before testing the material, check the product's MSDS carefully in case it contains any hazardous substance.

CREATING TONAL STRUCTURES AND THE AQUATINT METHOD

Several different methods may be employed to create prints which display a tonal range. Hard-resist drawing techniques (such as crosshatching, using steel wool or stippling, see test plate on p. 102) can make tiny, closely spaced scratches which print as shading and tone, as will grids and dots made in soft resist. The narrow lines and small pits can be bitten to different depths using the stage-biting process, providing a further range of tones.

Broad lines, large dots and wide areas of bare metal will etch as open bite. To create a tonal range within these areas the artist must employ an etching technique that will generate a pitted or finely reticulated surface which will be capable of holding ink. (The term 'reticulated' is used to describe a fine network.)

One of the earliest etching methods of creating a randomly pitted surface was to sprinkle flours of sulphur onto a copper plate. This corrosive substance attacks the metal and roughens the surface enough so that it holds a little ink and prints as a gentle tone (see p. 161).

Another classical method involves puncturing a dry layer of hard resist with sand or carborundum and etching the revealed metal. The resulting plate surface can be described as being scrobiculated (pitted) and each of the individual etched pits will hold ink. On inspection with a magnifying glass this dotted structure is evident on the tonal areas of the proof. Henri Goetz's method of 'carborundum etching' has a similar principle to the sand puncture technique (see p. 12). Soft resists can also be used to generate scrobiculated plate surfaces or a mezzotint-like grid.

The most widely used tonal technique involves creating an etched reticulated surface known as 'aquatint'. In the first stage of the method a multitude of tiny dots of resist are applied to the surface of the plate. The random pattern made by the dots of resist is dried and the plate is etched. The mordant bites the unprotected metal between the individual motes of resist and in this way a network of tiny crevices is etched in the metal. On close examination the tonal areas on aquatint prints are composed from the network of ink-holding crevices surrounding the dots of resist.

The most modern technique involves using a positive in conjunction with a photoresist to create a tonal structure on the plate. This approach has many creative possibilities, from directly drawn marks, images constructed of digital pixels to the use of random dot screens. The resulting tonal structure on the plate can be either reticulated or pitted (see pp. 191–192).

USING THE PUNCTURING METHOD

Acrylic hard resists provide crisp and clear punctures and are ideal for the exploration of sand, abrasive paper and carborundum image techniques. This method of creating a scrobiculated surface may be used on all metals and is particularly useful for imposing a tonal structure on aluminium plates etched in copper sulphate.

Equipment and materials required

Work on a clean workboard in the appropriate area for the chosen creative technique.

- a plate coated in a dry layer of hard resist
- some dry sieved sand, coarse carborundum, sandpaper or abrasive paper
- stencils
- a plastic sieve
- some clean drying cloths
- an etching press

Principle: the particles will puncture the layer of hard resist, creating a dotted pattern which can be etched to create tone.

Working method

- There are several possible starting points but, whichever method is selected, be careful not to leave any particles on the workbenches or on the press, as abrasive grit in etching inks will scratch polished plates.
- If sand is being used it should be sieved to ensure that it is free of sharp stones and lumps which could damage the press. The dry sieved sand is sprinkled directly on the plate in the desired pattern. Stencils can be used to shield areas of the resist.
- A second method involves using sandpaper (cut into a shape or used as a sheet) to generate a uniform tone. Different grades of abrasive paper will provide a range of effects on the plate.
- A third method is to use carborundum particles to generate painterly or calligraphic marks, photo images or text. An advantage of this method is that the final print will be the same way round as the carborundum image (i.e. not a mirror image). Firstly a piece of stiff smooth card is cut to the same size as the plate. An image is formed by painting with a water-based glue such as PVA or screenprinting with Lascaux medium mixed with screenpaste on the card. Before the sticky image dries, carborundum is sprinkled over the image. When the painting method is being used a guide drawing may be made. The image is usually painted and sprinkled in sections (due to the drying time) and the excess is repeatedly shaken off onto a piece of paper. The carborundum image must be dried thoroughly before use.
- The process of puncturing the hard resist takes place in the printing area.

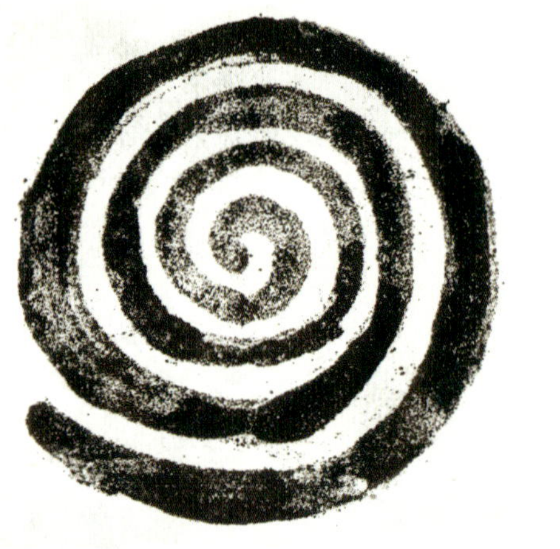
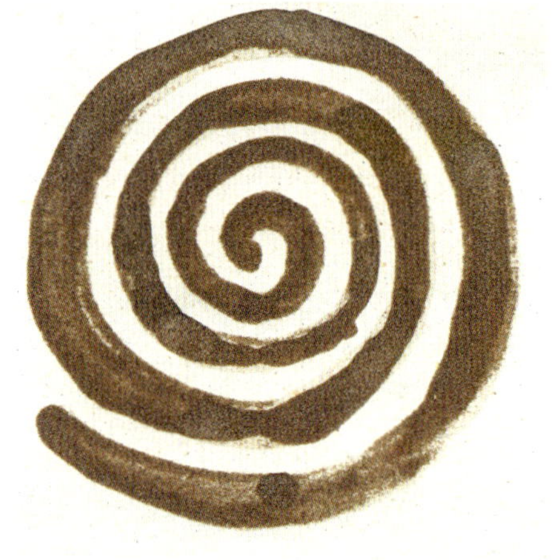

far left A print taken from an aluminium plate holding an etched image created using the puncturing method.

left The puncture sheet which was used to create the print (this reads the same way as the print). A spiral was painted on a piece of card with glue and then sprinkled with sand.

• Lay a sheet of tissue paper on the press bed, followed by the plate with either the loose particles, the sandpaper or the carborundum image. Lay a firm piece of card on top and then a sheet of tissue over the card. Carefully position the etching blankets and slowly roll the assembly through the press. Lift the blankets, remove the tissue and card, and discard them carefully (due to the particles). Lift up the plate together with the bottom tissue sheet and and place these on a workboard. Take this to the drawing area and brush away the excess particles from the plate onto the tissue. Fold up and discard the tissue. Rinse the plate in water to remove any remaining particles.

• The resist will be punctured according to the pattern made by the particles and the pressure exerted by the press.

• When the plate is dry it can be examined for flaws and any unwanted dots can be stopped out (see pp. 121–122). As the resist is clear and the punctured dots are often quite tiny, it may be helpful to flash bite the plate to darken the image.

• After any corrections have been made with stop-out resist (or if the stop-out resist has been used to make an image) the plate can be etched. Deeply etched dots will hold more ink and will print as a dark tone. The tonality of specific areas can be controlled by stage biting. After etching the plate can be worked further or can be stripped and proofed.

CREATING A SCROBICULATED SURFACE USING SOFT RESIST

A finely scrobiculated surface can be generated on the plate using soft resist and sugar. This method can be used to create an ink-holding structure over the entire plate or in broad open lines which have been created with hard resist, stop-out resist, soft resist, wash resist or photoresist. Rich blacks and a full range of tones can be created by step biting the plate or by using collagraphic techniques after etching is complete (see pp. 173–175).

Equipment and materials required

Work on a clean workboard in the drawing area.

• a plate freshly coated in a layer of Lascaux Soft Resist
• a sheet of paper
• some caster sugar
• a sieve or tea strainer
• a soft brush

Working method

• Follow the application method given for Lascaux Soft Resist (see pp. 114–116).

• After the cool plate has been coated with a thin and even layer of soft resist, caster sugar is immediately sprinkled onto the surface using a sieve. An even and dense layer should be

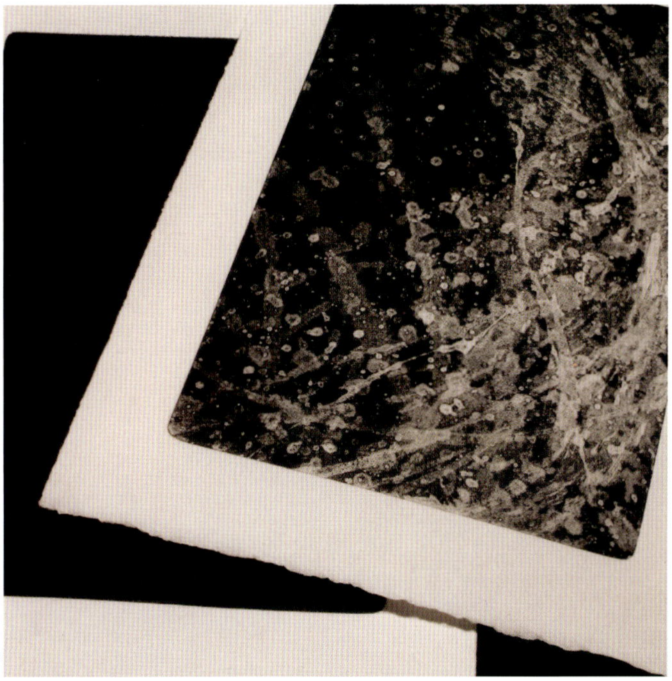

Lascaux Soft Resist was sprinkled with caster sugar to generate a dense mass of fine dots on a zinc plate. The resulting print (behind) is velvety and rich. The plate was added to, using collagraphic techniques (see pp. 173–175), and the resulting tonal print can be seen in the foreground.

laid so that the plate is covered by a small mound of sugar. Caster sugar gives a particularly good result but experiments can be made with other sugars and with salt.

- The plate should be left to sit for 5 minutes to allow time for the sugar particles to sink through the thin layer of resist. It may then be put in a warm place to dry undisturbed.
- When the layer of resist is dry, the mound of sprinkled sugar is tipped off onto a piece of paper and the plate immersed in a tray of warm water. After a few minutes a soft brush can be used to dislodge the dissolved sugar, revealing a multitude of dots of exposed metal. As these are often quite tiny it may be helpful to flash bite the plate to darken the image.
- The flash-bitten plate can be examined for flaws and any stopping-out can be carried out.
- A test print should be consulted to determine biting times before etching.
- A rich velvety surface can be created by stripping the plate after etching and repeating the process.
- The plate can be worked further with direct, etching or collagraph methods or it can be stripped and proofed.

CREATING AN ETCHED INK-HOLDING GRID USING SOFT RESIST

A complex ink-holding grid can be etched onto the plate surface using soft resist. The printed effect is rich and is similar to a hand-rocked mezzotint. A range of tones can be created by step biting the plate or by using collagraphic techniques (see pp. 172–175). The method can be used to create a tonal structure in broad open lines which have been created with a hard resist, soft resist, wash resist or photoresist.

Equipment and materials required

Work in the printing room.

- an etching plate coated in a layer of soft resist
- some tissue paper
- some cloth with an open weave (such as scrim)
- a sheet of PVC

Working method

- Follow the application for soft resist and working method 'Creating Collage-Type Impressions' (see pp. 111–113).
- The coated plate is laid on a sheet of tissue on the etching press bed and a flat piece of clean fabric with a grid-like open weave (such as coarse scrim or netting) is laid over the moist resist. The PVC sheet is laid over this, followed by several sheets of tissue paper and the blankets. The assembly is rolled through the press and the material is impressed into the resist.
- The blankets, tissue paper and PVC sheet are removed. The cloth should be peeled away carefully and the patterned soft resist dried and examined. The fibres in the cloth will generate

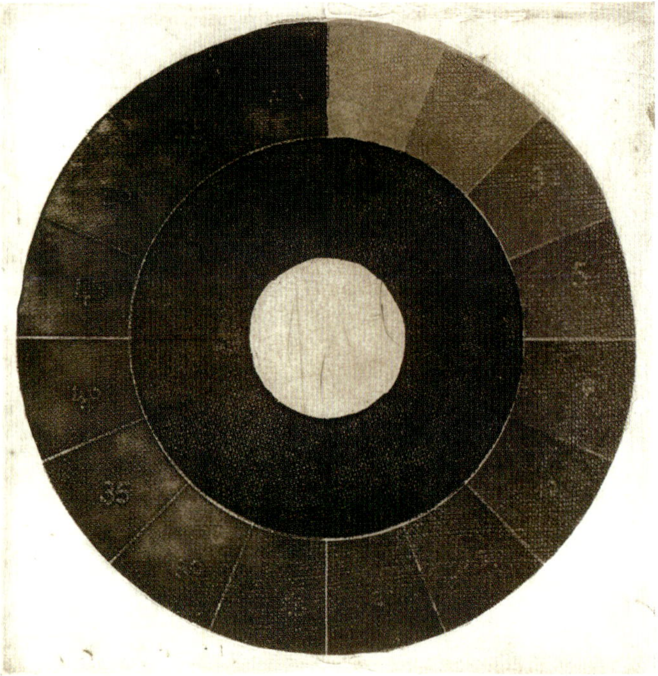

left An etched grid was created using Lascaux Soft Resist and a piece of scrim. The plate was then step-bitten to generate a range of tones which can be seen in this educational print.

opposite This print was taken from a copper plate to which a uniform aquatint was applied. Stop-out resist was painted on and then the plate was spit-bitten with ferric chloride. The lines were created subsequently using hard resist.

interesting lines with ragged edges. If there are clearly visible spaces between the lines, the cloth may be repositioned so that the line of the weave runs in a different direction. The process of impressing the plate is then repeated and the plate examined. This way of creating tone is comparable to the effect generated by rocking a mezzotint plate (see p. 92).

- The soft resist should be thoroughly dried, flash bitten and examined to check that the grid covers the plate. If all is well, a test print should be consulted to ascertain the length of etch required for the desired range of tones. The plate can then be bitten.
- To generate a very rich velvety black the process may be repeated using different angles.

CREATING AN AQUATINT

The technique of aquatint is used to create highly controllable, creative and predictable etched reticulated structures on the plate surface. These fine networks hold the ink and, depending on their structure and depth, print as a range of tonal effects.

The process can be used in a number of ways. An aquatint may be laid as an initial stage: for example, an etched tonal image created by spit biting, stage biting, scraping and burnishing or painting on collagraphic media. Alternatively the aquatint may be applied at a later stage in the development of an image and may be used in conjunction with any other resist such as a photoresist, hard resist, wash resist or soft resist. Some types of resist such as wash resist and the lift-solution method are dependent on the application of an aquatint.

To create an aquatint the artist first applies a multitude of tiny separate dots of acrylic resist to the prepared surface of an intaglio plate. A toothbrush, a diffuser, a simple powered spray gun or an airbrush can be used to apply the resist. A toothbrush or diffuser will generate large and irregular dots, whereas a powered spray gun or airbrush will produce smaller, closely spaced dots. The airbrush can be used to produce modulated tonalities, for example cloudy effects, tonal ranges, soft lines and blends. Stencils made from paper and lift solutions can also be used to enable the rapid assembly of complex patterns or images.

Acrylic resists are generally coloured so that the tiny dots are visible on the plate surface. These acrylic motes maintain their shape, dry very quickly and become waterproof and acid-resistant. The dried plate can be examined and checked with a magnifying glass and then etched. The mordant attacks the

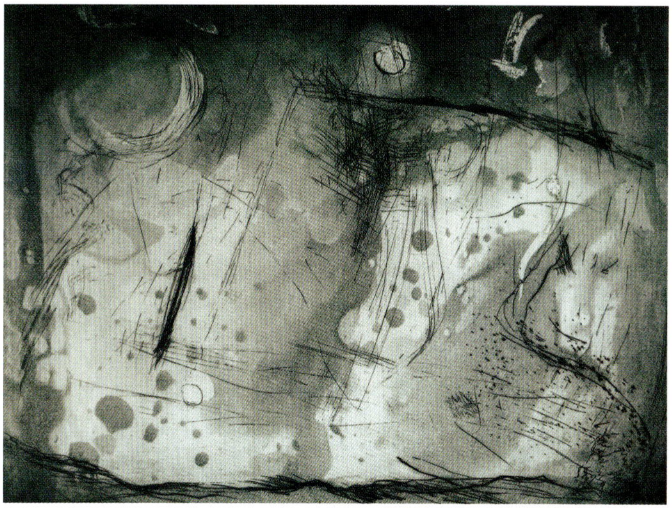

unprotected metal which surrounds each separate dot of acrylic resist and a fine network of fissures is etched in the surface of the plate. When the plate is inked up these interwoven crevices hold the ink. The tone and appearance of the print is controlled by the size of each of the particles of resist, the distance between the particles, the pattern in which the motes of resist have been applied, and the depth to which the network of unprotected metal has been etched (the stage-biting process may be used). For example, large irregular dots will create a tone with spots of sparkling white, whereas a multitude of evenly sized tiny dots positioned close together will provide a smooth deep tone with no noticeable light spots. Light areas can be created by stopping-out shallowly bitten sections during the etching process. Dense velvety tonal effects may be achieved by repeating the entire aquatint process several times with increasingly small particles.

An aquatint test strip should be made and printed for each type of aquatint and mordant to determine how the different depths of bite will hold ink and print (see overleaf).

below left Gabriela Seiler (Switzerland), 2005. The artist drew into Lascaux Hard Resist, etched, then stripped and proofed the plate to create this linear image.

below right Seiler then applied uniform aquatint to the entire plate and stopped out some areas. The plate was stage-bitten, stripped and proofed, transforming the image from linear to tonal.

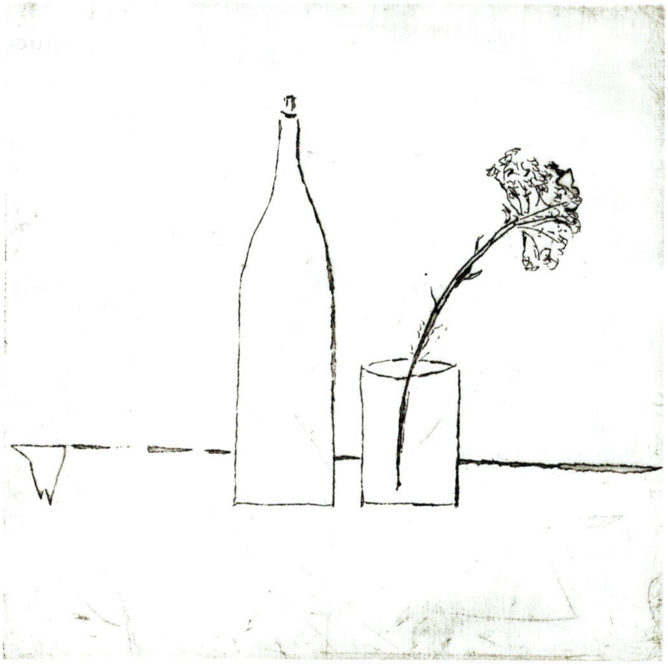

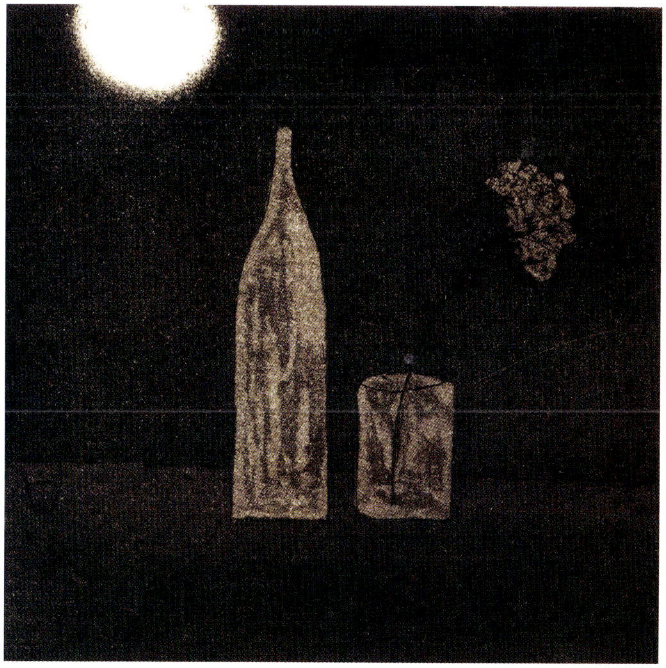

Equipment and materials required

Work at the workstation for spraying (see pp. 47–48). Wear an apron, gloves and a mask which is suitable for aqueous mists.

- a prepared dry etching plate
- a bucket of warm soapy water, sponges and clean drying cloths
- the selected resist
- several sheets of newsprint cut to the correct size
- a powered spray gun or airbrush (see pp. 47–48)

Principle: tiny dots of resist are sprayed onto the plate and dried; the area around the dots is then etched to form a reticulated ink-holding surface.

SPRAYING TECHNIQUE AND THEORY

Practise on clean newsprint (placed on the backboard of the spraying unit) in order to develop spraying skills, to explore the different image-making methods and to observe the results. Try spraying serpentine shapes passing over the plate at different speeds, with relaxed and tense body positions, and compare the positioning of the dots. Practise adjusting the tool to deliver fine, medium and coarse mists, and take into account that the density of the aquatint is also determined by the distance between the airbrush and the plate (the greater the distance, the further apart the dots). Spray different types of consistent, even coatings and experiment with stencils and making a sprayed image. Consider the fact that if the plate is sprayed too densely, little or no etching will be able to take place. Consider also that any parts of the plate which are not sprayed at all will etch as open bite unless stopped out.

The sprayed paper can be examined with a magnifying glass (note that if the paper is over-sprayed it will absorb the resist, whereas if the metal is over-sprayed the dots of resist will flow together, creating dribbles or closing the area).

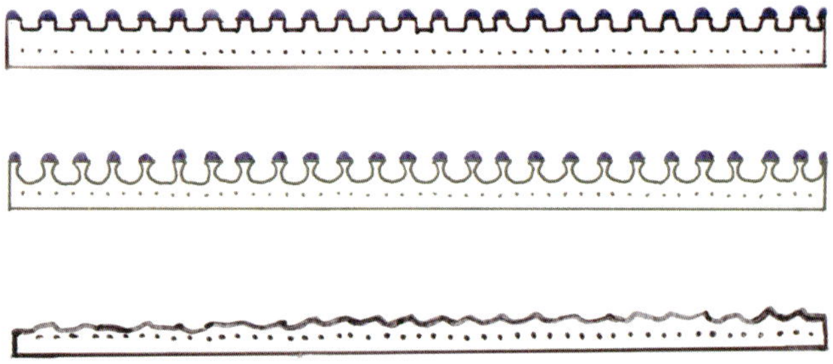

above Sections of an aquatinted intaglio plate with evenly sprayed dots of resist (blue colour) at different stages of biting.
1. Shallow etch.
2. Deep etch: the mordant is starting to undercut the dots of resist.
3. The dots of resist have been undercut and have floated free from the plate: this is now flattened and has a non-ink-holding (open-bite) surface.

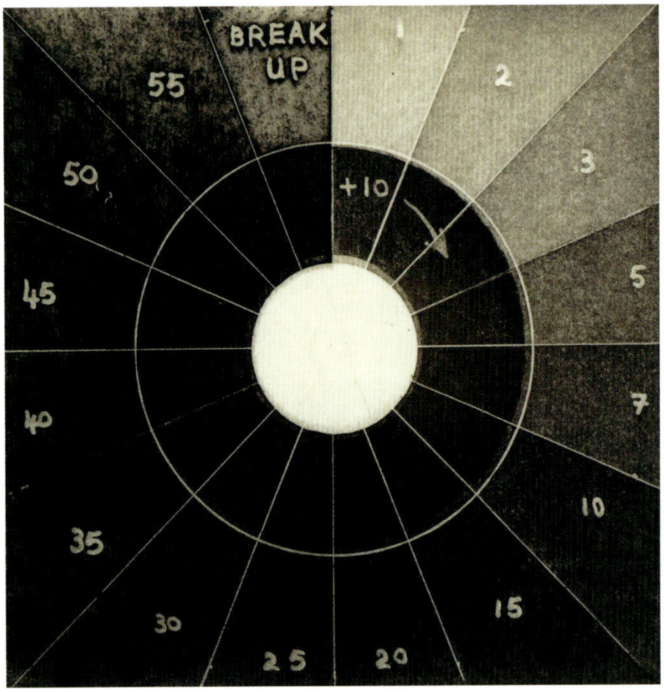

left This stage-bitten aquatint test print was stopped out in timed segments (the number of minutes etched is written in marker-pen resist). The point at which the tiny dots of resist were undercut by the mordant can be seen (the artist predicted this and wrote 'break-up'). A second aquatint was applied to the inner ring, and this was etched for another 10 minutes, creating a further tonal complexity (see plate on p. 122).

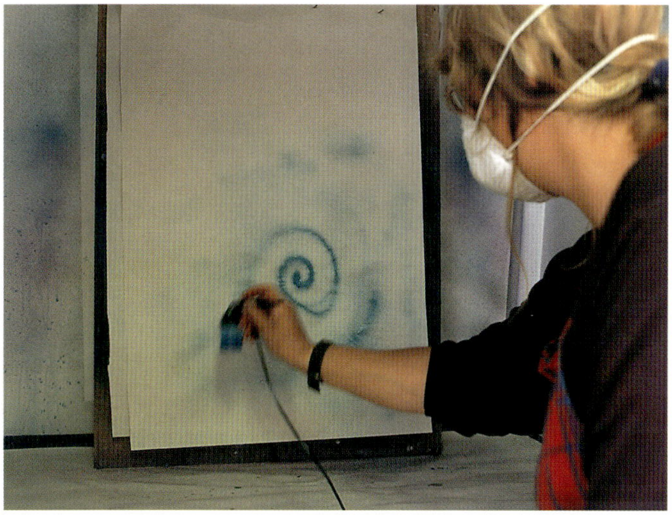

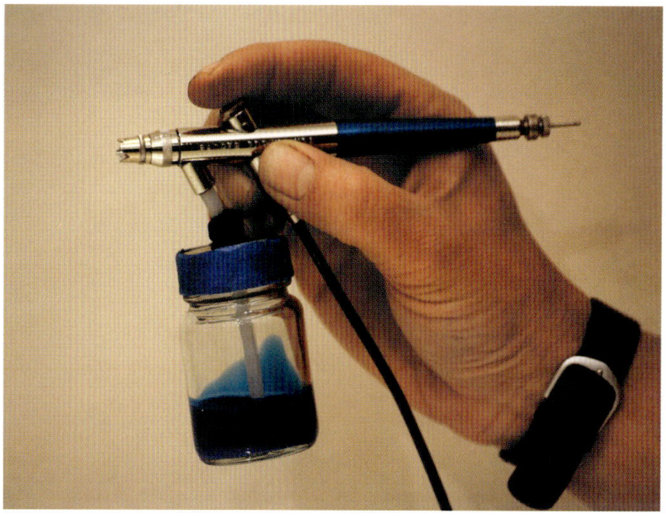

above left Practising by spraying marks on paper before applying a modulated aquatint to a plate.
above right Holding the airbrush.
below left Lascaux Lift Solution was painted onto the plate in the form of the tree and clouds. The plate was sprayed with a uniform aquatint of slightly diluted Lascaux Aquatint Spray Resist (this increased the dot size). The lift solution was removed (see pp. 135–136) and a second uniform aquatint (of undiluted Lascaux Aquatint Spray) was sprayed over the plate. This provided a fine dot and therefore the dense tone which can be seen in the tree and clouds.
below right The tree and clouds were formed on this plate using several applications of a modulated aquatint in conjunction with two sequential lift-solution paintings (using Lascaux products).

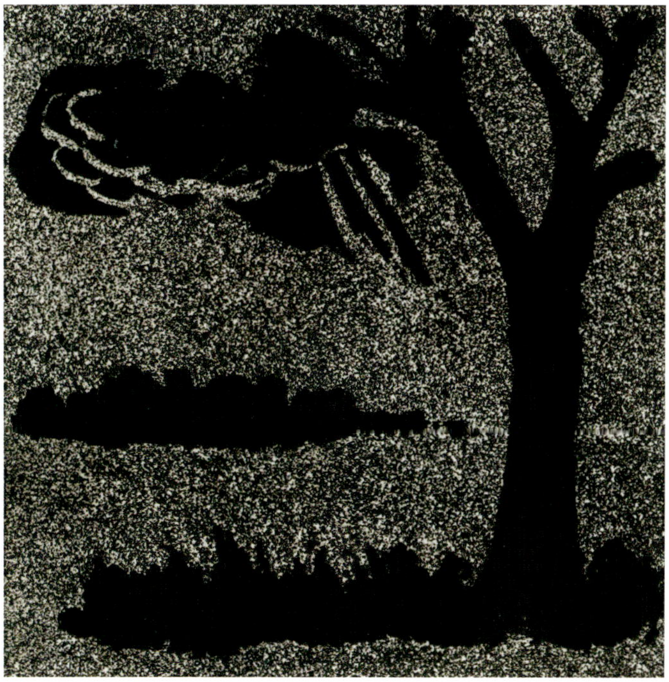

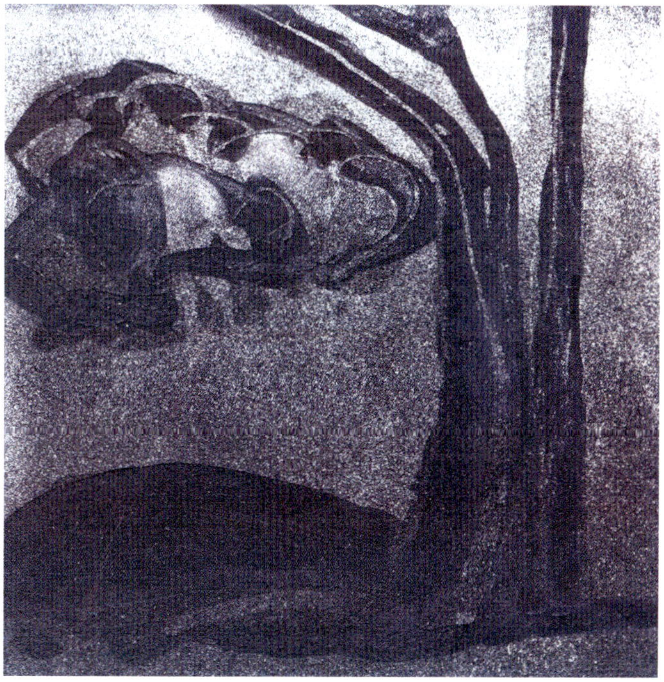

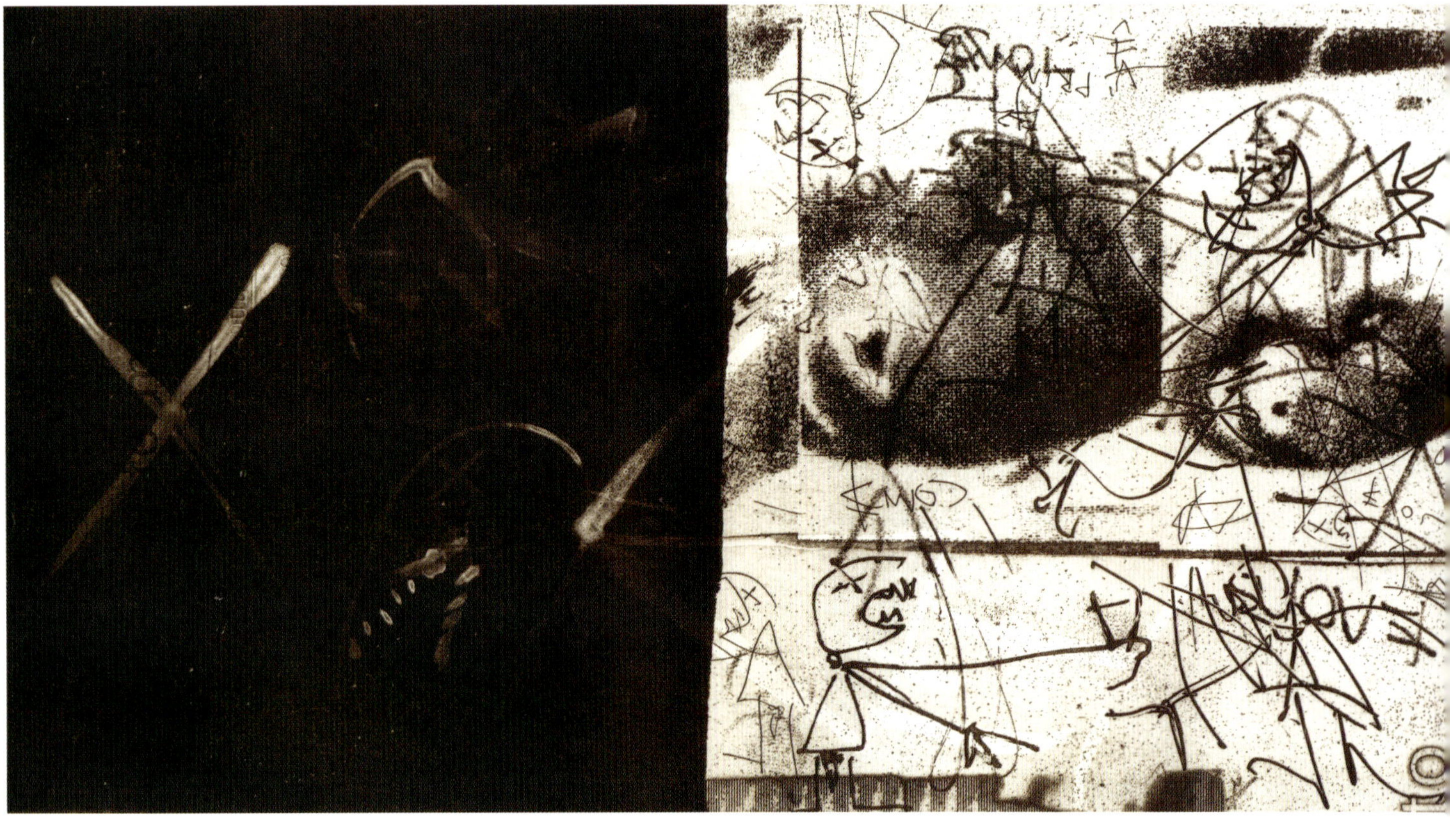

After experimenting and gaining confidence on paper, some test plates can be made. Place a clean sheet of newsprint on the backboard and position the plate upright on the shelf, leaning it back slightly against the paper-covered board. Test the airbrush on the newsprint, away from the plate, before spraying on the metal. When the metal has been sprayed and the resist has been dried, it should be examined carefully with a magnifying glass to check that there is a network of uncovered metal between the dots of resist. Dots made from Lascaux Spray Aquatint Resist are strongly coloured and clearly visible but other types of resist may be harder to see. In these cases plates can be flash-bitten to darken the areas around the dots.

Keep a sample of the sprayed newsprint to compare with the final printed tone. A collection of these samples with spraying details and biting times can be kept for future reference.

Giuseppe De Giacomi (Switzerland), *Untitled*, etching, 12 x 23 cm (4¾ x 9$^{1}/_{16}$ in.), 2005. This print is from a copper plate etched in Edinburgh Etch. Lascaux hard resist, soft resist, aquatint spray resist, stop-out resist, plate-backing resist and a screenprinted resist (defining the photographic elements) were used to generate the image. The pale areas in the left panel were created using collagraphic methods (see pp. 173–175).

UNIFORM AQUATINT

This type of aquatint is used when even tonality is required over the entire plate surface.

- Plates should be bevelled, backed, free of any oxidization or grease, and dry.
- Set up the area and adjust the spray gun or airbrush to deliver a fine mist. Practise spraying serpentine shapes on a clean sheet of newsprint.

• Place a clean sheet of newsprint on the backboard and position the plate on the shelf. Spray the plate in a steady serpentine shape, starting with a horizontal band at the top and spraying off the edge of the plate for a minimum of 10 cm (4 in.) before changing direction and spraying a parallel band below the first. Continue steadily spraying in this way until the entire plate has been covered.

• Allow the first coat to dry for a minute or two then rotate the plate through 90°, position it on the shelf and repeat the spraying process.

• Allow the second coat to dry for a minute or two and then carefully examine the plate with a magnifying glass. Check that there is a fine network of uncovered metal between the dots of resist. Generally the spraying process should be repeated but in some cases the plate may be ready to be fully dried and etched.

• Clean the airbrush, switch off the compressor and tidy up.

MODULATED AQUATINT

Creative airbrushing techniques can be used to generate tonal images on the plate.

• Set up the workstation and practise spraying the image on newsprint.

• Place a clean sheet of newsprint and position the plate on the shelf.

• Spray the plate as planned and, remembering that the metal is not absorbent like the paper, allow the layers of sprayed resist to dry for a few minutes before continuing to build up the image.

• Dry the plate and carefully examine the motes of resist with a magnifying glass before etching.

• Clean the airbrush, switch off the compressor and tidy up.

USING STENCILLING METHODS

Complex reticulated effects can be generated on the plate by using stencils in conjunction with aquatint spray resists. The stencils may be simple or complex and can be made from paper, plastic, card, metal, water, dishwashing detergent, Lascaux Resonance Gouache, water-soluble paints, sugar-lift mixtures, Lascaux Lift Solution or oily materials. Subtle tonal ranges or strong contrasts can be explored. Uniform or modulated aquatints may be applied over the stencils.

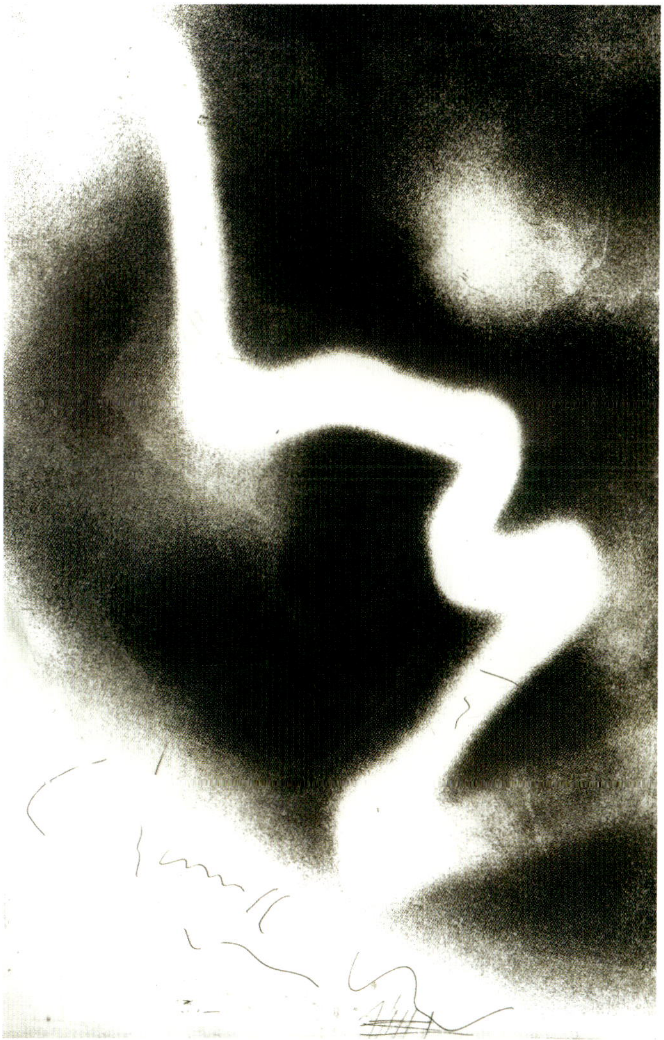

A modulated aquatint (Lascaux Aquatint Spray) was used to create this print. The artist drew with etching tools into some of the closed areas.

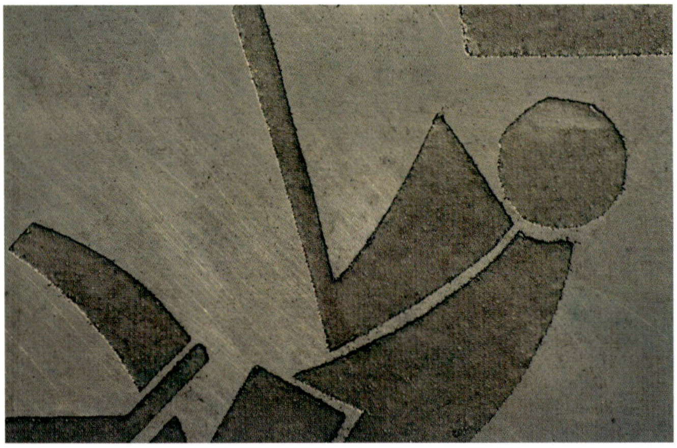

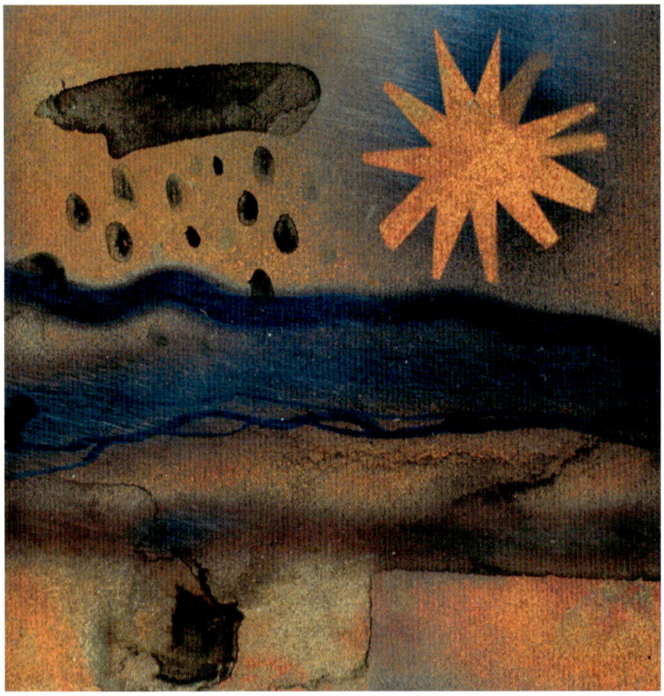

top This steel plate was created by spraying over paper stencils until the exposed areas of plate were completely protected by resist. The stencils were lifted and the plate was open-bitten, then a uniform aquatint was applied and the plate was etched again.

above A uniform and modulated aquatint (blue), in conjunction with stop-out resist (blue), wash resist (green) and the effect created by paper stencils (the metal), can be seen on this etched copper plate on which Lascaux products were applied.

PAPER, PLASTIC, CARD AND METAL STENCILS

Shapes, lines and tonal changes can be made using stencils cut from sheet materials. The area which is sprayed may be a cut-away section or a 'floating' shape. The stencils may have sharp or ragged edges.

• Lightweight materials such as tissue paper, Japanese papers, newsprint, doilies, greaseproof paper, tinfoil, netting, lace, very thin PVC sheet, acetate or plastic sheet make excellent stencils. Water may be used to slightly dampen the back of the stencils so that when they are pressed against the plate they will stick to the surface for a few minutes. Some Nepalese and Japanese papers will allow a certain amount of the resist to soak through onto the plate, creating characteristic textures. Stiff card, metal and waterproof stencils are impervious to the resist spray and can generally be re-used. Stencils made from these materials can be purchased in home-improvement stores or can be home-made.

• When the stencils have been arranged, the plate may be positioned vertically (if the stencils are lightweight and are adhering to the surface) or horizontally (if the stencils are heavier).

• On an unetched plate, when a uniform aquatint is sprayed over the stencils the exposed metal will be covered in dots of resist and, after etching, will print as an even tone (unless the plate is already covered with dry spray aquatint or another type of resist). If a white background is required, continue to spray the aquatint in layers, allowing each to dry for 1–2 minutes between coverings. This will result in a continuous film of resist which will prevent the unshielded areas of metal from etching.

• When the resist is dry, the stencils are removed carefully from the plate with an etching needle. The broad areas of plate which were shielded by the stencil will etch as open bite unless an aquatint is applied to them.

• An alternative method of working involves repositioning the stencils repeatedly during the spraying process to create complex tonal effects.

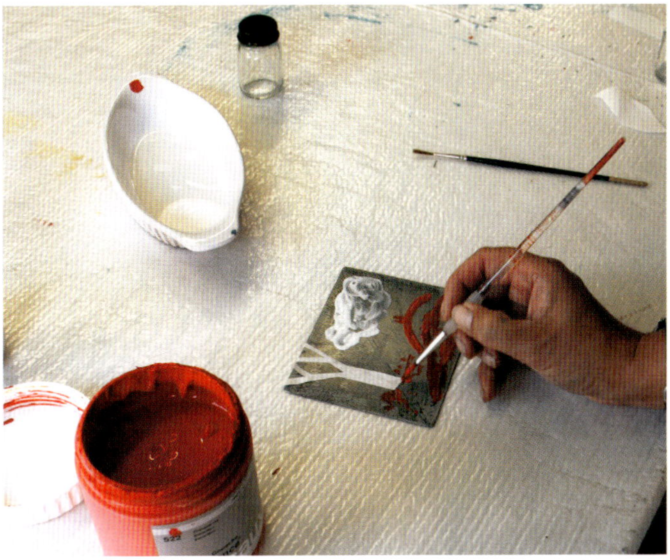

above Painting Lascaux Lift Solution and Lascaux Resonance Gouache on a plate.

below right A painting made on a plate with Lascaux Resonance Gouache was sprayed with resist, dried, soaked in water and rinsed off. The photograph shows the resulting areas of revealed metal which could now be etched as open bite or worked further using the same or another technique (e.g. uniform aquatint).

WET PAINTED STENCILS

Soft painted marks, broad lines, tonal changes, wash effects and textures may be made on the plate using wet stencils made from dishwashing detergent, water, toothpaste or Lascaux Resonance Gouache.

- When stencils are made using dishwashing detergent or water, the image is painted and the plate is immediately sprayed with resist. The plate can be worked on in a horizontal position if necessary. The water evaporates quickly, which allows some dots of resist to break through, creating textures where they bond with the plate surface. The resist will gather around the edges of the water stencils, often flowing along the shape and generating an unusual wash effect. Dishwashing detergent is more viscous, holding its shape better and drying more slowly. It can be made foamy to generate spotty textures.
- Stencils made from Lascaux Resonance Gouache (or bicarbonate toothpaste) hold their shape well and can be used to make more accurate marks. A thick layer of moist gouache shields the plate effectively and, as it absorbs some of the sprayed resist, bridging (joining together) is less likely to happen. When a white background is required, the successive layers of resist should each be allowed to dry for a couple of minutes to create a continuous film of resist which will prevent the metal etching.
- When the resist has dried, the detergent, toothpaste or gouache stencils are washed away. The plate may need to be soaked in warm water for 10 minutes if a heavy deposit of resist has been applied over gouache. The plate is then examined and considered. The broad areas which were shielded by the wet stencil will etch as open bite unless an aquatint is applied to them. The plate may be etched or the image worked further with other techniques.

DRY PAINTED STENCILS

Painted marks, interesting bold lines and tonal changes may be made on the plate using dry painted stencils made from water-soluble paints such as gouaches or Lascaux Resonance Gouache, sugar-lift mixtures or Lascaux Lift Solution. These materials are painted on the plate, dried and then used as stencils. It is important that the stencil is as dense as possible. The lift materials are able to absorb water and swell and it is this action which causes the resist (on top of the lift material stencil) to lift.

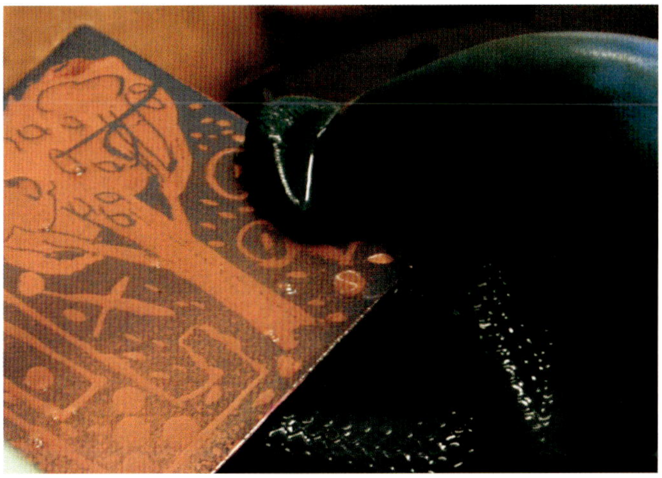

• Water-soluble paints such as the Lascaux gouaches hold their shape well and can effectively shield the plate.

• Lascaux Lift Solution provides an attractive bold broken line similar to sugar lift. The white liquid dries very quickly and becomes powdery and fragile. The dry image can be edited by scraping parts away.

• When the image is complete and dry, it is sprayed with resist. A uniform, modular or heavy spraying (to create a white background) may be applied. The paint stencils cannot absorb the resist so bridging is more likely. The lift solution is able to absorb the particles of resist to a certain extent but should not be heavily sprayed with a diluted resist.

• When the spray resist is dry, the plate is soaked in warm water for 20 minutes. The water-soluble stencils will dissolve, lifting the resist from the plate. A soft brush may be used to loosen the unstable resist. The plate is then examined and considered. It may then be drawn into, stopped out, aquatinted and etched. The broad areas which were shielded by the dry stencil will etch as open bite unless an aquatint is applied to them.

OILY STENCILS

Oil crayons, litho crayons, R & F Pigment Sticks, vegetable oil, melted margarine or etching ink may be used as stencils. It is important that the stencil is as dense as possible. This method of working is effective but the oily materials leave greasy residues which block effective etching and prevent further resists from bonding to the surface.

• Oil crayons, litho crayons and R & F Pigment Sticks can be used to make drawn marks on the plate. Painted stencils can be made with vegetable oil, melted margarine or etching ink. The margarine is easier to paint with when it is in liquid form and it can be melted easily by floating the container in a basin of warm water. When working with art materials it is good practice to wear gloves and an apron.

• When the image is complete, it is sprayed with resist. A uniform or modular aquatint or repeated spraying (to create a white background) may be applied.

• When the resist is dry, the oily stencils are removed with vegetable oil and the image is examined and considered.

• The oily residue on the etching area will inhibit biting and therefore the plate is degreased thoroughly with dishwashing liquid or an acidic degreaser (an alkaline degreaser may damage the resists). The plate may then be drawn into, stopped out, aquatinted and etched. The broad areas which were shielded by the oily stencil will etch as open bite unless an aquatint is applied to them.

TYPES OF ACRYLIC RESIST FOR AQUATINT

There are several different types of acrylic resist which can be sprayed onto plates to create aquatints. Each material has its own characteristics and uses.

LASCAUX AQUATINT SPRAY RESIST

This blue liquid resist is water-soluble and ready to use. It is compatible with other Lascaux resists and most photoresists. Lascaux Aquatint Spray Resist has been designed to be used in conjunction with both Lascaux Lift Solution and Lascaux Wash Resist.

It can be applied to finely grained or previously etched plates of all metal types with a toothbrush, diffuser, powered spray gun or airbrush. Uniform and modulated aquatints (including very fine tones) or a range of creative methods can be explored. The dots of resist are designed to maintain their individual integrity and have enough body to form tiny raised motes which do not spread out at the base. The dot size can be controlled and the resist may be diluted with water to generate a further range of possibilities. The resist dries rapidly on the plate surface, becoming waterproof and acid-resistant. It is strong enough to withstand repeated biting and rinsing. After etching it is easily removed from the plate.

Z*ACRYL HARDGROUND EMULSION

This may be used to create a range of fine aquatints. This tinted liquid resist is water-soluble and ready to use. It is compatible with other Z*Acryl resists and Z*Acryl photopolymer.

The manufacturer states that the resist can be applied to finely grained plates of all metal types. An airbrush may be used to create either uniform or modulated aquatints, or a range of creative image-making aquatint effects. The resist dries rapidly on the plate surface, becoming waterproof and acid-resistant. Plates can be flash-bitten to darken the areas around the dots of resist and then examined. After etching the resist is easily removed from the plate (see p. 214).

BADGER ACRYLIC AQUATINT SOLUTION FOR PRINTMAKERS

This black liquid resist is water-soluble and is diluted 50% with water before use. If the product is used undiluted it is very difficult to remove once dry. It can be applied to copper plates to create very fine uniform aquatints as well as modulated aquatints and stencil work.

The resist dries rapidly on the plate surface, becoming waterproof and acid-resistant, and is strong enough to withstand long etches. After etching the resist is removed from the plate (see the manufacturer's instructions).

ART MATERIALS USED TO CREATE AQUATINTS

Speedball Screen Filler can be sprayed onto a copper plate and used as a resist to create an aquatint. It must be stirred well before use and may be diluted with water (up to one part filler to five parts water) to create a variety of dot shapes and sizes. A toothbrush, diffuser or powered spray gun may be used to apply it (Speedball Screen Filler will tend to block the spray gun).

The resist can be used on finely grained or previously etched copper plates but as the filler is reddish-brown the dots are difficult to see on the surface. Uniform or modulated

Julie Arnall, *Untitled,* etching, 37 x 17 cm (14½ x 6¾ in.), 2002. A uniform aquatint and Lascaux Hard Resist were used to generate this plate, which was inked up with a white ink and printed on dark paper.

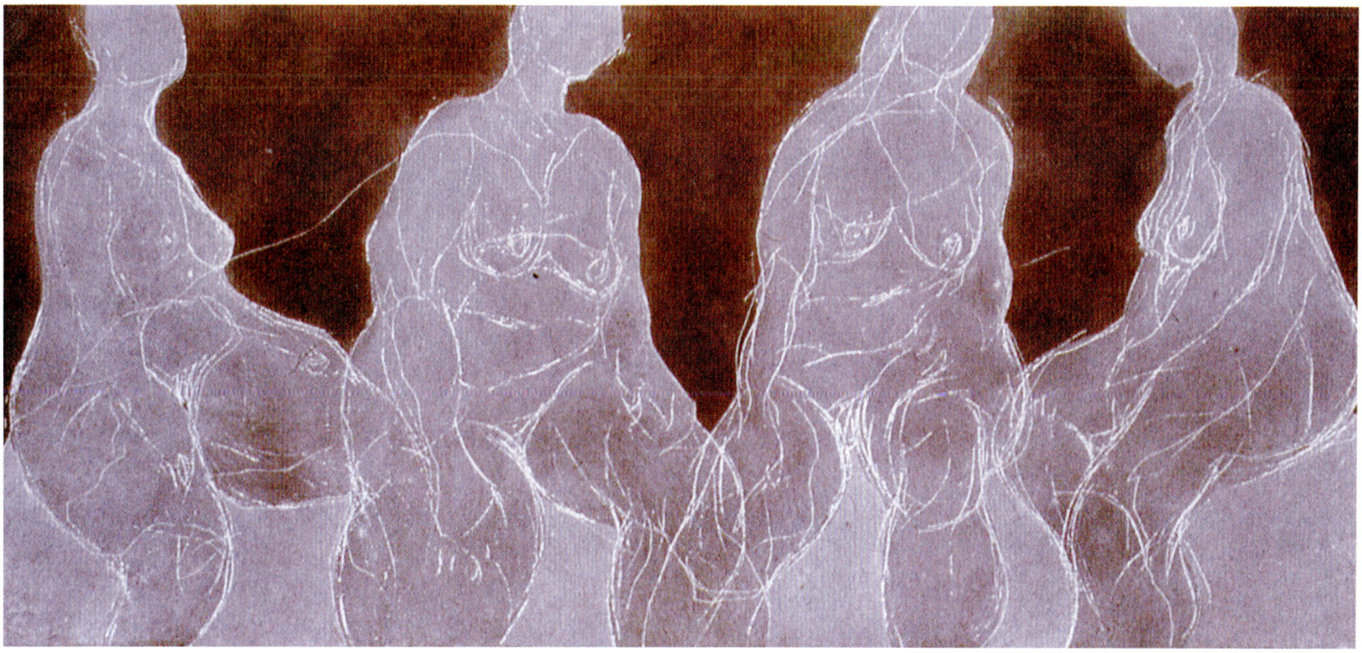

aquatints (including fine tones) or stencil work can be explored. The resist dries on the plate surface, becoming waterproof and acid-resistant. After etching it is easily removed from the plate (see p. 214).

WASH RESISTS

Acrylic wash resists can be used to generate a range of complex reticulated effects on the plate which will print to provide tonal effects similar to tusche or watercolour washes. To enhance the contrast of the printed image all wash resists are used in conjunction with a fine uniform aquatint.

PAINTING METHODS

Equipment and materials required
Work on a waterproof workboard.

- a prepared plate
- the selected wash resist(s)
- water
- a china or glass palette
- some soft brushes
- a container of water
- some tea or red wine (tannin)
- cotton wool
- a basin of warm soapy water, sponges and clean drying cloths

Working method

- Select a type of wash resist according to the metal being used and the effect that is required. New plates should be bevelled, cleaned, finely and evenly grained, degreased, backed and dry. Previously etched plates should be backed, dry and free of any residues of oxidization or grease.

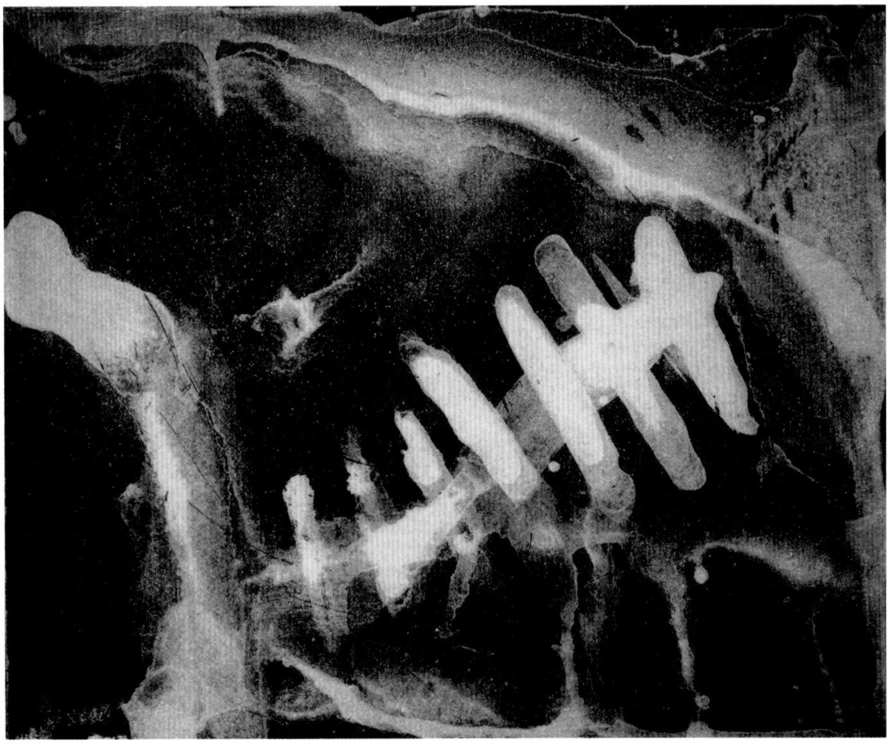

left This print shows the characteristic effect of Lascaux Wash Resist used in conjunction with Aquatint Spray Resist.

opposite Lascaux Wash Resist on copper before being aquatinted.

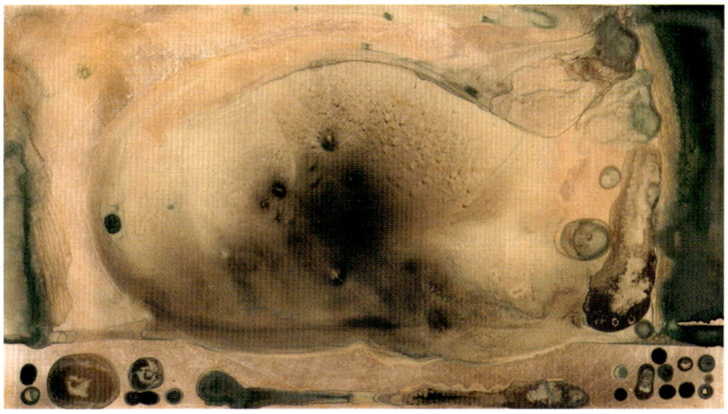

• Lay out the materials and make sure that the working area is clean and not dusty. Set out a basin of warm soapy water, some sponges and clean drying cloths so that it is easy to clean the brushes and other tools intermittently in soapy water. When working with art materials or dishwashing liquid, it is good practice to wear gloves and an apron.

• Shake the container or stir the diluted mixture and pour some wash resist into a clean palette. There are a number of creative painting techniques which can be employed.

• The first brushmarks of the image may be made on the plate with water; a brush may then be used to introduce the wash resist to the wet pools.

• The wash resist may be painted on the plate using soft brushes and left to reticulate.

• Water can be added to marks painted with wash resist.

• The resist may be diluted and painted on the plate and left to dry.

• Painting with tea or red wine instead of water will create different types of reticulated effects due to the tannin content in these liquids.

• The best results are achieved if the pools of liquid are left to dry after being brushed onto the plate, rather than overworking them.

• Another method involves allowing the wash resist to dry a little. When the outer edges of the brushstrokes have dried, some cotton wool can be used to absorb the wet centre. The image can be painted again with wash resist to create a contour effect. This process can be repeated several times to build up the image.

• An aquatint may be sprayed onto the wet washes on the plate to generate further textures.

• Brushes and tools should be washed in soapy water after applying acrylic resists and resist washes.

• After the image has been painted, the resist should be allowed to dry thoroughly and should then be sprayed with a fine uniform aquatint to provide a contrast (if an aquatint is not applied, some areas of exposed metal will etch as open bite and the wash effects will be difficult to see).

• A different image-making technique involves brushing and splashing the plate with wash resist. While the wash resist is still wet an R & F Pigment Stick (an oil paint in stick form) may be used to draw an image on the plate. The oily marks will repel the wash resist and act as a resist on the plate. An aquatint should be applied over the oily drawing and wash-resist washes.

• When the aquatint has dried, examine the plate with a magnifying glass and consider which areas are likely to etch. Check that the plate is not entirely covered in wash resist, as even the diluted resist is strongly acid-resistant and may prevent any etching from taking place.

• Consult an aquatint test strip to work out the optimum biting time for the dots of aquatint spray resist.

• The plate may now be etched for this period of time. After biting, the plate is removed from the mordant, gently rinsed and examined. In some cases the plate should be de-oxidized, dried and another uniform aquatint applied before a second bite (again with reference to an aquatint test strip). In other cases the plate will be ready to strip.

• When the etching process is complete, remove the resists, de-oxidize, rinse and dry the plate.

• Polishing the surface gently will heighten the contrast within the image.

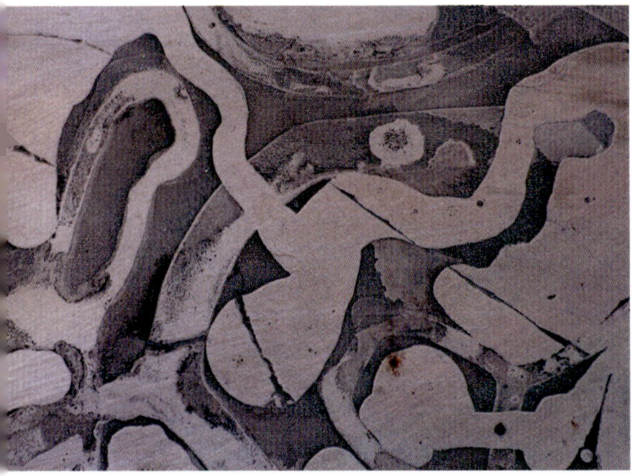

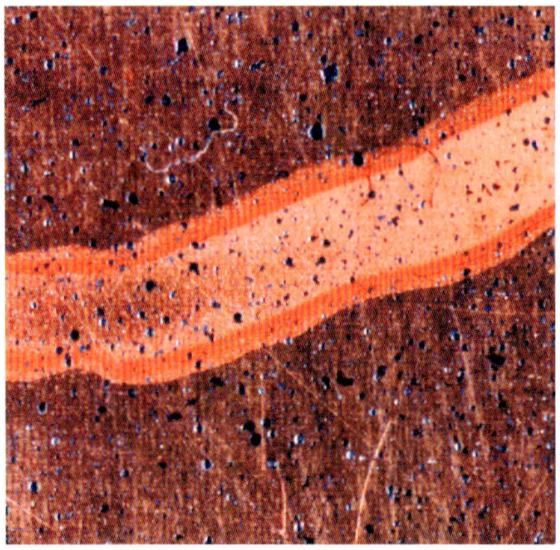

far left A Lascaux Wash Resist was used in conjunction with Lascaux Aquatint Spray Resist to create these etched textures.

left A magnified detail of a wash resist made from Speedball Screen Filler diluted in water. The centre of the line will break up more quickly than the denser edges.

TYPES OF WASH RESIST

The different materials provide a variety of wash effects.

LASCAUX WASH RESIST

This resist has been specially designed as part of the Lascaux acrylic-resist etching system and should be used in combination with Lascaux Aquatint Spray Resist. It is painted on etching plates to create washes and tonal effects, which are particularly effective on copper and brass but may also be used on steel and zinc.

The resist works due to the ability of the different elements in the solution (in the form of the painted marks) to separate before they dry. The mixture will therefore separate in the container and should be shaken vigorously for 5 minutes to distribute the particles evenly. Squeeze a small amount into a clean china or glass palette and stir regularly during the painting period. The resist has an ink-like consistency and can be painted, poured, spilled or splashed onto the plate surface using a variety of artist's tools, Chinese and other brushes. The resist may be used at full concentration or diluted with water, either on the plate or in a palette, to create a range of spectacular wash effects.

When the painted marks are dry, the plate should be aquatinted before being etched.

ART MATERIALS USED AS WASH RESISTS

Some types of acrylic paint, screen fillers and Graphic Chemical & Ink Company water-washable block printing inks can be diluted in water to create a range of wash resists which are suitable for use on copper. Digital scales should be used when making wash resists: as a guideline one part paint or ink to between seven and nine parts water generally works well. The mixtures will need to be stirred thoroughly before use.

The different materials provide a variety of washes. Green acrylic paints often form chain-like contours. Speedball Screen Filler provides very fine brown washes which are difficult to see on the copper plate but etch beautifully to create soft printed effects. Black block printing ink dries slowly on the plate to provide a granular wash. A fine uniform aquatint is applied to enhance the contrast before the plate is etched.

PHOTORESISTS

Photoresists (from the Greek *phos* meaning 'light') are light-sensitive materials which are applied to a plate, exposed to ultraviolet light (in conjunction with an image held on a positive) and processed to become acid-resistant. This photo-etching method may be used to build up an entire image or to introduce an element or text. Dry film photoresists may be applied to all commonly used metal plates, hold incredible detail, withstand long etching periods and can be removed easily from the plate. They are available in different thicknesses (shores) and are sold under a variety of brand names (such as ImagOn, Photec, Puretch and Z*Acryl). A thin film should be selected, as thicker films must be thinned in order to become suitable for photo-etching. The process of thinning the film is wasteful and complicated, and provides less predictable results.

There are several separate stages involved when working with photoresists. These are: the creation of a positive; the lamination of the light-sensitive dry film photoresist to the plate; the exposure of the coated plate and positive to ultraviolet light; the developing process; and curing and drying the photoresist.

The cured photoresist is too tough to draw into but in some cases an area may be scraped away. The image can be edited by stopping-out and if tonal areas are required an aquatint may be applied. However, some types of resist will degrade the photoresist and cause it to break down, resulting in foul bite. Lascaux acrylic resists are compatible with most types of dry film photoresist and Z*Acryl resists may be used with Z*Acryl dry film photoresist.

The roll or sheets of photoresist should be clearly labelled and stored in a cool dark place and they must be handled carefully as the film is easily cracked or spoiled. The delicate film of photoresist is held between two Mylar sheets to protect it from dust, grease and damage. One Mylar is more brittle than the other: this supports the film and is known as the carrier sheet.

below left Under yellow safe light, Lascaux Black Coating was painted over all of the carrier sheet of a plate coated with dry film photoresist. The shielded plate was then taken outside and the image was painted with water and drawn into. For broader areas the dissolving coating was wiped away with tissues and brushes. The layer of photoresist below was gradually exposed to the sunlight as the artist worked.

below right Jennifer Page (US), *From Venus*, etching and engraving, 40.5 x 51 cm (16 x 20 in.), 2004. The plate was laminated with Puretch dry film resist, and exposed to UV with the positives of the Venus flytraps and the face. After developing it was etched with ferric. The plate was again laminated with Puretch, and this time the positive of the flies' bodies was exposed and then etched for longer than the previous images. The plate was subsequently worked with a Dremel engraving tool to darken certain areas.

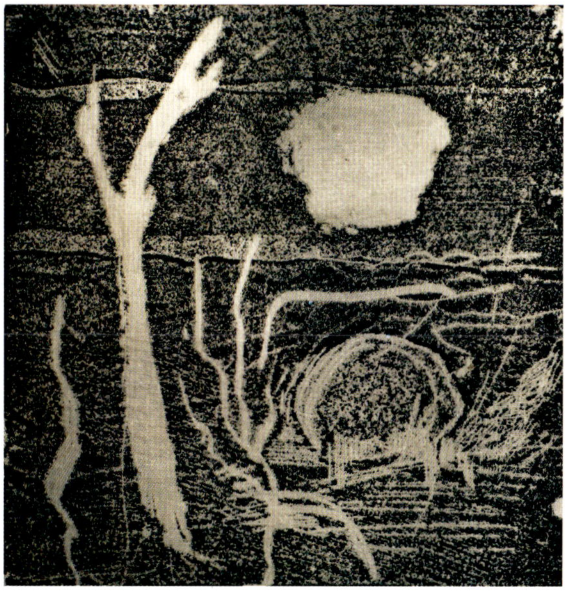

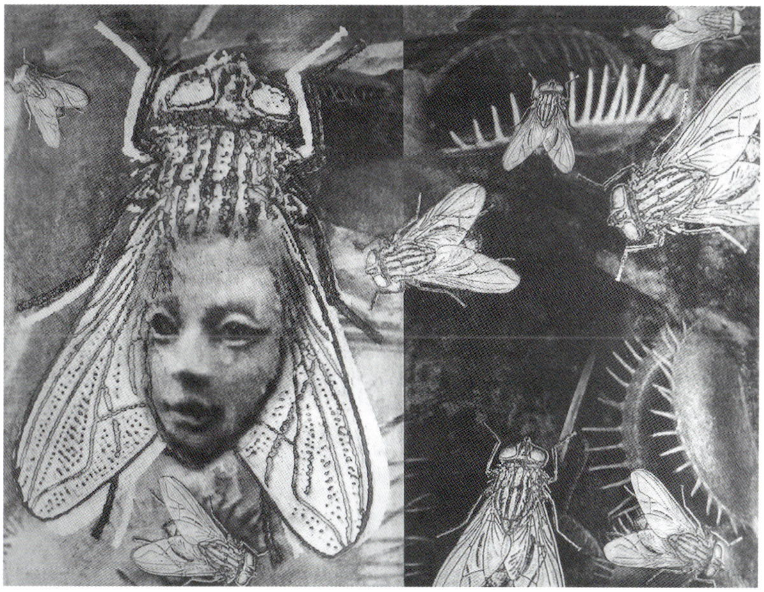

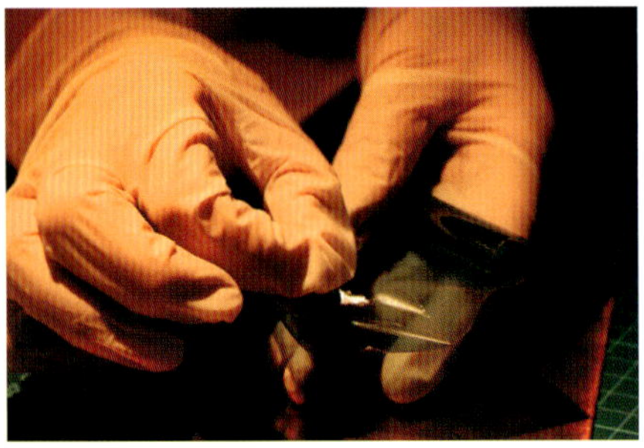

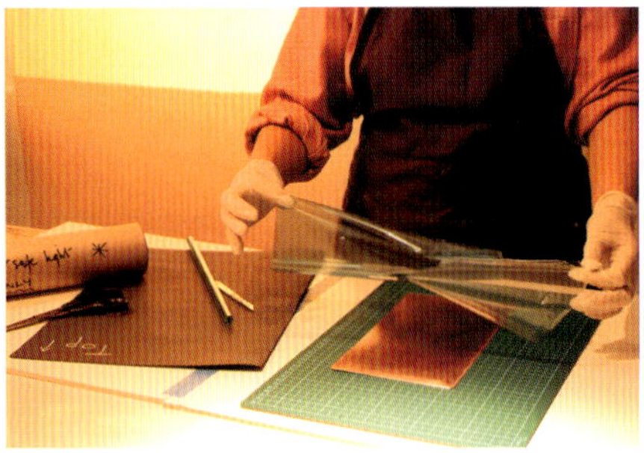

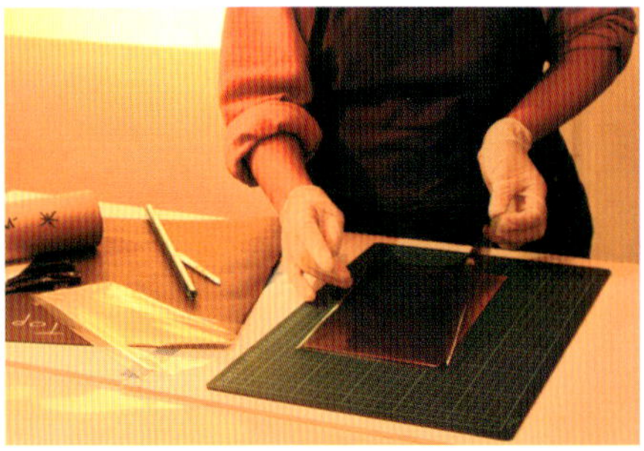

The soft protective Mylar is referred to as the slip sheet, as it is removed before application. The suppliers of dry film photoresists usually provide instructions regarding their recommended working methods as well as environmental and health and safety information. Surgical gloves should be worn, as skin contact with the film (including slip sheet and carrier sheet) and developing solution should be avoided. The film should not be burnt or heated excessively. Dry film photoresists can be laminated using a special machine and some practitioners recommend wet lamination but these methods (which involve heat) require ventilation equipment. A household iron may be used to laminate the dry film resist and a ventilated drying cabinet may also be used to warm the plate and film before lamination. The following dry lamination method does not involve heating the film-coated plate and works well for most types of dry film photoresist.

LAMINATION METHOD

The aim of this process is to attach a layer of photoresist film to the entire surface of the plate.

Equipment and materials required

Work in a yellow safe-light room (see p. 50). Wear an apron and surgical gloves, and tie up hair.

- a spray bottle containing water
- a bevelled, very finely grained (or polished), degreased, backed, dry plate (previously etched plates may also be used)
- a cutting board
- a smooth sheet of red or black cartridge paper folded in half to make a folder
- two sheets of hardboard (Masonite) taped along one edge to form a simple carrying folder for the plate
- a scalpel
- an etching press
- selected dry film photoresist
- a waterproof marker pen

Working method

- Plates should generally be very finely and evenly grained but some brands of dry film photoresist can be applied to highly polished plates or previously etched plates. Any burr on the surface will puncture the resist, causing tearing and ultimately foul bite unless the plate is stopped-out. The bevelled edges of the plate should be smoothed with fine abrasive paper as any fragments or spurs can also cause the delicate layer of dry film photoresist to rip or chip during the developing process.
- Work in safe yellow light. Spraying the air with a little water can help to dampen down any dust.
- The surface of the plate and the workboard should be free of any dust, fluff or hairs. Working on the cutting board, cut some small practice squares and a piece of film to fit the plate. The shape and size may be slightly larger than the plate or slightly smaller depending on the position of the image on the plate and personal preference. If the sheet of dry film photoresist is larger than the plate, it will need to be trimmed down

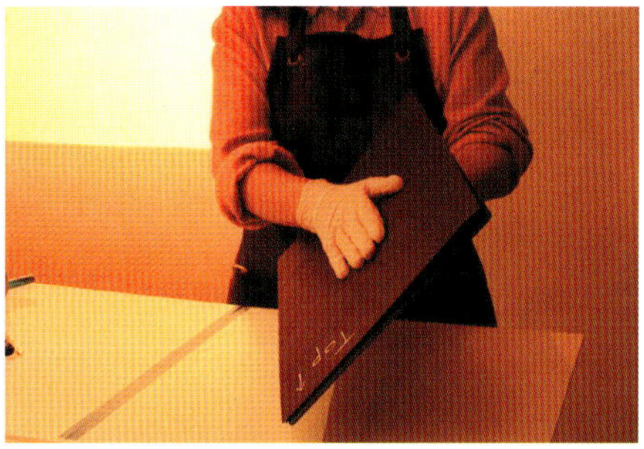

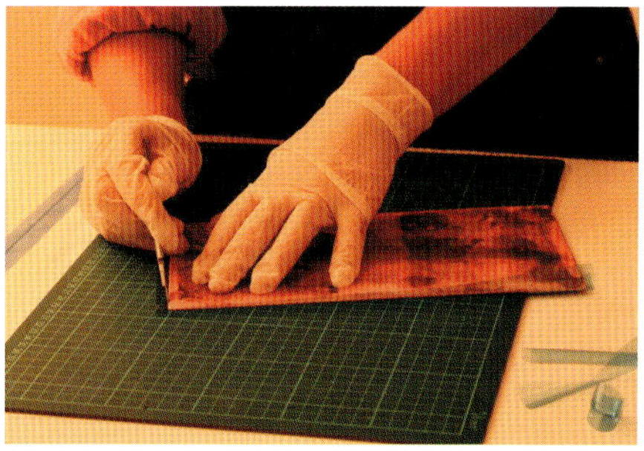

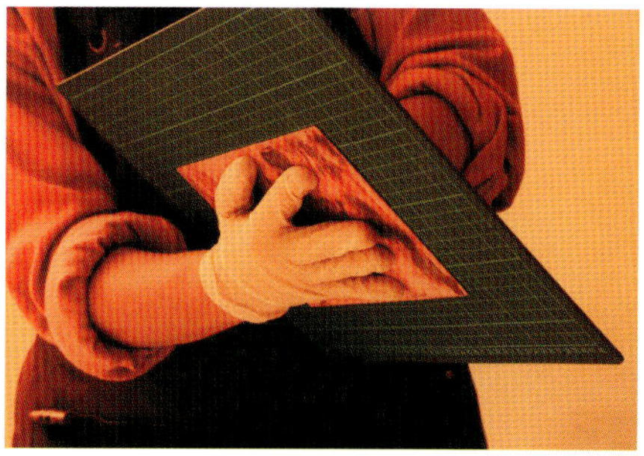

before lamination (the sides of the plate and any blemishes will require stopping-out). In cases where the sheet of dry film photoresist is smaller than the plate, the bond will be excellent: the unprotected border and the top corner of the plate will require some stopping-out (this is because the film will have been touched on the top corner and may be slightly damaged).

• On a practice square make a 1 cm (½ in.)-long slice down from the top edge of the right-hand corner of the dry film photoresist. Holding this flap firmly between two fingers, tear across to the right side. The aim is to create a rough rip so that the layers of materials will be visible to the eye. Identify the slip sheet (the soft Mylar) and carefully peel it away without touching the delicate, slightly sticky film, which remains supported by the carrier sheet. Practise removing the slip sheet from several of the small squares before attempting to work on the piece for the plate. Avoid removing the slip sheet with a large gesture, as the resulting static charge will attract any dust that is in the air, on clothing or on hair.

• Start to prepare the dry film photoresist for the plate as described for the practice squares (make a cut, tear, catch and peel away the slip sheet), lay the dry film photoresist down on the plate and move it into position. The carrier sheet should be facing up and this may be very gently stroked from the centre of the plate outwards to each corner to cause the resist to stick a little to the surface. If too much pressure is applied, the delicate film will stretch and distort or bubbles of air may be trapped between the film and plate. Large plates can be placed in the hardboard folder (as this makes it easier to flip the plate over).

1. Catching hold of the slip sheet.
2. Peeling the slip sheet away.
3. Positioning the photoresist with the carrier sheet upwards on the plate as it lies on the cutting board.
4. After placing a sheet of paper over the plate, the whole assembly is flipped over.
5. The plate (back facing upwards) is slid from the paper back onto the cutting board so the excess film can be trimmed away.
6. The trimmed plate is held firmly against the board and flipped over.

• The plate, covered with the sheet of dry film photoresist, can then be flipped over and laid on the cutting board (the back of the plate will now be facing upwards). The excess dry film photoresist should be visible and this can be cut cleanly away from the edges of the plate with a scalpel. Discard these pieces of waste film.

• Carefully place the plate inside the cartridge paper folder (against the spine). Place the paper folder in the hardboard folder. Mark one outside cover of the folder 'top' with a marker pen to indicate which way up the plate is facing inside the folder (this should guard against inadvertently exposing the light-sensitive film to daylight).

• Take the folder containing the plate to an etching press which is set for normal printing pressure. Lay down the hardboard folder on the press bed with the top side facing up, open it and slide the cartridge paper folder onto the middle of the press bed. Position the spine of the paper folder so that it is parallel to the side of the press bed rather than parallel to the roller. Remove the hardboard folder.

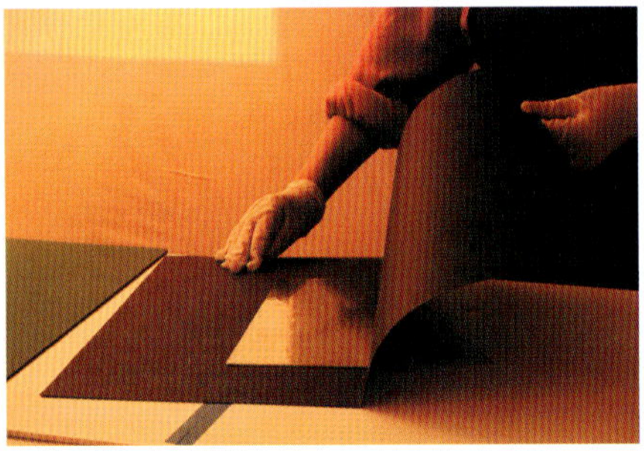

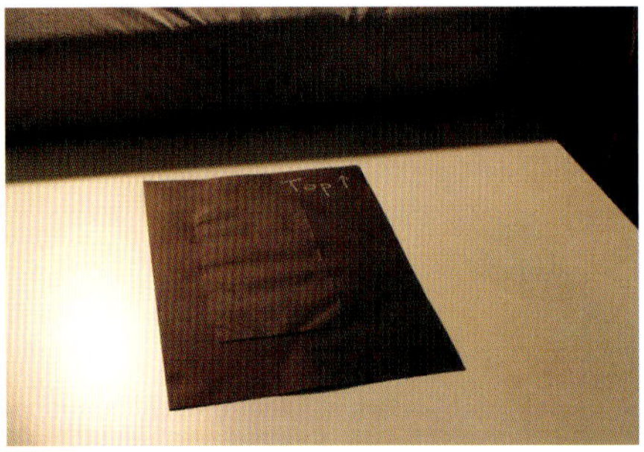

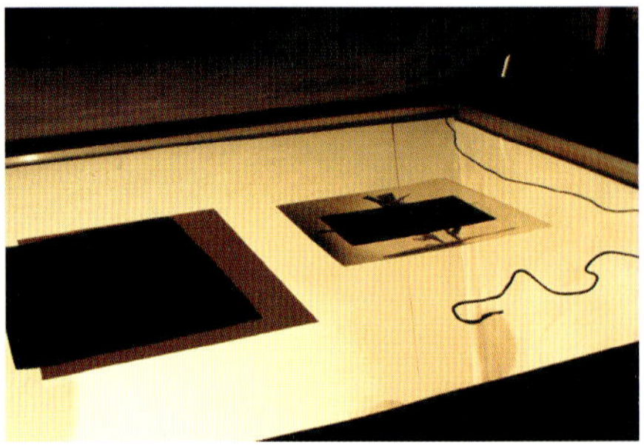

1. The plate and photoresist are placed in a lightproof folder.
2. The folder containing the plate (face-up) is run through the press to laminate the resist to the plate.
3. The laminated photoresist can now be exposed to a positive and UV light.

• Lay the press blankets over the paper folder (containing the plate) and roll this through the press three times to ensure a good lamination. A factor in the quality of the lamination is the smoothness of the cartridge paper layer between the film and the press blankets.

• Lift the blankets and place the paper folder (containing the plate) in the hardboard folder. This sturdy lightproof folder will provide safe storage for the plate until the exposure process. To check the lamination, return to the yellow safelight room and examine the plate and the layer of dry film photoresist (the carrier sheet is left on the laminated film at this point). If it appears that bubbles of air are trapped under the film, or the layer is wrinkled, the plate should be stripped and the lamination process repeated.

EXPOSING THE PHOTORESIST

After the artwork has been created in the form of a positive (a clear substrate holding opaque marks: see p. 181), the exposure process can be carried out. The positive is held in close contact with the dry film photoresist-coated plate while they are exposed to ultraviolet light. A UV exposure unit with vacuum and light integrator can be used for high-resolution images and predictable results. Exposures may also be made outside using sunlight. The UV light will pass through the clear areas of the substrate onto the dry film photoresist. These exposed areas undergo a chemical change (known as crosslinking or photopolymerization) and will not dissolve during the developing process. The areas of resist which are shielded from the light (by the opaque areas on a positive) will dissolve during the developing process, leaving the metal unprotected.

DETERMINING EXPOSURE TIMES

To get the best results from the exposure equipment, positives and photopolymer resists, a test plate can be made using an exposure calculator (such as a Stouffer 21 step guide wedge) or a positive. The effort taken to make a test, document the results and store the notated prints in a visual aid folder will help to produce successful stencils, and will save time and materials in the future. As the UV bulb in the exposure unit ages, the light emitted will become weaker and a new test may need to be made. Exposure calculators are inexpensive, reusable tools and are available with instruction booklets from intaglio companies such as Puretch and screenprinting manufacturers such as Autotype, Dirasol, Sericol and Ulano.

Some of these exposure tools have to be manipulated manually, whereas others have filters which simulate different exposures. A filtered exposure calculator is a film supporting a repeated identical image made up of lines and spaces, text and ranges of halftone dots. Generally all but one segment is coated on the back with filters of successively increasing density, which are designed to produce the effect of different exposure times. When a single exposure of the sequence is made, the resulting plate enables the user to select the particular segment which demonstrates the most accurate exposure, and from this result a calculation can be made to determine the length of the correct exposure. Once these tests have been carried out, a positive made from different materials and translucent substrates commonly used in the studio can be designed as an exposure test strip. Marks can be made with different materials, which might include pencil, compressed charcoal, roll-on tusche, photocopies or digital printouts. These should be applied to the supporting substrates (which might include tracing paper, smooth PVC or grained sheets). The photoresist may be etched and the resulting print can be compared with the positive. This useful reference information can be notated and stored in a visual aid folder.

EXPOSURE UNIT METHOD

Equipment and materials required

- a UV exposure unit with vacuum and light integrator
- a positive or opaque materials for other working methods (see pp. 181–192)
- a folder containing a plate laminated with a dry film photoresist (with the carrier sheet still in place)

Working method

- Both the positive and the glass should be clean and free of dust, grease and scratches. Scratches on the glass surface will cause the UV light to refract during exposure, causing unwanted open lines in the photoresist. Grease and dust can shield the UV light from the photoresist, creating pinholes and fisheyes which will etch.
- Switch on the safe light in the unit to illuminate the positive lying on the clear glass surface (assuming that the UV light source is located beneath the glass). The image on the positive should read as it is to print ('right-reading'). When the unmarked side of the substrate lies in contact with the glass, the opaque marks are on top, touching the photoresist-coated plate, creating a close contact and allowing an accurate exposure. If the positive is in the 'wrong-reading' position when an exposure is made, the contact is less close as the thickness of the substrate separates the marks from the photoresist. The light will bend fractionally, resulting in a loss of accuracy. The result may be the same if the positive has too much impasto.
- The edges of the positive will cause the light to refract, creating dotted or open lines in the photoresist. Composite images should be created bearing this in mind (see p. 188).
- The laminated plate is positioned face-down on the positive (with the carrier sheet still in place). To avoid any risk of scratching the glass, the plate should be moved directly from the folder onto the positive.
- A close contact is made between the glass, the positive and the photoresist-coated plate using the vacuum pump (this is switched on and allowed to take effect).
- Set the light integrator to release a measured amount of UV light (this measurement can be judged from the results of previous test strips) and switch on the UV light source. If using a unit without an integrator, the exposure can be measured in seconds and minutes.
- When the controlled exposure to UV light is made, the UV light passes through the glass top of the UV exposure unit and the transparent areas of the positive onto the laminated plate.
- After exposure, the UV light and the vacuum pump should be switched off. The exposed plate can be placed in the hardboard folder.

SUNLIGHT EXPOSURE FRAME

Equipment and materials required

- sunlight
- a sunlight exposure frame
- a sponge and basin of water
- a positive or opaque materials for other working methods (see pp. 181–192)

• a folder containing a plate laminated with a dry film photoresist (with the carrier sheet still in place)
• a darkened or yellow safe-light room

Working method
• Make some test plates and prints and keep notes of the time of year and weather conditions. The correct exposure time may be a matter of seconds rather than minutes.
• Prepare the positive and the plate as described above and then set up the sunlight exposure frame (see p. 51). Make certain that the contact between the positive and photoresist-coated plate is as close as possible and then take the assembly outside.
• Remove the cover and expose the plate for a timed period (according to previous test plates).
• After exposing the photoresist, cover the plate (to end the exposure) and return to the yellow safe-light room (see p. 50). The exposed plate may be removed from the sunlight exposure frame and stored in a hardboard folder.

SIMPLE SOLAR METHOD
• This is a very simple method but can be surprisingly effective. Make some test plates and prints and keep notes of the time of year and weather conditions. The correct exposure time may be a matter of seconds rather than minutes.
• Prepare the positive (ideally the artwork on the positive should be waterproof) and laminate the plate.
• Working in the yellow safe-light room use a soft sponge to wet the carrier sheet on the plate with a little soapy water (a drop of dishwashing liquid will help break any surface tension). Lay the plate face-up, position the positive on the wet surface and smooth out any air bubbles. Put the plate in the hardboard folder and take it outside.
• Open the folder and expose the plate for the selected time.
• After exposure, close the folder (to end the exposure) and return to the studio.

DEVELOPING THE PHOTORESIST
After exposure the plate is developed. The crosslinked areas will not dissolve but the areas of resist which were shielded from the light (by the opaque areas on the positive) will dissolve during the developing process, revealing the metal. A test plate can be made to illustrate the point when the metal surface is revealed (the 'breakpoint'). The test plate is drawn on with a water-soluble marker pen before the photoresist is laminated over the marks. When the test plate is developed, the ink will dissolve at the breakpoint.

Equipment and materials required
• surgical gloves, visor and apron
• a folder containing the exposed plate (with the carrier sheet still in place)
• a calibrated measuring jug
• developing solution (see opposite)
• a small, soft sponge or soft brush
• a tray larger than the plate
• a sink with water and hose

Working method
• Work in a shaded area rather than in full sunlight.
• Pour some developing solution into a jug from the storage barrel and fill a clean tray in or near a sink (this makes it easy to pour away the spent solution).
• Lay the plate in the solution with the photoresist facing up and use a gloved finger to feel for an edge of the carrier sheet. A gentle plucking motion along the plate edges will usually lift this film free of the photoresist. Peel away the carrier sheet, being careful not to tear the fragile photoresist in the process. Discard the carrier sheet in a waste container.
• The developing solution will now start to act on the unprotected photoresist and it is therefore important that the plate is covered by the solution. The surface of the plate is stroked gently with the sponge or soft brush until the image or pattern is clearly visible as exposed metal. The sponge or brush help to

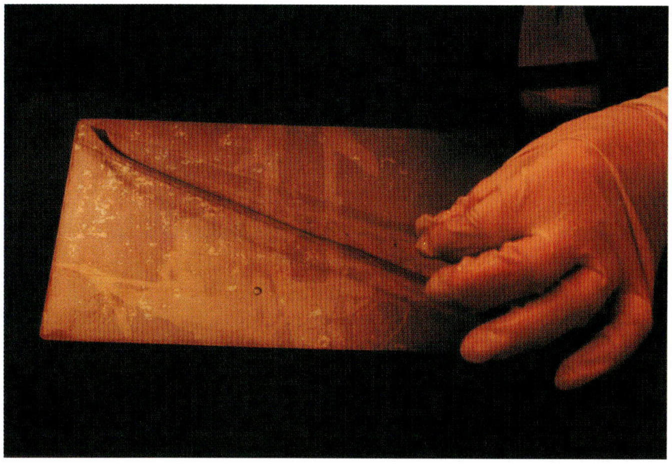

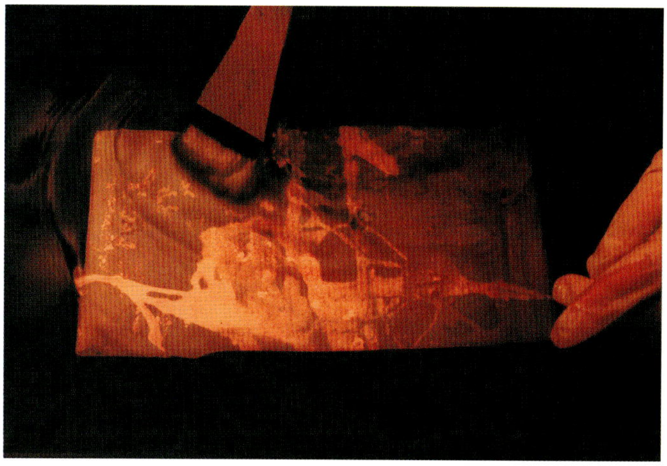

above left The exposed plate is laid in the developer and the carrier sheet removed. Note the air bubbles trapped under the photoresist: in this case these are caused by dust on the plate.

above right The photoresist is dissolving in the areas which were shielded by the image on the positive. Note how the trapped air bubbles have formed open areas where there should be texture. Instead of stopping-out the process would be repeated to achieve a better result.

remove the dissolving photoresist from the plate and leave the metal clean. Another technique involves repeatedly applying fresh developer with a sponge rather than working in the tray.

• The solution will become cloudy as the photoresist dissolves. If the photoresist is over-developed the polymerized film (which looks like a blue negative of the image and should remain as the resist on the plate) will start to break up, and ultimately it will dissolve completely from the plate.

• After developing the photoresist, rinse the plate thoroughly with some unused developing solution and then water. This practice will remove any polymerized and semi-polymerized photoresist particles from the metal which is to be etched. Even a thin film of these materials will inhibit etching.

MAKING UP THE DEVELOPING SOLUTION

A small quantity of sodium carbonate (anhydrous) is dissolved in water to make an alkaline developing solution. It can be purchased from supermarkets (for washing clothes) or from janitorial, chemical or swimming pool maintenance suppliers, and is also sold as soda ash or soda crystals. For the best results the solution should be discarded after each plate has been developed, as polymerized and semi-polymerized photoresist particles in the used solutions can redeposit on the etching surface and inhibit biting. Sodium carbonate is inexpensive and a large quantity of the developing solution may be mixed up and stored in a plastic brewing barrel (with a low dispensing tap).

Equipment and materials required

Work at the photoresist developing and rinsing workstation.

• gloves, visor, apron and dust mask
• precision weight-measuring scales (preferably digital read-out)
• a calibrated measuring jug
• sodium carbonate
• warm water
• a tray larger than the plate
• a sink with water and hose
• a brewing barrel with low dispensing tap

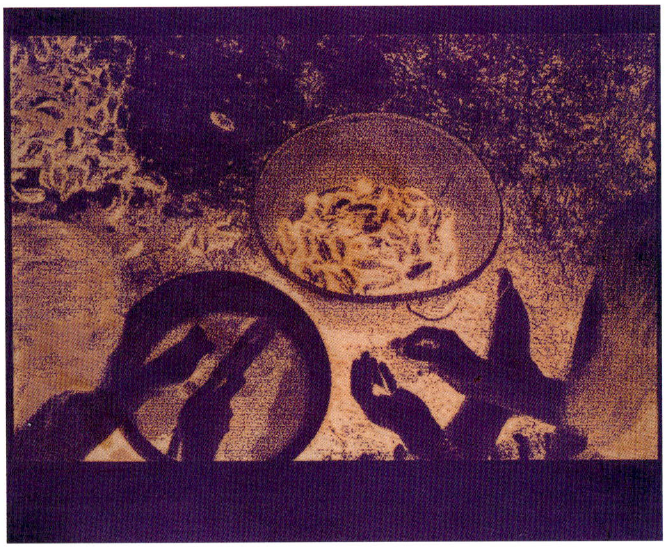

A plate which has been laminated with Photec photopolymer, exposed, developed and cured to a characteristic violet colour. It has not yet been edited with stop-out or aquatinted before etching (see etched plate on p. 123 and print on p. 59).

Working method

- Work out the capacity of the barrel and calculate the quantity of sodium carbonate required. The mixture for general use is 10g sodium carbonate to 1 litre of water (100g sodium carbonate to 10 litres of water).
- Half-fill the barrel with water.
- Wear an apron, gloves, eye protection and a dust mask when handling the dry sodium carbonate. Weigh the correct quantity of sodium carbonate on the scales.
- Dissolve the weighed sodium carbonate crystals in a jug of tepid water. Any spilt sodium carbonate can be cleaned up and the dust mask may then be taken off.
- Add the dissolved mixture to the barrel and top it up with water. The barrel can be stored in the area used for developing plates.

CURING, DRYING, ETCHING OR WORKING THE PLATE FURTHER

- Daylight can be used to cure (harden) and dry the photoresist, or the plate may be dried and given a further exposure on the UV exposure unit. The cured plate will deepen in colour.
- The image may be flash-bitten to check that it is etching well before being stopped-out or aquatinted. If it is not etching the plate may in some cases be developed further, or the light-sensitive layer should be stripped and the entire process repeated.
- If the flash-biting process reveals that the image is biting well, the plate may be etched. If there are broad open areas which require tone, the plate should be rinsed, de-oxidized, rinsed again, dried and an aquatint applied before the plate is etched.

OTHER TYPES OF RESIST

OILY RESISTS

A range of greasy materials can be applied to the plate and used to resist the action of the mordant. Oily resists are fragile as they are etched before they dry or harden on the plate.

Lines and marks may be drawn on the plate with oil crayon, oil bar, lithographic crayons, lithographic pencils and chinagraph pencils. Oil paint, Vaseline and etching ink may be painted onto the plate and wash effects can be created using lithographic tusches. R&F Pigment Stick can be applied and rolled out to cover the entire plate surface for use as a soft resist. Any repairs to these resists are difficult to manage: one technique is to use a small soft brush to apply a little oily resist.

These media can be used to create an image on a plate which has been polished or grained. A previously etched plate can be painted or drawn on with oily resists. They can also be applied to a plate holding an acrylic resist with an image or pattern (e.g. aquatint, punctured resist, soft resist or photo-resist).

Etching tools, paint shapers and brush handles will glide through many of these materials, exposing the metal, although consideration has to be given to any acrylic or photoresist beneath. Although these lines and marks may look clean, a greasy residue is often left on the metal and this inhibits the action of the mordant, making biting erratic.

Equipment and materials required

Work in the drawing area on a workboard covered with a clean sheet of newsprint.

- a bevelled, de-oxidized, degreased and backed plate (polished, grained or etched)
- selected oily materials
- brushes, rollers and other application tools

below left This print is from an aluminium plate holding an oil-bar drawing of a boat. This was etched in a copper sulphate solution. The mordant created irregular pits in the unprotected metal and it is these which hold the ink.

below centre A print from a steel plate which was roller-coated with a layer of oil bar and drawn into before being etched.

below right A print from a plate which was first coated in Lascaux Hard Resist. Two areas in the dry resist were scraped away and a marker pen was used to draw the pale areas of the faces. The marker-pen drawing was also drawn into with etching tools and a uniform aquatint was sprayed on the plate.

- etching needles or sticks for drawing into the resists
- some vegetable oil
- dishwashing liquid
- alkaline degreaser and plastic brush

Working method

- A bevelled, de-oxidized and degreased plate is used. The surface may have been polished, grained, previously etched or may hold an acrylic resist (e.g. aquatint).
- Painting and drawing techniques or soft-resist collage and drawing techniques may be used (see pp. 111–115). Contamination of the resist with dust, hair or fluff will cause foul bite.
- When working with crayons and greasy pencils, a greater quantity of resist can be applied if the plate is warmed in the drying cupboard before the drawing is made.
- Oily resists are etched when they are still moist so great care must be taken not to scratch or smudge the surface in the mordant tank or tray. Slightly longer than normal etching times may be required to allow the mordant to penetrate any residual greasy layer on the areas of metal to be etched. When monitoring the etching process, use cold water to rinse the plate as warm water may melt the resist.

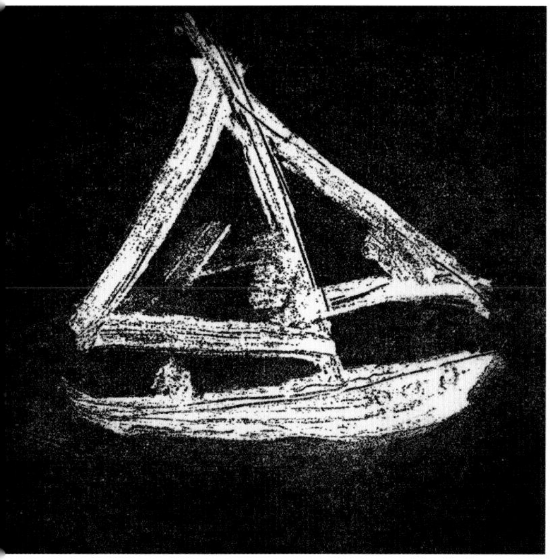

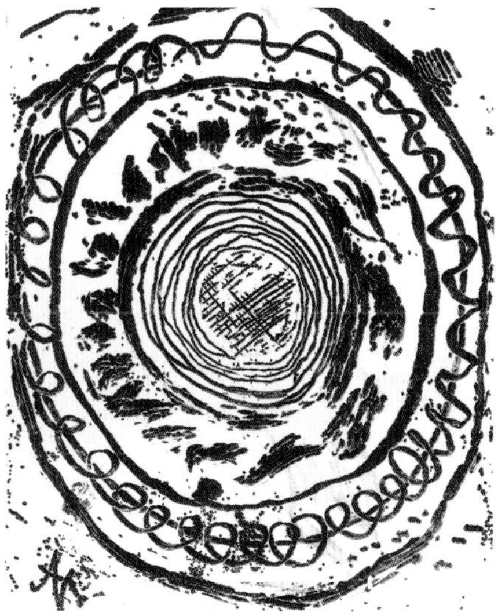

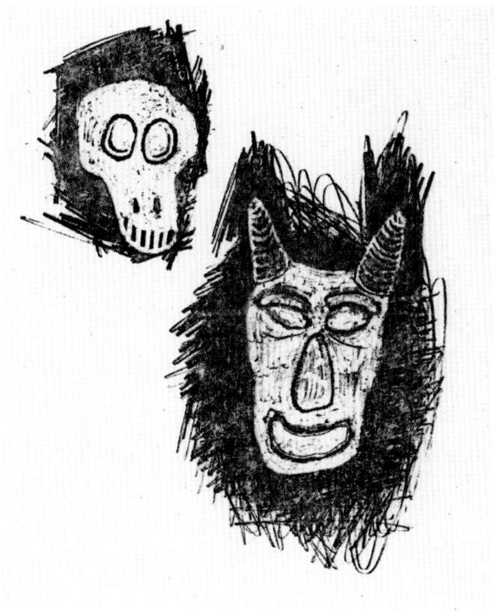

To generate the image on this etched copper plate a transferred photocopy of an enlarged engraving was used as resist. A uniform aquatint was sprayed on the plate and it was then etched.

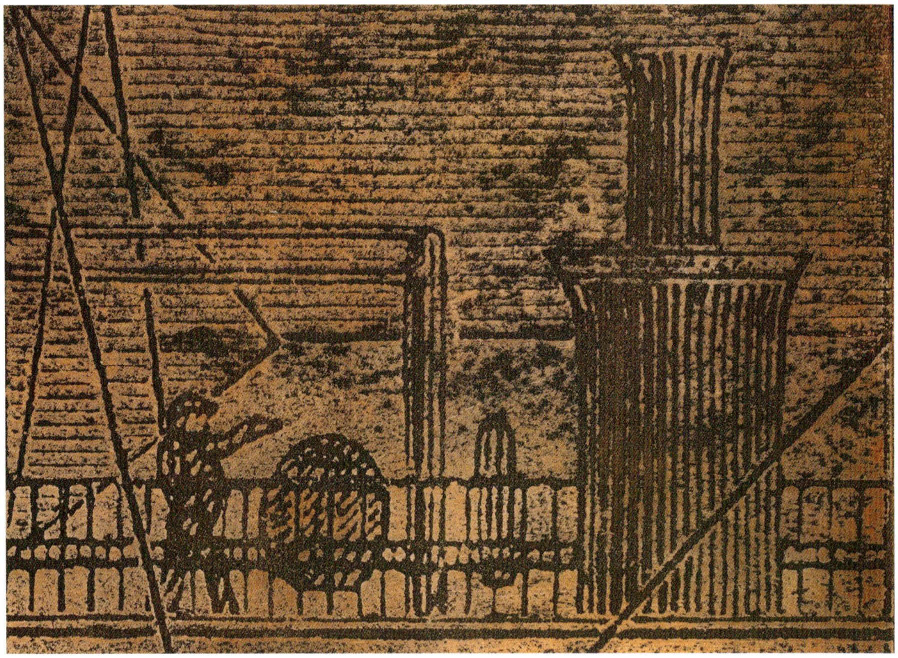

• When the etching process is complete, remove the oily resists and any acrylic resists from the plate (see pp. 214–216). This should then be degreased with an alkaline degreaser before working further or printing with water-based inks.

WATERPROOF MARKER PENS

Some types of waterproof marker pen may be used as resists. A drawing is made on the plate surface and then an aquatint is applied. When the dots of sprayed resist have dried, the plate may be etched. When the etch is finished, the plate can be rinsed and de-oxidized, and if further etching is required the plate may be dried, the image re-drawn, and a further aquatint applied. After etching, the waterproof pen marks can be removed by lightly polishing the plate surface.

PHOTOCOPY TRANSFERS

A photographic, autographic or digital image, or found materials (such as ephemera, fabrics or leaves) may be photocopied onto ordinary photocopy paper. The resulting image may then be transferred from the photocopy to the plate using the following method.

Equipment and materials required

Work on a clean workboard in the drawing area.

• a fresh photocopy holding rich tones
• a clean, bevelled, grained plate
• masking tape
• a cotton tea towel
• a domestic clothes iron
• equipment for aquatint application

Working method

• As the toner will prevent etching, the dark areas of the image will not etch. If the reverse effect of this is required, an inverted photocopy of the image should be made and used. For best results a freshly made photocopy should be trimmed so that it fits onto the plate.
• Position the plate face-up on the workboard and place the

photocopy face-down on the plate surface. Adhere the corners with small pieces of masking tape.
• Lay the tea towel over the photocopy and iron (on a medium heat) steadily for 5 minutes. The toner will offset onto the plate.
• Carefully remove the photocopy from the plate.
• An aquatint is applied to the plate (this will secure the toner).
• When the sprayed dots of resist have dried, the plate may be etched. It should be disturbed as little as possible while it is etching as the toner tends to break up in the mordant and may wash away when the plate is rinsed after biting.
• The toner may be polished from the plate after etching.

ADHESIVE TAPES

Some types of adhesive tape, such as parcel tape, carpet tape and masking tape, may be used as resists. These materials are useful for stopping-out panels of test plates. However, the glue can sometimes be awkward to remove from the plate.

ETCHING THE PLATE

MORDANTS

For centuries artists have etched metal plates with acids or corrosive salts. When these chemicals are diluted with water or formulated into etching solutions, the different mixtures are referred to as mordants. All of these corrosive mixtures are hazardous but some are more dangerous to use than others. Acrylic resists, photoresists and oily resists may be used successfully in many different types of mordant. However, it is possible to get a full range of bites with mordants which do not release toxic fumes and these should be selected for use (see pp. 154–161).

Mordants which release toxic or flammable fumes during the mixing or etching process are the most hazardous to use and should be avoided. These risks were understood by medieval artists who tried to protect themselves by covering their noses and mouths with scarves. More recently printmakers have used powerful and expensive ventilation systems in the mordant area and personal respirators in an attempt to protect themselves from the fumes. However, these precautions are often not entirely successful, and gases vented outdoors create hazardous pollution which can be drawn back into another part of the building. It is also often the case that toxic fumes are redirected into other rooms within the building, harming unsuspecting individuals. As a result of these findings, recent legislation has prevented some studios from using mordants which give off toxic fumes. Others have had to add filtration devices to their extractors: the filters are expensive and have to be replaced frequently.

The most dangerous chemicals traditionally used in intaglio printmaking mordants are nitric acid, hydrochloric acid, potassium chlorate, cupric chloride solution, potassium dichromate and sulphuric acid. It is not necessary to use these substances but many etchers still employ them as mordants; as it is likely that artists will encounter these chemicals in colleges and print studios we have included some information about them (see pp. 152–153).

Whichever mordant is chosen, local authority regulations and an up-to-date MSDS must be consulted before purchasing or using a particular chemical. The MSDS will provide information about the chemical, the health hazards, fire risks, how to deal with any spillage and the correct disposal of waste. Guidance concerning safety clothing (e.g. which type of gloves should be worn: nitrile, rubber or plastic), studio equipment and procedures should always be followed. In most cases eye protection, rubber boots and a chemical-resistant apron or overalls are essential. It is important to follow good studio practice to avoid accidental ingestion which can easily occur by smoking, touching the mouth or failing to wash hands before eating. Repeated intakes of small amounts of these chemicals over time can be very damaging.

Some of these chemicals are available in anhydrous (powdered) or solution (liquid) form and the MSDSs will vary accordingly. Powdered forms present many more hazards and it is preferable to seek out a liquid form.

MORDANTS WHICH ARE NOT RECOMMENDED

Full personal protection and powerful fume extraction systems are essential, as all of these chemicals are dangerous substances to work with. They should only be used by trained staff in studios which are equipped with specialist acid rooms with a safety shower, an eye-wash fountain (rather than hand-held solution), copies of MSDSs for each chemical and wash-room facilities close by. The acid room should be well lit and equipped with non-slip acid-resistant flooring, a powerful ventilation system, specialist storage facilities, protective shields between the different baths, rinsing trays and clear safety information. Some authorities recommend that a NIOSH-approved respirator with acid gas cartridges should be worn and that air-purifying respirators should not be used with nitric acid: nitrogen dioxide cannot be detected by odour and it is therefore not possible to detect any odour breakthrough with charcoal cartridges.

The storage requirements for these chemicals is important and the information provided on the MSDS should be followed carefully. When making up mordants, concentrated acid should always be added to the water, not the other way around, as this can cause a violent reaction. It is also important that solutions should never be mixed in bottles, as the heat generated in a confined space could cause an explosion.

Used acid solutions containing copper must be disposed of by a professional waste disposal company. Acidic solutions may be diluted with water and neutralized with sodium bicarbonate (baking soda).

NITRIC ACID (HNO_3)

This mineral acid was traditionally known as aqua fortis and is sometimes called azotic acid. The acid is added to water in different concentrations to etch copper, zinc and steel (each type of metal must have its own bath). Nitric acid has a characteristic rough bite which is caused by lateral erosion.

It is a strong oxidizer, highly corrosive and generates noxious gases (nitrogen tetroxide, oxides of nitrogen, zinc and ammonium nitrate, and hydrogen) and heat when it etches metals. These gases form bubbles on the surface of the plate which act as a barrier to the etching process and so must be continually brushed away with a feather. The need for repeated feathering and monitoring the bite forces the printmaker to open the ventilation unit frequently. This practice results in inevitable exposure to toxic fumes and the risk of acid splashes unless full personal protective equipment is worn each time. The practice of drawing into the ground or resist while the plate is biting in nitric acid is highly dangerous. The noxious gases tend to be heavier than air and any release from the acid unit can harm other artists working in the studio.

Another considerable risk is that when large open areas of exposed metal (or many plates in a single acid bath) are etched, the temperature of the bath will increase, accelerating the rate of bite, which in turn generates more heat. This exothermic reaction can go out of control. Traditionally a bath of cold water was placed beside the acid bath and overheating plates would be lifted from the acid and cooled in the water. Exothermic reactions will result in a coarse line of poor quality and will tend to break up the resists, causing foul bite.

Typical mordant recipes for etching zinc are one part nitric acid added to ten parts water (1:10) for a fast bite; 1:16 (medium); 1:20 (slow). For copper typical dilutions are: 1:2 (fast); 1:4 (medium). For steel 1:4 (fast); 1:10 (slow): this bath is quickly exhausted and needs replacing after etching. Spit biting (using a brush to paint the acid on the plate) is particularly dangerous because of the risk of inhaling fumes and splashes from the acid.

Contact with nitric acid and exposure to its vapours can result in severe damage to the eyes, respiratory system, skin and teeth. This can take the form of pain and discolouration of the eyes, delayed pulmonary oedema and bronchitis, skin irritation and burns, and dental erosion.

HYDROCHLORIC ACID (HCl) AND DUTCH MORDANTS

Synonyms for hydrochloric acid are anhydrous hydrogen

chloride, hydrogen chloride, aqueous hydrogen chloride, chlorohydric acid, spirit of salts and muriatic acid. Traditionally hydrochloric acid was added to water and used to etch zinc (rough bite), aluminium (very slow) and steel (fast or slow bite depending on dilution). Hydrogen gas is produced when these metals are etched. Hydrochloric acid does not etch copper unless the mordant is warmed.

Dutch mordants were invented in the mid-nineteenth century for etching copper. Examples of these mixtures are Frank Short's bath (10 parts hydrochloric acid, 2 parts potassium chlorate and 88 parts water) and Buckland Wright's bath (20 parts hydrochloric, 4 parts potassium chlorate and 80 parts water). Dutch mordant is chemically an acid salt of hydrochloric and is similar in its reaction to ferric chloride. When this mordant is mixed, toxic chlorine gas is released but during etching no bubbles are formed. Plates need to be bitten for several hours but the bite is more accurate than with nitric acid. When a new solution is made up, the acid must always be added to water, never the other way around. It is also important that solutions should never be mixed in bottles as the heat generated in a confined space could cause an explosion.

Exposure to this acid can cause glottic oedema or circulatory collapse, both of which can result in death. Damage can include conjunctivitis, corneal burns, permanent optical damage, dermatitis, skin burns and dental erosion. It can also cause inflammation and ulceration of the respiratory tract, hoarseness, a feeling of suffocation, cough, choking, bronchitis, pulmonary oedema, rhinitis, laryngitis and tracheitis. Other symptoms may include dehydration, abdominal pain, diarrhoea, nausea, vomiting, lethargy or hypotension. The acid is harmful to the environment and is classified as a hazardous substance. Waste must be removed by a specialist agency.

POTASSIUM CHLORATE ($KClO_3$)

Potassium chlorate is an ingredient in Dutch mordant and should never be mixed with any other chemicals. Synonyms for potassium chlorate are chloric acid potassium salt, chlorate of potash and Berthollet salt. It is normally supplied in powder or crystal form and is a strong oxidizer and a respiratory, skin and eye irritant. Gloves, apron, eye protection and a particulate respirator should be worn when working with the powder or crystals. When the potassium chlorate is made into Dutch mordant, the safety information given under 'Hydrochloric acid' above should be followed.

CUPRIC CHLORIDE SOLUTION ($CuCl_2$ IN H_2O)

Cupric chloride in its pure form consists of fine, light blue-green crystals which smell slightly of hydrochloric acid. Its synonym is copper (II) chloride. The material is dangerous to work with in powder form and should be purchased as a green aqueous solution. It must not come into contact with acids as it may release toxic chloride fumes.

It is diluted in water to etch aluminium, 1:3 (for a fast bite) and 1:8 (for a slow bite). Splashes in the eye can result in severe irritation with blurred vision, redness, pain, discolouration and possible eye damage. A chemically resistant apron, plastic gloves and eye protection must be worn.

OTHER ACIDS AND ACID COMBINATIONS

Traditionally aluminium was etched in a mordant consisting of water, potassium dichromate, sulphuric acid and grain alcohol. Mild steel would be etched in a mixture of water, hydrochloric acid, nitric acid and methylated spirits. Copper was sometimes etched in a combination of water, potassium dichromate, sulphuric acid and hydrochloric acid. These mordants are highly toxic and have been superseded by safer alternatives.

In an attempt to improve biting, etchers modified nitric mordants with ferric chloride in order to reduce the tendency for etched lines to widen. Another technique was to add sufficient nitric acid to Dutch mordant to create bubbles, revealing any foul bite taking place. Acetic acid was sometimes mixed with nitric acid and water to make a diagnostic etchant for photo-etching.

MORDANTS WHICH ARE RECOMMENDED

FERRIC CHLORIDE SOLUTION ($FeCl_3$ IN H_2O)

Traditionally ferric chloride has been used to etch copper, brass and zinc accurately. Its synonyms are iron chloride solution, iron perchloride solution and iron (III) chloride solution. The advantages of this mordant are that it can be measured by Baumé; it bites with very little lateral etch; it gives off no noxious fumes; it tends not to displace the resists; and it is stable and long-lasting. A precipitate is formed in the lines during the etching process and this can impede or arrest the bite. To prevent this deposit building up, the plates may be etched face-down in a tray of mordant (the plate is supported on wooden stands or hung from a frame) and the tray is rocked gently. Another traditional method involved pouring the etching solution repeatedly over the plate. In the modern circuit-board industry the ferric chloride is sprayed onto the plate within a vertical tank. This method has been adapted by printmakers who hang the plate in a vertical tank which is filled with the mordant. A flow of air bubbles inside the tank circulates the mordant, dislodging the precipitate from the lines.

Ferric chloride should always be purchased as an aqueous solution. In powdered or crystalline form it is hazardous to handle and dangerous to dissolve in water, giving off heat and toxic hydrogen chloride fumes. Ferric chloride solution is a corrosive material and contact with eyes can result in blurred vision, redness, pain, discolouration and severe burns. Skin contact may cause sensitization, irritation, rashes and burns. Although no noxious gases are given off when etching copper, the mordant should be used in a well-ventilated area. To avoid the risk of splashes and skin contact, eye protection, aprons and gloves should be worn. Ferric chloride solution is stable under ordinary conditions of use and storage. Note that aluminium plates should never be bitten in ferric chloride as this would result in a hazardous chemical reaction and the generation of hydrogen gas.

Ferric chloride solution is not classified as a hazardous waste. However, once the mordant has been used to etch copper or brass the classification changes because the waste mordant will contain dissolved copper which is dangerous to aquatic life. These solutions should be disposed of in accordance with local environmental regulations.

MAKING UP FERRIC CHLORIDE MORDANTS

A separate mordant must be made for each different type of metal. The concentration or specific gravity of a ferric chloride and water solution will affect how strongly the mordant will etch the metal. The specific gravity can be measured in Baumé (Bé) with a hydrometer. This is a simple procedure: the solution is placed in a tall, clear, narrow, calibrated container and the long, slim hydrometer is floated in the solution. A reading can then be taken from the calibrations on the hydrometer.

The solution can be adjusted by adding small measured quantities of water, and after being stirred the Baumé may be retaken. After calculating the quantities required, a larger volume of mordant may be made up, stirred and its Baumé checked. This technique enables artists to make up precise mordant recipes consistently as well as monitoring the condition of existing mordants.

A hydrometer is held in front of a container of ferric chloride solution. The water is for diluting the ferric to the correct Baumé.

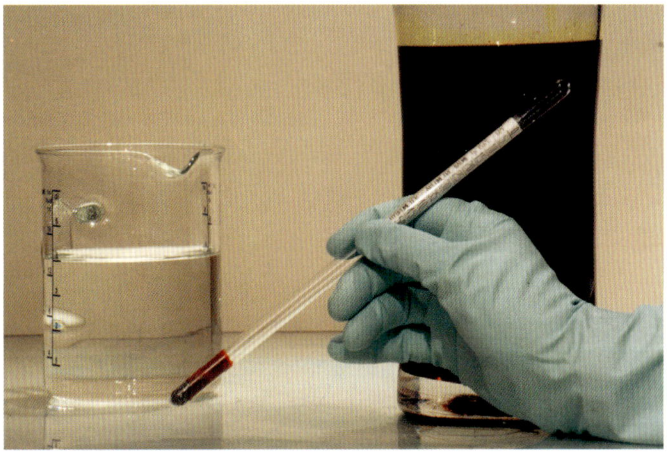

The solution of industrial-grade ferric chloride which is purchased from chemical or intaglio suppliers is usually 45° Bé. This concentration was used traditionally to etch copper slowly. When the temperature of the mordant is below 60° F (15° C) the etch will become very slow. An addition of water to the purchased solution of ferric chloride will make the mordant etch more vigorously because of the reduced viscosity. Traditionally 35° Bé would be used for a fast etch on copper. After a dilution of 35° Bé has been reached the biting action of the mordant becomes weaker.

Traditionally zinc was bitten in ferric chloride of three strengths 33° Bé (fast), 35° Bé (fairly fast) and 45° Bé (slow). The plate would be supported face-down and the bath rocked gently to remove the dark, viscous deposit of ferric hydroxide which forms on the plate during etching. The formation of this precipitate could be repressed by adding up to 10% of hydrochloric acid to the solution. This clarified the mordant and plates could be bitten face-up in the tray. It is now considered unsafe to etch zinc in ferric chloride mordants unless a fume-extracting etching unit is used.

A small amount of hydrochloric acid was also often added to the copper bath. This method was documented by Jack Shirreff and by Ross, Romano & Ross in the 1970s. Citric acid can be used as a safer alternative to hydrochloric acid and will act in a similar way. In 1996 Friedhard Kiekeben added citric to a saturated ferric chloride solution to create his mordant 'Edinburgh etch'. His recipe involves dissolving 400g of anhydrous citric acid powder into 1.2 litres of hot water and adding this to 6 litres of ferric chloride solution with a Baumé of 42–45 Bé.

Equipment and materials required

Work in a ventilated, warm, well-lit and equipped mordant area (see pp. 48–49).

- nitrile gloves, dust mask, waterproof apron and visor
- ferric chloride solution (45° Bé)
- a plastic syphon
- some water
- some calibrated plastic jugs
- a notepad and pen
- a hydrometer
- a tall, narrow, plastic measuring container
- some buckets
- a tray or tank suitable for the mordant
- a sacrificial piece of plate metal
- a timer
- some test plates
- digital scales if citric acid powder is being used

Working method

- Before purchasing tools and materials source an MSDS for all of the chemicals which are being used. Check with the local authority about drainage legislation and the correct disposal of spent chemicals which have been used for etching (copper deposits will generally require professional disposal).
- Work in the mordant area and always wear the correct safety equipment. Use a siphon to transfer the liquid ferric chloride from the industrial container into a bucket or a jug held in a bucket. Be aware and take care not to splash any mordant on anyone else who is also working in the space.
- Make up the mordant for each metal as explained above by measuring the Baumé, and fill a tank or tray. If citric acid is to be added wear gloves, a waterproof apron, a dust mask and a visor when handling and weighing (on digital scales) the powder.
- The mordant must be labelled clearly with the name, the recipe, the date when it was made and the type of metal which may be etched in the bath (e.g. copper only).
- Bite a small sacrificial piece or offcut of copper to take the sting off the mordant, as the first bite is often erratic and may damage resists. When the mordant is stable, make some test plates for aquatint and line work. Note on the test print the type of resist, the etching times for each panel, the room temperature, the date and the Baumé of the etching solution at the time of etching the plate. Mordants can often last for several years, only requiring the occasional addition of a small

quantity of water to counteract evaporation. A wipe-clean board or piece of paper near each mordant is useful for notating the date and results of any further checks of the Baumé.

• A lid to help reduce the evaporation of the water can be placed over the mordant once it is made up. The lid must always be removed during etching.

ETCHING WITH FERRIC CHLORIDE MORDANTS

The plate is flash bitten as a preliminary test etch (see 'Working method'). After flash biting, the standard etching procedure which is described below can be followed.

Equipment and materials required

Work in a ventilated, warm, well-lit and equipped mordant area (see pp. 48–49).

- nitrile gloves, waterproof apron and visor
- a tray or tank containing the mordant
- plate holders if a tray is being used
- a rinsing tray
- a waterproof marker pen
- a timer
- some test plates
- plate to be etched
- scissors
- a handling strip
- parcel tape
- a room thermometer

Working method

• The plate should be backed and hold resists on the front side. Attach a PVC hanging strip onto the back of the plate with parcel tape. Make sure that this is secure and write the time and an identifying note on the end of the strip with a waterproof marker pen.

• Work in the mordant area and always wear the correct safety equipment. Be aware and take care not to splash any mordant on anyone else working in the space.

• To make a flash bite, examine the plate and note the colour of the exposed areas of metal; carefully immerse the plate into the mordant for one or two minutes; lift out the now slightly etched and darkened plate and check for any areas of shiny metal. These bright spots reveal that the plate is not etching in these areas and it should be rinsed and examined. A thin layer of resist or grease may be causing the problem. The plate should be deoxidized with a solution of vinegar and salt, and the problem addressed and solved before trying to etch the plate again.

• When all the exposed areas of the metal are biting correctly, the plate may be etched so that the indentations will hold ink. The length of time it is etched will determine the depth of the bite and ultimately the darkness of the tone on the print. If the

below left A dip tank with a plate on a hanging strip being etched in the Edinburgh Etch mordant. The sink on the right contains a tray of copper sulphate solution.

below right A copper plate lifted from the mordant is ready to be rinsed and examined (see detail of print, p. 97).

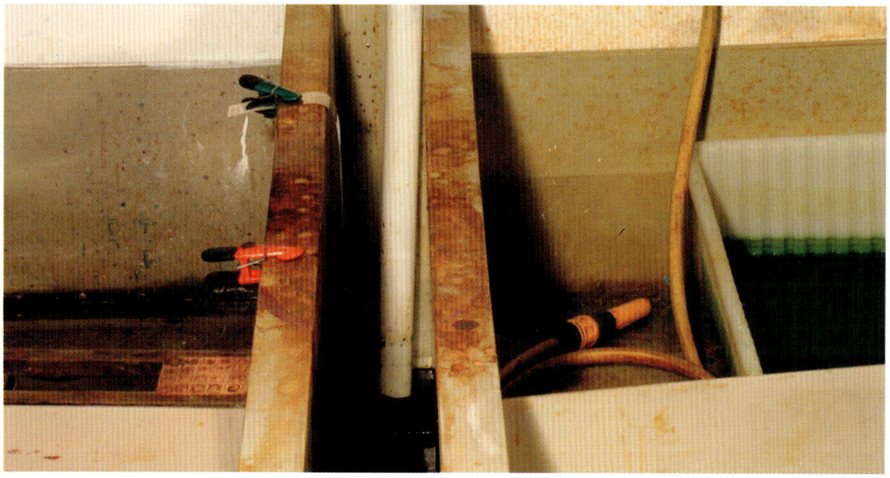

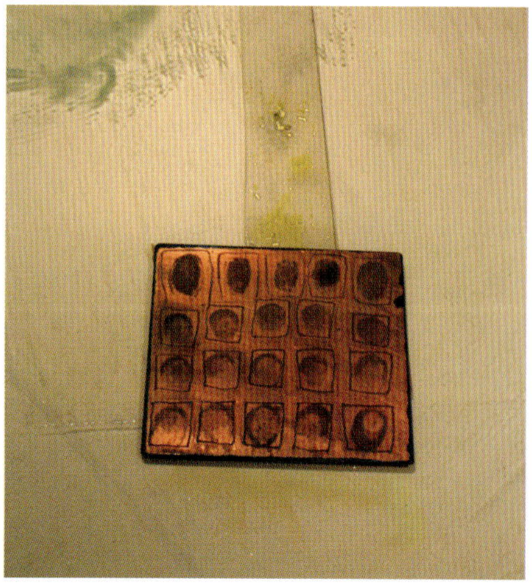

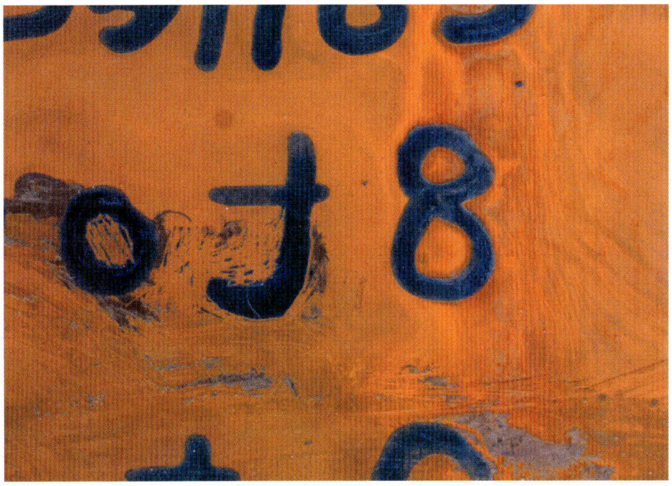

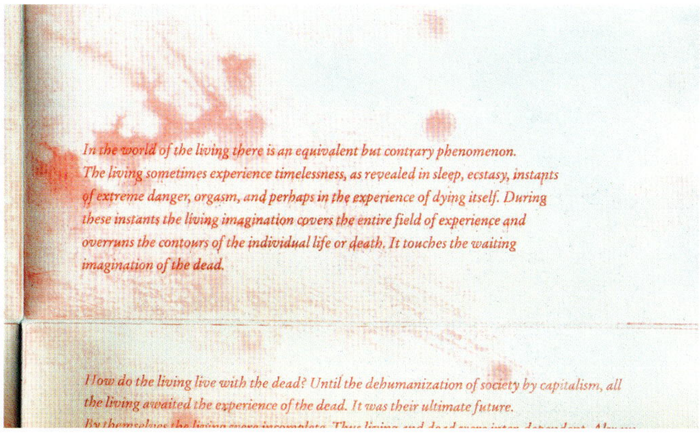

plate is over-etched the resists may break up or the lines may become undercut or dots detached. To determine the optimum time, previous test plates and prints should be studied.

- A note should be made of the planned duration of the etch and this can be monitored with a timer.
- After etching the plate, it can be rinsed with water. Care should be taken to avoid splashing when the plate is rinsed, especially if the handling strip is removed at this stage. A safer way of rinsing the plate is to place it in a tray of water and to remove the handling strip underwater.
- If further resists such as an aquatint or stop-out (for the stage-biting process, see pp. 122–123) are to be added to the plate, it should be de-oxidized, neutralized and dried.
- The resists can be stripped after the plate has been rinsed and de-oxidized.
- The stripped plate is then de-oxidized, neutralized and dried before adding further resists or inking-up and printing.
- Remove safety clothing and wash hands thoroughly after finishing work in the etching area.

SPIT BITING WITH FERRIC CHLORIDE SOLUTION

Soft etched effects can be created by painting ferric chloride mordant directly on a plate sprayed with an aquatint. The painted-on mordant will etch between the fine dots of resist,

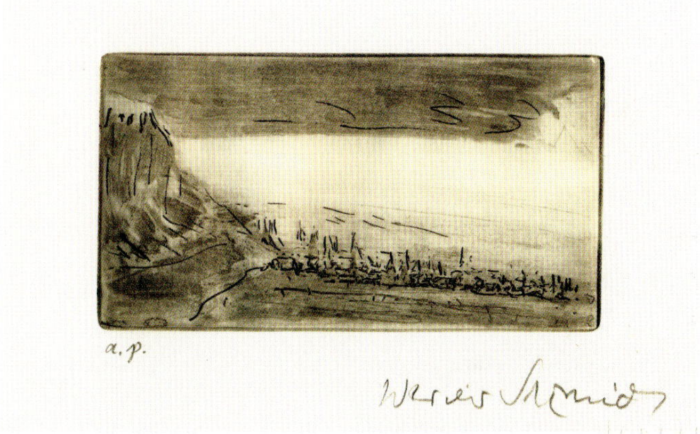

top left Oxidization after open-bite etching a relief copper plate holding stop-out resist (see stripped plate on p. 120 and print on p. 59).

top right The text on a group of brass plates was etched in a mordant bath, after which the soft marks were made by spit biting the assembled piece, which was then printed as a whole: this illustrates a detail (see print on p. 228 and a plate detail on p. 96).

above Werner Schmidt (Germany/Switzerland), *Untitled,* etching, 18 x 9 cm (7 x 3 in.), 2005. The soft edges of these fine aquatints were created by using Lascaux Resonance Gouache to contain the ferric chloride mordant during the spit-biting process (the brass plate can be seen on p. 62). The lines were drawn through Lascaux Soft Resist and the plate was bitten in a dip tank.

creating a reticulated structure which will hold ink and print as soft tonal marks.

Equipment and materials required

Work in a ventilated, warm, well-lit and equipped mordant area (see pp. 48–49).

- nitrile gloves, waterproof apron and visor
- a plastic workboard
- a small container of ferric chloride solution measuring between 45° Bé and 35° Bé
- a rinsing tray
- a timer
- some aquatinted test plates
- a plate (holding a fine uniform aquatint)
- paintbrushes
- a room thermometer
- a notepad and pen

Working method

- Work in the mordant area and always wear the correct safety equipment. Be aware and take care not to splash any mordant on anyone else working in the space.
- Some test plates should be made to ascertain the correct biting times. The etching time is generally longer than when the plate is immersed in a mordant of the same Baumé.
- The plate should be backed and hold a fine uniform aquatint on the front face. Areas which are to remain white or pale may be protected with stop-out resist, waterproof marker pens or oily crayons and other media. Lascaux Resonance Gouache can be used to contain the painted mordant and, as this material is not a true resist, a lively soft edge can be generated.
- The plate is laid on the waterproof workboard. The workboard or a notice should make it clear that the plate is being etched so that other studio users can take care.
- Some mordant can be poured into a china or glass dish. Some soap flakes can then be added to make a bubbly mixture which provides a different type of bite.
- The darkest areas of the image are painted on the plate with paintbrushes and left to etch.
- The mid-tone areas of the image are then painted on the plate and the darker areas repainted to strengthen the bite.
- After etching the plate, it is rinsed with water. Care should be taken to avoid splashing when the plate is rinsed. A safer way of rinsing the plate is to place it in a tray of water after etching.
- The rinsed plate is then de-oxidized, neutralized and dried before being worked further.
- Remove safety clothing and wash hands thoroughly after finishing work in the etching area.
- Resists should be removed from the plate before printing.

COPPER SULPHATE ($CuSO_4$)

The synonyms for this material are blue vitriol, cupric sulfate, copper (II) sulfate 5-hydrate, copper sulphate electroplating, BCS copper fungicide and blue stone. It is purchased as a blue, odourless, crystalline solid and it is soluble in water. The solution can be used to etch zinc, aluminium and steel and unusually the metals can be etched in the same bath.

Nik Semenoff and Cedric Green have been responsible for promoting the use of copper sulphate as a safer mordant. Previously it was not commonly used by printmakers, although it has been suggested that Goya may have used it as an etchant.

Although it is used by organic farmers as a pesticide, copper sulphate is classified as very toxic to aquatic organisms and may cause long-term damage in the environment. When farmers spray this chemical (as Bordeaux mixture), the fine mist presents a health hazard and can result in a condition known as 'vineyard sprayer's lung'. Symptoms include weakness, malaise, loss of weight, a cough and greenish-brown sputum. Swellings may occur in the liver and lungs. For this reason the mordant should never be sprayed in a fine mist.

Dust from copper sulphate crystals is harmful by inhalation and may cause irritation to the mucous membrane. Particles in the eye could cause inflammation, damage to the tissue, corneal opacity and possible adhesion of the eyelid to the eye. Prolonged skin contact with the material may cause irritation and possible sensitization or dermatitis. Local ventilation should be used when plates are being etched.

MAKING UP A COPPER SULPHATE MORDANT

This recipe is based on the innovative work of Semenoff and Green. It is Semenoff's weak recipe for aquatint and delicate resists minus 'Sani Flush'. Green does not add 'Sani Flush' but his Bordeaux etch contains more copper sulphate than this mordant. It is used in a flat tray and plates are bitten facing up. This mordant will etch zinc, aluminium and steel reliably without attacking the resists. Other recipes which contain a high quantity of salt tend to break down many types of resist. Aluminium has a rather unusual behaviour when etched with copper sulphate (see below).

Equipment and materials required

Work in a ventilated, warm, well-lit and equipped mordant area (see pp. 48–49).

- nitrile gloves, waterproof apron and visor
- a tray suitable for the mordant
- copper sulphate powder
- sodium chloride (table salt)
- digital scales
- a notepad
- a plastic syphon
- some calibrated plastic jugs
- a waterproof marker pen

Recipe

10 litres of tap water
500 gms of copper sulphate
125 gms of sodium chloride (table salt)

Working method

- Use a calculator to determine the quantities required to fill a flat tray. Make a note of the recipe and of the date.
- Position the tray which is to become the etching bath in its correct place in the etching area.
- Measure the water using a clean measuring jug and pour it into the flat tray.
- Weigh out the quantity of sodium chloride (salt) required using digital scales and dissolve this in the water.
- Work in the mordant area and put on gloves, a waterproof apron, a dust mask and a visor before handling and weighing (on digital scales) the copper sulphate crystals. Close and put away the copper sulphate storage container.
- Carefully add the copper sulphate crystals to the water and salt solution in the tray.
- Stir the mordant with a plastic spatula until the blue copper sulphate crystals are dissolved. The mordant is then ready to use. A lid can be placed over the mordant when it is not in use.
- Tidy up the area before taking off the dust mask.
- The mordant must be labelled clearly with the recipe, the date when it was made and the metals which may be etched in the bath (e.g. zinc, steel and aluminium).

ETCHING WITH COPPER SULPHATE

Some test plates for steel, zinc and aluminium should be bitten and the prints taken from these may be displayed nearby to show biting times and the characteristic etched effects. On aluminium plates linework and tonal areas created with the puncturing method (see pp. 125–126) work well but broad open lines or marks and aquatinted areas generally do not perform well.

As an approximate guide, biting times at normal room temperature (20°C) will give a strong line or open bite in 20 to 30 minutes. A deep aquatint is usually around 15 minutes.

Equipment and materials required

Work in a ventilated, warm, well-lit and equipped mordant area (see pp. 48–49).

- nitrile gloves, waterproof apron and visor
- a tray containing the mordant with lid

- a notepad
- a rinsing tray
- a handling strip
- parcel tape
- a waterproof marker pen
- a timer

Working method

- Work in the mordant area and always wear the correct safety equipment. Be aware and take care not to splash any mordant on anyone else working in the space.
- The plate should be backed, have a handling strip and hold resists on the front side. To create controllable tonal areas on aluminium plates the puncture method should be used.
- The first stage is to flash bite the plate. When all the exposed areas of the metal are biting correctly, the plate may be etched so that the indentations will hold ink.
- A note should be made of the planned duration of the etch and this can be monitored with a timer.

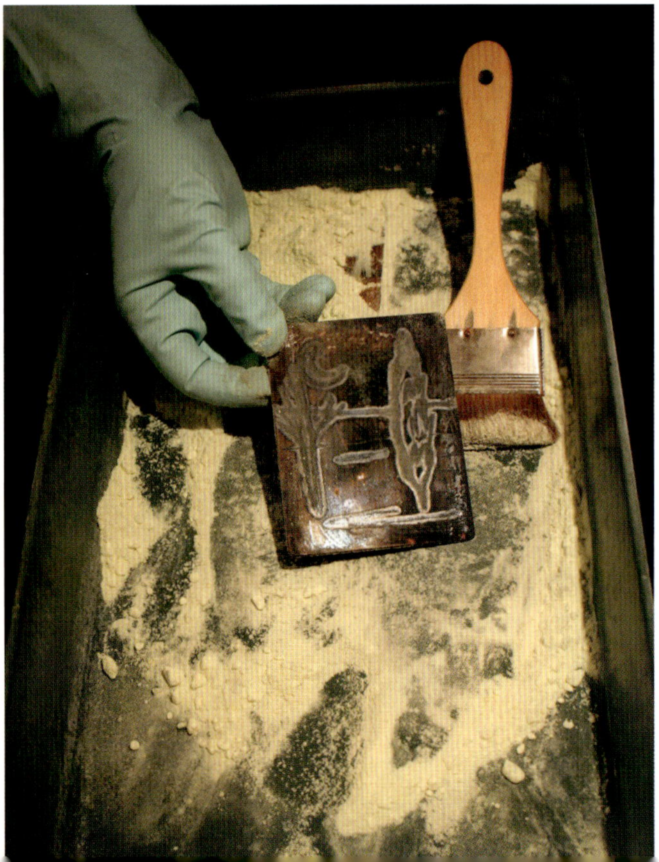

- During etching a thick, dark precipitate will form on the plate surface but this does not seem to inhibit the action of the mordant so feathering is not necessary.
- After etching the plate, it can be rinsed with water which removes the precipitate. Care should be taken to avoid splashing when the plate is rinsed, especially if the handling strip is removed at this stage. A safer way of rinsing the plate is to place it in a tray of water and remove the handling strip underwater .
- If further resists such as an aquatint or stop-out (for the stage-biting process, see pp. 122–123) are to be added to the plate, it should be de-oxidized, rinsed with a neutralizing solution and dried.
- The resists can be stripped after the plate has been rinsed and de-oxidized.
- Remove safety clothing and wash hands thoroughly after finishing work in the etching area.

SULPHUR (S)

'Flours' of sulphur is ground rhombic sulphur and is not readily available. However, 'flowers' of sulphur is the sublimed substance formed when sulphur (S) is purified by distillation and may be purchased from pharmacies or organic garden centres. It is used as an insecticide (the material is mildly toxic to aquatic organisms). The powder is slightly toxic if ingested or inhaled and is irritating to skin and eyes.

This yellow powder, which has a faint odour of rotten eggs, will lightly etch the surface of a copper plate over a number of days. The powder should be used in a well-ventilated (but not draughty) area. It should not be allowed to come into contact with moisture or oxidizers.

ETCHING WITH SULPHUR

Equipment and materials required

Work in a ventilated, well-lit studio.

A copper plate being removed from sulphur powder after etching for three days.

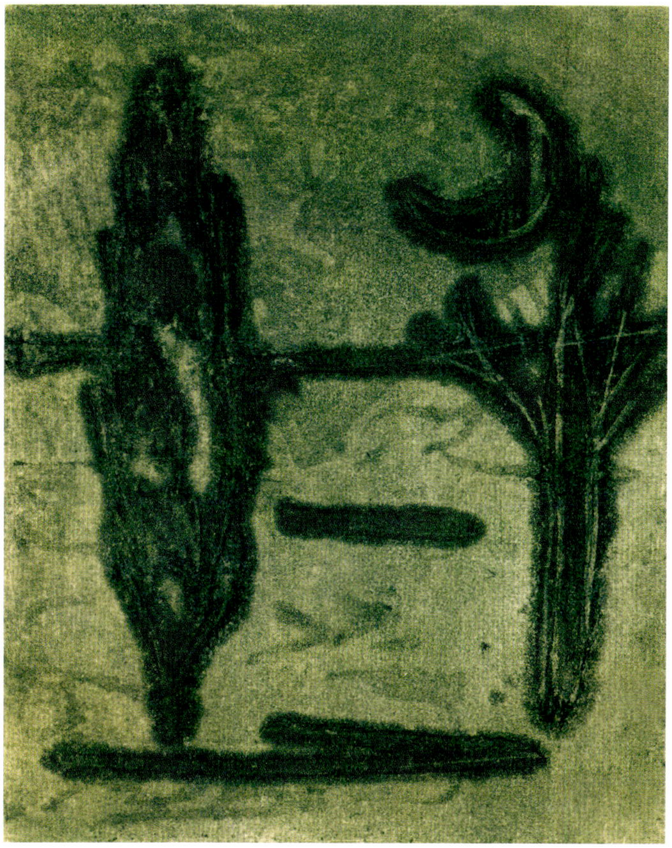

The plate illustrated opposite was inked up with water-washable oil paints and printed on cream paper.

- a polished, worked copper plate or plate holding resists (e.g. aquatint)
- some conté crayons, compressed charcoal or charcoal powder
- some paintbrushes
- some virgin olive oil
- some flowers of sulphur (sulphur sublimed BPC)
- a plastic tray
- a lid

Working method

- Prepare the plate and apply any resists that are required (acrylic resists will be unaffected by the virgin olive oil). Paint the oil in the form of the image or on the area to be etched. Interesting results may also be obtained by painting with a mixture of oil and conté crayon dust: this combination makes a grainy black paint which is easy to see on the plate and provides a different effect. Alternatively, a crayon can be used to draw directly on the plate. The finished drawing should then be painted over with oil. Historic recipes involved painting the image on a polished plate with lavender oil or olive oil, then sprinkling the oily image with powdered sulphur before leaving it to etch. The oily areas etched very lightly and the unprotected copper remained unharmed. Other recipes have suggested mixing the oil with the sulphur, then painting with the resulting paste, and one recipe suggested using honey as the painting medium.
- Lay the worked plate in the dry plastic tray.
- Put on gloves, an apron, a dust mask and eye protection before carefully covering the plate with a thick layer of flowers of sulphur. The sulphur is soluble in oil and therefore will only etch the oily areas.
- The plate should be left undisturbed for at least several hours so that it can absorb the sulphur powder (this helps prevent loose oil running or smearing). The plate may then be tilted so that the excess sulphur falls from the unpainted areas of copper into the tray. The lines of the image will be coated with a wide, thick crust of yellow sulphur powder.
- For good results leave the plate to etch for three days or more. Store the tray in a safe dry place and label it clearly (with the name of the chemical, the fact that a plate is being etched, and the date).
- After several days lift the plate from the powder (wear protective clothing). Use a soft, wide brush to remove all the loose sulphur from the plate.
- The plate may be wiped with a soapy disposable rag and deoxidized.
- The etched image can then be examined before any resists are removed, or the plate is worked further (i.e. with direct or collagraphic methods) or is inked-up and printed.

COLLAGRAPHY

COLLAGRAPHY

Collagraphy is an additive process which may be used to make intaglio plates. The method is often associated with vigorously made work which has rough textured surfaces and collaged elements. However, collagraph plates can be made which hold fine lines, textures, a range of controllable tones, offset marks and delicate impressions. The prints may resemble fine linear etchings, mezzotints, aquatints, deeply etched open bite or photo-etchings.

Collagraph plates can be made from metal, plastic, wood or heavy card. The plates may be new, or may have been worked with direct methods, or may have been previously etched. New plates should be grained and then coated with a layer of Lascaux Hard Resist or an acrylic varnish. This practice seals the plate, allows accurate control over the background tone and makes a good base to which the acrylic media can bond.

The image is formed by building up the plate surface and working into the added media. This may involve adding a medium (acrylic varnish, paint, resist, gesso, texture gel, medium or glue) or another material (paper, photopolymer, abrasive paper, adhesive tape, feathers, wood, metal, fabric, plastic, plant material, sand or carborundum) to the plate. The natural characteristic of the added media may be ink-holding, non-ink-holding or both. Ink-holding materials include acrylic gesso, texture gels and modelling pastes. Non-ink-holding media include acrylic self-levelling gels, Lascaux resists, Speedball screenprinting filler, acrylic varnishes, PVA, smooth acrylic painting aids and some types of acrylic paints. Materials which have both smooth and ink-holding areas include fabric and textured papers.

In some cases, parts of the added layer are removed or displaced using direct methods, or are dissolved during the photocollagraphic process. However, in this additive process (unlike subtractive processes), the original supporting plate surface remains intact. Collagraphic techniques can be used singly or in combination with one another.

The durability of collagraph plates depends on the choice of plate substrate (metal plates are stronger and easier to ink up), preparation of the substrate, media used (some media may re-wet or become sticky), the construction of the plate (embedded materials must be securely held), inking up and printing pressure (some materials may peel, flatten or crack). For best results the finished plate may be sealed with a thin layer of a durable material such as Lascaux Hard Resist or Lascaux Varnish. If acrylic media are used, this intaglio method can be employed by all artists including children and

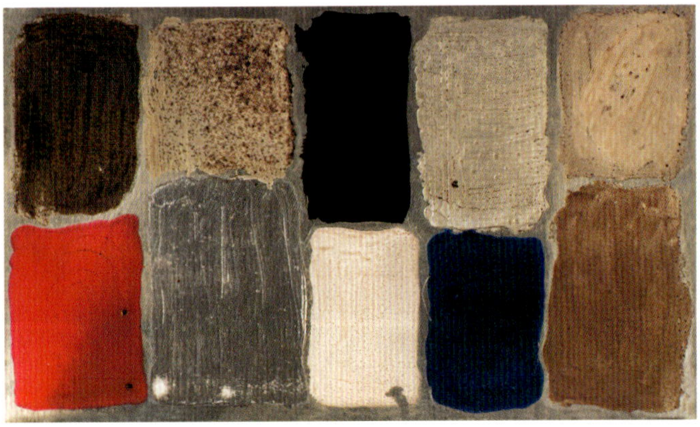

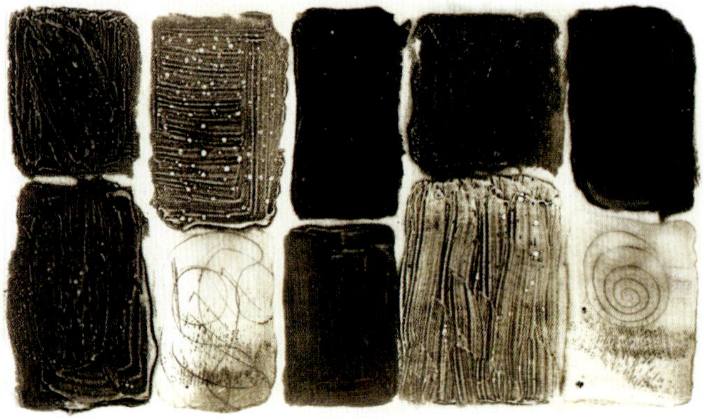

right The first zinc plate for *Bellini Wall* holds collage elements and a range of collagraph media, including Lascaux Gesso and Plate-Backing Resist. It was inked up in a yellow ochre ink and printed.

centre right The second plate for *Bellini Wall* is a photocollagraph. The artist painted a positive, which was then exposed in conjunction with a random dot screen to a zinc plate laminated with a layer of Photec. The developed and cured plate was printed with a sepia ink in register on the ochre print.

below right Victoria Crowe (UK), *Bellini Wall*, collagraph, 23.5 x 41.5 cm (9¼ x 16⅜ in.), 2004: the finished two-plate collagraph print.

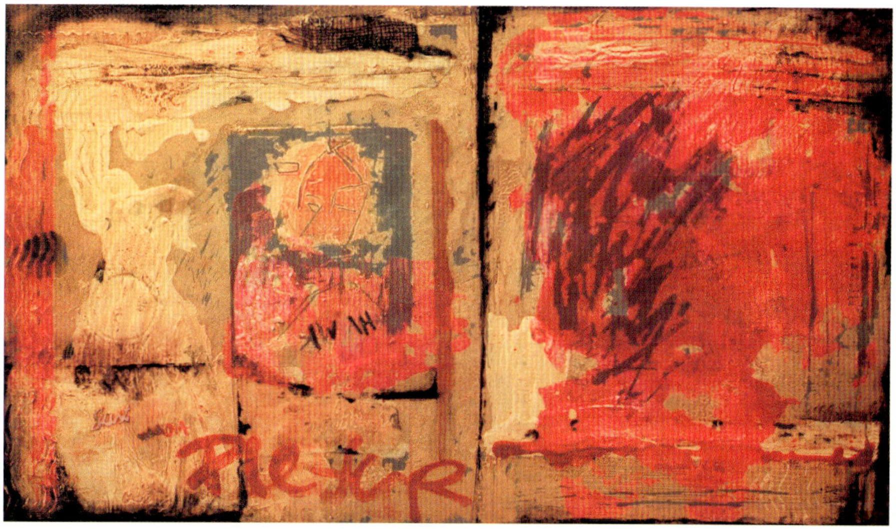

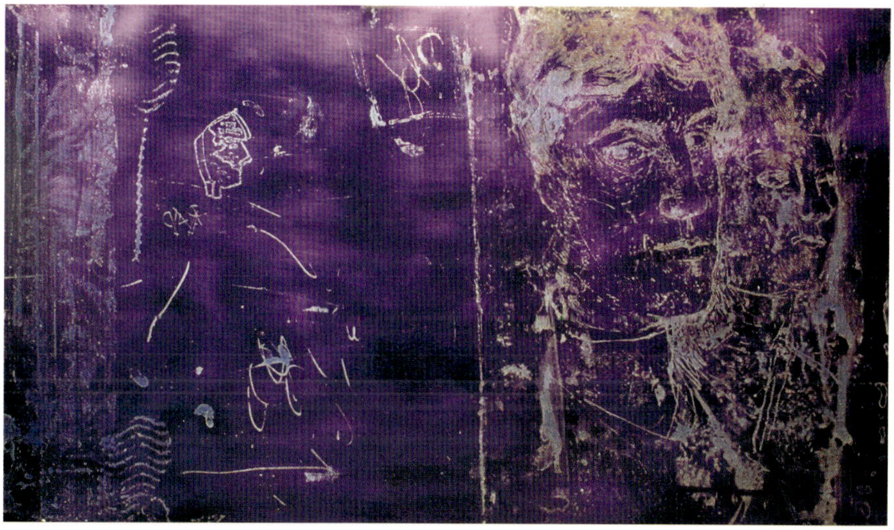

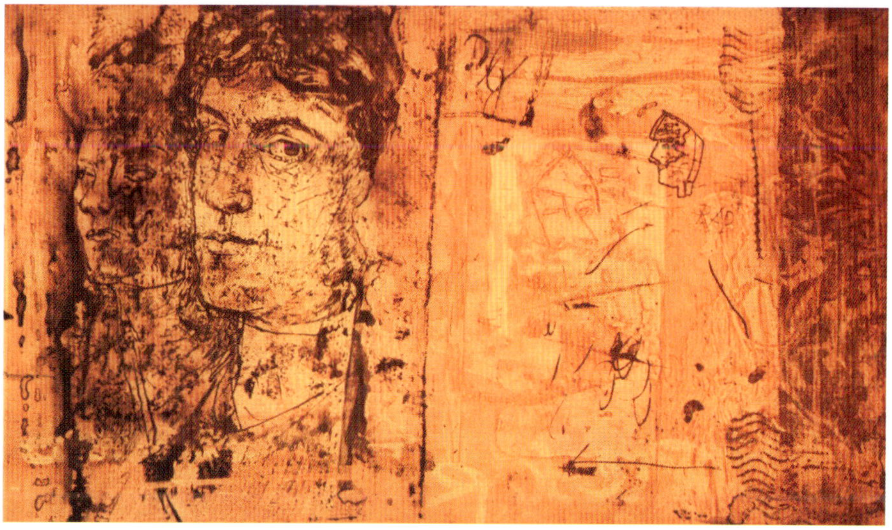

opposite left Lascaux modelling pastes, impasto gel, gesso, pastelground, plate-backing resist and stop-out resist were painted in small panels on this sealed zinc plate. The plate was made to test the different media.

opposite right The print from the test plate demonstrates how the materials printed.

high-risk groups. Acrylic media can also be stripped from metal plates after use, which makes this way of working economical (see p. 215).

CREATING FINE LINEAR WORK

Precise lines, clean sharp marks, impressions and delicate drawings which resemble finely etched lines can be made using collagraph media. Dark lines on a pale-toned or white background may be created either by using a photocollagraphic process or with the following method.

There are two stages involved: the first is forming a smooth substrate and the second is creating the image.

Equipment and materials required for forming the smooth surface

Work on a clean workboard in the drawing area.

- a prepared plate
- a clean, damp, flat sponge which is smaller than the plate
- a clean, wide, square-ended, flat, soft, fine-haired brush such as a sable or watercolour brush or a 5 cm (2 in.) Prolene brush made by ProArte
- Lascaux Hard and Soft Resists
- a china or glass palette
- a basin of warm soapy water, sponges and clean drying cloths
- a waterproof permanent marker pen
- a brush rest
- a drying cabinet

Principle: repeated layers of resist are painted on the plate surface to create a thick smooth surface which will not hold ink and may be worked into.

Working method for painting a base layer of non-ink-holding media

- A copper, brass, zinc, steel or aluminium plate may be used. Plates should be bevelled, cleaned, finely and evenly grained, and degreased, and may be backed with a varnish (to reduce colour contamination from the metal).
- Lay out the materials and make sure that the working area is clean and not dusty. Set out a basin of warm soapy water, some sponges and clean drying cloths so that it is easy to clean the brushes and other tools intermittently in soapy water. This practice will prevent the acrylic resist drying on the tools. When working with water-soluble resists or dishwashing liquid, it is good practice to wear gloves and an apron.
- Apply the first base layer of resist in exactly the same way that it is applied to be used in the etching process (see pp. 104–105). Dry the coated plate in a drying cabinet and then apply a second base layer. When this is thoroughly dry, apply the final image-making layer of either hard or soft resist.
- After the third layer is applied the image can be created using techniques suited to working into a wet layer, or the coating can be dried thoroughly and drawn into with etching needles.

Equipment and materials for making the image

Work on a clean workboard in the drawing area.

- the coated plate
- some feathers, leaves, fabrics, paint shapers, etc.
- etching needles, scrapers, roulettes, wire wool and wire brushes
- paintbrushes
- magnifying glass
- a china or glass palette

Principle: the impressed marks or lines drawn into the wet coating or scratched-away lines and marks in the dry coating will hold ink depending on their depth and width; any wide areas will print with an open-bite effect.

Working into the wet coating

- While the third layer of resist is still moist, feathers, leaves, lace, embossed wallpaper and other textured materials may be pressed into the coating to leave an impression which when

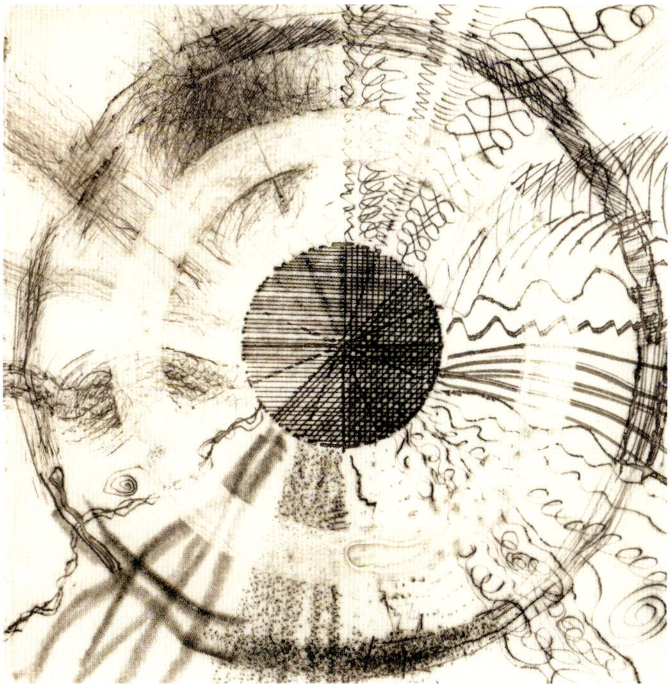

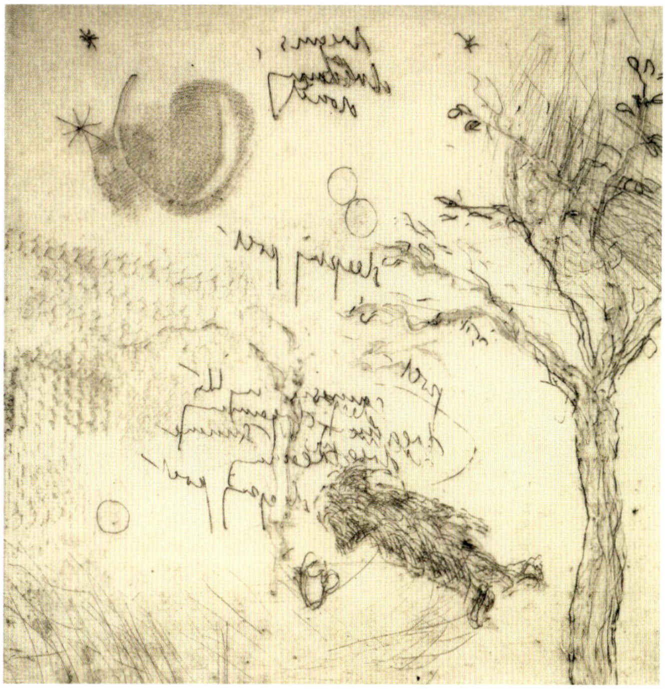

above left A print of lines and marks which were drawn into dried Lascaux Hard Resist. The inner concentric ring (which is lighter in tone) was formed by painting a final thin layer of stop-out resist over the marks to reduce their tonality.

above right A print taken from a plate on which fingerprints, impressions of netting and pencil marks were made in a layer of moist Lascaux Soft Resist.

dry will hold ink. Drawing into the coating with a brush handle will generate soft lines and marks. Water can be applied with a small brush to make marks and textures in the coating.

- Drawing errors may be repaired by filling carefully with some hard resist and redrawing.
- Other collagraph techniques may be used to build up the image.
- When the image is complete, the plate should be thoroughly dried before being inked up and printed in the same way as an engraving or fine etching.

Drawing into the dried coating

- The coating on the plate should be thoroughly dry.
- A guide drawing may be made on the plate or a coloured coating can be applied to the surface (see pp. 103 and 108).
- A range of etching tools such as needles, scrapers, points, roulettes, steel wool and wire brushes may be used to work into the layers (see p. 103). Tonal areas and marks can be created using techniques such as crosshatching and stippling.
- The waxy resist is easy to draw into and the excess can be brushed from the plate without smearing. It is not necessary to expose or scratch into the metal. The tonal quality of the lines and marks will be determined by their depth.
- Errors may be carefully filled with some hard resist. The plate is then dried and the correction can be redrawn.
- Other collagraph techniques may be used to build up the image.
- When the image is complete, the dry plate may be inked up and printed in the same way as an engraving or fine etching.

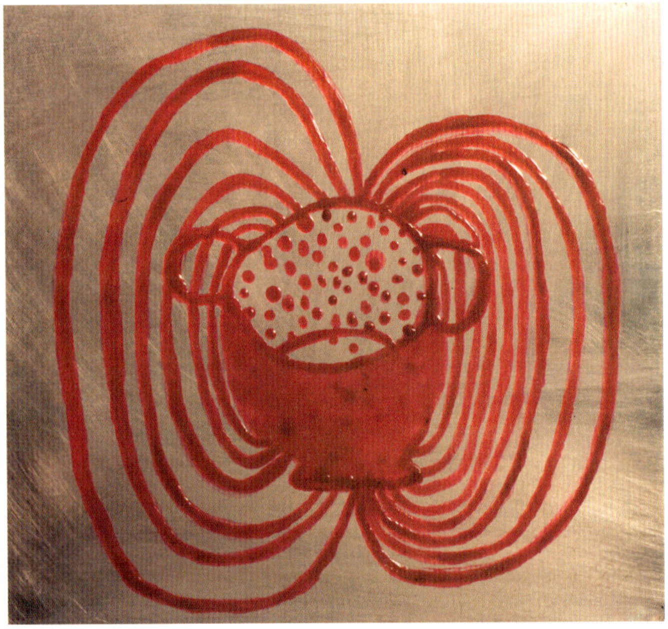

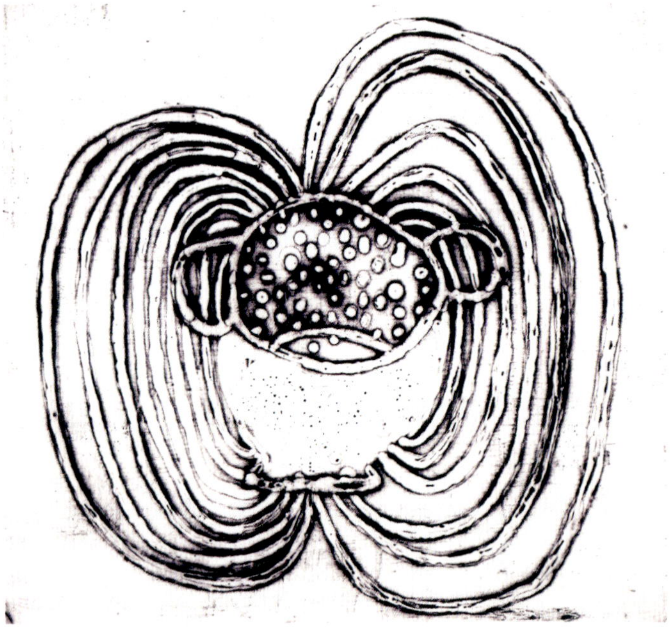

above left Lucy Cobb built up this image of a colander by painting onto a sealed zinc plate using Lascaux Plate-Backing Resist, which dried to form a smooth non-ink-holding surface.

above right When the plate was inked up and printed, the ink was held only on the outside edges or contours of the painted image.

CREATING CONTOUR LINES

Collagraphic media which dry with a smooth surface can be used to generate images constructed of contour lines which resemble the printed effect normally associated with open bite on a deeply etched plate (see p. 97).

Equipment and materials required

Work on a clean workboard in the drawing area.

- a prepared plate
- some soft paintbrushes
- Lascaux Stop-Out Resist, Lascaux Plate-Backing Resist or PVA
- a china or glass palette
- a basin of warm soapy water, sponges and clean drying cloths
- a waterproof permanent marker pen
- a brush rest
- a drying cabinet

Principle: each painted mark will only hold the ink around its contours: these thin lines will form the printed image.

Working method

- Plates should be bevelled, clean, degreased and dry. Scratches and marks on a plate surface will print: if a white or pale-toned background is required, the surface can be coated in several layers of Lascaux Hard Resist or other smooth-drying resilient media (see p. 164).
- Lay out the materials and make sure that the working area is clean and not dusty. Set out a basin of warm soapy water, some sponges and clean drying cloths so that it is easy to clean the brushes and other tools intermittently in soapy water. This will prevent the acrylic media drying on the tools. When working with water-soluble resists or dishwashing liquid, it is good practice to wear gloves and an apron.

• Paint the image so that it sits up in high relief on the plate. If stop-out or plate-backing resist is used, the image can be dried quickly and repainted until the correct height is achieved. A thick deposit of PVA may be painted onto the plate but the centre of each mark may take a long time to dry. If the plate is printed before the PVA has completely dried, the image may be squashed flat by the press. Images painted with PVA will often re-wet during the inking-up and printing process so it is important that the finished plate is sealed with an acrylic varnish (which does not become sticky).
• When the plate is thoroughly dry, it may be inked up and printed.

CREATING TEXTURES, TONES AND PATTERNS

Offset and impressed patterns and textures may be made using a variety of collagraphic media and techniques.

Some types of media dry to form a surface which feels evenly textured and will hold ink. These ink-holding media may be painted or offset directly onto the collagraph plates. They may also be drawn into to create lines and marks or worked into to create impressions or to hold collage elements. These media include acrylic gessos, acrylic texture gels, acrylic mediums mixed with fine carborundum grit and polyfiller (for repairing plaster) strengthened and made more flexible by adding PVA. It is important to select a material which can bond well to many types of substrate, is pleasant to paint with, can be worked into, maintains the definitions of marks made in it, provides a good even tonal range, dries quickly without cracking, becomes durable enough for printing and does not re-wet or become sticky during the printing process.

Lascaux Acrylic Gesso fulfils all of these criteria and dries to create a white surface which has a similar texture to an etched plate which has been finely aquatinted. There are different creative approaches: the image may be painted onto a smooth plate with gesso or the plate may be coated with a uniform layer of gesso and worked into. The tonality can be controlled by painting on thin layers of acrylic varnish (see 'Creating a Contrast', p. 172).

Photocollagraphs can also be made when textures are required, and screenprinting techniques can be used to introduce collagraphic marks to plates (see p. 176).

CREATING PAINTED AND OFFSET LINES AND MARKS

Equipment and materials required
Work on a clean workboard in the drawing area.

• a prepared plate
• some artists' brushes, decorators' brushes, toothbrushes and other tools
• some feathers, leaves, textured fabrics, etc.
• Lascaux Acrylic Gesso
• Lascaux Hard Resist
• a china or glass palette
• a basin of warm soapy water, sponges and clean drying cloths
• a brush rest
• a waterproof marker pen

Principle: an ink-holding medium is painted or offset onto the plate to create a range of linear and tonal effects.

Working methods

• Copper, brass, zinc or steel plates may be used. New plates should be bevelled, cleaned, grained, degreased and backed. Aluminium may be used if the metal is grained and sealed thoroughly with Lascaux Hard Resist before the gesso or other acrylic medium is applied. Previously etched plates should be clean and degreased (deep marks on these plates will show as embossed areas on the print). Plastic substrates and hardboard may also be used.
• If a pale-toned or white background is required, the plate should be coated with smooth layers of Lascaux Hard Resist (see p. 164). Acrylic gesso will bond well to the hard resist.

Alternatively the plate may be coated with gesso if the image is to be dark and close-toned.

- A guide drawing may be made on the plate with waterproof marker pens, conté crayons or pencils (and tracing paper) depending on the surface.
- Lay out the materials and make sure that the working area is clean and not dusty. Set out a basin of warm soapy water, some sponges and clean drying cloths so that it is easy to clean the brushes and other tools intermittently in soapy water. This will prevent the gesso drying on the tools. When working with water-soluble artists' materials or dishwashing liquid, it is good practice to wear gloves and an apron.
- Create the image on the plate by painting with gesso, off-setting gesso from leaves or paper shapes, using stencils, impressing fabric or feathers into the painted marks, working into the marks with water, or by spattering, dribbling and splashing with diluted gesso.
- When the gesso is dry, the tonality can be altered by painting thin even layers of Lascaux Hard Resist (see 'Creating a Contrast', p. 172).
- The dry plate can be drawn into (see p. 171), worked further with other collagraph media, or proofed and printed as an aquatint would be. Any high areas should be scraped down to prevent damage to the printing paper.

CREATING A BASE LAYER OF INK-HOLDING MEDIA TO WORK INTO

A layer of gesso or other ink-holding media can be used for drawing into, making impressions or embedding collage elements. Acrylic painting media can also be used to hold collage elements. The use of smooth non-ink-holding base layers suitable for drawing into is described on p. 164.

Equipment and materials required

Work on a clean workboard in the drawing area.

- a prepared plate
- a clean, damp, flat sponge which is smaller than the plate
- a clean, wide, square-ended, flat, soft, fine-haired brush
- Lascaux Acrylic Gesso
- a china or glass palette
- a basin of warm soapy water, sponges and clean drying cloths
- a brush rest
- a drying cabinet

Principle: three layers of gesso are painted on the plate surface to create a level ink-holding surface which may be worked into to create a range of marks.

Working method

- Copper, brass, zinc, steel, plastic, hardboard (Masonite) or card plates may be used. New plates should be bevelled, cleaned, grained, degreased and backed. Previously etched plates should be clean and degreased (deep marks on these plates will show as embossed areas on the print).
- Lay out the materials and make sure that the working area is clean and not dusty. Set out a basin of warm soapy water, some sponges and clean drying cloths so that it is easy to clean the brushes and other tools intermittently in soapy water. This will prevent the acrylic gesso drying on the tools. When working with water-soluble artists' materials or dishwashing liquid, it is good practice to wear gloves and an apron.
- Apply the first base layer of gesso in exactly the same way that Lascaux Hard Resist is applied in the etching process (see p. 105). Dry the coated plate in a drying cabinet and then apply a second base layer. When this is thoroughly dry, apply the final image-making layer.
- After the third layer is applied the image can be created using techniques suited to working into a wet layer or the coating can be dried thoroughly and drawn into.

DRAWING AND WORKING INTO THE WET MEDIA

Equipment and materials required

Work on a clean workboard in the drawing area.

• the plate, painted with gesso
• paintbrushes
• a basin of warm soapy water, sponges and clean drying cloths
• a brush rest

Principle: the impressed marks or lines drawn into the ink-holding layer will hold ink depending on their depth and width (printing as a close-toned image).

Working method
• While the third layer of gesso is still moist, leaves, feathers, lace, embossed wallpaper and other textured materials may be pressed into the coating and removed carefully to leave an impression which, when dry, will hold ink.

below left A proof taken from a plate coated with Lascaux Gesso which had been impressed while it was moist with ferns and netting.

below right The tone of the high areas of the plate was then reduced (see p. 172) and this proof was taken to assess the change.

• Brush handles can be used to draw into the coating to make lines and marks.
• Water can be applied to make textures and marks in the coating.
• Errors may be carefully filled with gesso and re-worked.
• Other collagraph techniques may be used to build up the image.
• When the completed plate has been dried, it may be worked further or inked up and printed in the same way that an aquatint would be treated. The marks and textures will print as the same tone as the surface gesso, so if a contrast is required see p. 172.

ADDING COLLAGE ELEMENTS

Low-profile collage materials (such as paper stencils, Japanese papers, crumpled tissue paper, tinfoil, doilies, lace, embossed wallpaper, dried skeleton leaves, gaskets, string, thread, wool, straw, grass, scrim and other fabrics) may be adhered to the plate surface or embedded in an acrylic layer. When the plate is dry, it can be inked up and printed to create collage effects and texture.

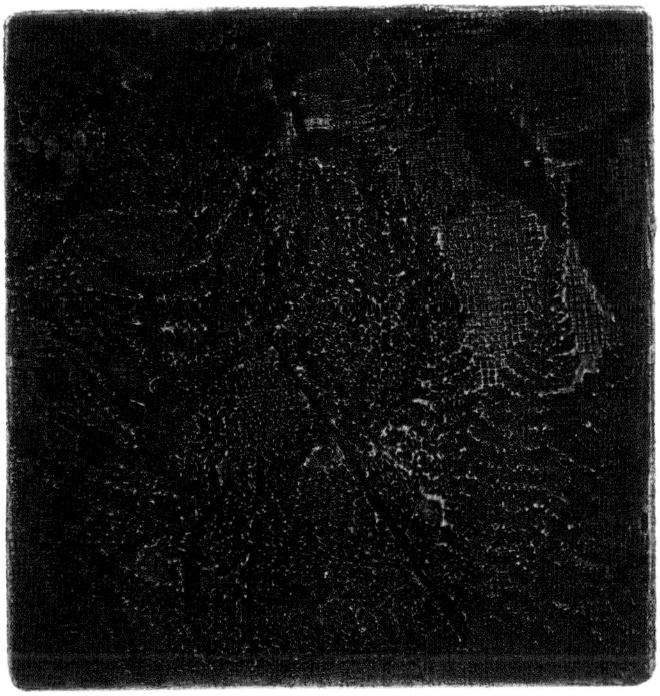

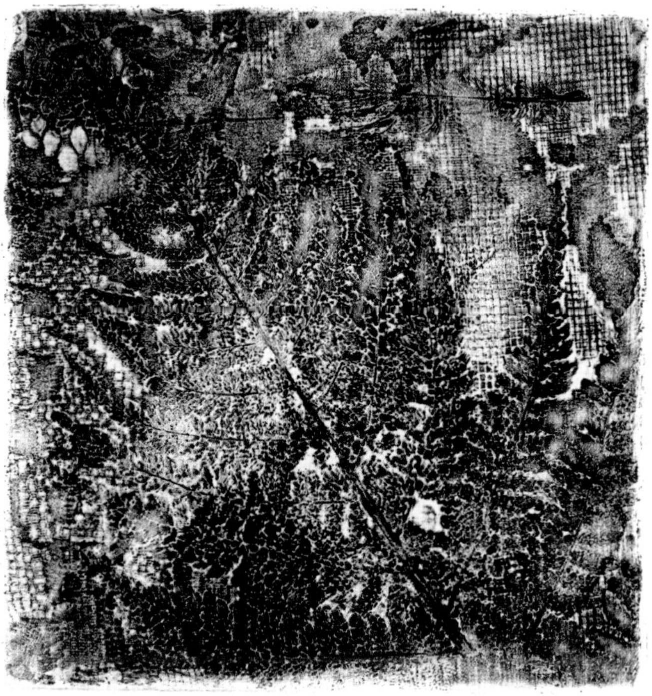

Equipment and materials required

Work on a clean workboard in the drawing area.

- a prepared plate
- low-profile collage materials
- decorators' and artists' brushes
- Lascaux Acrylic Gesso, Structura or Medium
- PVA
- a china or glass palette
- a basin of warm soapy water, sponges and clean drying cloths
- household dishwashing detergent
- a brush rest

Principle: low-profile collage materials are adhered to the plate, inked up and printed.

Working method

- Plates should be bevelled, cleaned, degreased and dry.

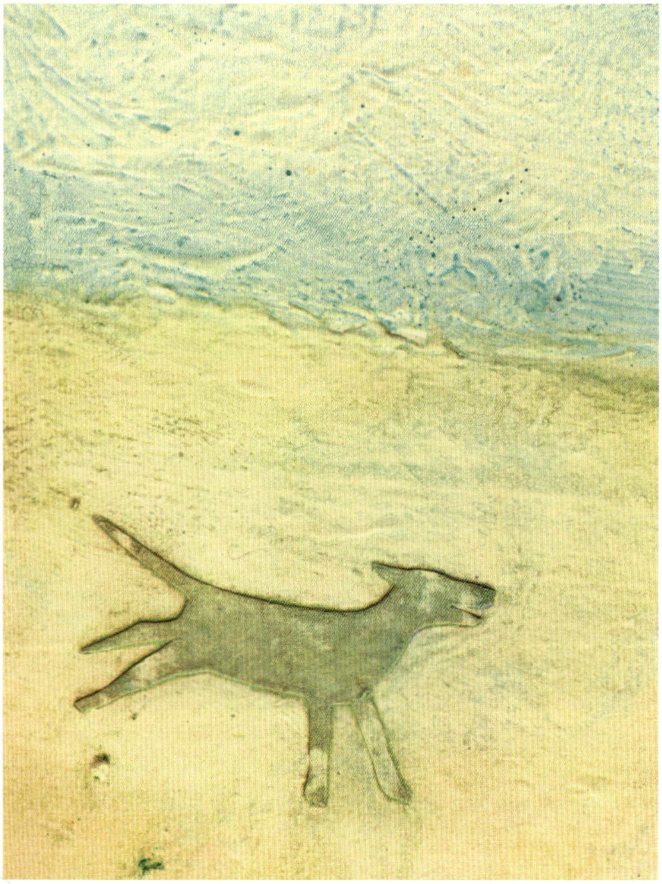

- Lay out the materials and make sure that the working area is clean and not dusty. Set out a basin of warm soapy water, some sponges and clean drying cloths so that it is easy to clean the brushes and other tools intermittently in soapy water. This will prevent the acrylic or PVA glue drying on the tools. When working with water-soluble artists' materials or dishwashing liquid, it is good practice to wear gloves and an apron.
- The collage materials will hold the ink in different ways and a wide range of printed effects can be achieved. The collage does not need to be in high relief to work well. For best results the added material should not only be adhered firmly but should also be embedded in the layer of gesso, medium or PVA on the plate.
- If a pale background is required, delicate materials may be embedded in a smooth layer of Lascaux Medium, whereas heavier materials will need a bed of Lascaux Structura or PVA to hold them. If PVA is used it must be dried overnight and then sealed with Lascaux Hard Resist or an acrylic varnish which will not become sticky during printing.
- If a tonal background is required the materials should be held in position in a bed of gesso or texture gel. Test plates can be made to experiment with these factors.
- If a mezzotint-effect background is required, a fabric with a grid-like structure should be selected. The ink will be held in the squares between the fibres, allowing a range of options to be explored by using different fabrics. Screenprinting mesh (recycled from screens which have been damaged) works well. The fabric should be adhered so that it covers the entire substrate in a flat layer. It can be held in a range of media but it is important to apply the layer very evenly to the substrate to prevent areas of the grid becoming filled (and therefore becoming non-ink-holding). Some practitioners use diluted black acrylic paint to hold the fabric or paint the fabric-covered plate black after it has dried. The image is then painted with a white acrylic paint which fills in the grid and dries to provide a smooth non-ink-holding layer (other heavy-bodied, non-ink-holding materials may also be used).

opposite A detail of a print from a plate which was made by painting with Lascaux Gesso and Structura. A cardboard dog shape was embedded into the media.

right Frances Kiernan (UK), *Conception* (from boxed piece entitled *String Quartet*), collagraph, 18 x 18 cm (7 x 7 in.), 2003 (detail). A spiral of string that was embossed to create this print, which is one of four pieces linked by string.

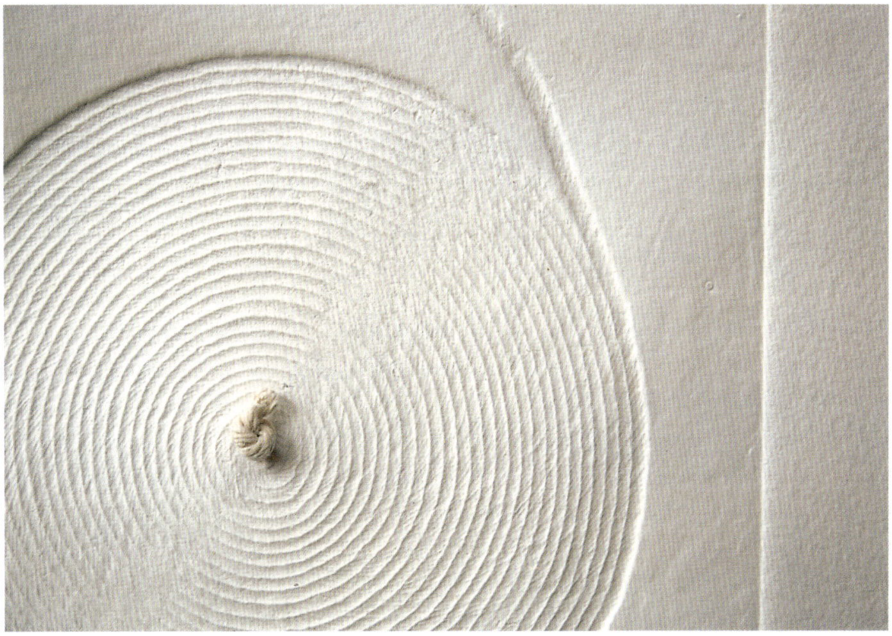

• Once the plate is dry it can be worked further or proofed and printed.

CREATING DRAWN LINES AND MARKS IN THE DRY, INK-HOLDING MEDIA

Equipment and materials required

Work on a clean workboard in the drawing area.

- the plate, painted with gesso
- etching needles
- paintbrushes
- a magnifying glass
- Lascaux Acrylic Gesso
- a china or glass palette
- a basin of warm soapy water, sponges and clean drying cloths
- a brush rest

Principle: scratched-away lines and marks in the dry, ink-holding layer will hold ink depending on their depth and width (printing as a close-toned image).

Working method

- The plate should be thoroughly dry before work begins.
- A guide drawing may be made on the gesso by tracing or drawing directly with pencils, conté crayons or a waterproof marker pen.
- The dry ink-holding media may be worked with direct methods such as drypoint. A range of etching tools such as needles, scrapers, points, roulettes, steel wool, wire brushes and abrasive paper can be used to work into the gesso to form ink-holding pits and indentations (see p. 103). It is not necessary to expose or scratch into the substrate which is holding the gesso.
- Any drawing errors can be corrected by filling in the mistake with gesso, drying the plate and then re-drawing.
- The tonality of the drawn image can be altered by laying down layers of Lascaux Hard Resist (see overleaf).
- Other collagraph techniques may be used to build up the image.
- When the image is complete, the plate may be inked up and printed in the same way as an aquatint.

CREATING A CONTRAST

The marks made in the gesso will print as the same tone as the surface gesso and will therefore be difficult to see. A contrast can be created by filling the tiny ink-holding indentations in the surface gesso with a thin film of Lascaux Hard Resist. The deeper lines, marks and textures of the image will not be filled and will remain ink-holding, printing as the darkest tones.

The coating has to be applied to the textured plate with care, as any excess resist will fill the deeper indentations and reduce the image's clarity and tonality. The instructions for applying a brush-on hard resist (see pp. 104–107) can be followed. One application of hard resist will reduce the tone of the top surface substantially. If, when the first layer is dried, a second layer is applied, the tone will yet again be reduced. Four layers will usually render the top surface smooth and incapable of holding ink.

CREATING, LINES, WASHES AND TONAL AREAS WITH CARBORUNDUM

Carborundum grains, pumice powder or sand can be used to create reticulated ink-holding surfaces on the plate. The ink is

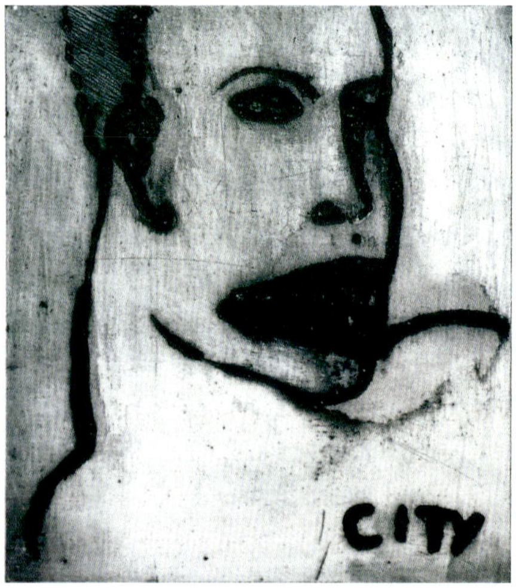

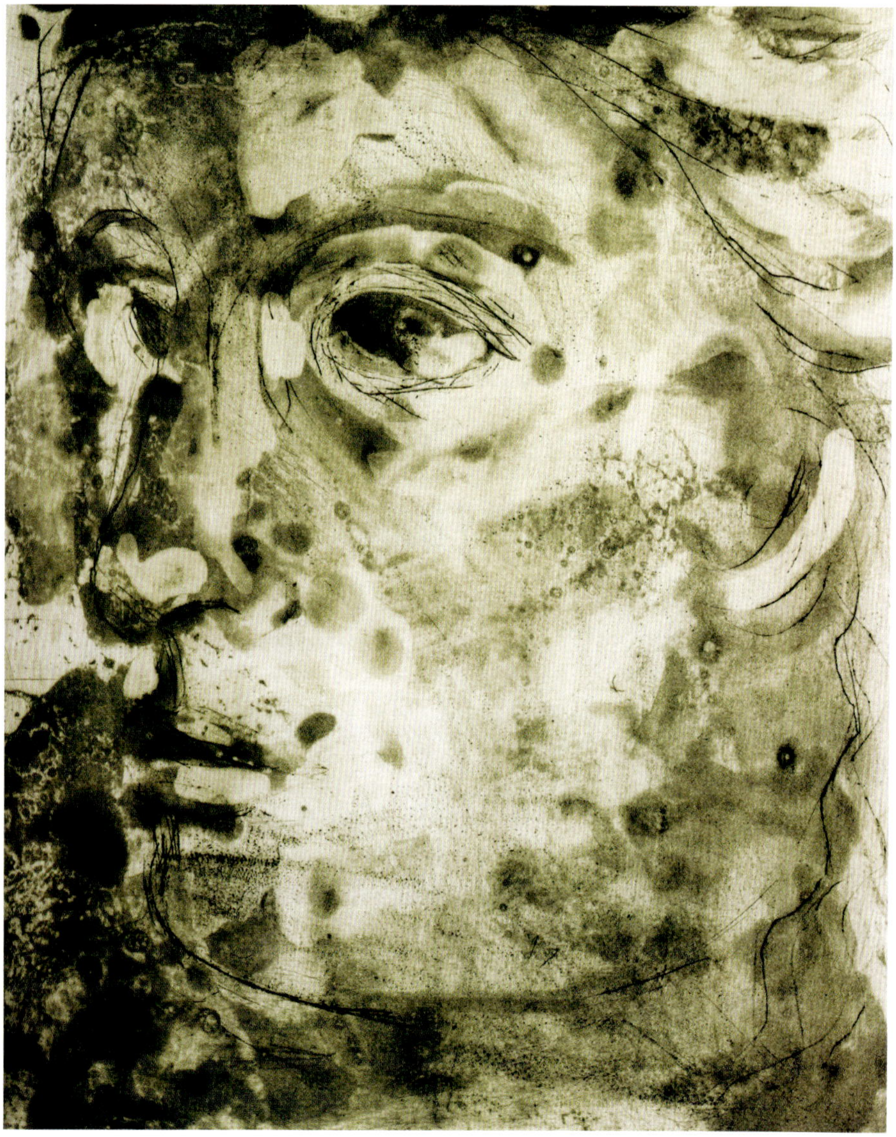

above Carol Robertson (UK), *City*, collagraph, 58.5 x 46 cm (23 x 18 in.), 1986. A print taken from a cardboard plate made by sprinkling sand onto lines painted with PVA glue.

right Sandra Casey (UK), untitled stage proof of collagraph, 19.7 x 24.5 cm (7¾ x 9⅝ in.) 2002. The zinc plate was painted with a layer of Lascaux Hard Resist which was dried and drawn into with etching tools. The artist then painted washes made with a solution of water, a little hard resist and a fine carborundum. Diluted hard resist was applied to introduce some lighter tones.

held between the particles and bold lines, subtle marks and tonal effects can be generated with great control. The tonality of these surfaces is determined by the size of the particles. The density and quantity of the grains will also control the tonal range: the theory of aquatint and halftones relates to this (see pp. 124 and 191). If the grains are fine and evenly spaced, the tone will look like a delicate aquatint; larger particles will create tones which are richer and heavier. Wash effects can be generated by suspending some particles in a solution of 250 mls of water and a few tablespoons of Lascaux Hard Resist.

The sand, carborundum or pumice must be very securely adhered to the plate or particles will detach during editioning. Gritty particles which become loose will become caught in scrim and can scratch the surface of intaglio plates. For this reason, separate inking-up materials should be used when particles are adhered to intaglio plates.

Equipment and materials required

Work on a clean workboard in the drawing area.

- a metal, plastic or hardboard (Masonite) plate
- dry sand, carborundum or pumice powder
- decorators' and artists' brushes
- Lascaux Acrylic Gesso, Medium or PVA
- wash solution as described above
- a china or glass palette
- a basin of warm soapy water, sponges and clean drying cloths
- household dishwashing liquid
- a brush rest

Principle: small, hard particles are adhered to the plate to create an ink-holding surface; the ink is held in the network of gaps between the particles.

Working method

- Plates should be cleaned, degreased and dry.
- Lay out the materials and make sure that the working area is clean and not dusty. Set out a basin of warm soapy water, some sponges and clean drying cloths so that it is easy to clean the brushes and other tools intermittently in soapy water. This will prevent the acrylic or glue drying on the tools. When working with water-soluble artists' materials or dishwashing liquid, it is good practice to wear gloves and an apron.
- A guide drawing may be made on the plate and either of the following methods can be used to create the ink-holding image.
- A section of the image is painted with medium, gesso or PVA and then the selected grain is sprinkled over the wet marks. The plate is then shaken and examined. The next section is painted, sprinkled and shaken and so on until the image is completed. The grains do not need to be in high relief to work well (examine and consider an aquatinted plate). A range of media and grains may be used to build up the complexity of the image.
- A wash solution can be mixed together and painted or poured onto the plate to create wash effects.
- Once the plate is dry it can be worked further or proofed and printed.

CREATING MEZZOTINT EFFECTS AND PALE TONES

Media which dry to create a smooth surface can be painted onto plates with an existing tonal structure to generate glowing whites and pale tones. A range of plate surfaces are suitable and include rocked plates for mezzotint, etched plates with a reticulated or scrobiculated surface, a photo-etching with a dotted surface, a photocollagraph with a dotted surface, a gesso-coated collagraph plate or a plate covered in a fine mesh.

Lascaux Hard Resist can be painted on to fill the indentations and create a smooth, non-ink-holding line or mark. This acrylic material is water-soluble, pleasant to paint with, and self-levelling. It dries quickly without bubbles, is highly durable, is unlikely to crack or flake, and does not become sticky during printing. The technique is highly controllable and artists can make up three (or more) different dilutions of

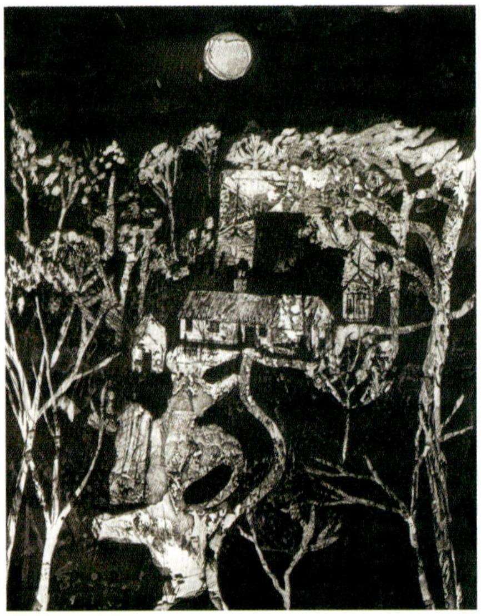

A detail from a print from an etched plate. Lascaux wash, hard resist, soft resist, aquatint spray resist and stop-out resist were used to generate the image.

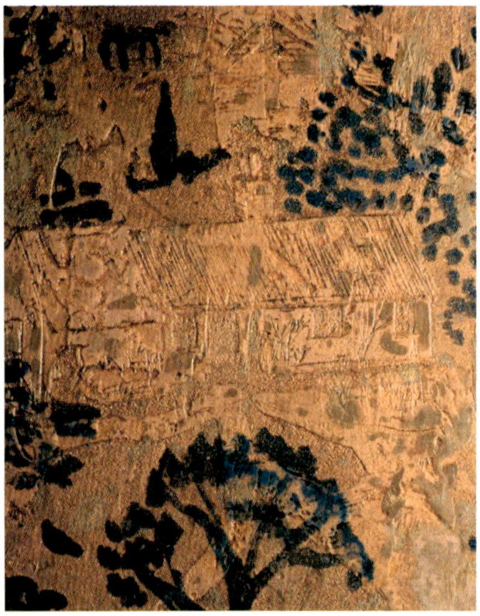

A detail of the surface of the same etched copper plate to which different dilutions of Lascaux Stop-Out Resist and water have been added by painting. Note the blue horse. The sky area was altered by polishing the aquatint down to reveal earlier stages.

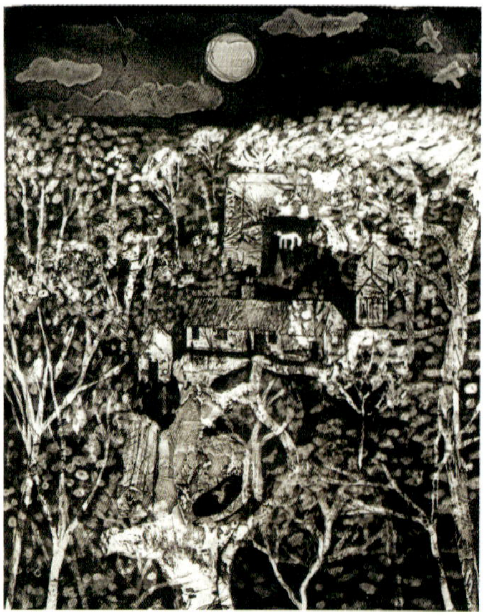

A detail of the print from the plate with the non-ink-holding collagraph media. Note the white horse, darker goose and sky.

hard resist and water to achieve a range of complex tonalities. Undiluted hard resist painted on a pre-rocked mezzotint plate will generate a line which will print as a glowing white. Wash effects can also be created on very finely textured surfaces. After editioning, the resist may be stripped from aquatinted and grained plates so that the plate may be re-used.

Experiments may be made with Speedball screenprinting filler, Lascaux stop-out and wash resist, and white acrylic paints and varnishes which are known (through test plates) to form a smooth, non-ink-holding surface when dry and be durable enough to print from.

Equipment and materials required

Work on a clean workboard in the drawing area.

- a plate holding a tonal structure
- some fine artists' brushes such as sable or Prolene Plus
- a magnifying glass
- Lascaux Hard Resist
- a china or glass palette
- a basin of warm soapy water, sponges and clean drying cloths
- household dishwashing liquid
- a brush rest

Principle: lines and marks are painted (with a smooth, self-levelling, non-ink-holding material) on an ink-holding plate surface to fill the indentations and to lighten the tonality in controlled increments.

Working method

- Plates should be cleaned, degreased and dry.
- Lay out the materials and make sure that the working area is clean and not dusty. Set out a basin of warm soapy water, some

sponges and clean drying cloths so that it is easy to clean the brushes and other tools intermittently in soapy water. This practice will prevent the acrylic drying on the tools. When working with water-soluble artists' materials or dishwashing liquid, it is good practice to wear gloves and an apron.

• Create the image by painting the hard resist on the plate (see above). The marks do not need to be in high relief to work well. The tone is dependent on how the indentations are filled and the smoothness of the painted marks. The self-levelling nature of the hard resist generates a smooth surface. The plate should be dried if further layers are required to make whites. Deeply bitten plates may require several layers, whereas the indentations on a pre-rocked mezzotint can be filled with a single brushstroke.

• The dry plate can be printed in the same way as a mezzotint or an aquatint.

Lucy Cobb (UK), *Drawing on Sound*, mezzotint and collagraph, 12 x 15 cm (4¾ x 5⅞ in.), co-published by Graal Press, 2004. The pale tones were created by painting three different dilutions of Lascaux Hard Resist onto a pre-rocked mezzotint plate. After the resist had dried the plate was printed.

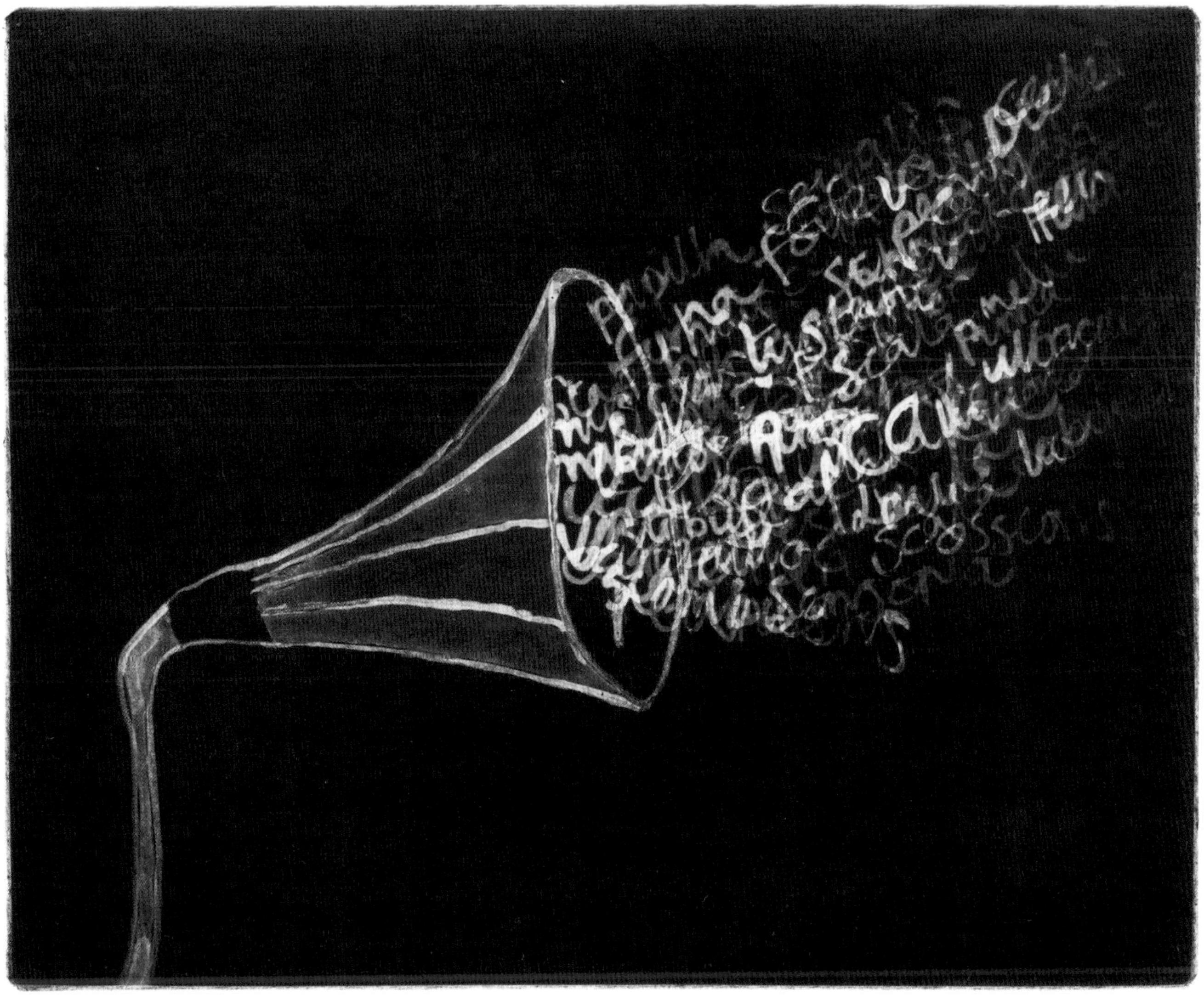

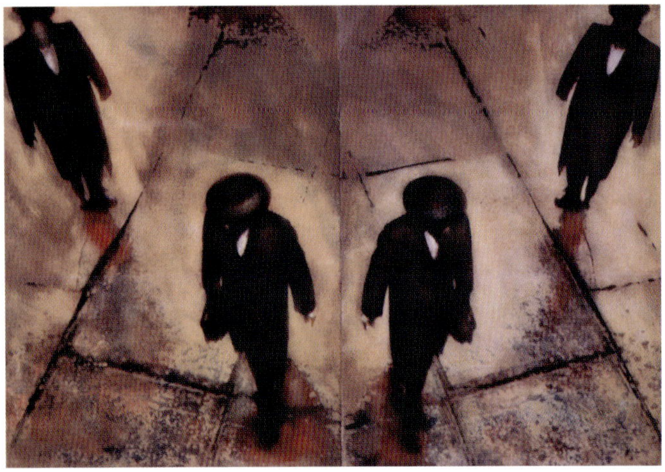

Karen Cunningham (US), *Underneath the EL,* collagraph, diptych, 76 x 152.5 cm (30 x 60 in.), printed and published by the artist at the Lower East Side Printshop, Inc., 2000. The artist screenprinted her own photopositive onto a Plexiglas plate using Rostow & Jung Carborundum Medium. She then inked up the plate using Akua inks to create this unique print.

USING SCREENPRINTING TECHNIQUES

Autographic, photographic, photocopied or digital imagery may be screenprinted onto collagraph plates which have a smooth or finely textured surface. Acrylic media which dry to a smooth finish can be printed to generate pale images, or acrylic gesso may be printed through a coarse mesh (40 T) to create tonal marks and lines.

Another tonal technique involves printing the image onto the plate with a sticky acrylic medium and immediately dusting on carborundum powder. The carborundum will stick to the wet lines and marks. After 10 minutes, the excess carborundum is shaken from the plate, and the plate is dried thoroughly. It may then be inked up, wiped and printed intaglio in the normal way. The carborundum-coated areas print with a dense, velvety appearance.

PHOTOCOLLAGRAPHY

Autographic, tonal, digital, photographic and photocopied marks and images can be held on a photocollagraph plate. The light-sensitive plate is exposed to ultraviolet light in conjunction with an image held on a positive and processed to create indentations in the surface. These pits and lines will hold the intaglio ink and the remaining smooth surface of the plate will wipe clean. The surface topography of a photocollagraph plate can be compared to an etched plate (see p. 61) and the printed results resemble photo-etchings or photogravures.

Once the plate has been cured and dried some artists use direct drawing methods and polishing techniques to work the surface but the processed light-sensitive layer is very tough.

However, collagraph materials and techniques can be used to build up the surface to create further complexity. There are many possibilities: collage elements may be added; painted layers of varnish can be used to lighten areas; gesso (or carborundum) may be applied to the surface to introduce marks or tone; or a further layer of light-sensitive film can be laminated to the plate.

The durability of a plate during editioning depends on the materials which have been selected and the quality of the processes involved. The process of making a photocollagraph print involves several stages.

- The artwork is generated in the form of a positive. A positive is a transparent substrate holding opaque marks which have been generated autographically, photographically, digitally or with a photocopier (see 'Positives', pp. 181–192).
- A sheet of light-sensitive film is laminated onto the plate (see pp. 142–144) or a plate may be purchased with a light-sensitive coating (see below).
- The light-sensitive plate is exposed to UV light in conjunction with the positive. A halftone screen is first exposed to the plate if tone is required in areas which otherwise would print with an open-bite effect.
- The UV light passes through the transparent substrate onto the light-sensitive plate. These exposed areas undergo a chemical

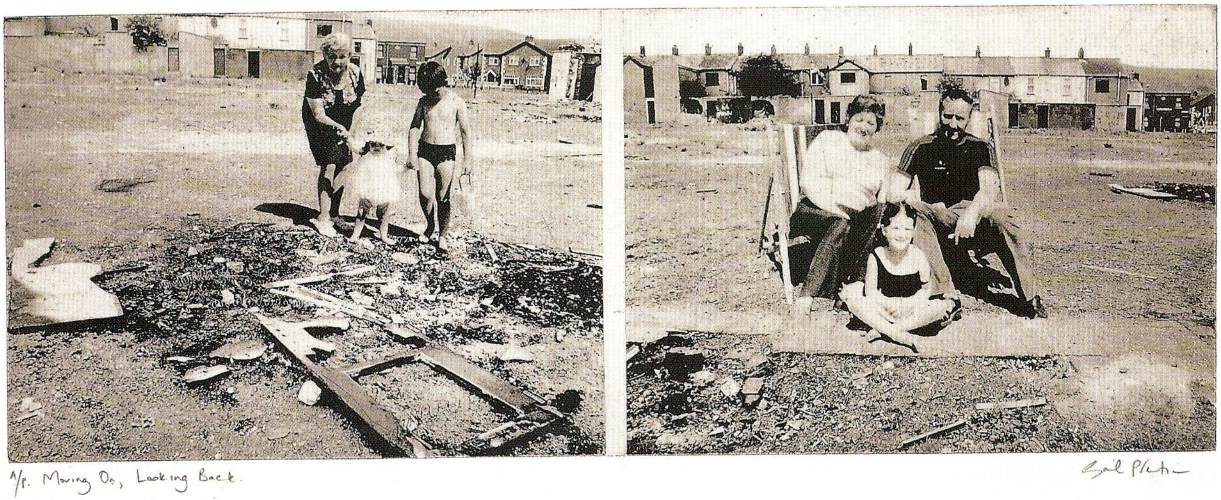

Gail Prentice (Northern Ireland), *Moving Forward, Looking Back,* 16 x 45 cm (6¼ x 17¾ in.), co-published in an edition of 25 at Seacourt Print Workshop, 2004.

change (known as crosslinking or photopolymerization) and will not dissolve during the developing process. The areas which are shielded from the light (by the opaque areas on a positive) will dissolve during the developing process, creating a range of indentations in the light-sensitive layer, which will hold ink depending on their depth. The plate holding the light-sensitive layer is unaffected by the process.

- The plate is cured and dried so that the layer becomes durable. The plate may be proofed and editioned or worked further with other methods.

USING DRY FILM PHOTORESIST TO CREATE PHOTOCOLLAGRAPH PLATES

Dry film photoresists are normally used to make photo-etchings but can also be used to create photocollagraphs. These materials are available in different shores, or thicknesses, and are sold under a variety of brand names (such as Photec and Z*Acryl: see pp. 140–141). Thin films which are suitable for photo-etching can be used, but if possible a thicker film should be selected for collagraph techniques as this will hold deeper indentations which can accommodate richer deposits of ink.

These films should be used in a ventilated studio, are developed easily in a mild alkaline solution, hold incredible detail, can be stored in the studio and can be removed easily from the plate (which can then be reused). Gloves should be worn when handling the film and when working on and inking up the plates.

LAMINATION METHOD

The film may be laminated onto finely grained metal plates, plastics, previously laminated photocollagraph plates and – to some degree – other materials such as varnished hardboard (follow the lamination method on pp. 142–144).

EXPOSING THE PLATE

After the artwork has been created in the form of a positive (see pp. 181–192), the exposure process can be carried out. A UV exposure unit with vacuum and light integrator can be used for high-resolution images and predictable results. Simple exposures may also be made outside using sunlight. See pp. 144–146 for detailed information on the various methods of exposure.

The image on the positive should be considered before the exposure process in order to judge the length and type of exposure that will be required. The correct exposure time can be determined accurately using a test plate and an exposure calculator such as a Stouffer 21 step guide wedge (for details see p. 144).

Broad or flat opaque areas on positives will ultimately print as an open-bite effect. These areas can be given a dotted structure which will hold the ink and print tonally if a halftone contact screen is used in conjunction with the positive which holds the image. This involves exposing the plate initially to a halftone contact screen (or a random dot aquatint screen) before exposing it to the positive. Halftone contact screens and positives are described in 'Positives' (see pp. 191–192). The standard method is to calculate the length of exposure required for the positive holding the image (e.g. 4 minutes) and then to expose the halftone contact screen first for double this length of time (e.g. 8 minutes). Theoretically if the plate were to be developed, dried, cured and printed at this stage it would print with an all-over tone. After the plate has been exposed to the halftone contact screen the positive holding the image is exposed to the plate.

The unshielded areas of the light-sensitive plate are exposed to UV light and become smooth and hard. These areas cannot hold ink and will not print. The areas which were shielded by the opaque image on the positive retain the tonal dotted structure from the initial exposure to the halftone contact screen. These pitted areas will hold ink and print, forming the image.

DEVELOPING THE PLATE

The developing method for photo-etching (pp. 146–148) may be followed, with the difference that the plate surface of a photocollagraph does not need to be revealed as the ink is held in the very shallow indentations in the light-sensitive layer. During the developing process it is very important to rinse the plate thoroughly with fresh solution and water as the indentations can be filled by residues in the developing solution. When photocollagraph plates are being made for the first time artists are often surprised at how much ink is held in such a fine surface.

Ettie Spencer (UK), work in progress, 25.8 x 14.3 cm (10⅛ x 5⅝ in.), 2004. The artist exposed her photocopy positive to a zinc plate coated with a layer of Photec. She developed, dried, cured and printed the plate with water-washable inks to create this print.

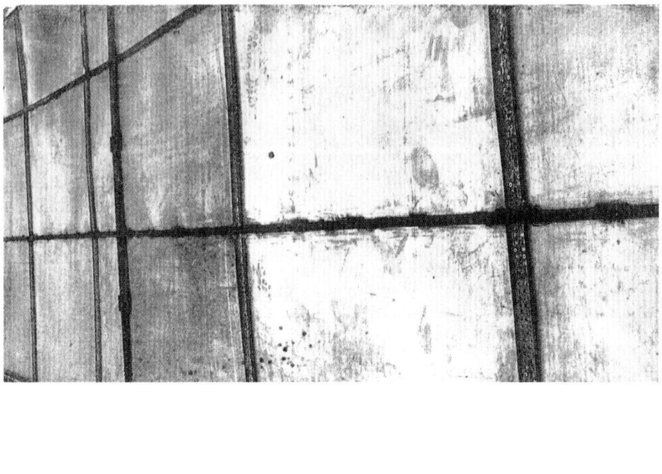

Spencer then worked the plate further by painting on gesso and hard resist. Carborundum was also sprinkled onto painted marks to create the dark tones. This print shows the changes the artist made.

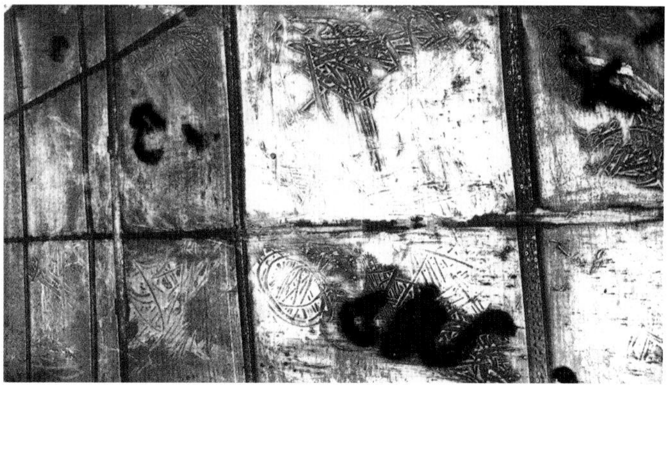

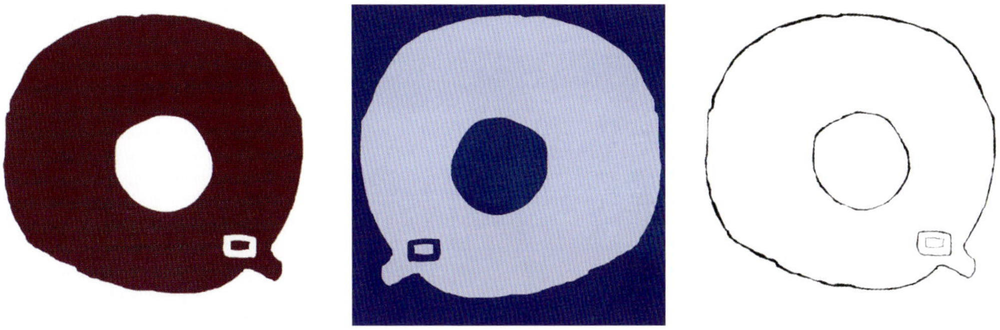

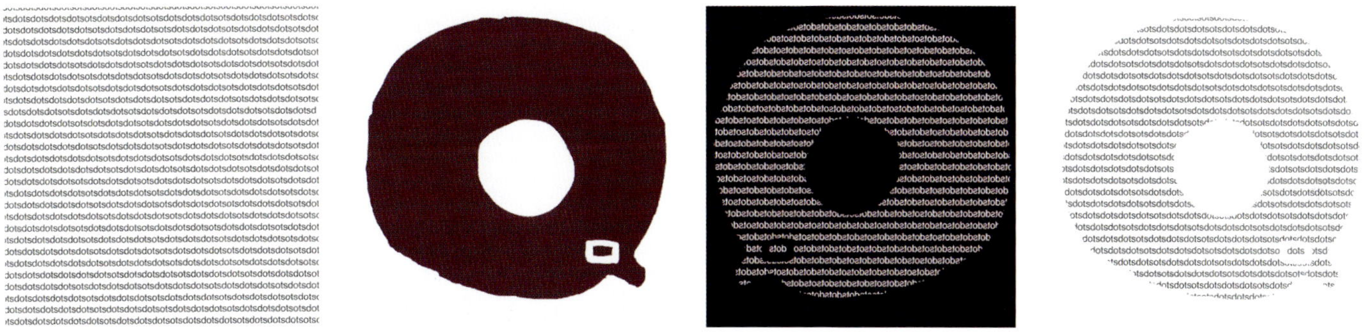

top row A schematic representation of the single exposure process. The upper three images (from the left) show:
1. a painted positive
2. the resulting photocollagraph plate after exposure, developing, drying and curing
3. the open-bite print from the plate.

bottom row A schematic representation of the double exposure process with a halftone contact screen. The lower four images (from the left) show:
1. a halftone contact screen or random dot screen
2. the same painted positive as above
3. the resulting photocollagraph plate after exposure to both the dot screen and the painted positive, developing, drying and curing (note the text – which represents the dots – within the Q shape)
4. the tonal print from the plate (again, note the text which represents the tone within the Q shape).

USING FLEXOGRAPHIC WATER-WASHABLE PHOTOPOLYMER PLATES AS PHOTOCOLLAGRAPHS

Light-sensitive flexographic plates which were developed for the commercial printing industry can also be used: these are very popular with printmakers although we do not use them in our practice. They are described by the industry as a 'laminated sheet containing water-soluble, photosensitive resin' and brand names include Solarplate (Torelief), Printight KM73 and Nylograv WSA52. Each plate consists of a steel or polyester plate which is firstly coated with an adhesive and antihalation layer, followed by a layer of photosensitive nylon resin which is protected by a cover film. After exposure the layer of nylon resin is developed in water.

These materials differ from dry film photoresists and during the developing and drying process a strong and unpleasant odour is released. Thereafter the plates give off an odour and therefore cannot be stored safely in the studio. They contain hazardous ingredients such as polyvinyl alcohol, derivatives of acrylates and methacrylates and photo-initiator and other additives. These include caprolactam, methyl alcohol, methyl acrylate and methyl methacrylate. The MSDS for Toyobo Company's products Printight KF-M, KM-M Type states that 'the prolonged inhalation of fumes or gases generated from the material during the processing operations may cause headache, respiratory irritation. Main symptoms: dizziness, headache, irritation to eyes and skin.' The MSDS also recommends that the following personal protective equipment is worn: 'a suitable gas mask depending upon the task, impervious rubber or plastic gloves, safety glasses, goggles or face shield and impervious clothing to prevent skin from contacting the material'.

EXPOSING PRELAMINATED FLEXOGRAPHIC PLATES

• Follow the guidelines given on pp. 177–178 but, before the flexographic plate is exposed, peel off the cover film with one continuous motion. Place the cover film in the waste container. Lightly dust cosmetic talcum powder over the tacky surface of the pre-laminated light-sensitive nylon polymer layer with a soft, wide brush. This prevents the positive from adhering to the plate during the exposure process.

DEVELOPING PRELAMINATED FLEXOGRAPHIC PLATES

The method of developing flexographic plates is different from working with dry film photoresists.

Equipment and materials required

- ventilation
- yellow lighting or shade is important
- gloves, visor, apron and respirator
- a folder containing the exposed plate
- a sink with water and hose
- water
- a thermometer
- two plastic jugs
- a tray larger than the plate
- a soft, clean scrubbing brush
- some sheets of newsprint

Working method

If the exposure has been made out of doors, work in the shade or wait until nightfall to develop the plate.

• Some artists have found that they achieve better results if the plate is left in the warm drying cabinet for 15 minutes before it is developed. The cabinet must be fitted with extraction if this procedure is followed.

• Before developing the plate, study the positive carefully, taking note of delicate lines which could be easily damaged and broader areas which will require more vigorous handling.

• Wear an apron, gloves, eye protection and a respirator.

• Make up two jugs of water with a temperature of between 68° to 78° F.

• Place the plate in the tray and pour a little water over the surface. Begin to scrub the plate gently with the brush. The bristles of the brush must be firm enough to be effective but should not damage the polymer which is to remain on the plate. Keep pouring on water and scrubbing. Keep a careful eye on the image as it develops and take care to work the surface equally. The process may take as long as 5 minutes.

• When the indentations look correct, lift the plate from the tray and rinse it with water.

• Blot the plate dry with some newsprint as water marks may print as blotches. Dust and hairs can become stuck on the surface of the plate at this stage and these can be removed by rinsing with water. The plate may then be placed in a ventilated drying cabinet or outside in the sun to dry.

• When the plate is dry, it should be exposed to the sun or UV light in an exposure unit until the surface does not feel tacky.

• The brush should be washed to remove any polymer from the bristles.

• The dried cured plate can be worked on further or can be proofed and printed.

POSITIVES

USING POSITIVES IN LIGHT-SENSITIVE INTAGLIO PRINTMAKING

When an image is to be transferred to an intaglio plate using a light-sensitive method, a positive has to be made. A positive is a translucent substrate which supports opaque marks in the form of an image or a pattern. There are a number of different types of positive: autographic (marks made by hand), photographic, digital, photocopy and contact screens.

Positives which hold lines, or broader areas which are broken up into dot or linear stuctures, can be exposed and developed faithfully onto light-sensitive plates used for photo-abrading (see pp. 94–95), photo-etching or photocollagraphy. However, a solid opaque mark (on any type of positive) will expose to create an area on the photoresist plate which will etch and print as open bite unless an aquatint is applied. When a photocollagraph plate is exposed to the same positive, the printed effect will be similar to open bite unless the plate is initially exposed to a contact screen holding a tonal structure such as a random dot screen (aquatint screen) or a halftone contact screen (see p. 191).

The positive used to make the plate shown on p. 141.

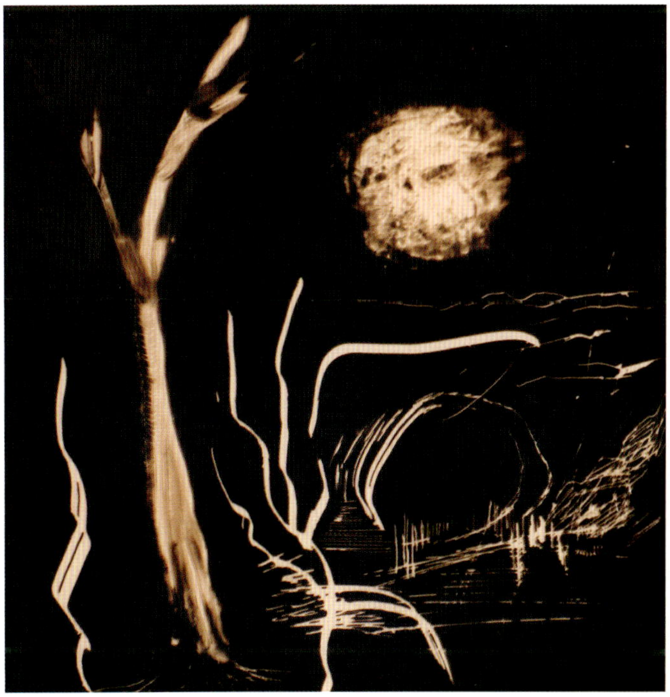

SUBSTRATES AND MATERIALS USED FOR POSITIVES

The substrate selected should be translucent or transparent so that the UV light will pass through easily. Substrates made from PVC and other types of sheet should measure around 240 microns thick. This is sufficiently thin to minimize light refraction during exposure and robust enough for the artwork to tolerate handling and re-use. Creased substrates and impasto marks will prevent a close contact being made between the positive and the light-sensitive plate, resulting in blurred images.

Black or colours from the red end of the spectrum are used, as these colours absorb UV light. Other colours may be experimented with but are generally less reliable, although there are exceptions. Blue highlighter pens can be used to make notes on positives, as the UV light will pass through this translucent ink.

The substrates and materials which are commonly used for each method of working are discussed below.

AUTOGRAPHIC POSITIVES

Positives can be built up entirely using drawing, painting and stencilling techniques or autographic marks may be added to photographic or digitally produced positives. Elements made using different types of positive may be collaged together and worked into to form an image.

Artists can employ the full range of techniques normally used when painting or drawing with pencils and crayons. Marks must be opaque to shield the light-sensitive plate from the UV light. Painting and drawing materials should be chosen with this in mind. Good quality pigment-rich materials such as soft pencils (4B and softer), conté crayons, compressed charcoals, some types and colours of acrylic paint and specially designed products such as Lascaux tusches are ideal. Overhead-projector pens, waterproof pens, metallic gel pens and dip pens with traditional ink can also be used. Correction pens for typing errors can be used on smooth PVC sheet to produce a characterful opaque white line which exposes well. Some brands will block the light more than others, and test strips should be made.

Broad animated lines can be drawn with R&F Pigment Sticks but these oily materials are very slow-drying and the image tends to be damaged by the exposure process. The positives are also difficult to store.

Tone can be introduced to a line image positive by drawing a series of close parallel lines, crossed by another series of parallel lines. The closer the lines are to each other, the darker the resulting tone. This is known as 'crosshatching'. Pencils and conté crayons can create tonal marks directly if they are used on a textured material such as grained tracing paper, drafting film or True-Grain. The graphite or pigment sits on the raised areas of the textured surface and the grooves (which remain clear) break the line into fragments. The tonality of the mark will vary according to the pressure with which the drawing tool is applied to the substrate, as this affects the proximity of the drawn fragments to each other.

Painted marks on textured substrates also break up into tonal gradients as the pigment settles into the cavities of the grainy surface. Smooth PVC sheet can be painted onto with Lascaux tusches (which contain suspended opaque particles), as the particles will reticulate into tonal wash patterns as they dry.

Another method of creating tone is to use an airbrush to spray patterns of opaque dots onto a positive. The areas where the sprayed dots are closest will print darkest. A similar but cruder effect can be achieved by splattering the positive using a toothbrush or stiff paintbrush.

All these dotted structures have similarities to the use of halftone (see p. 191) and are comparable to the process of aquatint in etching.

SUBSTRATES

Suitable substrates include flat sheets of tracing paper, clear smooth PVC sheet, clear grained PVC sheet, grained drafting films and specialist film such as True-Grain. These materials are available from graphic arts materials and paper suppliers. The prices of some comparable materials vary considerably so it is worth researching the cheapest source. Rolls of film or tracing paper are unsuitable as they tend to curl.

Tracing paper is inexpensive and useful for drawn marks and frottage. Heavyweight tracing paper is more robust and tends to have a better drawing surface than the smoother lightweight equivalents. Tracing papers are unsuitable for painting on as any contact with moisture will cause them to buckle and crease: the resulting poor contact during exposure between the tracing-paper positive and the light-sensitive plate will cause any creases to appear on the plate as open lines, and parts of the image may be blurred and distorted.

Drawings and paintings can be made on drafting films, grained plastics and True-Grain. These substrates have a 'toothed' surface similar to the texture of watercolour paper or a lithographic stone, and this rough surface breaks up the marks into a dot-like structure. Drawing on these sheets with pencils and crayons flattens the texture of the substrate and painted marks are often difficult to remove from the toothed surface without damaging the sheet, so these films are not easily re-used. A lightbox is useful to see through the grained sheet to the guide drawing or map beneath.

Smooth, clear PVC sheet accommodates the broadest range of exposure times, is inexpensive and is easy to see through. It is ideal for collage methods and for painting on

right Barbara Rae painted with Lascaux Tusche Water-Soluble on a smooth clear PVC sheet. The dry image was then painted over with a layer of Lascaux Tusche Waterproof. When this was dry, the first tusche was washed away with warm water.

below right Metal and plastic stencils were laid on a smooth clear PVC sheet and sprayed over with Lascaux Tusche Wash Spray.

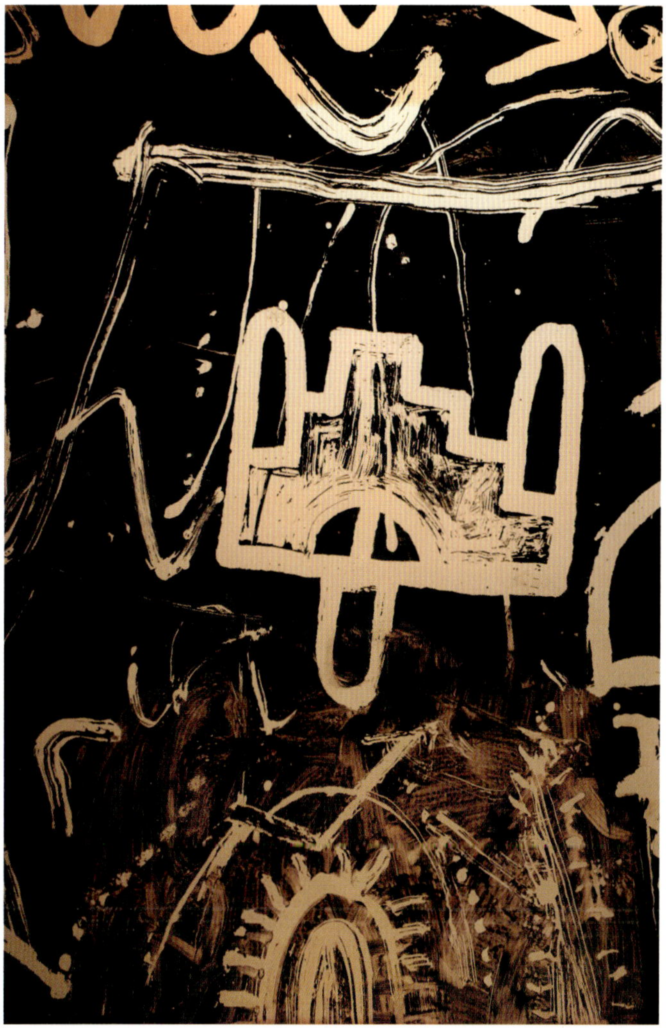

with a wide range of materials, including some types of acrylic paints and the Lascaux tusches. All of these materials bond well with the surface and images can be removed if necessary without damaging the sheet. Clear PVC sheet should be used when drawing into painted or rolled-on marks (made using the appropriate Lascaux tusches), as the smooth surface will allow a clean line. Due to its smooth surface pencils or conté crayons cannot be used in the normal manner. However, if the PVC is first dampened with spray-type window cleaner, a conté crayon can be used to draw rich fluid lines.

Some PVC or grained sheets may be greasy, repelling tusche or paints. This problem can be solved by degreasing the surface using a sponge and some household cleaner. Dry the sheet with a clean rag before starting work.

STENCILLING METHODS

Various materials can be used to block the light and these may be arranged on a PVC sheet to form a positive. Red or black paper, doilies, Japanese papers and fabrics (such as lace, scrim or netting) can be cut or torn to form shapes and textures. Found materials with a thin profile (for example, leaves, feathers and gaskets) can also be used. These stencils or objects may be kept and rearranged to generate new compositions.

TUSCHES

Lascaux manufacture specially designed tusches for creating autographic marks on positives of all types, including photographic and digital. These materials are unusually versatile, safe to use, water-soluble, opaque and easy to apply. The tusches are coloured differently so marks can be identified on the sheet.

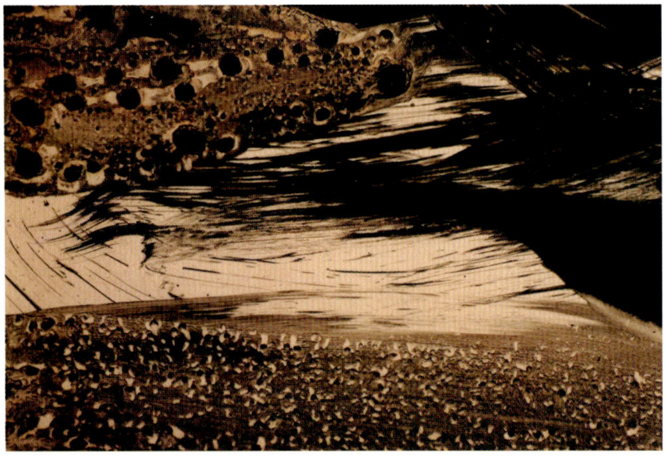

Washes generated using Lascaux Tusche Wash.

The tusches can be used to explore a range of painting techniques, including dry brush marks, wet washes, splattering, spilling, pouring, sponging, offsetting, dribbling, stippling, stencilling and scumbling. Brushes, rags, paper, rollers, airbrushes, stencils and paint shapers may be used to create marks.

They can be painted on in a smooth and even coat and then drawn into with paint shapers and other tools. Some types of tusche can be drawn into when the positives are dry to create non-printing lines.

Several of the Lascaux tusches enable artists to make positives which contain marks usually found in traditional printmaking media. Printmaking-type marks include aquatint-like tonal effects, soft-ground impressions and drawings, and sugarlift, hard-ground and monotyping effects.

Lascaux Tusche Waterproof can be used to make a range of characteristic marks. It is used when durable image areas are required on a positive. The waterproof nature of the tusche can be used as part of a painting method. For example, an element of the image is painted with Lascaux Tusche Waterproof and allowed to dry before other tusches are painted over it. The Lascaux Tusche Waterproof will remain unaffected by this overpainting without re-wetting.

Lascaux Tusche Water-Soluble can be used to make a range of painted marks and washes. The tusche is easily manipulated and it can be re-wet to remove selected areas, or to make soft edges, or to create delicate, non-printing lines. For example, a smoothly painted layer of tusche may be allowed to dry before the surface is drawn into with etching tools. The thin, delicate lines on the positive will not print, but the surrounding areas of tusche will. To protect the fragile image, any editing to the lines should be made on the reverse of the sheet.

TUSCHE WASHES

Lascaux Tusche Wash and Lascaux Tusche Wash/Spray can be used to create washes that resemble lithographic, aquatint and watercolour tonal gradients. The tusche particles are opaque, so even dispersed or delicate tonal washes may be exposed and printed accurately. All of the Lascaux tusches may be diluted to create different types of reticulation by adding water, tannin, Lascaux Diluting Liquid or clear window cleaner. Drying time is affected by dilution (water will take the longest time to dry).

Small amounts of fine carborundum powder may be sprinkled onto wash images on the PVC sheet to create further reticulations. Lascaux Tusche Wash/Spray may also be used in an airbrush to create tonal effects similar to an aquatint or a random dot screen.

LASCAUX TUSCHE SOFT-GROUND EFFECT

This working method is closely related to the soft-ground method in traditional etching but the impressed marks will ultimately print as pale tones. The tusche is slow-drying, viscous and capable of a broad range of marks. One technique involves using an etching press to take impressions of fabric, leaves, feathers and other material. The collage will lift off some areas of tusche and the resulting print will replicate the tonality of the positive. The sharpness of the impressions is affected by how dry the layer of tusche is on the PVC sheet.

In a simple version of this method, the tusche can be applied by brush and an impression taken using hand pressure, but the following method makes use of a roller and an etching press.

- The transparent PVC sheet is masking-taped to a lightbox, glass bench or clean drawing board. A piece of white paper should be placed below the PVC sheet.
- The tusche is laid out (using a plastic spatula) on a clean glass inking slab and is rolled out using a hand-roller. The tusche is applied thinly and evenly to the PVC sheet.
- The tusche-covered PVC sheet is detached from the bench and positioned on the etching press bed. A collage of low-profile textured materials, such as feathers, leaves, threads and paper shapes, can be laid on the top of the tusche. Avoid using wire, chain links or other hard objects that may cause damage to the blankets or press. Once the collage is complete, a second PVC sheet is laid on top, then a sheet of blotting paper and finally the press blankets.
- The collage is rolled through the etching press at normal pressure (the lack of an etching plate means that the normal setting exerts less pressure). After it has passed through the press, the blankets and blotter are lifted, and the top PVC sheet is carefully peeled away. (An image will have offset onto this sheet and may be used as a positive if desired.) The collage will be flattened and embedded in the tusche layer on the lower PVC sheet. An etching needle may be used to peel each item carefully away. Once the collage has been removed from the tusche, the positive can be examined on a piece of white paper or on a lightbox. The aim is to produce a positive with defined contrast; enough tusche should remain on the sheet to block the light. Positives often appear faint but expose to produce effective images.

A positive made using Lascaux Tusche Soft-Ground Effect, which was then edited with another tusche.

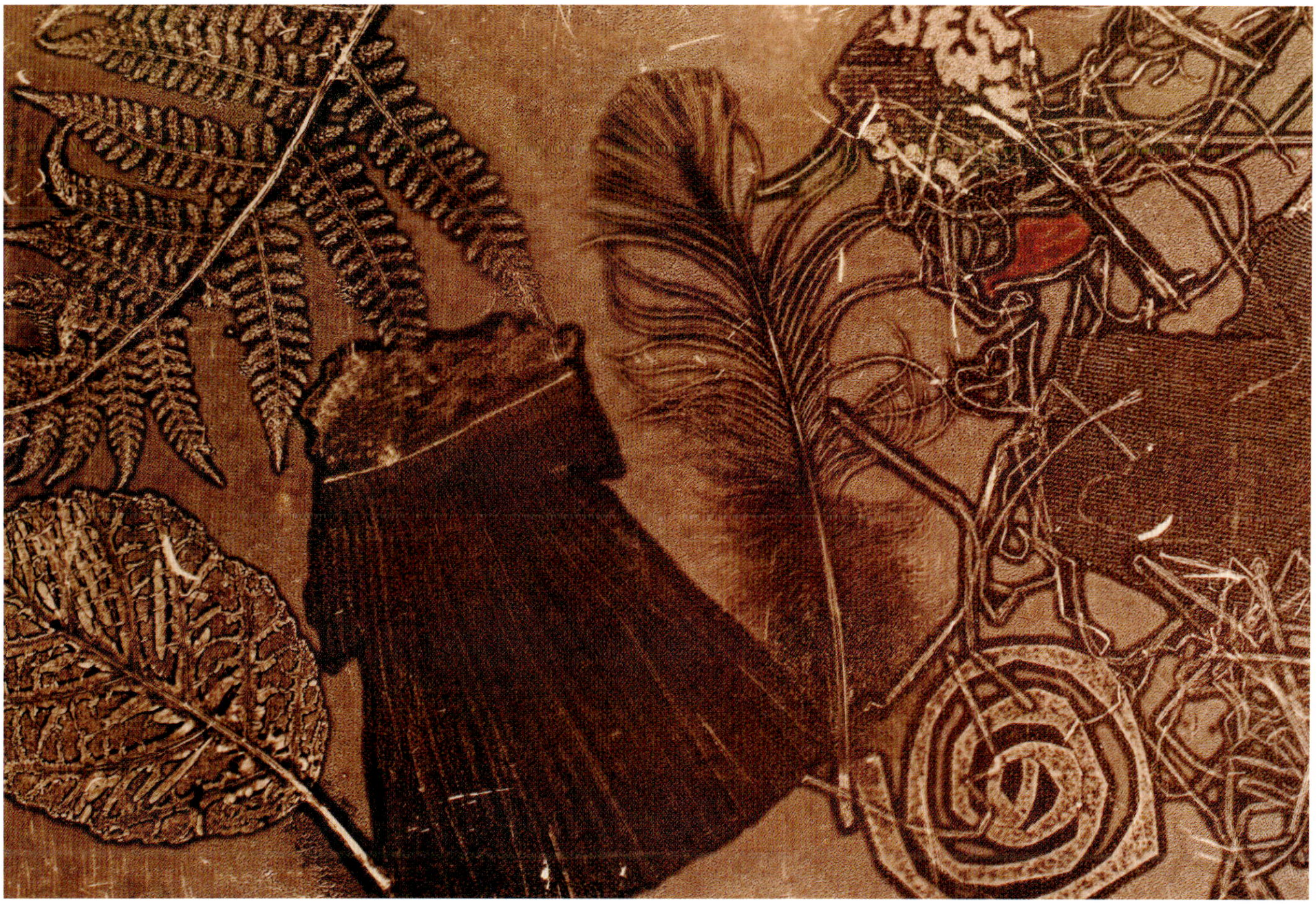

• The results will vary depending on how dry the tusche was when the collage was run through the press. If the impressed marks do not allow light to pass through, either the tusche was applied too thickly or the etching press pressure was insufficient. If the background allows light to pass through, either the tusche was applied too thinly, the pressure was too great or the covering material was not sufficiently glossy to repel the tusche and so too much was removed from the lower PVC sheet.

• Alterations can easily be made to the positive before exposure. When the image is still moist, brushes and paint shapers can be used to wipe away areas and make marks. The tusche will dry slowly and can be drawn into with etching tools at any stage. The tusche may be re-wet to create washes or to remove areas of the image. Marks can be added at any stage using any of the other tusches.

• When the tusche is dry, alterations to the image can be made on the reverse of the sheet. This method protects the fragile image and allows accurate editing. When the collage image is printed, the tusche areas will print as dark tones. In etching an aquatint may be required and in photocollagraphy a dot screen can be used to provide a tonal structure.

LASCAUX TUSCHE SOFT-GROUND EFFECT
USED TO CREATE DRAWING MARKS

This tusche can be used to make drawn marks similar to the traditional etching soft-ground method. The drawings have a soft atmospheric character with the appearance of foul bite across other parts of the image. The lines will print as pale tones.

• The PVC sheet is masking-taped to a glass bench. The tusche is laid out (using a plastic spatula) on a clean glass inking slab and is rolled out using a hand-roller. The tusche is applied thinly to the PVC sheet.

• A sheet of tissue paper is laid over the PVC and its corners lightly taped to the workboard to hold it securely.

• Position the map, key drawing or textured paper on top and hinge the top edge to the workboard with a strip of masking tape. The paper's surface will determine the type of mark.

• A pencil or crayon can be used to draw vigorously on the drawing paper (this strong paper is used as it will not rip and its texture will animate the drawn line). Drawing papers with different textures will give different results. The tissue below will not be damaged and is sufficiently absorbent to lift the tusche where pressure has been applied, leaving the PVC clear.

• When the image is complete, hinge back the drawing paper and carefully peel away the tissue. The tusche drawing will be clearly seen on the tissue, and if the positive is held up to the light, these areas should now be clear of tusche.

• When the tusche is dry, other tusches may be painted on the image side or on the back of the sheet.

Positives can be made by using monotype techniques (see p. 203). Lascaux Tusche Soft-Ground Effect can also be rolled up on linocuts, woodcuts and etching plates, allowing these to be printed onto clear smooth PVC sheet to make positives. The tusche can be used as a painting tusche and may be diluted with water, Lascaux Diluting Liquid or spray-type window cleaner to create wash effects.

LASCAUX LIFT SOLUTION

This is used in combination with Lascaux Tusche Wash/Spray. The method is comparable to using the sugarlift technique in traditional etching and is good for bold line imagery. The painted line tends to have a particular character.

• An image is painted on the substrate using Lascaux Lift Solution and is allowed to dry and become chalky. A substantial deposit of solution is necessary.

• Lascaux Tusche Wash/Spray is airbrushed over the lift-solution image and the area of the PVC sheet which is to print. This should be allowed to dry thoroughly. A single, even layer will create a light tonal effect; many layers will create denser tones. If many layers are to be used, each must be allowed to dry before the next is applied. Should the sprayed layers become too wet, the lift-solution image will be damaged.

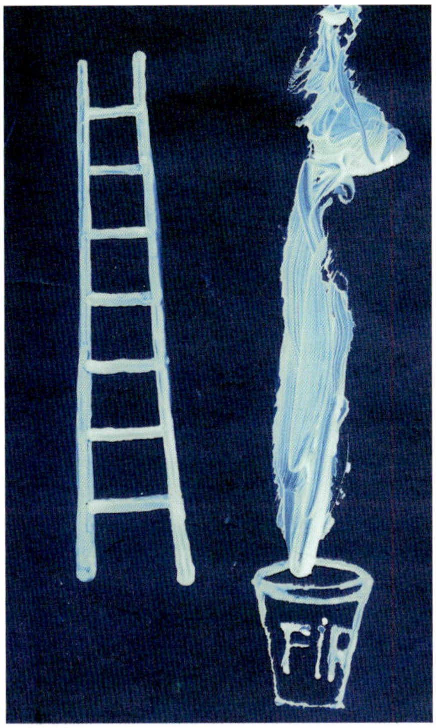

Anti-clockwise from left:
1. A Lascaux Lift Solution painting on a clear sheet of PVC which is lying on a blue work board.
2. The lift solution has been sprayed with Lascaux Tusche Wash Spray. The spray on the lower half was allowed to dry and then re-sprayed to create a flat field.
3. The lift solution was washed away with water. The texture created by the spraying process can be seen clearly.
4. A detail of the zinc plate which was coated with a layer of Photec, exposed to the positive, developed, dried and cured. An aquatint spray resist or other tonal technique would be applied before etching unless an open-bitten effect was desired.

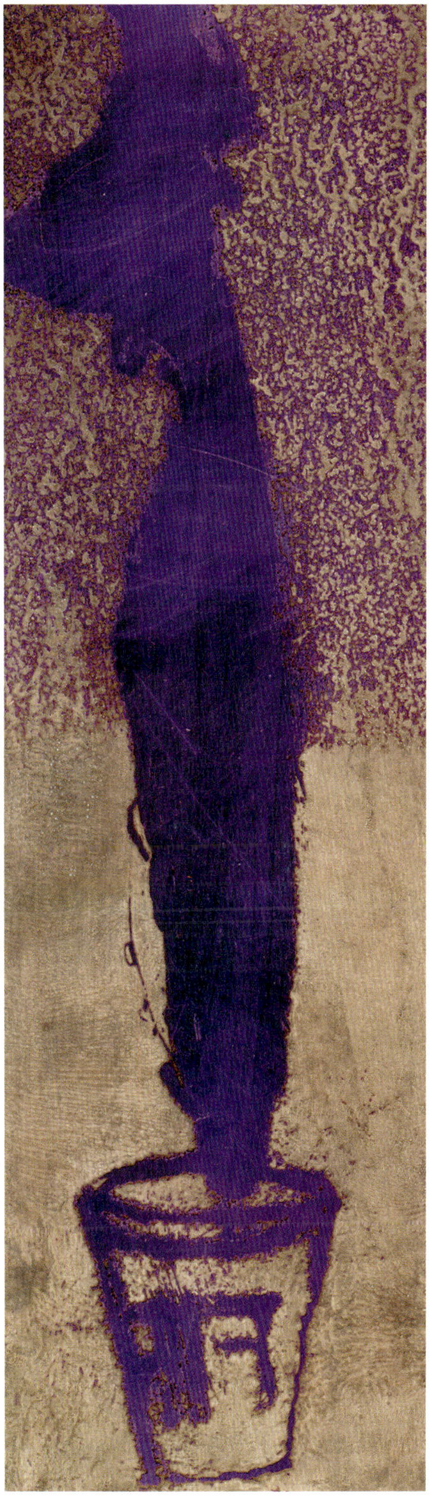

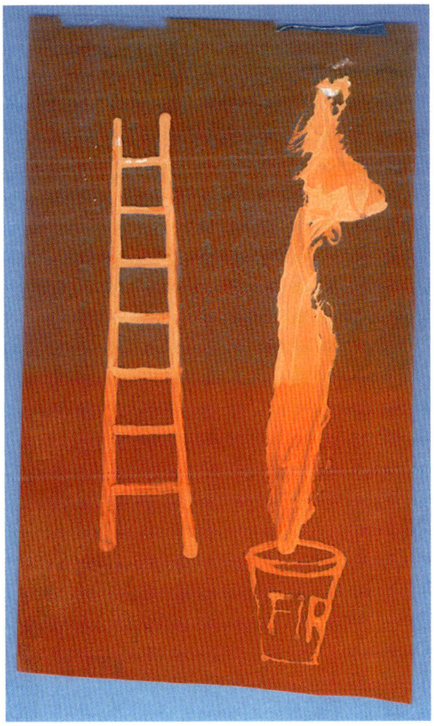

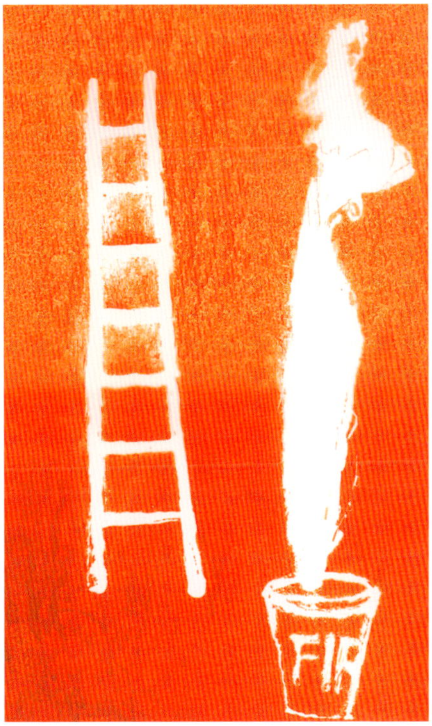

• When the tusche layers are dry, the positive is immersed in a tray of warm water for 10 minutes. The lift solution will start to dissolve, lifting the layers of sprayed tusche. The painted lift solution will eventually lift away, leaving the substrate clear in the form of the image. The remaining airbrushed tusche on the positive will print.

MAKING AN AUTOGRAPHIC POSITIVE

The following instructions include information for a wide range of methods (e.g. drawing, painting, using tusches or stencils).

Basic equipment and materials required

Work in the drawing area or painting studio.

- a lightbox (useful for checking positives) or a white-surfaced bench covered with PVC or hardened glass
- a guide drawing or map
- a suitable transparent substrate
- any additional positive element (e.g. photocopy, digital positive)
- clear adhesive tape
- ceramic bowls or palettes
- selection of artists' tools depending on method (e.g. roller, brushes, scissors)
- selected drawing, painting or stencil materials
- a horizontal rack or drying cabinet for positives
- a basin of warm soapy water, sponges and dry cloths
- storage for dry positives

Working method

- Set up the area with materials and tools required, and a basin of water.
- The transparent sheet is laid on the working surface and its corners taped down firmly with masking tape. A guide drawing (mapping out important areas of the image and the edges of the plate) may be placed beneath the transparent substrate. If a photographic, digital or photocopy positive is to be added to the autographic positive, the element should be carefully attached with clear adhesive tape to the back of the transparent substrate. The sheet is then turned over and the autographic marks are painted or drawn on the front of the substrate. If the intention is to merge the elements seamlessly, the mark-making should relate to the character of the added element.
- The image is drawn or painted on the substrate. The positive can then be slid onto a workboard (the corners should be taped to the board) so that it can be carried horizontally to a drying area.

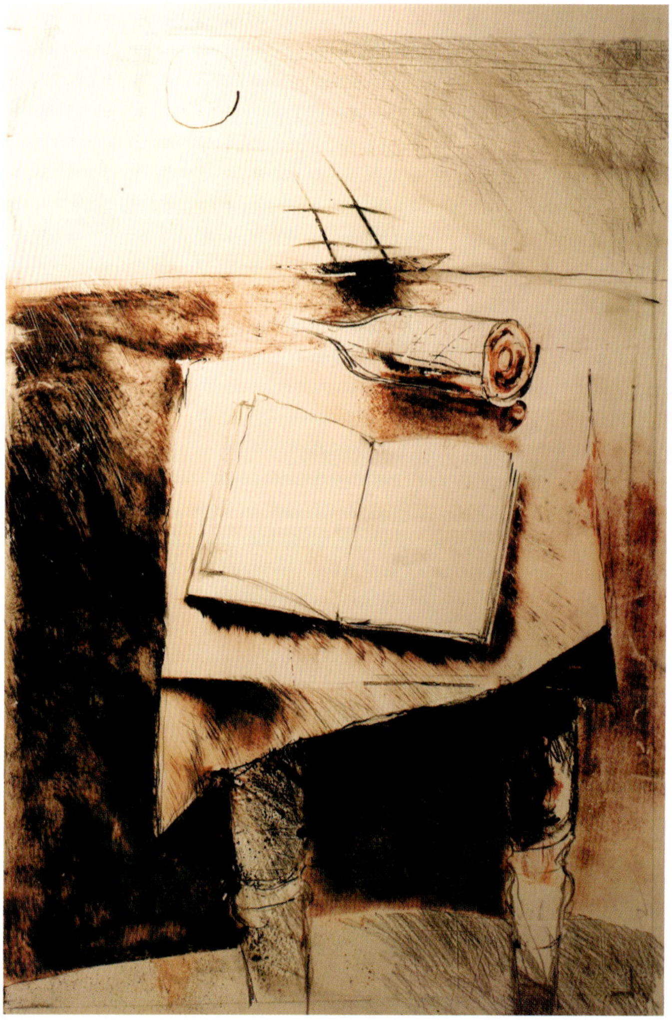

opposite A positive made on drafting film using conté crayons, Indian ink, acrylic paints, soft pencils and an eraser.

right A smaller photopositive (with the image of the rowing boat) has been attached to the back of this autographic positive painted with Lascaux Tusche Wash: they were exposed simultaneously.

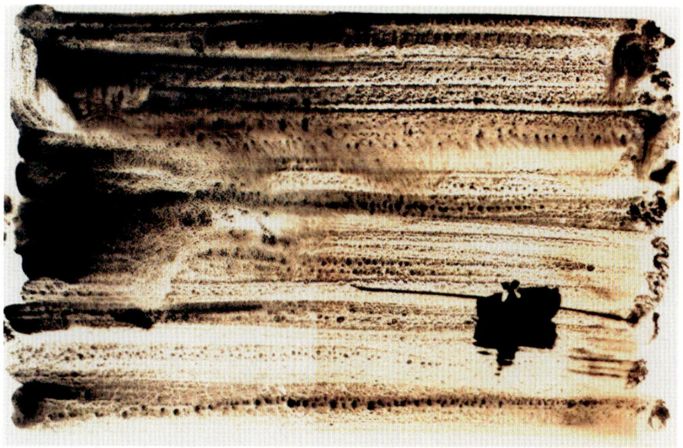

- When the positive has dried, it may be examined on a lightbox or held up to a window to check the image and that the marks are sufficiently opaque to block the light. If several positives have been made, they may be stacked on top of each other on the lightbox to check the register. Any necessary alterations may be made.
- When the work is finished, the positives may be exposed. They may then be stored flat between tissue in a drawer in case another exposure is required.
- Acrylic and gouache paints and Lascaux tusches are water-soluble, and painted areas and brushes can be cleaned with warm soapy water. China or glass dishes should be used as palettes, as dry acrylic and tusches can be removed from these by soaking them in hot water. Dry materials can be removed from smooth PVC sheet with a plastic non-scratch household cleaning pad and Lascaux Remover, Mystrol or Cif cleaner (see p. 215).

PHOTOGRAPHIC POSITIVES

Photographic positives can be made with an ordinary darkroom enlarger or a process camera. An understanding of black and white photographic processing is necessary and these skills can be learned from books, the internet and darkroom courses.

An enlarger can be used to make positives from photographic negatives onto transparent positive film (lith film), rather than an ordinary photographic paper. Polyester lith films are usually handled in red safe-light conditions. Test strips should be made to ascertain the optimum exposure time. The dark opaque areas on the film will become the part of the image that will dissolve when the light-sensitive plates are developed. Grainy negatives may not require the use of a contact screen to establish a printable tonal gradient. This is because the intrinsic graininess of the image on the negative may be sufficient to fragment the tone into random dots, if the enlargement is great enough. Photographs can be taken deliberately on high-speed film to enhance this effect.

With a process camera original photographs, digital output, found material, collages, drawings or painted marks can be enlarged and reproduced as line or halftone images on lith film. When a process camera is used, light is reflected off the original artwork, through the lens, and onto the sensitive lith film. Normal darkroom procedures are followed to develop and fix the lith film.

These photographic processes use toxic chemicals to develop and fix films, so safety clothing should be worn and the darkroom should be equipped with good extraction and ventilation equipment. Suppliers of lith films and related chemicals offer up-to-date health and safety advice.

Process cameras can be purchased second-hand or from specialist suppliers. This way of working offers high contrast and superb detail, but is becoming less common due to the possibilities offered by – and the availability of – digital processes and photocopiers.

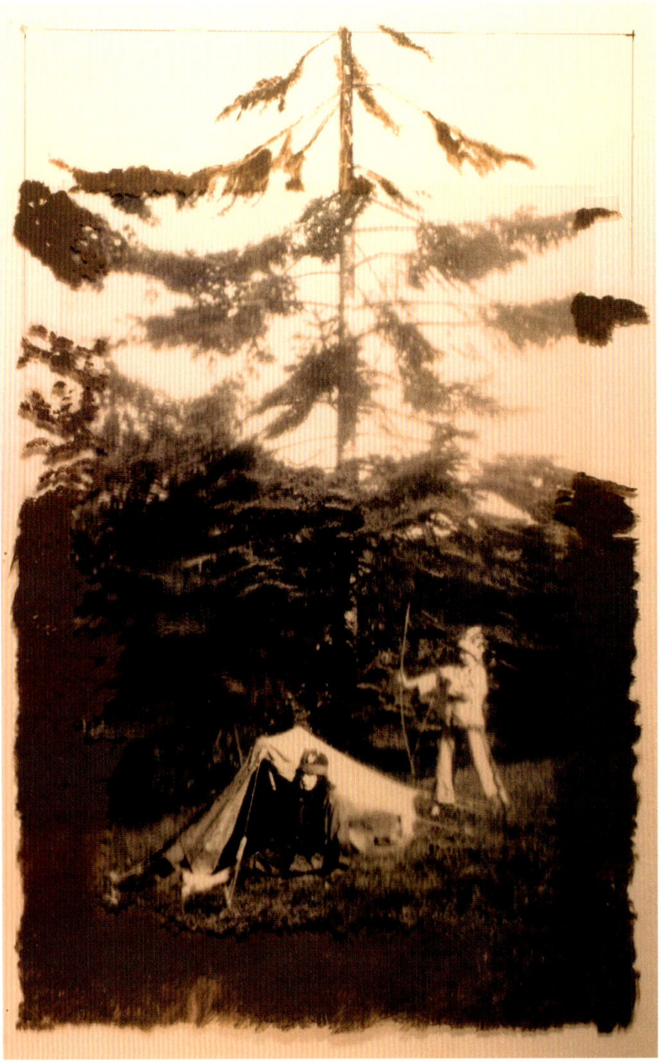

Lascaux Tusche Water-Soluble has been used to edit and extend this photocopy positive (which is attached to the back of a larger clear sheet of PVC). The image had been manipulated digitally, printed onto paper with an inkjet printer, and then enlarged onto acetate using a photocopier.

DIGITAL POSITIVES

Photographic positives have been almost completely superseded by digital processes. An understanding of digital imaging techniques is necessary and these skills can be learned from computer software tutorials, books, the internet and courses.

A conventional mouse or a pressure-sensitive pad and pen (stylus) can be used to make original images. A scanner can be used to input drawings, paintings, photographs, text, collage or found materials. A scanner with a backlit lid enables the artist to scan photographic negatives and transparencies into a programme for manipulation. Similarly images can be captured and input from the internet, or with digital still and video cameras. Existing images can be colour-separated to make reproductions or to create new images.

The artwork can be manipulated using applications such as Adobe Photoshop (some artists write their own programmes). The tonal structure may be altered and different types of halftone can be applied (see opposite). The resolution of the image is usually expressed as dots per inch, or dpi. The higher the resolution at which an image is captured, the greater the amount of detail that is stored. This resolution cannot subsequently be increased but may be decreased. Storing and manipulating images at high resolutions requires more computer memory, which slows the process down.

OUTPUTTING POSITIVES

Different output devices produce printed images in varying resolutions, and the more sophisticated the machine, the more capable it will be of printing very fine detail.

Completed artwork up to A4 (29.7 x 21 cm/11⅝ x 8¼ in.) can be printed using a home printer onto clear acetate or OHP acetate (for use with overhead projectors). These sheets are sold by office suppliers.

Larger-format images should be stored on a DVD, a CD or a Zip or Jaz cartridge and taken to a bureau for output onto a transparent substrate. Before embarking on an image, it is a good idea to visit the bureau to find out what kind of substrates they will print on, the estimated cost, the file type they require (e.g. TIFF), the form of disk (e.g. DVD), the format (e.g. PC or Mac) and to check that the emulsion side of the clear film can be up (rather than down).

PHOTOCOPY POSITIVES

Photocopiers can be used to make positives from text, drawings, painted marks and found objects (e.g. bus tickets and other ephemera, string, jewelry, patterned cloth). They can be used to magnify, reduce, reverse or alter the contrast or tone of an image (for instance, a pale drawing on a positive can often be rescued by photocopying it and then exposing it successfully). Reprographic companies often offer other special effects.

Some machines will print on good quality tracing paper, and clear photocopy acetates are available which make excellent substrates. Most photocopiers have a maximum size of A3 (29.7 x 42 cm/11⅝ x 16½ in.), but many reprographic agencies are able to make large copies on tracing paper.

Photocopy positives can be drawn and painted on. However, positives that have been altered with tusches and paints often show extreme changes of tone and fail to look homogenous. A good technique to avoid this is to make any changes to a paper copy using typing correction pens, fineliner pens, and black and white acrylic paints. A final single photocopy of the modified artwork can then be made on a translucent substrate (for use as the positive).

Colour photocopiers are able to make basic colour separations which can be used for four-plate colour printing. The colour control on the machine is set to one colour (for example, magenta); then a photocopy of the magenta areas is made on a transparent substrate (using the black toner cartridge). When this is processed to become an image on a plate, it may be printed with magenta ink. This process is repeated to make plates for yellow, cyan and black. When these plates are printed with the correct colour and in register, the original image is rebuilt. Experimental work using alternative colours can be explored.

HALFTONE CONTACT SCREENS

The original halftone screens of the 1890s were used for translating the tonal structure of a continuous tone photograph into a series of dots which would mimic the original tonal gradient. These early contact screens consisted of two glass plates, each of which was etched with a series of closely spaced parallel lines. The lines were inked up with a dark pigment to make them opaque, and then the two plates were glued together face to face so that the etched lines intersected at right angles, forming a grid of small squares. The number of parallel lines to the inch on the screen would determine the fineness of the tonal reproduction.

The screen was placed in close contact with the lith film and the negative was projected onto these. As the light shone through the grid each square acted as a tiny lens, breaking the image up into a series of dots. The size of these dots was affected by the brightness of the light.

As a result the darkest areas on the finished print were where the black dots were largest and merged, and the lightest areas were where the dots were small and scarce, and the light tone of the paper could predominate. This halftone system meant that a single black ink could print a scale of tones from black, through grey, to white. Similarly, any colour that was printed would show a range of tones.

Contemporary artists can apply a wide range of halftone effects and frequencies (the number of dots to a given measurement) to an image, using digital software such as Adobe Photoshop, and this programme offers a choice of dot shape, such as round, elliptical, square, cross, line and diamond.

Even if the artist does not apply a halftone to a digital image, an inkjet printer will automatically impose a form of random dot in order to simulate tonal changes. This is referred to as 'dithering', and the dithered dot structure generally transfers successfully to a light-sensitive plate, eliminating the need for a halftone. Using Adobe Photoshop, it is also possible to impose a specified dither on the image itself, using different values to create a variety of effects.

Modern halftone contact screens are also used to impose a tonal structure on photocollagraph plates in order to avoid an open-bite effect. The light-sensitive plate is exposed to the halftone contact screen which consists of a clear substrate holding a very fine geometric grid or a dot structure. Different halftone configurations include grey screen (cross-line image), straight line, wavy line, mezzotint and random dot (aquatint effect). This last type is the most commonly used by artists for aesthetic reasons: as its name implies, the arrangement of dots is not geometric or mechanical.

Contact screens are difficult to make by autographic means but can be made photographically or digitally. They are normally purchased from specialist suppliers and are available in fine or coarse grades. They are expensive and require careful handling to avoid damaging their surface.

After exposure to the contact screen, the light-sensitive plate is then exposed to the positive holding the image. This second exposure is usually half the length of the contact screen exposure (for example, the contact screen might be exposed for 30 seconds and the image positive for 15 seconds).

When the plate is developed after the second exposure, all the areas of the light-sensitive coating which were exposed to the UV light remain on the plate, becoming strong, smooth and non-ink-holding. The shielded areas will dissolve away.

As a result of the second exposure, only the image areas on the developed plate will have an ink-holding pitted or reticulated surface (generated by the contact screen).

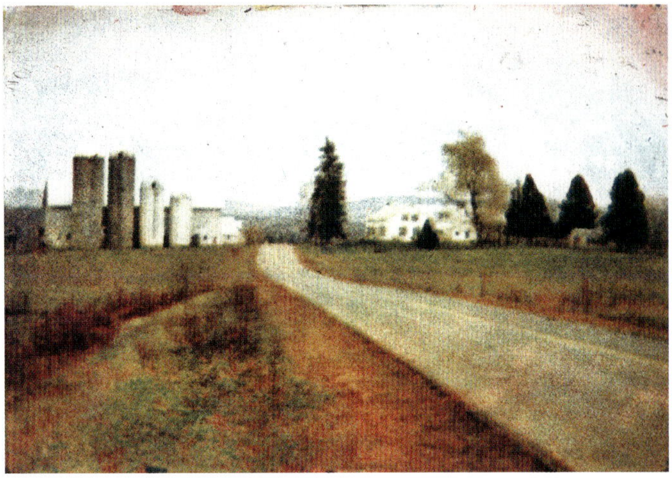

Ryan Laurey (US), *Farmhouse,* photocollagraph, 7.5 x 12.7 cm (3 x 5 in.), 2004. A photograph was taken with a plastic Holga camera and the image was digitally separated to generate four positives. The positives were exposed to four plates, which were developed and dried. The plates were inked up intaglio using process colours, then printed in sequence and in register on Hahnemühle copperplate paper.

COLOUR SEPARATION AND PROCESS PRINTING

An image can be divided by colour into a set of four halftone separations (positives). Each represents a different colour. These four positives are used to generate four intaglio plates. The plates can be made using either the photo-abrading, photo-etching or photocollagraphic processes. When the four plates are inked up (intaglio) with process colours and printed in perfect register, the image will be re-assembled (see 'Registration Methods', pp. 208–210 and 'Multi-Plate and Process Printing Registration Method', p. 210). Accurate registration is essential throughout the various stages: this includes the creation of the positives and plates and applies to the printing process as well. Care is also required to avoid cross-contamination of the colours when printing (e.g. from scrims and work surfaces).

The colour separation process was developed as a method of colour reproduction for printing, and separations were originally created using a photographic technique. This involved the use of a process camera with different colour filters and a halftone screen. Nowadays commercial images are generally separated digitally. Artists can make colour separations photographically or digitally, or basic separations can be created using a colour photocopier.

The separated colours are usually the four translucent process colours: cyan, magenta, yellow and keyline black (CMYK) but other colour systems may be employed, such as RGB (red, green and blue – the additive primaries). When the finished print is examined with a magnifying glass, it is evident that the translucent coloured dots overlap and blend to form additional colours.

INKING-UP AND PRINTING METHODS

APPROACHES TO PRINTING

Intaglio plates may be inked up so that the indented areas hold ink (intaglio method) or so the high, smooth areas hold ink (surface or relief method), or both. A single ink may be distributed to the entire surface of the plate or a range of inks may be applied to selected areas of the plate, as in à la poupée for an intaglio method and monotyping for a surface method.

The planned method of printing can influence how many plates are needed for a single image or how the surface of a plate is constructed (e.g. a viscosity plate should have at least three separate depths). In other cases different printing methods and substrates can be experimented with. These test prints are known as proofs. The proof that is selected as the best is called the BAT (*bon à tirer*). The intaglio printmaker can then print an edition (a set of nearly identical prints based on the BAT). Varied editions can be created by printing the plate in a variety of ways.

Collage materials such as tissue papers, thin papers or leaf skeletons can be adhered to the printing paper and printed onto: this method is known as chine collé. Intaglio and surface printing techniques may be combined on a single plate to create roll-overs or complex viscosity prints.

Several intaglio plates may be designed to be printed in register to form a complex coloured image. For example, process colours may be used: the first plate may be the magenta areas of an image, the second may be the yellow areas, the third may be blue and the fourth may be black. The resulting print will show pure colours as well as browns, greens, oranges, purples and deep tone. Other coloured inks may be used if a more experimental approach is being followed.

Oil-based and water-based inks (including a range of process colours), as well as printing papers, are specifically manufactured for intaglio printmaking. Some inks can be printed onto dry papers but generally the paper is dampened and blotted before printing.

THE INTAGLIO INKING-UP AND PRINTING METHOD

When the plate is inked up using the intaglio method, the narrow lines, the pits and the edges of plateaux on the surface hold and retain the ink while the smooth areas are wiped clean (the nature of plate surfaces is discussed in detail in 'The Principles of Intaglio Printmaking', pp. 59–65).

Equipment and materials for inking up

Work in the printing area (see pp. 52–56) and wear appropriate gloves and clothing for the type of ink. (The printing paper is generally prepared, see p. 54, before inking up.)

- an intaglio plate
- inks and additives for intaglio printing
- a palette knife
- a dauber, cut card or squeegee blade
- some tarlatan or scrim
- some squares of tissue paper (15 cm/6 in. square)
- a sheet of blotting paper
- substrates for printing on
- materials for cleaning up
- some tinfoil
- a waterproof marker pen
- a notebook and pen

Working method

- The marks on the plate surface may be originated using direct, etching or collagraphic methods. The plate should be clean and dry, and it is important that it is bevelled with no

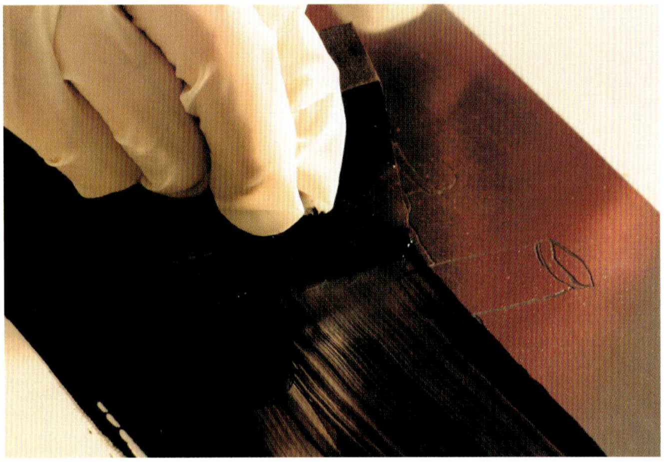

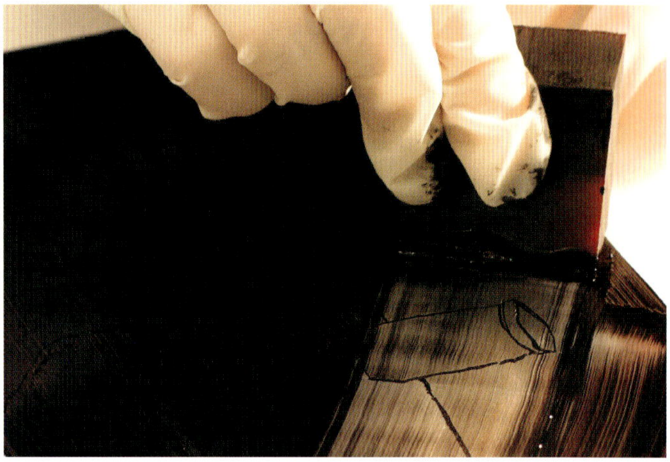

1. Applying ink to the plate with a squeegee.
2. Making sure that the ink has been applied to the surface evenly and in all directions.
3. The ink is lifted from the smooth surfaces of the plate with a ball of scrim.
4. Finally a sheet of tissue is used to remove any remaining ink from the smooth surfaces of the plate.

sharp edges. Ragged unfiled edges can cut hands during inking and the paper and blankets during printing.

• The etching press should be set at the correct pressure for the thickness of plate (consult studio staff, the press manual, the press manufacturer or a printing engineer if in doubt about operating a particular press). A good method of checking press pressure is to take a plate of the same thickness as the one that is to be inked up and printed and emboss this onto a sheet of blotting paper. The back of the print should be examined to check that the pressure was even on both sides and sufficient without being excessive.

• A suitable ink and any additives should be selected according to the type of plate surface (e.g. specialist inks are available for plates which hold fine aquatints and drypoints, and soft finely pigmented inks should be used for delicate plates) and the particular printing substrate. The choice is also influenced by the artist's intentions and the studio set-up.

• The ink and any additives are mixed up and applied to the plate (at room temperature). This is preferable to the practice of warming the plate on an etcher's hot plate, which often results in unpleasant fumes from the heated inks and waste materials on the hot plate being released into the studio.

• The first stage in the process is to fill all the indentations with intaglio ink. The choice of applicator depends on the plate surface. The ink may be applied using a leather dauber (or dabber or doll), a piece of stiff card (4 cm/1½ in. square), an offcut of screenprinting squeegee blade or a toothbrush. Soft squeegee blade is useful for carborundum collagraph plates as it will not leave fibres on the abrasive surface. A toothbrush may be needed to reach into the deep areas on roughly bitten etched plates or heavily textured collagraph plates. A cleanly cut card, leather dauber or cloth doll is used to apply ink to drypointed and etched plates as their delicate surfaces can be damaged easily. Daubers are available from printmaking suppliers or can be homemade.

• The intaglio ink is applied systematically to the plate in parallel bands. When the entire surface of the plate is covered with the ink, the artist turns the plate through 90° and repeats the process. The plate is then turned again through 90° and a third application of ink is moved across the surface. This technique ensures that every indentation is filled and no empty pockets remain. Delicate plates must be daubed gently. If card is used,

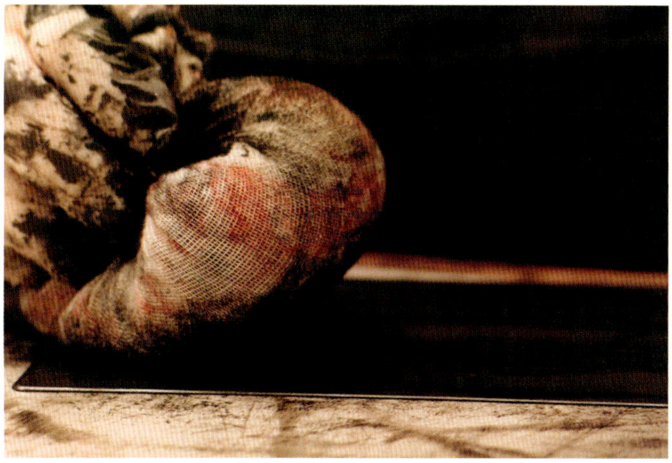

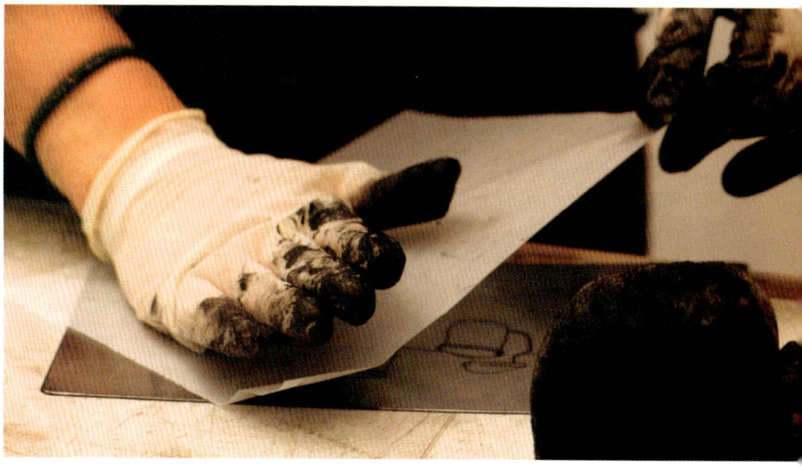

several pieces may be required to complete the task. A steady and thorough approach can be remembered and replicated to make the edition consistent. The technique for printing à la poupée is slightly different as only localized areas of the plate are filled with ink (see p. 198).

• The second stage of the process involves wiping the ink from the smooth areas of the plate without disturbing the ink in the indentations. Three tarlatan (scrim) pads of different softness are used to begin with (on all types of plates). This inexpensive open-weave cloth is available in rolls or sheets from printmakers' suppliers. The closeness of the weave and the quantity of starch varies and some suppliers sell a range of scrims. Some printmakers also use cheesecloth.

• To make a pad for wiping the plate, a length of scrim (approximately 1 metre/3 feet) is cut from the roll and the starch removed. This can be done by scrubbing the cloth vigorously as though washing it or by passing it through a metal loop attached to the wall (a door handle may be fitted for this purpose). The etching press wheel or handle should not be used for this task as this is considered to be a hazardous practice, plus the starch will clog up the mechanism of the press. The starch may also be washed from the cloth. When the cloth has been sufficiently softened, it can be fashioned into a ball (or pad) which is around half the size of a grapefruit. The artist holds the ball where the fabric edges meet and the crease-free round side is used to wipe the plate surface. Any creases or wrinkles can pull the ink out of the indentations. This may also happen if the tail ends of the scrim are allowed to drag over the plate surface during the wiping process.

• The first pad to be used should be made from the coarsest, most starchy scrim. A previously used and heavily soiled pad (the inks must be compatible) is often used and some etchers will add some ink to the surface of a new pad before starting to wipe. The pad is used with a gentle consistent stroking motion and the plate is wiped systematically from one side to another. The movement should travel off the edge of the plate to prevent a build-up of ink around the edges. If too much pressure is applied, ink will be pulled from the indentations. In the same way as when the ink was applied, the plate is turned and stroked in different directions to ensure an even and predictable effect. This pad is used until the plate surface can be seen faintly under a film of ink.

• The second pad may be softer and of a finer weave. It should hold less ink on its surface than the first pad but is used in the same way. After the plate has been wiped with this pad the smooth surfaces of the plate should be quite visible. In cases where the tarlatan pads are shredded by rough textures on collagraph plates, a cotton rag may be used to wipe the smooth areas clean. A good technique involves wrapping the cloth around a hand with a finger outstretched and then using the cloth-covered fingertip to wipe away the ink. The excess cloth should be held firmly in the palm of the hand to prevent it dragging over the plate, which will pull ink from the indentations.

- The third pad is the softest and is used to remove streaks, smears and smudges of ink from the smooth areas of the plate. When this process is complete, a thin 'plate tone' of ink is left on the surface which prints with an atmospheric effect.
- When a warm or cool tint is required on an image, a 'loose' translucent coloured ink is applied with a clean ball of scrim, allowed to sit and interact with the 'leaner' ink for a moment, and then the plate is printed. However, if a greater contrast is required the wiping process should be continued.
- Tissue paper can be used to lift the remaining film of ink from the smooth surfaces of the plate. The tissue paper is laid (with the most absorbent side down) on the plate. The paper can be drawn slowly towards the printer as the other hand moves with a light circular motion. The entire plate surface is worked in this way and the tissue paper is replaced whenever it becomes soiled or rips. The plate is turned and the process repeated. Because of health concerns, this way of working is preferable to the practice of handwiping where the plate is stroked with the pad of the hand. In this wiping technique a little French chalk (or magnesium carbonate) may be used to draw more ink from the smooth surfaces but care must be taken not to 'overwipe' the plate.
- When the plate surface has been wiped, the edges and back are wiped clean with a soft rag. Care has to be taken not to mark the inked-up surface.
- The plate may now be printed, or the process of retroussage may be employed to create a slightly richer print. This method involves drawing the ink from the indentations by flicking a slightly inky rag over the surface.
- After inking up, gloves should be removed and hands should be cleaned before handling paper or printing (unless working with a clean-handed assistant).

Equipment and materials for printing

- an etching press
- an inked-up plate
- a registration sheet
- some sheets of tissue paper
- the printing paper
- clean grips (folded card or PVC)

Working method

- The pressure should have been set for the type of plate that is being printed (see above).
- The prepared registration sheet (see p. 208) is laid on the press bed and covered with a sheet of tissue. The lines and arrows (drawn with a waterproof marker pen) on the registration sheet should be clearly visible through the tissue.
- The inked-up plate should be handled with gloves, or held using folded card grips, to keep hands clean. The plate is picked up and carefully 'dropped' onto the middle of the sheet of tissue.
- The sheet of tissue is held (with completely clean hands) by two corners and moved so that the plate lies in register with the

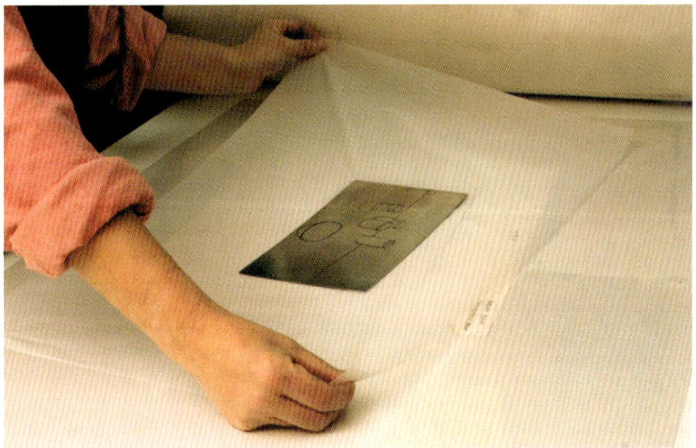

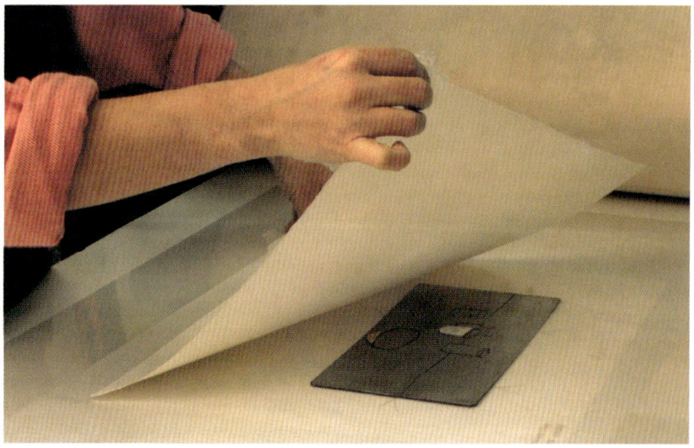

lines and arrows on the registration sheet which correspond to the position of the plate.

• The prepared paper is lifted by two diagonally opposite corners (clean folded card or PVC grips should be used, as even clean fingers can mark the paper). The paper should be allowed to sag in the middle. The top corner is carefully lined up with the marks on the registration sheet which correspond to the paper. When the corner is lined up correctly, it can be held in place with the card grip (or by placing a thumb on the back of the paper). The paper can then be pivoted so that the sides and bottom line up with the lines on the registration sheet. When this is correct, the plate can be laid down gently on the inked plate (if the printing paper is moved after this stage it will be marked by the moist ink).

• Two sheets of clean tissue are then placed over the printing paper to protect the blankets from absorbing any leaks of ink and some of the size and moisture which will be squeezed from dampened printing paper during the printing process. The felts or interfacing will require less drying and also less washing (to remove the size) if this good practice is followed. Newsprint should not be used as it contains acid which will be transferred from the blankets onto the acid-free printing paper, causing yellow stains to appear on prints.

• The blankets are placed on top and are smoothed flat.

• The assembly is rolled slowly and steadily through the press. The enormous pressure applied by the press rollers forces the ink from the plate into the fibres of the paper, creating characteristic prominent inky lines and rich velvety tones. The printing process embosses the textured plate into the softened paper and the printed marks will be a mirror image of the marks on the plate. If the press is operated with too much speed, prints are often poor and this practice can be hazardous.

• After printing, the blankets and tissue are lifted away. The corner of the printing paper is picked up (again using folded grips) and peeled away carefully from the plate surface. This reduces the risk of the paper ripping if the plate has deep cavities or the lifting of the plate if it is light (aluminium or card). Tiny rips which appear as white flecks are quite common and a small, dry, firm paintbrush can be used to redistribute some ink over these marks.

• The print should be laid on a clean sheet of tissue or hung up to look at before being dried and flattened.

• The plate should be lifted from the press bed (using the tissue beneath it to protect hands from ink) and placed on the inking-up work surface. The tissue should be discarded and any marks on the press wiped away. The registration sheet should be put away if other printmakers are using the press.

1. The inked-up plate is laid on a sheet of tissue and positioned on the registration sheet.
2. The dampened paper is laid over the plate in register with the marks on the registration sheet (in this case the registration sheet corresponds exactly with the size of the printing paper). Two sheets of tissue are then laid over the printing paper.
3. The press blankets are carefully laid over the paper.
4. After printing, the blankets are lifted and the print carefully peeled from the plate.

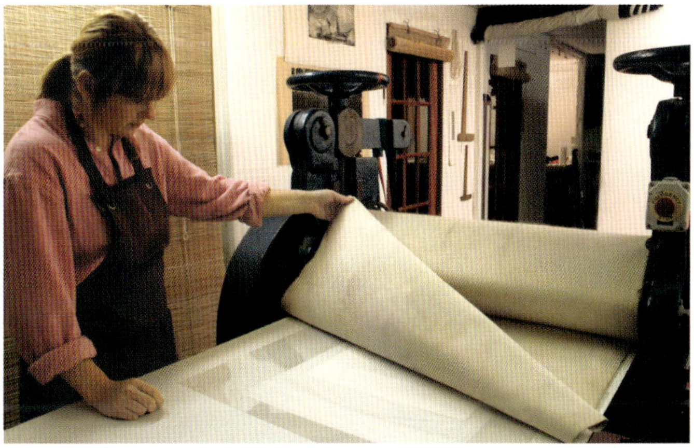

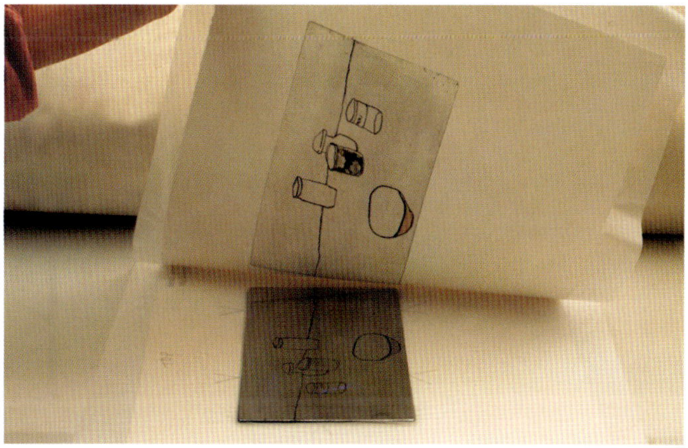

• The plate may either be inked up for a second print or cleaned and stored (see p. 224).

• If printing is finished for the day the inking-up workstation should be cleaned up (see p. 216). The ink may be stored by wrapping it in some tinfoil and labelling this with a waterproof marker pen.

À LA POUPÉE

Several colours can be printed simultaneously from a single plate with this intaglio method. Each ink is applied to the plate with its own inking pad or doll (poupée). The plate is then wiped with clean scrim and tissues (so as not to muddy the colours) and a print is taken. This method is generally most effective when the plate has been designed to be inked in this way.

EMBOSSING

A clean, dry, deeply bitten plate or a richly textured collagraph plate may be impressed into a soft heavyweight paper to create an emboss.

The impression is often sharper if a dry paper is used but this method can cause creasing from the corners of the plate outwards to the edges of the paper. To avoid creases the paper should be the same size as the plate (a bleed print).

If a pristine effect is required it is important that both the plate and the paper are immaculately clean as any blemishes or marks will show up. Some artists ink the plate (either intaglio or with a roll-over) with a white or cream ink to increase the sense of depth.

When a damp paper is used, care must be taken not to flatten the print too much when it is dried.

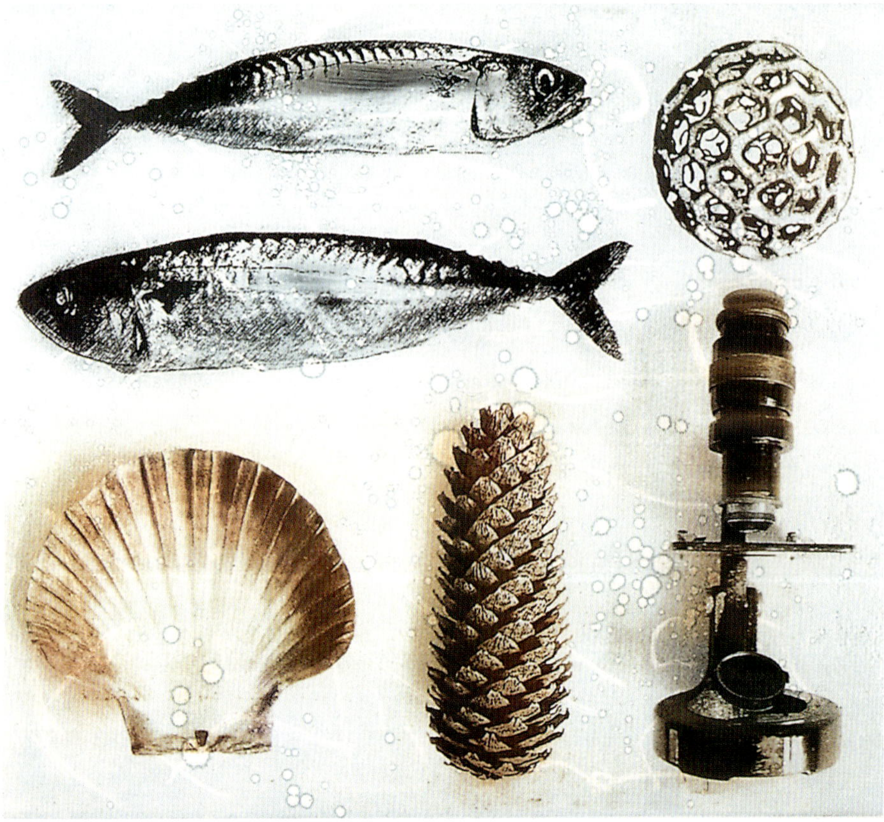

left Rebecca Vincent (UK), *Still Life with Microscope*, 35 x 39 cm (13¾ x 15⅜ in.), 2004. This photocollagraph was inked à la poupée and the Imagon-coated plate was also rolled over with a pale blue ink.

opposite Robert Callender (UK), *Coastal Collection*, detail of embossed print, 61 x 91.5 cm (24 x 36 in.), made at Graal Press, 1999 (see etched plate illustrated on pp. 12 and 71).

CHINE COLLÉ

This technique was popular in the late eighteenth and nineteenth centuries and it can be used when printing any type of intaglio plate as a means of introducing interesting colours, textures and tones to the print.

The name chine collé describes the working method. This involves glueing (collé) the back of delicate sheets – or cut-out shapes – of paper from China, Japan and India (chine is the French term for China), laying these on an inked-up intaglio plate (with the glued side facing upwards), then positioning a sheet of dampened heavyweight intaglio paper over the plate and paper elements. The paper is then covered with several sheets of tissue paper and the blankets of the press. The assembly is run through the press and the pressure laminates the collaged sheets onto the support sheet at the same time as printing the image onto both. The resulting image has a unified and often complex appearance.

Oriental papers accept intaglio ink well, and the heavier paper provides support for these delicate sheets. Modern printmakers use all sorts of thin paper for chine collé: coloured tissue paper, wrapping paper, pages from magazines, sweet wrappers and screenprinted paper.

Traditionally a glue or wheat paste was used but in some cases the different papers were only held together by the pressure from the printing press. The French method involved applying paste to the elements, allowing these to dry, positioning them on the plate and then during printing the adhesives became active.

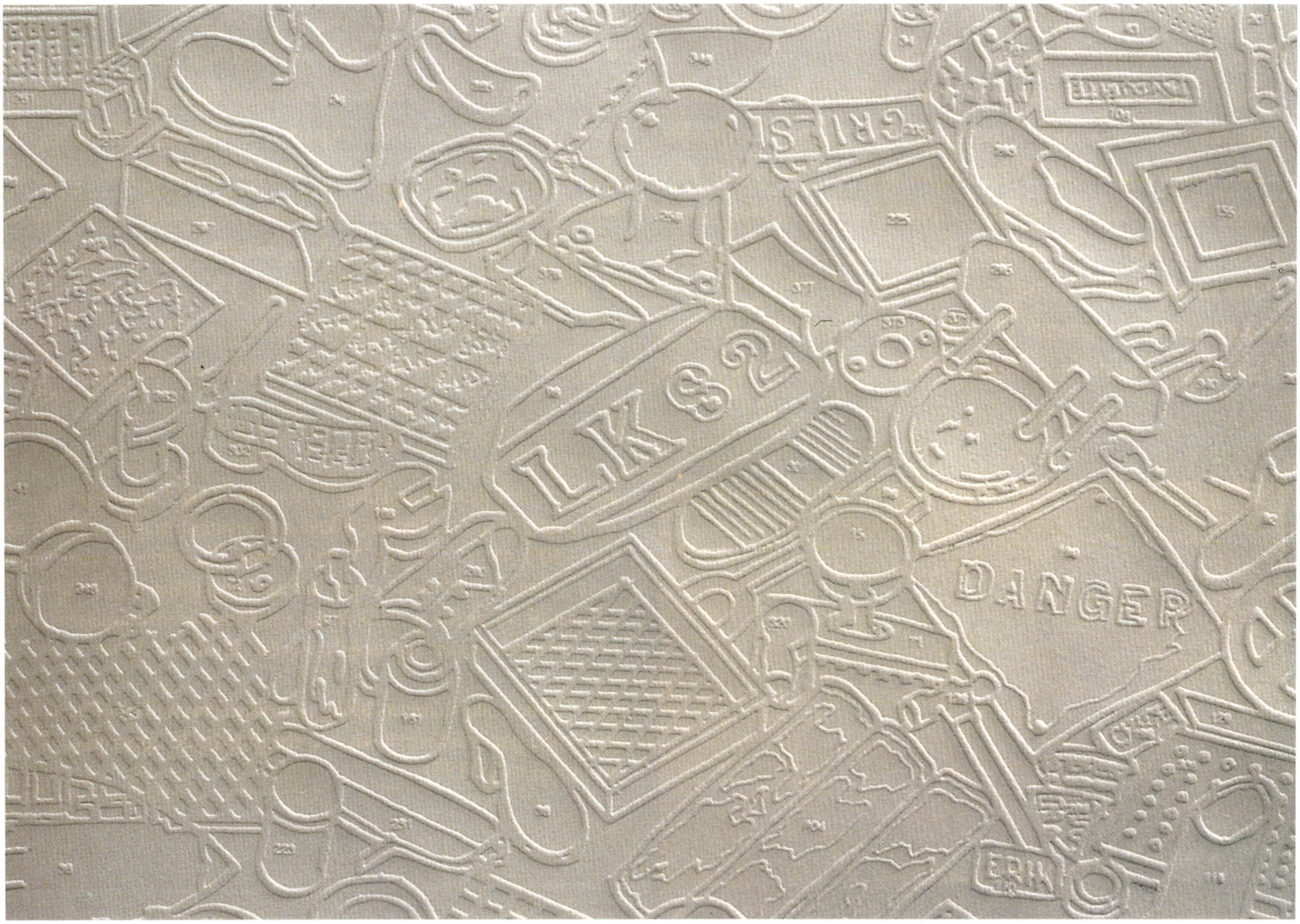

Equipment and materials required

- an inked-up intaglio plate
- a range of thin papers
- a suitable glue (see below)
- a brush
- two sheets of PVC
- a dampened sheet of heavyweight intaglio paper
- a basin of soapy water

Working method

- Design a plate for the chine collé method or make a plan for the elements to fit an existing image. A proof can be taken and used to work out the required shape. In some cases the collage may be assembled in advance on sheets of Chinese or Japanese paper; alternatively the spontaneous approach described below may be successful.
- Cut or tear the thin paper to the shapes required and lay these elements on a clean sheet of PVC.
- Select a glue and prepare it for use. Professional printmakers normally choose acid-free materials such as Rhoplex N-580, Lascaux Medium, PEL White Neutral pH Adhesive or YES Paste. Artists also use wallpaper paste (methocellulose), rice paste or Jin Shofu wheat paste.
- Ink up the intaglio plate.
- Lay out the fragments of paper to be glued on a sheet of PVC, orienting them carefully so that they are glued on the correct side. Apply the glue, working from the centre outwards. An excessively thick deposit will be squeezed out during printing, so judging the amount of glue to apply is a skill which develops with experience.
- Prepare the dampened intaglio paper.
- Position the plate on the press bed and carefully place the glued elements on it with the adhesive facing upwards. Cover with the dampened intaglio paper, several sheets of tissue and the blankets. Run this through the press slowly and steadily.
- Lift back the blankets and tissue paper and slowly remove the print from the plate (making sure that the printed collage is attached to the support paper). The print can be dried between boards in the normal way (see p. 220).
- Chine collé prints should be transported and mailed flat.

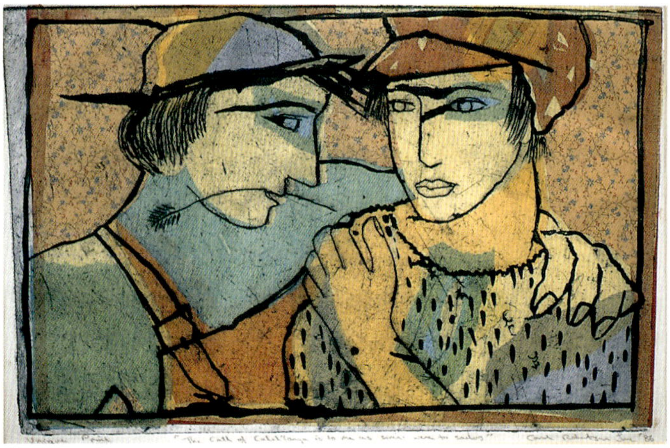

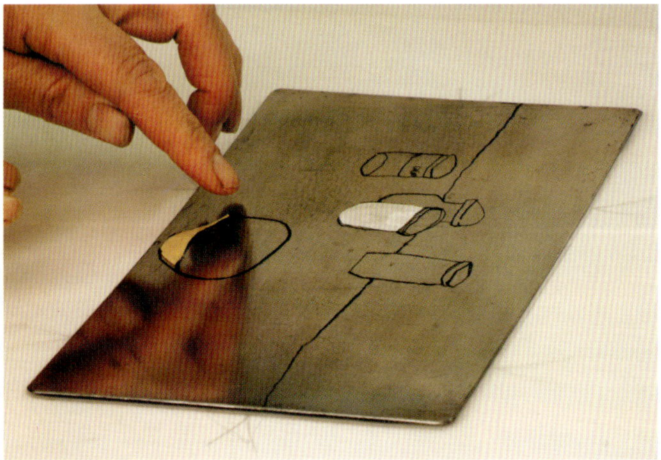

above Carol Robertson (UK), *The call of Cala Longa is to me as sirens were to sailors*, linocut inked and printed intaglio with chine collé, 30 x 45 cm (11¾ x 17¾ in.), 1986. The complex elements were adhered to Chinese paper before being printed in a varied edition of 30. A foam blanket was used to prevent damage to the press from the thick and deeply worked linoleum sheet.

left Chine collé elements being positioned on a plate. The patterned paper is face down and the glued side uppermost (see print on p. 197).

ROLL-OVER AND VISCOSITY PRINTING METHODS

When a deeply indented plate is inked up using a roller (brayer), the highest smooth surfaces on the plate hold the ink and print (as in relief printing). The narrow lines, pits and deep areas which lie below the surface are not filled with ink and cannot print. When an etching press is used to print the plate, these indented areas will generate raised white lines and other embossed textures, and this technique is described as a roll-over.

Viscosity printing is based on the principle that oily inks containing different proportions of oil will reject each other and will separate consistently on the plate surface. The artist adds copperplate oil to selected inks to alter their viscosity. The process involves making an intaglio plate with a range of depths and applying several separate layers of coloured ink with rollers which vary in their softness ('durometer' or 'shore').

This specially conceived plate is firstly inked up in the intaglio manner with a lean ink ('lean' is the term used to describe an ink which does not contain much oil). The second stage involves applying a slightly looser (more oily) coloured ink with a soft roller. This inky layer lies in the next group of low declivities. A harder roller is then used to apply a still looser third coloured ink which will lie on the next range of indentations. Finally a hard roller is used to apply a fourth loose ink which will lie on the surface of the plate. The plate is then left for several minutes to allow time for the inks to react to each other and to settle on the plate surface.

For example, a plate may be inked with a black intaglio followed by a blue roll-over, then a magenta roll-over and finally a yellow layer. The resulting print will show a range of colours, including some greens, purples and browns where the colours have blended together. Editions can be printed if care is taken to avoid transferring the colours from the plate onto the rollers and inking slabs. If this type of contamination occurs, the prints will look muddy and dull.

Stencils made from PVC sheet can also be used to control where the layer of rolled-on ink is positioned on the plate.

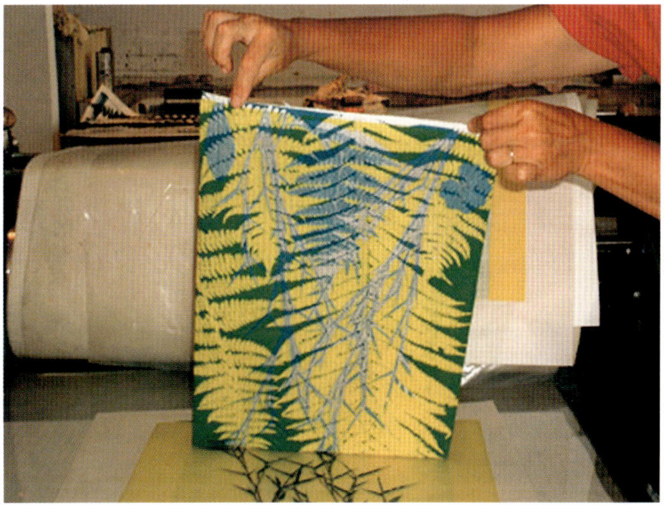

On the etching press at Zea Mays Printmaking in Massachusetts, Anita Hunt uses a roll-over technique to create multicoloured monotypes.

Equipment and materials required

Work in the printing area (see pp. 52–56) and wear appropriate gloves and clothing for the type of ink (see p. 210). A large inking bench will be required if the viscosity method is being used.

- an intaglio plate with deep or varied indentations
- inks and additives for intaglio printing
- inks and additives for relief printing
- some palette knives
- a glass or stone inking slab
- some rollers
- paper for printing on
- materials for cleaning up
- some tinfoil
- a waterproof marker pen
- a notebook and pen
- an etching press
- a registration sheet (see p. 208)
- registration blocks

• some sheets of tissue paper
• the printing paper

Working method

• The marks on the plate surface may be originated using direct, etching or collagraphic methods. The plate should be clean and dry and it is important that it is bevelled with no sharp edges as these can cut hands, rollers, the paper and blankets.
• The etching press should be set at the correct pressure for the thickness of plate. The un-inked plate may be printed on an old blotter and the emboss inspected. The back of the print should be looked at to see that the pressure was sufficient and even on both sides.
• The indentations in the plate surface may be left free of ink or may be inked up in the intaglio method (follow the inking-up instructions given on pp. 193–198).
• The ink and any additives for roll-over methods (see pp. 210–212) are mixed up and rolled out on a glass inking-up slab. This reservoir of ink should be a neat, even square of ink as any lines or marks will be transferred to the plate surface and will print. Any PVC stencils which are being used should be taped into place over the plate before the ink is applied by roller.
• The roller is used to apply an even, thin layer to the cool plate. Any lines created by the action of the roller will print.
• A wide roller with a sufficiently large diameter should allow the ink to be deposited on the plate in a single pass without creating any repeat lines.
• If the viscosity method is being used, several inking slabs and rollers of different shore will be required. The rollers must be cleaned after each roll-up. After the plate has been rolled up, it should be allowed to sit for five minutes before it is printed. A note can be made of the ink recipe and how the plate was inked up.
• The plate is printed on the etching press (follow the instructions given on pp. 196–198). After printing, the print should be dried on a rack until the oily ink has dried. When the ink is dried, the print may be dampened, flattened and dried between boards (see p. 220).

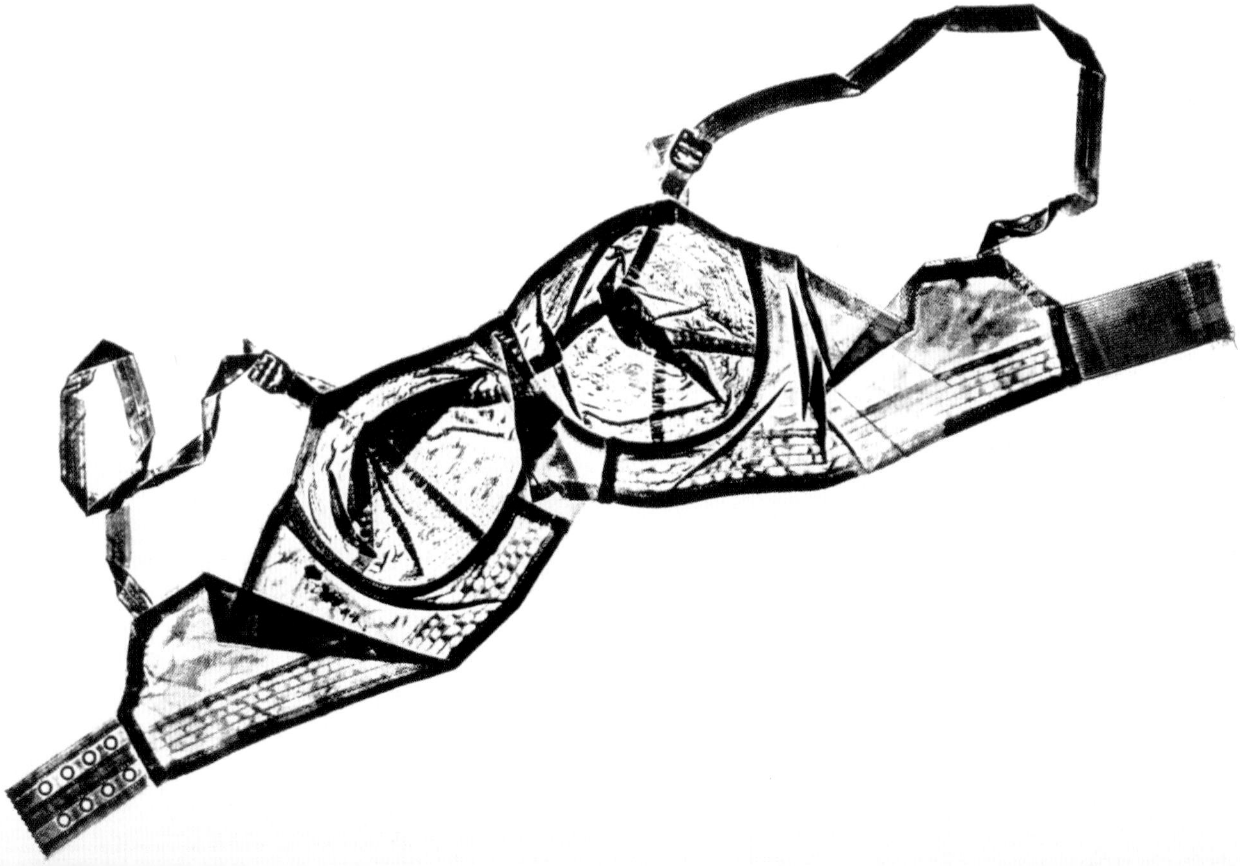

opposite Miriam Schaer (US), *Phantom Armour*, collagraph monotype on paper, 51 x 66 cm (20 x 26 in.), printed and published by the artist at the Lower East Side Printshop, Inc., 2001.

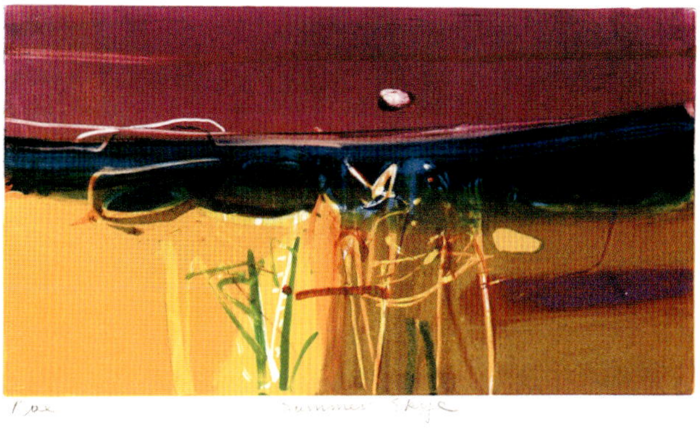

right Barbara Rae (UK) *Summer Skye*, monotype, 17 x 32 cm (6¾ x 12⅝ in.), 2004. This monotype was made by drawing back into rolled-out layers of colour. The artist printed the different layers of colour in register onto dry paper using the paper-trapping registration method (see p. 210).

• The plate should be lifted from the press bed and placed on the inking-up work surface. The tissue should be discarded and any marks on the press wiped away. The registration sheet should be put away if other printmakers are using the space.

• If printing is finished for the day the plates, palette knives, rollers and inking-up slabs should be cleaned up with vegetable oil (see pp. 215–216). The inks may be stored in some tinfoil and these packets can be labelled with a waterproof marker pen.

MONOTYPES

These painting, drawing and colour-layering techniques may be combined with intaglio inking and printing methods to introduce colour, texture or additional elements. The effects which can be generated may resemble a pencil drawing, an oil painting, watercolour or pastel, or the results may be unique to this medium. Some artists make monotypes to develop their ideas before creating an image on an intaglio plate. It is also possible to use the methods to generate positives which may be used in conjunction with light-sensitive intaglio plates (see p. 181). Monotypes can be printed by hand, with a roller, with a PinPress or by using an etching press.

There are several different working methods which may be used on their own, in conjunction with other monotype plates or with an intaglio plate. Plate monotyping techniques may be used on a plate which holds an indented image or on a plate which has a finely grained surface. A tooth will help to hold the ink during the printing process. Plates may be made from metal, plastic, varnished card or wood. Many printmakers favour clear Plexiglas, which allows a registration device such as a map or guide drawing to be placed under the sheet.

Oil-based intaglio inks, lithographic inks, relief inks, pigment sticks, water-miscible oil paints and oil paints may be used to create an image on the plate. Alternatively, water-soluble materials such as gouaches, watercolours, water-based intaglio inks, acrylic paints, Golden, Createx, Akua Kolor and water-soluble crayons and pencils – such as Caran D'Ache pencils – may also be used for monotyping.

TRACE MONOTYPING

The characteristic drawn lines associated with this offsetting method (see p. 16) can be explored by making positives.

DRAWING INTO A ROLLED-OUT LAYER OF INK

Wiped-away lines, marks, textures, tonal effects and complex coloured layers can be printed using the following method.

Equipment and materials required

Work in the workstation for inking up (see p. 55).

- a map or guide drawing
- a plate or plates
- inks for monotyping techniques
- a roller
- cleaning materials (depending on the type of ink)
- paper for printing on

Working method

- Any necessary registration may be considered (see p. 208).
- Roll out some ink on an inking slab to form a reservoir. Apply the ink to all or selected areas of the plate using a roller or dabber. It is good practice to wear gloves and an apron when working with artists' materials.
- Draw into the layer of ink with a blunt stick, paint shaper or the end of a paintbrush. Textures, marks and tonal areas can be created by pressing fabric, netting, feathers, leaves or card shapes into the ink. Gloved fingers and brushes can also be used to work into the layer.
- Other monotyping methods can be used if required.
- Depending on the type of ink, the image on the plate is printed on dry or dampened paper. Follow the printing instructions on pp. 196–198.

PAINTING METHODS

Many different techniques may be used, including making dry brush marks, wet marks, splashes, washes, diluting, offsetting and roller marks.

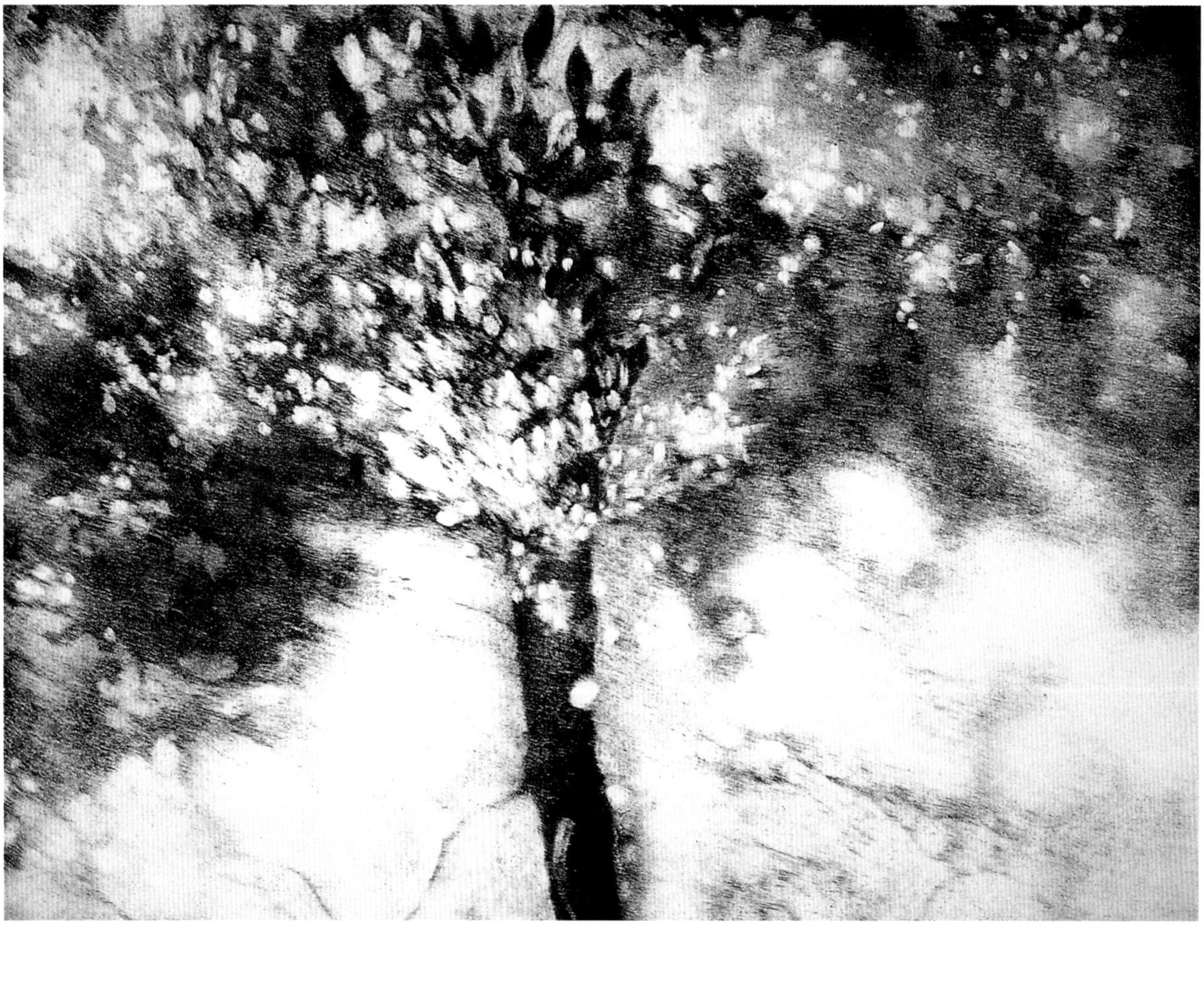

Equipment and materials required

Work in the workstation for inking up (see p. 55).

- a map or guide drawing
- a plate or plates
- inks for monotyping techniques
- some brushes
- some different sized rollers
- cleaning materials (depending on the type of ink)
- paper for printing on

Working method

- Any necessary registration may be considered (see p. 208).
- Make a palette of slow-drying or re-wettable inks. Paint the image onto the plate, avoiding depositing too thick a layer or covering previously painted marks. It is good practice to wear gloves and an apron when working with artists' materials.
- The image may be drawn back into with a blunt stick, paint shaper or the end of a paintbrush. Textures, marks and tonal areas can be created by pressing fabric, netting, feathers, leaves or card shapes into the ink. Gloved fingers and brushes may also be used to work into the layer.
- Other monotyping methods can be incorporated if required.
- Depending on the type of ink, the plate is printed on dry or dampened paper (see p. 219).

DRAWING WITH OIL-BASED MEDIA

Bold drawings can be made using oil-based pigment sticks.

Equipment and materials required

Work in the workstation for inking up (see p. 55).

- a map or guide drawing
- a plate or plates
- R&F oil-based pigment sticks
- cleaning materials
- paper for printing on

Working method

- Any necessary registration may be considered (see p. 208).
- The drawing is made on the plate surface. It is good practice to wear gloves and an apron when working with artists' materials.
- Other monotyping methods can be incorporated if required.
- The plate is printed on dry or dampened paper (see p. 219).

DRAWING WITH WATER-BASED MEDIA

Drawings can be made using water-soluble crayons and pencils.

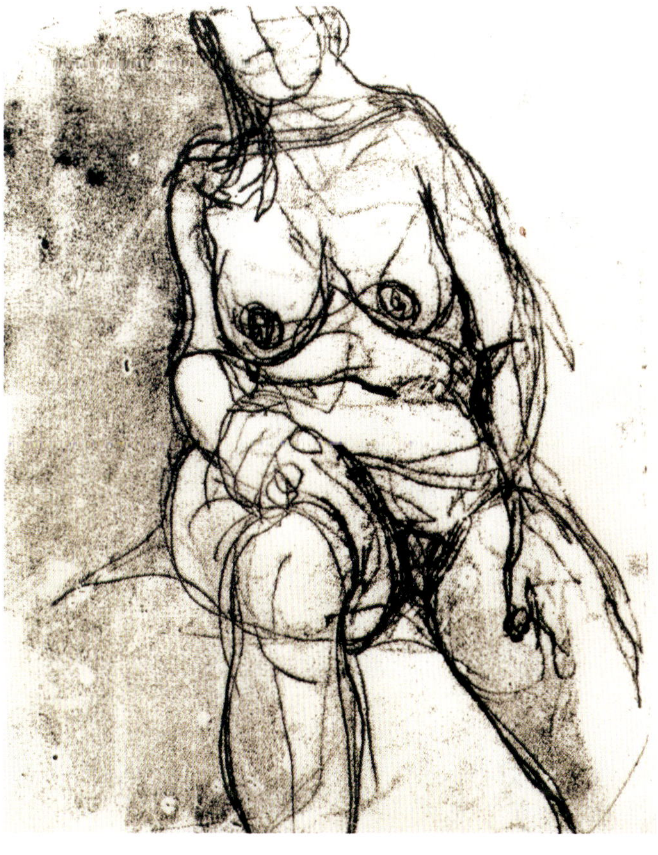

opposite Anita S. Hunt (US), *Shimmer*, monotype, 45.7 x 61 cm (18 x 24 in.), 2002. The artist rolled up a clear plastic plate with a black ink. She started the image by creating lines in the layer using the trace monotyping method. The remaining ink on the plate was then worked into with cotton buds and a small roller. The plate was printed onto dampened Somerset paper.

right Julie Arnall, untitled, trace monotype, 26 x 32 cm (10¼ x 12⅝ in.), 2002.

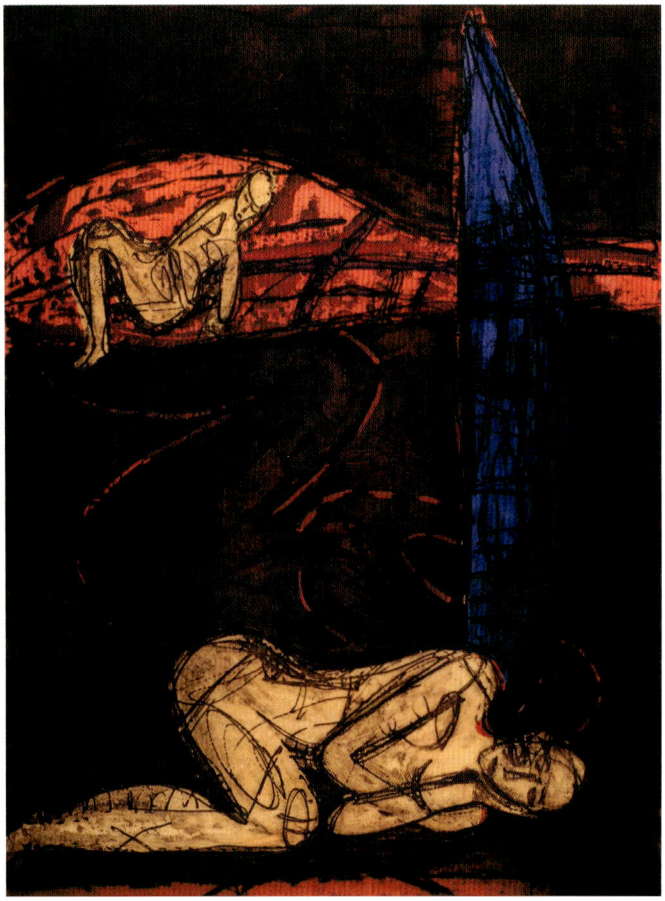

Margaret Hunter (UK/Germany), *Dreamings,* etching, dyed paper, chine collé and screenprinting, 76 x 56 cm (30 x 22 in.), 2002. This etched steel plate was inked intaglio and bleed-printed onto paper which had been dyed red. Blue and cream chine collé elements were incorporated, and a final blue cross was screen-printed with water-based media on the upper red shape.

Equipment and materials required

Work in the workstation for inking up (see p. 55).

- a map or guide drawing
- a plate or plates
- water-soluble crayons and pencils
- a releasing medium (see below)
- cleaning materials
- paper for printing on

Working method

- Any necessary registration may be considered (see p. 208).
- When working with water-soluble crayons or pencils, many printmakers prepare the plate by coating the surface with a thin layer of a loosening agent. This will re-wet during the printing process, releasing the drawn marks and ensuring that the drawing is completely transferred to the paper. Gum arabic, wallpaper paste, water-based screenprinting paste and water-resoluble acrylic mediums are suitable.
- When the coating has dried, the plate may be drawn into. It is good practice to wear gloves and an apron when working with artists' materials.
- Other monotyping methods can be incorporated if required.
- The dampened printing paper may be positioned over the plate and the blankets laid down. If this is left for a few minutes before operating the press, the releasing layer will have time to re-wet and the resulting print will generally be more successful.

COMBINING INTAGLIO WITH OTHER MEDIA

Colour and further imagery may be introduced to intaglio printing by combining it with other media such as drawing, painting, monotyping, screenprinting, lithography, digital work, photocopying, photography and collage methods.

If the intaglio plate is printed onto an image made using another medium, a number of factors will affect the success and quality of the resulting print. These include the ink-holding capability of the plate, the type of ink which has been applied to the intaglio plate, the different substrates and the inks already present on them. Oily and sealed surfaces will reject the intaglio ink, making the print pale and indistinct. Absorbent surfaces are generally better to print on.

Some artists draw, paint, screenprint or offset photocopies onto their intaglio prints.

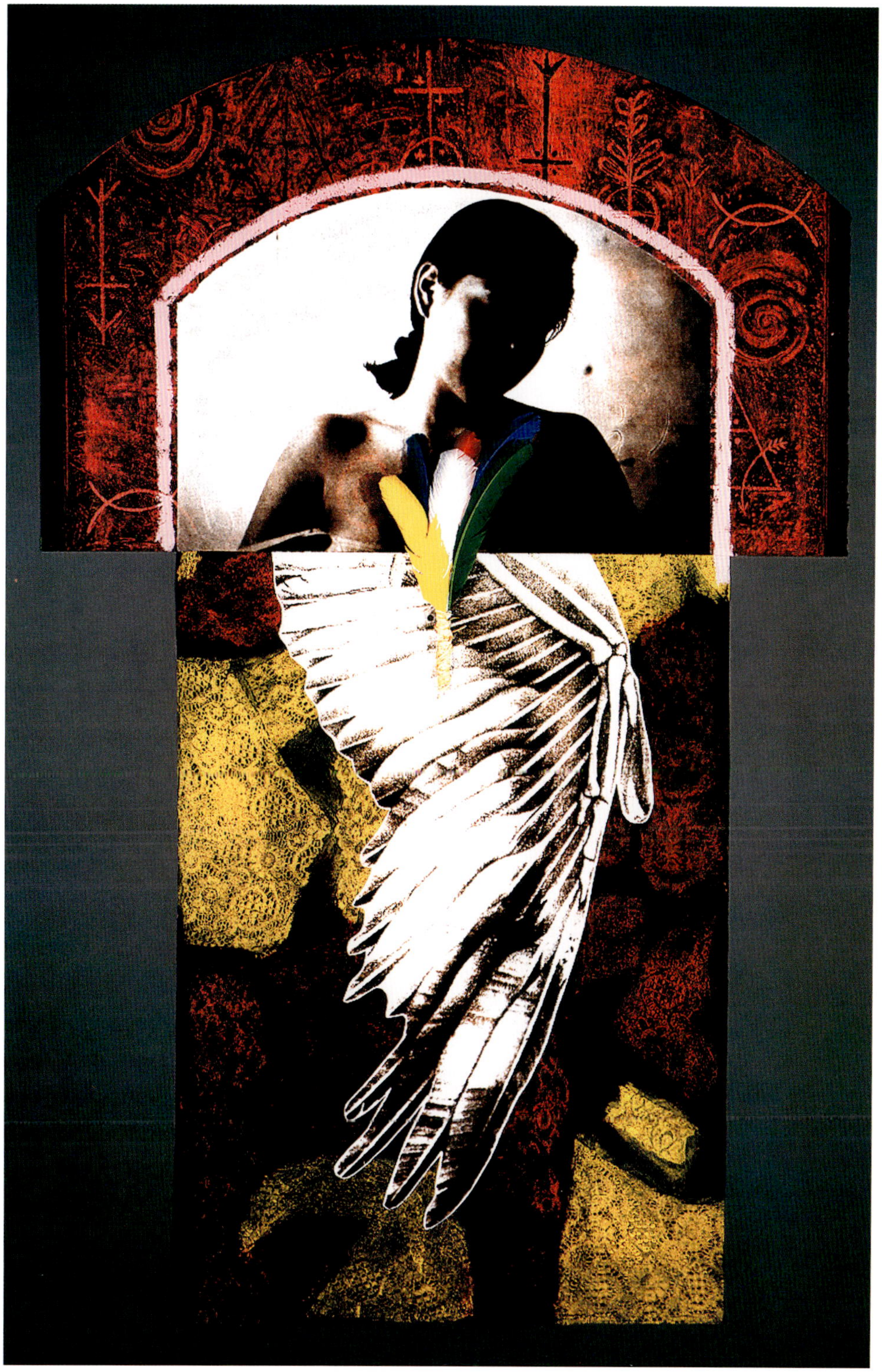

Juan Sanchez (US), *Victoria de Samotracia (Afro-Taina)*, collagraph, photolithograph, handcolouring, feathers and raffia, 172.7 x 109.2 cm (68 x 43 in.), printed at Wildwood Press in an edition of 16, 2000.

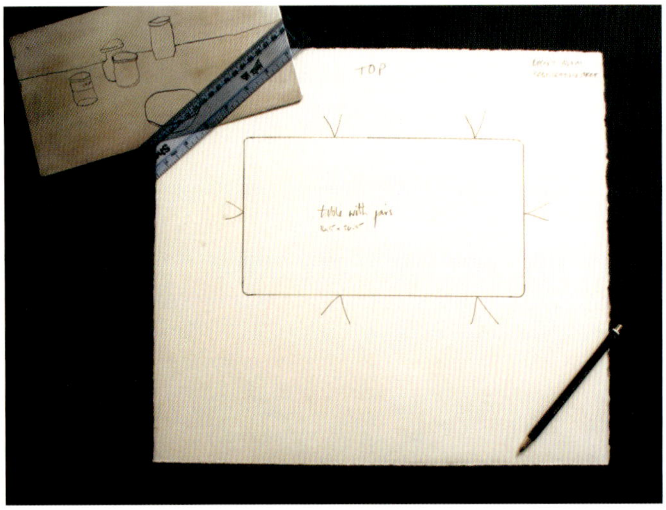

left A registration sheet (in this case a sheet of the editioning paper so the paper size does not need to be marked).

below left White magnetic registration blocks in use on a steel etching press bed (see print on p. 22).

REGISTRATION METHODS

In order to print the plate or plates in exactly the correct place on the paper a registration system is used. The resulting prints will look consistent and professional, and will be easier to frame and display.

A traditional and accurate method is to use one sheet of the editioning paper as a registration device. To make this registration sheet, the clean plate which is to be printed is positioned on the paper in the correct place (use a ruler to measure the distance from the plate to the edge of the paper). The plate is then drawn around with a waterproof marker pen, and arrows or V-shaped marks are drawn up to the plate edges to facilitate registering the plate to the lines. The corners and edges of the registration sheet can be coloured with a waterproof marker pen so that they can be easily seen against the white press bed when registering the printing paper to the registration sheet. The name of the plate and its dimensions can be written on the registration sheet with a waterproof marker pen.

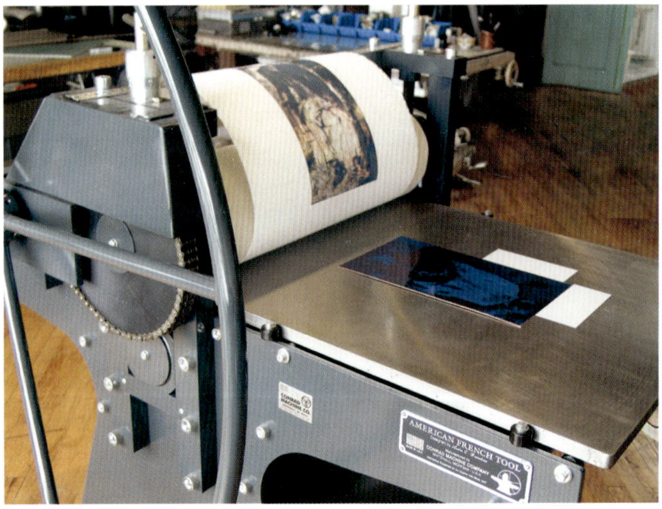

The registration sheet should be dampened and blotted in the same way that the editioning paper is treated (see p. 219). This practice ensures that the registration sheet is the same size as the damp printing papers. When long editions are being printed or the air is very dry, the registration sheet may have to be re-dampened occasionally.

The dampened and blotted registration sheet is laid on the press bed and covered with a sheet of tissue paper. The inked-up plate is then laid on the tissue paper, which is picked up by the corners and moved so that the plate slides into register with the drawn lines and arrows on the registration sheet below. The prepared printing paper is then lifted by diagonal corners and brought to the press. It is lined up with the coloured edges of the registration sheet and the top corner is laid down in register. A thumb can be used to anchor the paper and it can be swivelled into position without its under-surface touching the inky plate. This type of registration sheet can be stored and used again.

An alternative method is to protect the registration sheet with a larger sheet of PVC on which the tissue and plate are laid. In this case the registration sheet is not dampened, and allowance is made for expansion of the dampened edition printing paper.

David Jay Reed (US), *A Decetive Lives Here*, photocollagraph, 30.5 x 40.7 cm (12 x 16 in.), 2002. A photograph was taken, altered digitally to include graffiti, and separated into four positives. These were exposed onto four copper plates, each laminated with ImagOn Ultra film, then developed, dried, inked up intaglio and printed in sequence (cyan, magenta, yellow and black) to create the final intaglio print.

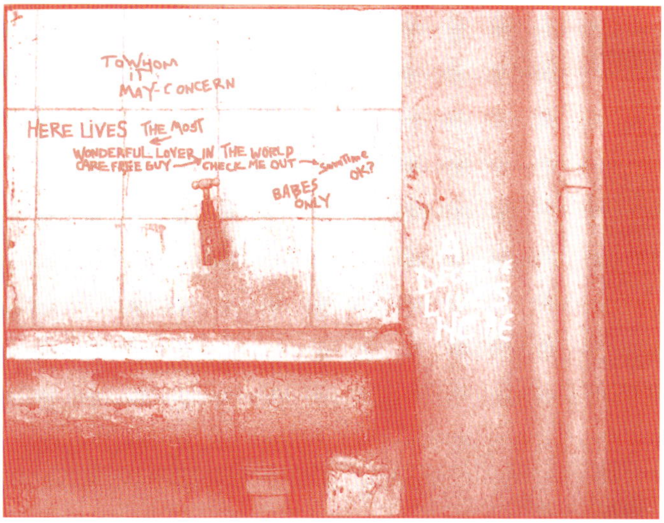

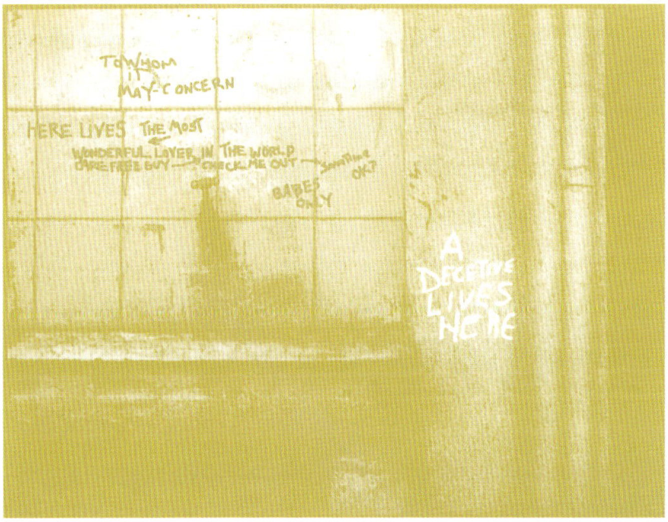

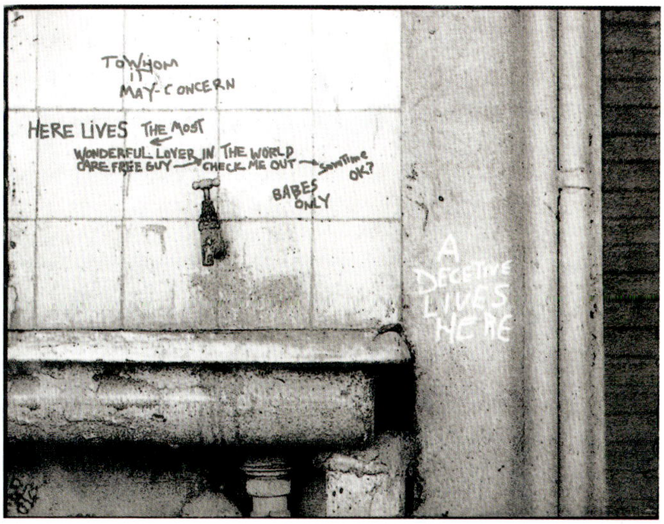

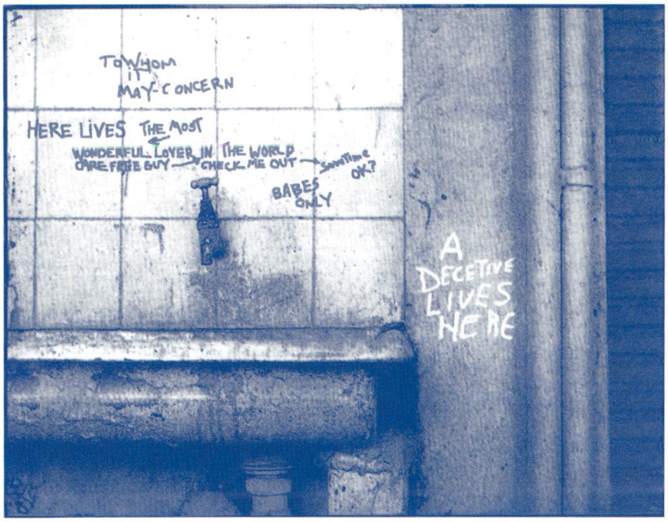

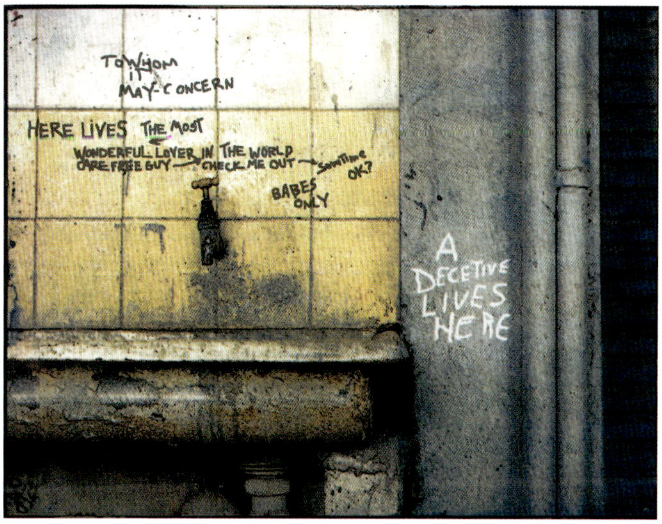

Some etching press beds hold an image of a grid. This bold black-and-white linear image is beneath a sheet of PVC which keeps it clean and dry. The plate is laid on tissue and moved so that it lines up with the grid. The paper can then be positioned on top of the inky plate using the lines on the grid for reference.

Another method involves using a metal, plastic or magnetic template with a cut-away section to hold the plate. Marks are made on the registration device to show where the paper should be positioned. These sheets can be home-made or purchased from intaglio suppliers such as Z*Acryl. They can be wiped clean after use and kept for plates and papers of the same size.

MULTI-PLATE AND PROCESS PRINTING REGISTRATION METHOD

The plates which are used must be precisely the same size. After cutting in the guillotine they may be held together in a vice and bevelled so that they are identical. This makes accurate registration easier and prevents a series of coloured lines appearing on the print around the edges of the image. All of the plates are normally inked up before the printing paper is prepared, and for this reason an ink which dries slowly on the plate is used. For four-colour process printing, special process colour inks are used (see p. 192).

The paper should have large margins as this makes the process of trapping the printing paper easier.

The first plate and the paper are placed accurately on the press bed with the aid of a registration sheet. These are rolled through the press, and the artist carefully traps the last few centimetres of printing paper under the roller. The blankets are lifted up over the roller and the printed paper is very carefully peeled from the plate (to avoid moving the plate), curled back and laid over the blankets and roller. Several magnetic or heavy metal blocks with straight edges are then placed against the edges of the used plate to mark its position. The first plate is carefully removed and replaced between the blocks with the second inked plate. The registration blocks are removed and any dirty marks on the tissue can be covered with small clean pieces of tissue. The print is uncurled back so that it lies in position over the plate. A sheet of tissue is then placed over the print, followed by the blankets. This second plate is printed, and again the last few centimetres are trapped under the roller (this time at the other end of the printing paper) and the process repeated until the print is complete.

INKS AND ADDITIVES

In the early days of intaglio printmaking artists such as Hercules Seghers used both water-based and oil-based inks. The modern printmaker can make inks from powder pigments mixed with oils or water-soluble media or can purchase a wide range of oil-based intaglio inks, water-based intaglio inks and water-miscible oil paints, as well as a wide range of additives for intaglio or surface printing techniques.

Inks should be mixed up on a clean glass or stone slab, and palette knives and other tools should be clean and free of dust. Plates should be inked up on a glass slab or an inert, wipe-clean work surface (see p. 55). Zinc and aluminium plates will react with a number of pigments, causing their colour to change. Copper reacts to fewer pigments and can be steel-faced. The use of newsprint in the wiping process can also adversely affect colour quality.

Good studio practice should be followed when working with all artists' materials: gloves or barrier cream should be worn when inking up and cleaning plates (especially if there are cuts and abrasions on the skin). The use of any toxic pigments (e.g. cadmium), hazardous additives (cobalt driers) or solvents (turpentine and white spirit) should be avoided. Hands should be washed before eating or smoking. Water-based inks can be cleaned up with soapy water and oil-based inks may easily be removed from the plates using an inexpensive vegetable oil (see p. 215).

OIL-BASED INKS FOR INTAGLIO METHODS

A wide range of coloured copperplate inks and specialist additives for intaglio printmaking are made by manufacturers such as Charbonnel, Gamblin, Graphic Chemical, Gerstaecker and Faust. Products include ranges of economy inks, blacks, coloured inks, process colours, metallic inks, graphites and greys, fine rich specialist inks, low viscosity inks and transparent inks.

The inks are manufactured to a high standard and are richly pigmented. They are ground until they are smooth, as the plate surface can be scratched by rough pigments. Intaglio inks are generally compatible and can be mixed to generate further ranges of colours.

When a translucent colour is required, a tiny touch of pigmented intaglio ink is added to a transparent base such as Charbonnel Transparent Lake or Graphic Chemical Tint Base Extender. This is then mixed up and the colour tested on a piece of paper. The process is repeated until the colour and translucency are correct.

Corn starch and magnesium carbonate may be used to stiffen inks, and additives such as eugonol (oil of cloves) can be used to retard the drying time.

Inking up and cold wiping can be aided by adding a little Graphic Chemical Easy Wipe Compound or Daniel Smith Miracle Gel Reducer into the ink before printing. These additives do not alter the body of the ink, the colour or the lightfastness. Charbonnel clear linseed oil, copperplate oil or a little raw linseed oil may also be used. When raw linseed oil is added to the ink, the lines and area of aquatint are enriched, but if too much is added it will cause yellow staining on the print. The quantity of additive which is required depends on the viscosity of the ink and the types of pigment which have been used.

Depending on the manufacturer, inks are available in tubes, cartridges (for use with a standard caulking gun), slip-top metal cans and screw-top plastic containers. Tubes and cartridges last well but when using open-top containers care must be taken to avoid gouging into the ink. A wedge-shaped palette knife should be placed in the container and moved in a full circle like the hands of a clock to remove the ink. A little water added to this type of open-topped container will help prevent the inks drying out. Mixed colours can be wrapped in tinfoil or greaseproof paper and stored for a short time.

Intaglio inks are absorbed by the printing paper and dry by oxidation: they may take as long as two weeks to dry thoroughly.

OIL-BASED INKS FOR SURFACE PRINTING METHODS

Lithographic and relief printing inks may be applied to the surface using a roller.

The ingredients in inks made for offset lithography vary widely so it is important to check the MSDS before purchasing or using these types of ink. Many types of ink are made with pigments which are not lightfast or of artist's quality, causing some colours such as yellows and reds to fade in only a few years. Lithographic inks are classed as either petroleum oil-based inks (usually containing driers), soy and vegetable oil-based inks (environmentally friendly), rubber-based inks (petroleum-based with added cyclized rubber) and waterless inks. Some of these types of inks contain hydrotreated naphthenic oil, butyl ester, methyl ester, terpene phenol resin, rosin ester, toxic driers and other hazardous additives; while other varieties, such as Daniel Smith's Lithographic Inks, are made especially for artists and contain only oils, magnesium carbonate and high-quality lightfast pigments. Daniel Smith Miracle Gel Reducer can also be used to decrease the tackiness of the ink, which reduces the possibility of roller marks.

Relief inks are made for woodblock, linoleum and intaglio relief printing and they generally contain copperplate oils and pigments. These inks are slow-drying and some manufacturers add cobalt driers or suggest adding driers (no more than 5% by volume). Many colours are available and a transparent base can be used.

STIFFENING INKS

Magnesium carbonate is a powder that may be added to increase the body of intaglio, lithographic and relief inks (a dust mask should be worn).

WATER-WASHABLE INTAGLIO INKS AND OIL PAINTS

A range of oil-based intaglio inks which are water-washable are made by the British company Caligo. These high-quality inks have a good range of blacks and colours, and a set of process colours specially designed for intaglio printing. Water-washable oil paints can also be used, although these are much looser than the specially made Caligo inks.

WATER-SOLUBLE INKS FOR INTAGLIO METHODS

Akua-Intaglio are water-soluble inks which have been specially designed for modern intaglio printmaking by Rostow & Jung. The ink can be easily cleaned from the plate, tools and working surface with dishwashing liquid and water. Akua-Intaglio ink dries on the paper from between 24 hours to a 2-week period, depending on the deposit of ink.

WATER-BASED INKS FOR SURFACE PRINTING METHODS

Traditionally watercolour paints were painted or rolled onto the plate with a rubber roller to create transparent luminous colours.

There are a number of water-soluble relief inks on the market with wide ranges of colour. Some brands of ink have a long open time and allow a very thin layer to be applied. Most of the inks dry to a waterproof finish. The inks can be cleaned up from plates and tools with dishwashing liquid and water.

MAKING INKS FOR INTAGLIO METHODS

Intaglio inks can be made from dry, finely powdered pigments mixed with oils or water-soluble media. Pigments are divided into two main categories: inorganic pigments (such as pigments derived from natural earth deposits, burnt or calcined earths, minerals and metallic compounds) and organic pigments (which are derived from vegetable or animal matter or processed from chemicals). Specialist suppliers such as Kremer offer a comprehensive range, from semi-precious minerals (such as lapis lazuli) to inexpensive modern synthetic colours. The range also includes metal powders (such as tin, stainless steel and copper) and pearlescent pigments.

A traditional black ink for intaglio was made from one-third heavy French black (vine black) pigment and two-thirds Frankfurt black pigment. Vine black is made from charred vegetable matter and has a bluish tinge. It is quite opaque, has good lightfastness, absorbs a high volume of oil and is slow-drying. Frankfurt black is no longer accepted as a pigment in its own right: it was more of a dark grey colour than a black and printmakers often now substitute it with ivory black or bone black. These blacks are made by charring animal bones (at one time ivory black was made from carbonized walrus tusks, hartshorn and elephant tusks). Bone black has a brownish tinge, is lightfast, fairly opaque and also has a high

Materials for making an oil-based intaglio ink, together with a glass muller, a palette knife and a storage tube.

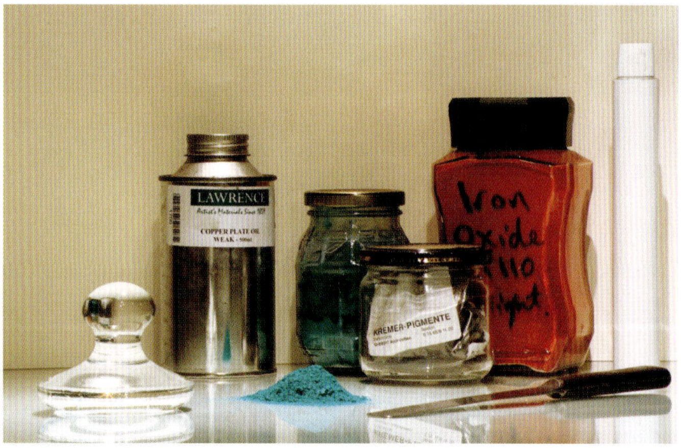

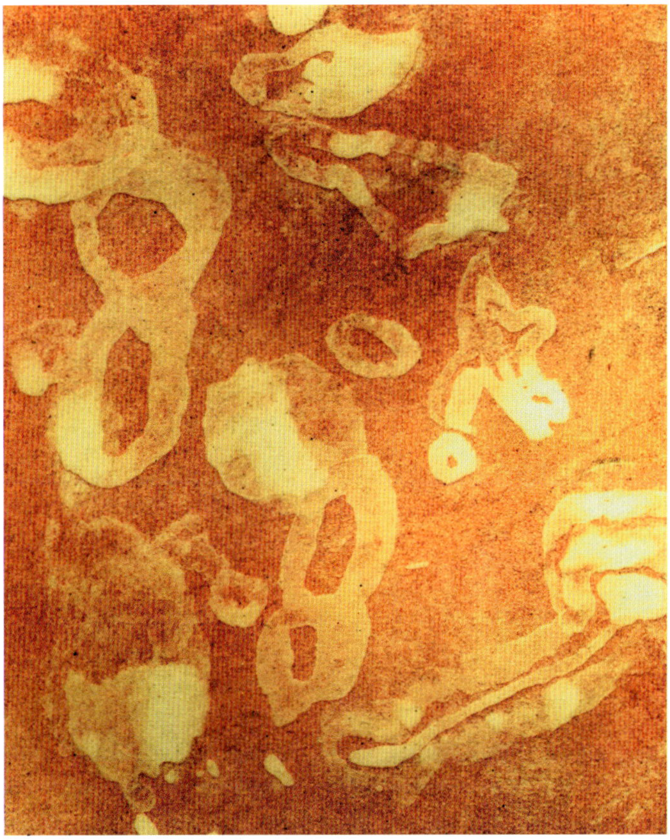

As part of an experimental ink-making project, an artist inked up this plate with chocolate spread and printed this image. The plate was made using wash resist and aquatint, and was etched in ferric chloride.

absorbency of oil and slow drying time. Lamp black and carbon black are very fine, greasy powders which are made from the soot produced by the burning of petroleum products.

Pigments must be stored in containers with lids and handled with care. Gloves, an apron and a particulate respirator must always be worn when handling powder pigments. Once the powder has been totally combined, the printing mixture is safer to handle (unless toxic pigments have been used). Some pigments such as cadmium are highly toxic, while others such as zinc and aluminium powder are very reactive and can be flammable. Information about the safe handling of different pigments can be sourced from specialist suppliers or from articles on the internet.

MAKING AN OIL-BASED INTAGLIO INK

Heavy, medium and light copperplate oils and raw linseed oil are mixed with the pigments to form an oil-based intaglio printing ink. Copperplate oil has a golden yellow appearance and is made by 'burning' linseed oil; heavy copperplate oil has been heated until it is heavy and sticky, and light copperplate oil has only been slightly heated. A clear oil is sold by Charbonnel. The temperature of the studio affects the behaviour of the oils: a heavy oil would normally be chosen for warm environments and a light oil used by artists working in a colder climate.

The finely ground powder pigment is placed in a mound on a glass slab and a well is made in the centre. Heavy copperplate oil is poured into the well and some light oil is added to make the mixture more pliable. A palette knife is used to make a paste, which is then ground to become a thick smooth cream. A glass muller with an abraded base diameter of 7–10 cm/3–4 in. is ideal for this purpose (traditionally mullers were made from porphyry). A plate which holds linear work, some fine aquatint, some areas of plate tone and open bite, as well as polished areas, should be used to test the qualities of the ink, and careful adaptations can be made to the mixture if necessary.

Coloured pigments may grind down more easily than some blacks; the mixture can be made more fluid and will benefit from the addition of Graphic Chemical Easy Wipe Compound. Once the ink has been made it will be long-lasting if it is stored (sealed from the air) in a tube, cartridge or container.

MAKING A WATER-BASED INTAGLIO INK

Experimental water-based intaglio printing inks may be made by mixing dry powder pigments with a range of acrylic media.

REMOVING RESISTS, COLLAGRAPH MATERIALS AND INKS FROM THE PLATE

Z*Acryl resists, floor polish, Speedball Screen Filler, Graphic Chemical & Ink Company Water-Washable Block Printing Ink, acrylic paints, painting media, and Lascaux tusches and acrylic resists are water-soluble and can be cleaned from brushes, tools, palettes, plates and surfaces with warm soapy water before they dry.

When these media dry and become waterproof, they are removed either with sodium carbonate stripping solution or with Lascaux Remover or Mystrol (see below). Materials which remain water-soluble after drying such as gouaches, water-resoluble mediums, screenprinting paste, tempera, water-soluble crayons and watercolour paints can be cleaned up with soapy water. Oil-based materials can be cleaned up easily using vegetable oil (see below).

SODIUM CARBONATE STRIPPING SOLUTION

Dried layers of photoresists, Z*Acryl resists, floor polish, Speedball Screen Filler, Graphic Chemical & Ink Company Water-Washable Block Printing Ink and some other materials can be removed from the plate with a sodium carbonate stripping solution.

Equipment and materials required

Work in the resist-removal area (see pp. 49–50).

- gloves, dust mask, visor and apron
- sodium carbonate
- digital scales
- water and calibrated jug

Working method

- It is good practice to wear an apron, gloves and visor (and a dust mask while mixing the powder).
- Make up the stripping solution of sodium carbonate and water (50–100 grams of sodium carbonate to 1 litre of water). Follow the mixing instructions given on p. 148 and then pour the stripping solution into a tray (this solution cannot be stored in a tank as the mixture crystallizes). Make a note of the components for future reference. Label the tray clearly so that it is not mistaken for a tray of developing solution (a newly exposed photoresist will be ruined if placed in this strong solution).
- Immerse the plate in a tray of the solution. The resist will dissolve after ten to twenty minutes.
- After removing the resist the plate should be rinsed thoroughly and examined for any remaining resist. The process may be repeated until the plate is clean.
- The plate should be degreased (see p. 78) before working further with other resists or printing with water-based inks.

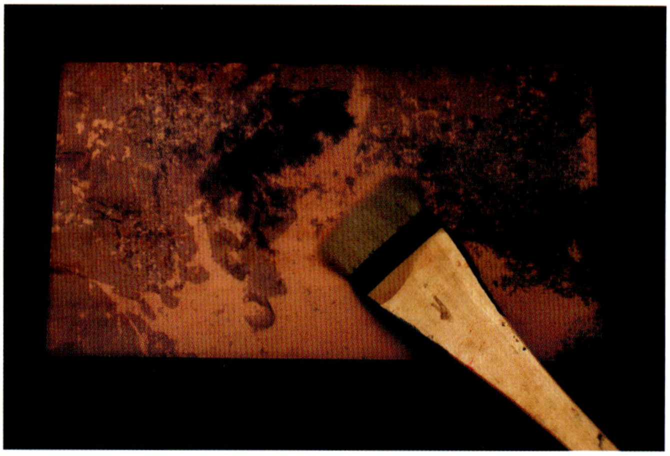

A layer of exposed photoresist breaks away easily from this copper plate in a tray of sodium carbonate stripping solution.

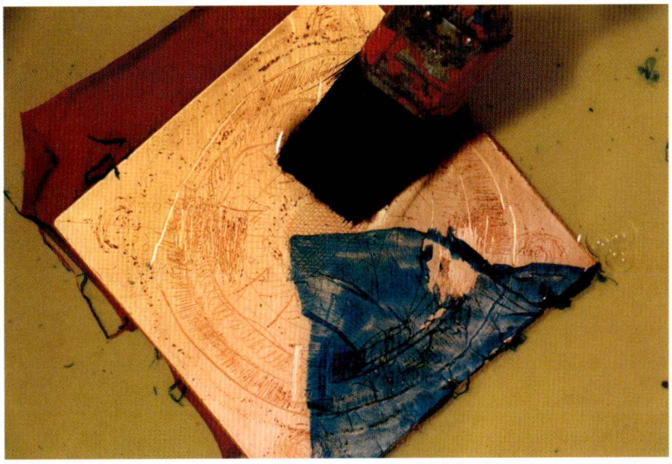

Degreasing the stripped plate with an acidic degreaser will remove inorganic compounds such as hard water deposits.

LASCAUX REMOVER AND MYSTROL

Dried layers of Lascaux acrylic resists, some types of acrylic paint, water-based intaglio inks and certain other materials may be removed with Lascaux Remover or Mystrol. These removers, rather than dissolving the resist, alter the crosslinked structure, causing the formerly tough layer to be weakened and lifted easily from the plate. The layer(s) of resists may become wrinkled and shrivelled or may appear unaltered, but can be loosened and brushed from the plate. Mystrol is a household cleaner which is classified as safe to the user and the environment and is a fast-acting resist remover. Brushes with deposits of dry resist can be soaked in the remover, washed in soap (Marseilles soap is ideal) and then thoroughly rinsed.

Equipment and materials required

Work in the resist-removal area (see pp. 49–50).

- an apron, gloves and a visor
- a tray or tank of Lascaux Remover or Mystrol
- a non-scratch plastic cleaning pad

Lascaux stop-out and plate-backing resists are weakened by the remover and become detached from the plate.

Working method

- The plate (or plates) should be immersed in a tray or tank of the selected remover for around 10 to 20 minutes. The tray or tank should have a cover (to reduce evaporation) and it is good practice to wear an apron, gloves and visor.
- After soaking, one plate at a time is removed from the tray and the weakened resist is immediately rubbed from the plate surface with a brush or non-scratch plastic cleaning pad (with an open weave). The weakened resist should not be allowed to dry on the plate as it will become tough again.
- The plate is rinsed in warm water and examined for any remaining resist. The entire stripping process may be repeated until the plate is clean. The plate should then be degreased with an acidic degreaser (see p. 78) before working further with other resists or printing with water-based inks.

VEGETABLE OIL

Oily resists and inks can be removed with vegetable oil.

Equipment and materials required

Work in the inking-up area for oil-based materials. It is good practice to wear an apron and gloves when working with oily art materials.

- some vegetable oil (the most inexpensive brand from a catering supplier)
- a non-scratch plastic household cleaning pad
- a china bowl for storing the pad
- dishwashing liquid
- some degreaser (alkaline)
- a plastic dishwashing brush with soft bristles
- some clean cloths

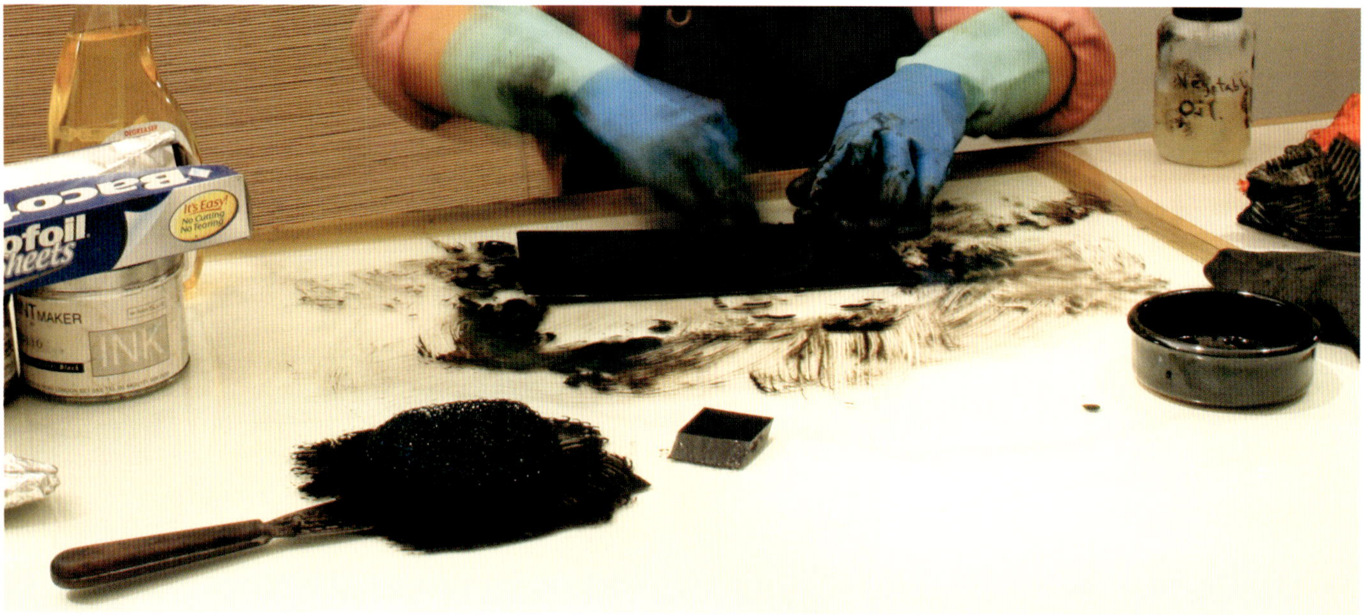

Working method

• Coat the soiled plate, work surface and any greasy tools with a layer of vegetable oil and leave for a few minutes (especially if the plate has a textured surface or deep indentations). Then use a non-scratch plastic household cleaning pad (with an open weave) to loosen the oily material. Store the soiled pad in a bowl for future use.

• Use a series of cloths to absorb the oil which is carrying the loosened oily resist and wipe the plate, surfaces and tools until they are clean. Deeply bitten plates which look very clean (i.e. have no ink or oil on the surface, edges or back of the plate) may be printed onto a piece of blotting paper to remove any vegetable oil and ink from the indentations.

• The plate, working surface and tools will look clean but will be coated in a greasy residue of vegetable oil. This can be removed with some soapy water. Everything should then be dried with clean cloths.

• The plate should be degreased with an alkaline degreaser, de-oxidized and neutralized (see pp. 70 and 78) before being worked further (e.g. the application of acrylic resists, or polishing) or printing with water-based inks.

above The vegetable oil is applied to the plate and tools with a non-absorbent pad (lying on the spatula) and gloved fingertips.

below After a few minutes the oil and ink is wiped up with rags or absorbent tissue.

• Unless an area for working with oily materials has been designated in the studio, the work surface and workboard should be degreased, rinsed and dried. This will prevent plates being contaminated with oily residues.

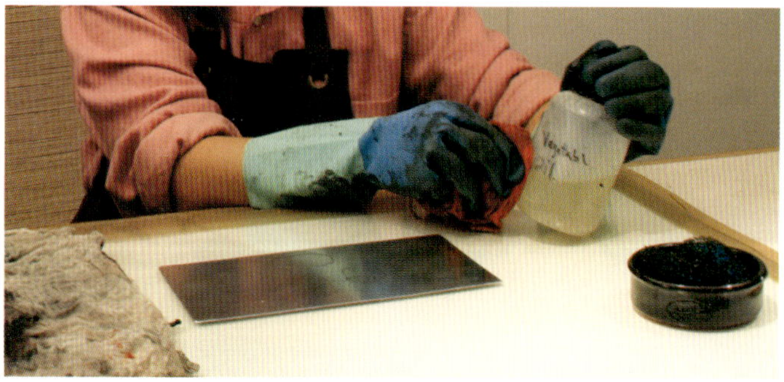

PRINTING SUBSTRATES

PAPER

Paper is made from a number of different materials, such as wood, cotton, linen and other vegetable matter, which are broken down into a mass of cellulose fibres. The pattern in which the fibres are laid down during manufacture will affect the way in which the paper expands when dampened for printing. For instance, if the fibres are randomly mixed – as in a handmade paper – expansion will be fairly consistent in every direction. When the fibres are predominantly parallel – as in most machine-made papers, such as cartridge or newsprint – expansion will be more directional. Mouldmade fine art papers are the most commonly used for intaglio printmaking and fall between these extremes.

The extent to which a paper will absorb printing ink depends on how it has been 'sized'. This refers to the addition of chemicals and glues such as rosin, gelatin, starch, aquapel or polymers at the manufacturing stage. Watercolour paper and other papers which have greater water resistance are known as hard-sized; papers which are more absorbent, or unsized, are called waterleaf.

Many papers will yellow or decay in time. This can be due to acidity, which may result from sizing with hide glue or alum. Artists who are concerned about the longevity of their work should use papers which are classified as acid-free or pH-neutral, together with high-quality inks.

Papers are available in rolls or in flat sheets of different sizes. Flat sheets are more suitable for printing and merchants generally stock a range of standard sizes. These vary from one country to another. Smooth papers are classified as hot pressed ('HP'), referring to the process which created the surface. Papers with textured surfaces are called 'ROUGH' and medium-surfaced papers can be labelled 'CP' (cold pressed) or 'NOT' (not hot pressed). Many of these watercolour and printmaking papers have beautiful surfaces and attractive feathered (deckled) edges.

Modern tests on the fibres of ancient prints have shown that many papers were blue in the fourteenth century. It is known, for instance, that Hendrik Goltzius printed on blue paper. Blue paper was also used for eighteenth-century French crayon manner prints, and later papers were dyed to look blue or purple.

Modern printmakers tend to use white, cream, pinkish or greenish papers. Art material shops and specialist paper merchants are able to supply swatches of different printmaking papers, and detailed catalogues are available. Printmaking papers from Italy, France, Germany and England are readily available, and many other countries have traditions of paper manufacture. The manufacturers will suggest which of their papers are suitable for intaglio: for instance, Fabriano Papers recommend Uno, Esportazione, Tiepolo, Rosaspina, Pescia and Umbria. Some examples of commonly used specialist papers for intaglio printing are listed below. The weight of the paper is generally described as grams per square metre (gsm or gm^2) or in pounds where metric measurement is not used.

- Arches paper has been made in the same French mill since 1492. Arches Cover is a versatile, acid-free paper made with 100% cotton and is available in white, cream or black, with four deckle edges.
- The German Hahnemühle etching paper is often used for printing aquatints and drypoints. This acid-free 300 gsm mouldmade paper has four deckles and is made from 75% cotton and 25% high alpha cellulose. As it is a waterleaf paper it is generally prepared by spraying the sheet with water rather than soaking it.
- Copperplate paper made by Zerkall of Germany is a white 250 gsm acid-free mouldmade paper with two natural deckles

and two tear deckles. It is made with a 25% cotton and 75% sulphite blend. As it is also an unsized paper it is generally prepared by spraying the sheet rather than soaking it.

- Somerset paper is made in England. These papers are made with 100% cotton and are often used for embossing, colour work and printing deeply etched plates or collagraphs.
- Rives papers are made in France, and are popular and useful for intaglio and for printing monotypes. Rives BFK 270 gsm is 100% cotton, acid-free, buffered and has four deckle edges.
- Magnani Pescia paper is a mouldmade 100% cotton 300 gsm paper from Italy. The sheets are available in a range of colours, including pale blue, soft white and grey. This absorbent paper is lightly sized and is prepared for printing by spraying with water.
- Domestic Etching Paper is machine-made in the USA with 50% cotton fibres and cut edges. It is warm white in colour, sized, acid-free and weighs 175 gsm.

A wide variety of papers are made in the Indian subcontinent, Japan and other countries in the Far East. These thin papers can be printed on and used for chine collé. Papers which contain leaves, flower petals, silk, glitter and feathers may also be used, but sometimes the particles can detach from the paper surface. Graphic suppliers, art shops and gift shops sell decorative papers, including types which are patterned, metallic, opalescent, gloss-coated and holographic. These papers may also be used for chine collé but are not acid-free and their colours may be fugitive.

Cotton linters are sheets of rag cotton which are used by papermaking mills as a component of intaglio papers. They are rough unsized sheets with variable surfaces and edges but can be effective for printing plates with deeply textured areas.

When multiple plates are being printed in register to create one print, the expansion and contraction of paper due to variations in print-room humidity may cause registration difficulties.

When the paper is smaller than the plate (so that the deckles are printed), the resulting print is known as a bleed print. It is important to cover the paper and plate with a second sheet to protect the blankets from the uncovered inky edges of the plate.

Samples of papers and prints, with notes recording paper type, paper weight and printing mixture recipe can be kept in a visual aid folder for future reference.

HANDLING AND TEARING PAPER

Sheets should always be lifted by diagonally opposite corners to distribute the weight equally, and to minimize the risk of denting and creasing. The potential damage to a sheet of paper can be demonstrated by repeatedly lifting and laying down a perfect sheet of cartridge paper, using only one hand. When the paper is examined, half-moon-shaped dents (dinks) can be clearly seen. Dinks in the paper are generally permanent and will be visible when the print is framed.

If the editioning paper is to be smaller than a standard sheet, it will need to be reduced in size. It is normal printmaking practice – for aesthetic reasons – to tear down paper rather than cut it. The paper is torn from the back of the sheet, using a steel straight-edge.

USING TISSUE PAPER

Acid-free white tissue paper should be used to protect the press bed and blankets, to interleave between drying prints and dried editions, and for packaging when mailing prints in tubes. Used tissue can be dried and cut into small squares for inking up plates.

USING BLOTTING PAPER

Acid-free white blotting paper is used to absorb the excess moisture from the intaglio paper before printing. It is more economic in the long term to use heavyweight papers of 300 gsm as these last longer than thinner sheets, which will quickly disintegrate and become unusable. A protective sheet can be placed over the blotter during use. When the blotter becomes wet, it can be dried between boards or hung up. Some printmakers use white cotton towels which are then washed and dried.

PREPARING THE PAPER FOR PRINTING

Intaglio plates may be printed on a wide range of papers and the way in which these are prepared will affect the quality of the print. The sharpness of line, depth of tone and intensity of colour will vary according to the qualities of the selected paper, so the choice of paper for both editioning and proofing is important. The preparation of the paper must be carried out carefully for each print. Faulty proofs can mislead an artist, causing them to re-work or alter a plate in the wrong way.

Some inks will print successfully on dry paper, especially if a bleed print is made, but generally the paper is dampened and prepared in the traditional way. This allows the paper to take on the form of the plate without creasing or tearing.

Equipment and materials required

Work in the paper-soaking workstation (see p. 54).

- paper for editioning
- a sink with a tray of water
- a spray bottle containing water
- a vertical draining screen (see pp. 54–55)
- some sheets of heavyweight acid-free blotting paper
- a protective sheet of strong paper or card
- several sheets of acid-free tissue paper

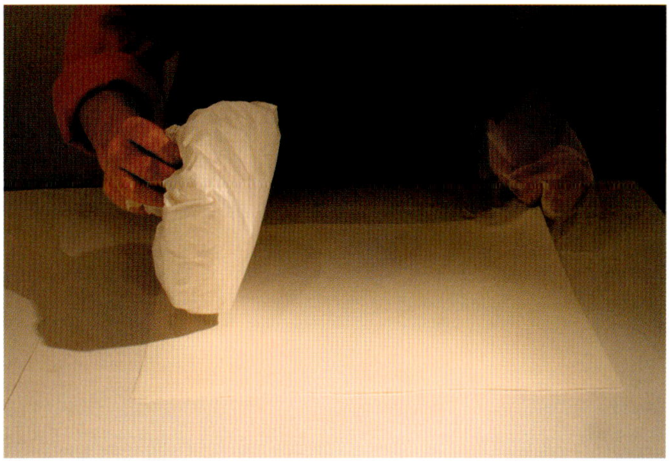

A pad of tissue is used at the end of the blotting process.

Working method

- The printer's hands and apron should be spotlessly clean.
- After deciding on the dimensions of the editioning or proofing paper, the correct number of sheets are torn to size and a registration sheet is made (see p. 208).
- Delicate papers (Japanese and Chinese papers, decorative papers, cotton linters and papers which contain very little size) are laid on a clean blotter and carefully sprayed all over with water. A second sheet of blotting paper can be laid over the dampened paper. The protective sheet is then laid over the blotter and the excess water is squeezed from the printing paper by gently pressing with the hands from the centre outwards in a circular motion. The protective sheet prevents the blotter from being abraded excessively by the movement of the hands. When the paper has been blotted, it may be printed.
- Intaglio printmaking papers are generally soaked before use. Each piece of paper is submerged in the tray of water and left to soak. Different papers will require soaking for different lengths of time: some may require only a few minutes, while others – such as heavily sized papers – will benefit from several hours in the water. After the paper has been soaked it can be treated in different ways. The first method involves lifting the paper from the water and placing it on the draining board for a few minutes. This allows much of the unwanted water to flow away, extending the life of the blotting papers. The printing paper is then placed on a blotter and overlaid with a second sheet of blotting paper. The protective sheet is laid over the blotter and the excess water is squeezed from the printing paper by gently pressing with the hands from the centre outwards in a circular motion. The protective sheet prevents the blotter from being abraded excessively by the movement of the hands. Some sheets of tissue can be rolled into a large ball and this can be swept gently over the front

and then the back surface of the paper. Used in this way, the tissue brushes up the nap of the paper, making the surface more receptive to the ink (a soft brush could alternatively be used). It also lifts up any hairs or fluff, and allows the artist to detect any areas of the paper which may still be holding too much water (the tissue paper will catch). If the printing paper remains too wet it should be blotted on a drier blotter. When the paper is ready, it may be printed on. The wet blotter should be put aside to dry.

• The second method involves thoroughly wetting each sheet and then stacking the sheets in a neat pile. The stack is then wrapped in a polythene bag and placed between boards. A weight is positioned on top. The paper can be stored in this way for several days (but if left too long it will become mouldy). The artist takes a sheet as needed and prepares it for printing by blotting as described above.

• After printing, the damp prints are dried between absorbent boards (see p. 56)

Prints are dried, protected by sheets of tissue paper, between absorbent boards. A card label used to locate prints can be seen projecting from the boards.

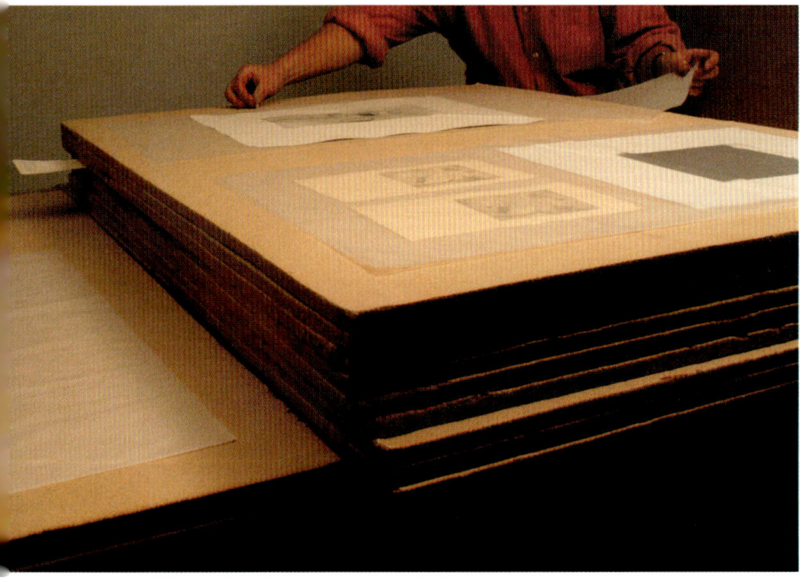

OTHER SUBSTRATES AND PRINTING INTO PLASTER

Historically it is known that some artists have printed on linen and other materials. Contemporary artists sometimes print on unusual substrates such as interfacing, silk or foils. Test prints can be made on a particular material to discover the most appropriate ink and best method of preparation and printing.

An interesting and effective technique involves using plaster to make a cast of an inked-up plate. Every subtlety of the plate will be evident on the resulting plaster print, and the plate itself will suffer none of the wear associated with being printed under enormous pressure. An obvious advantage of this technique is that it allows intaglio prints to be taken without the need for a press.

Equipment and materials required

Work on a glass surface in the drawing area.

- an intaglio plate inked up with an oily intaglio ink (see p. 211)
- some plaster of Paris
- a trowel or mixing spatula
- a basin to mix the plaster in
- some acrylic strengthening medium
- a dust mask, gloves and an apron
- some light wire netting for use as an armature (for larger plates)
- four balls of Plasticine
- four straight pieces of wood (such as old framing moulding) which measure slightly longer than the plate and have cleanly cut ends
- a glass surface
- a jug
- a plastic spatula
- a basin of soapy water and cleaning materials

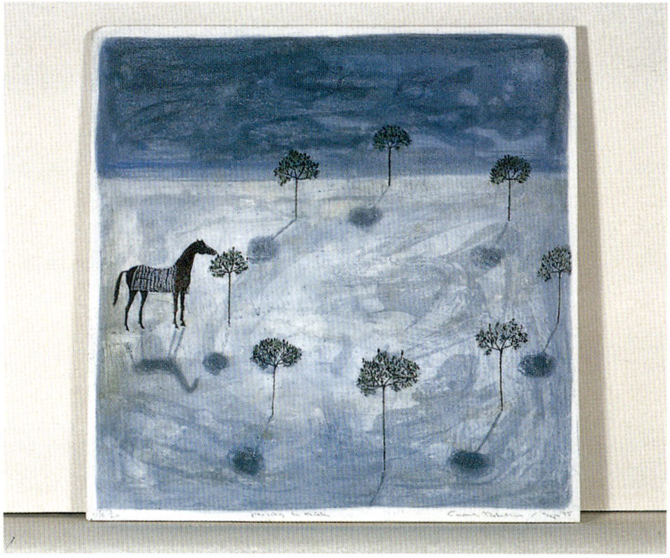

Carol Robertson (UK), *Entranced*, etching and collagraph printed on plaster, 36 x 38 cm (14⅛ x 15 in.), 1994. Lascaux acrylic paints and varnishes were used as resists and the plate was etched in a tray as well as being spit-bitten. Speedball Screen Filler was used as a collagraph material on the etched plate to generate pale delicate washes. The plate was inked à la poupée and printed into plaster.

Working method

- Lay the inked-up plate on the glass surface facing upwards. Collagraph plates must be well-varnished with a non-rewetting material.
- Position the pieces of wood around the plate so that they fit tight to the edges. Use a strip of Plasticine to wedge each piece of wood against the plate.
- Make up the plaster according to the instructions and add some acrylic strengthening medium. Wear a dust mask, gloves and an apron when working with the plaster.
- Put the plaster into the jug and, as it begins to set, pour it onto the plate very carefully, avoiding creating any bubbles. If the plaster requires a strengthening armature, lay a piece of the wire netting (cut smaller than the plate) on the plaster once the layer is around 1 cm (½ in.) deep. Pour the remaining plaster into the mould, covering the armature.
- Smooth the back of the plaster with a plastic spatula and for best results leave it to dry overnight.
- The next day remove the wooden framework. Place the plate and plaster in a warm place such as a drying cabinet for a few minutes to loosen the ink. Hold the plaster-coated plate vertically and carefully insert the point of a knife to release the plate from the plaster layer. The finished plaster print will show every detail of the plate. When the plaster has hardened, any rough edges may be softened down with a file or a knife.
- The plate may then be cleaned and inked up again.

COLLATING AND PRESENTING INTAGLIO PRINTS

When the prints are flattened and dry, they should all be taken to a clean, dry work area. There they should be collated before signing and embossing with the printmaker's stamp (the chop). Prints on unusual substrates should be prepared for exhibition according to their particular characteristics.

COLLATING INTAGLIO PRINTS

Collating an edition printed on paper involves examining and comparing the prints, and determining the final number of the edition. Any dented, damaged, badly printed or out-of-register prints should be put to one side as proofs. Minor blemishes can be cleaned from margins using a scalpel or a soft eraser. Fluff and dust may be removed with a large, soft, dry, spotlessly clean brush. The prints should be handled with the care used when handling drawn or painted works on paper. Each sheet should be picked up by opposite corners to prevent denting. The perfect prints should be counted and a note made of this number. From this group the following proofs are selected:

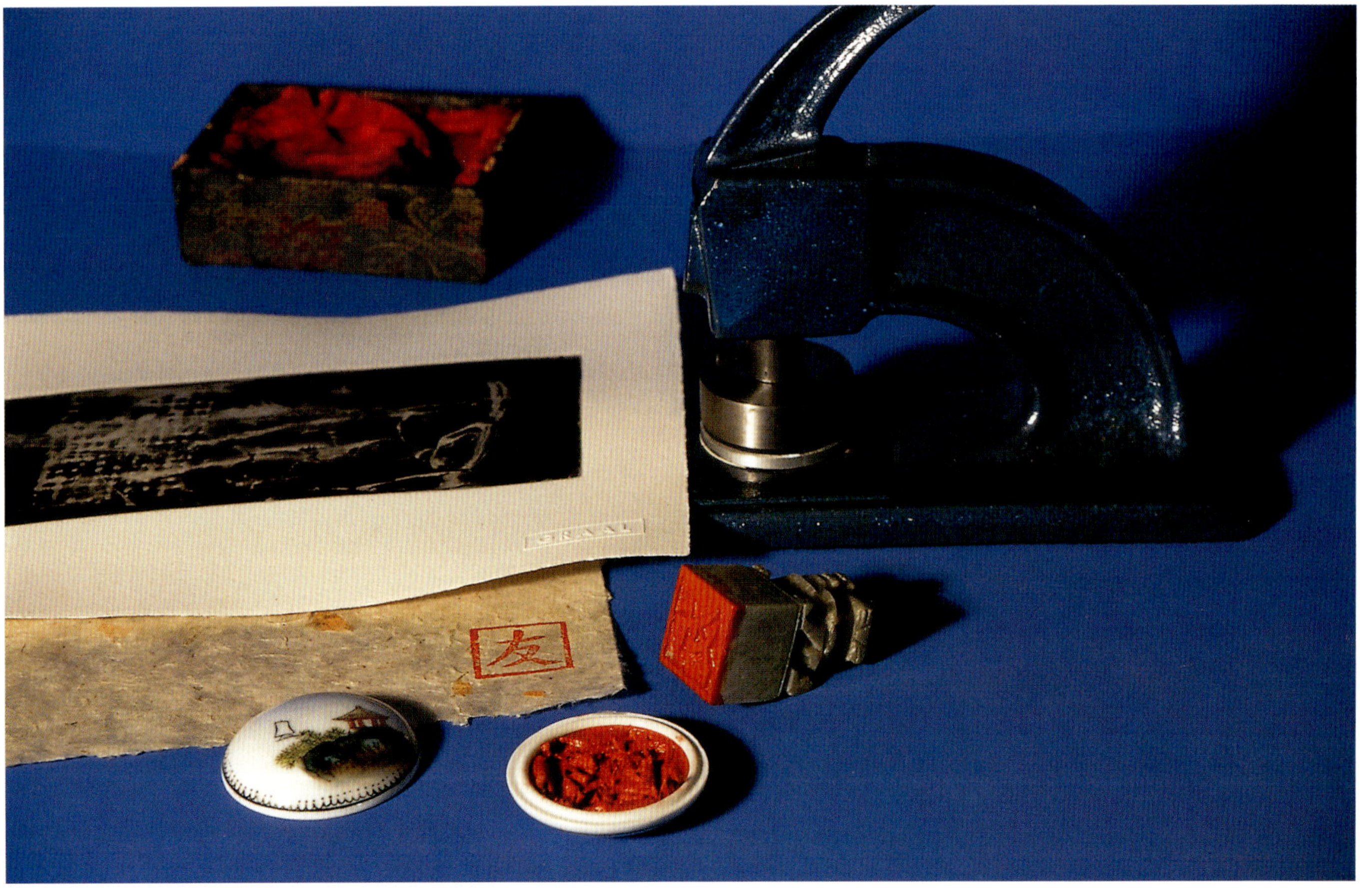

opposite A studio embossing chop and a Chinese chop with its own special ink pot.

right Kari Holopainen (Finland) presents his series of intaglio prints in specially made portfolios.

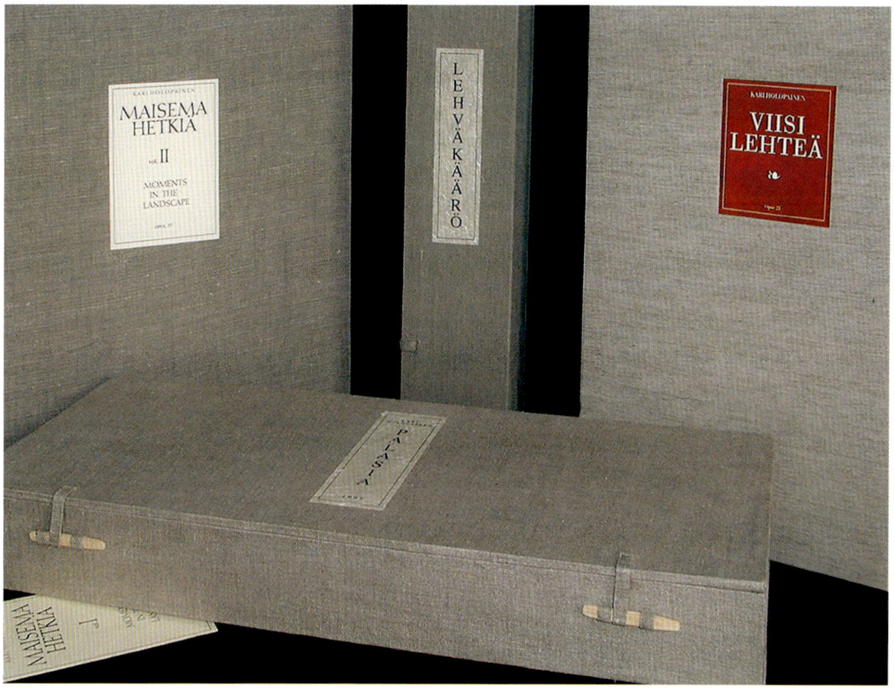

• When an artist has worked in collaboration with a publishing studio, a printer's proof (PP) is given to the intaglio printmaker who printed the edition.

• A proof is retained for the studio archive and this is used for display purposes when promoting and selling the edition. This proof is marked HC, which originates from the French *hors de commerce*, meaning 'not for sale'.

• Up to 10% of the remaining prints may be designated artist's proofs (APs). These belong to the artist or may be shared with the publishing studio. If a BAT proof (see p. 193) has been used as a working guide when printing, it may have been annotated by the artist or may have become marked during the printing process. Some collectors have an interest in these prints, so they should not necessarily be discarded.

• The remaining prints are counted and form the edition. These and the proofs are signed in a soft graphite pencil. If the print is a bleed print, it should be signed within the image. A soft coloured pencil may be used if necessary. The signature is usually placed in the lower right corner of the print. The edition is numbered, in the lower left corner. Conventionally the total edition number is preceded by the number of the print, for example 5/30. The artist may write the title of the work in the centre, level with the number and signature.

• In the case of a collaborative print, the studio chop is used to emboss or stamp the prints to identify their origin. The chop is usually applied to the lower right corner of the print, close to (or on top of) the signature. Some artists have their own personal chop.

• The collated prints should be interleaved with sheets of acid-free tissue and stored in a polythene bag in a plan chest.

• A document of authenticity for the edition should be drawn up for the use of galleries or purchasers. The document may specify the artist's name, the title of the work, the date, the medium, the paper size and image size, the number of prints and proofs in the edition, and the selling price. The document can also briefly describe how the print was made (for example, 'two-plate intaglio print, first plate etching with aquatint, second plate collagraph, both printed with water-based inks on Arches 200 gsm acid-free paper'). This information is also essential for the artist's own records and should be stored in a notebook or computer, together with details of the location and sales of each print in the edition. The artist's records should be updated as sales are made.

PRESENTING INTAGLIO PRINTS

The artist should judge the most appropriate way in which the work should be presented. Framing and hanging a print is not necessarily the only option. Prints have been made which were designed to be turned into lanterns, pop-up images and origami forms, or as part of an installation. Plates have also been used to create wall pieces, and have been incorporated as elements within larger sculptures and performance pieces. Some artists have exhibited inked-up intaglio plates.

Intaglio prints on paper should be framed according to the style of the work, rather than following the general perception of how prints should be framed. Some images will suit a black lacquered frame but others will look much better in an entirely transparent Plexiglas or Perspex frame, a lime-waxed wooden frame or a specially treated finish which is normally reserved for paintings. Artists who do not frame their own prints should seek out a good framer who is used to dealing with fine art work.

Prints may be float-mounted, window-mounted or float-mounted within a window-mount. Heavy prints can be suspended from the mounting board using self-adhesive Velcro (plastic hook-and-loop fastener), which allows fine adjustments to be made. To frame a print to conservation standard, the appropriate materials should be used, including acid-free mount board, tapes and backing board. The print surface should not be in contact with the glass, which should ideally filter out UV light.

Prints to be mailed or transported in cardboard or plastic tubes should not be rolled too tightly. The print should be laid on a large sheet of tissue which overlaps its edges. Another sheet of tissue should then be laid over the surface of the print, and these should all be rolled together to form a cylinder. The overlapping tissue should be tucked into the ends in order to secure the print and prevent it from unrolling. The roll can be placed inside a light plastic sack (such as a waste-bin liner) to protect it against moisture while it is in transit. A ball of crumpled tissue should be placed at the bottom of the mailing tube and the rolled print should then be inserted, together with a sheet with the recipient's and sender's addresses (in case the external labelling is damaged). Finally, another ball of tissue should be placed on top of the print and the tube should be firmly sealed at each end with parcel tape.

STORING PLATES

When a plate has been editioned, it is usually 'cancelled' so that it cannot be printed from again. This is to respect the implicit agreement between the artist and prospective purchasers that the printed edition will remain limited to the number noted by the artist on each print. The form of cancellation varies: the plate may be scored diagonally with a drypoint needle; a hole may be drilled through each corner of the plate; or a small section of a corner may be sliced off.

If the editioning has not been completed and a plate is to be stored, it should be cleaned thoroughly so that it is free of any resists, ink, chemical residues, de-oxidizing solution, degreaser, grease or oxidization. Some artists recommend that a light coating of oil or petroleum jelly will protect a metal plate from corrosion, but there is some evidence to suggest that this can lead in the long term to unwanted marks on the surface.

After the plate has been cleaned and thoroughly dried, it should be handled carefully, wrapped in acid-free tissue paper and placed in a polythene envelope. PVC sleeves should not be used as they can tarnish metal. The envelope should be labelled with the print title, the artist's name and the date, and stored vertically in a dry place.

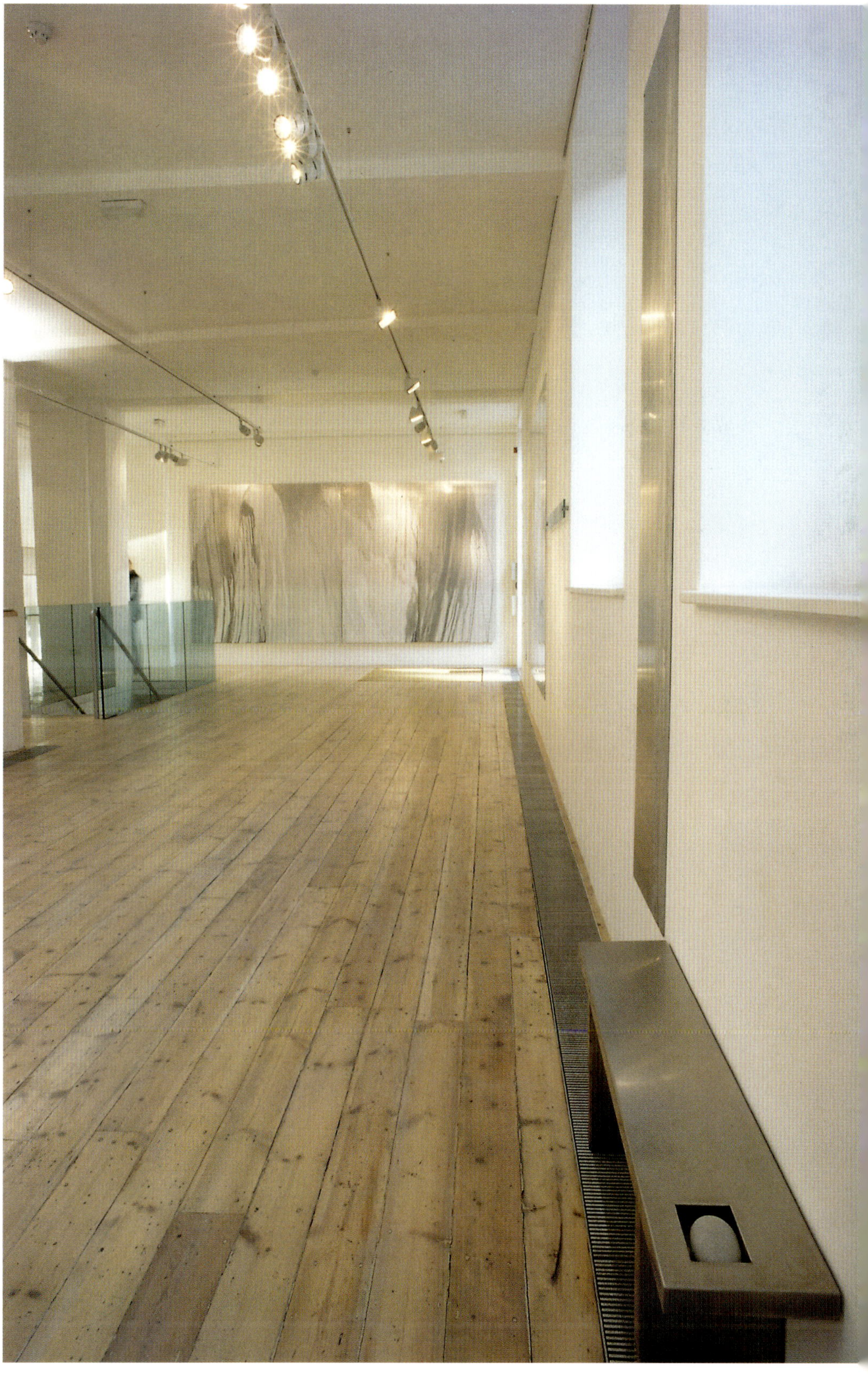

Elizabeth Ogilvie (UK), *Oceanus 1*, four etched aluminium plates made at Graal Press in 1999.

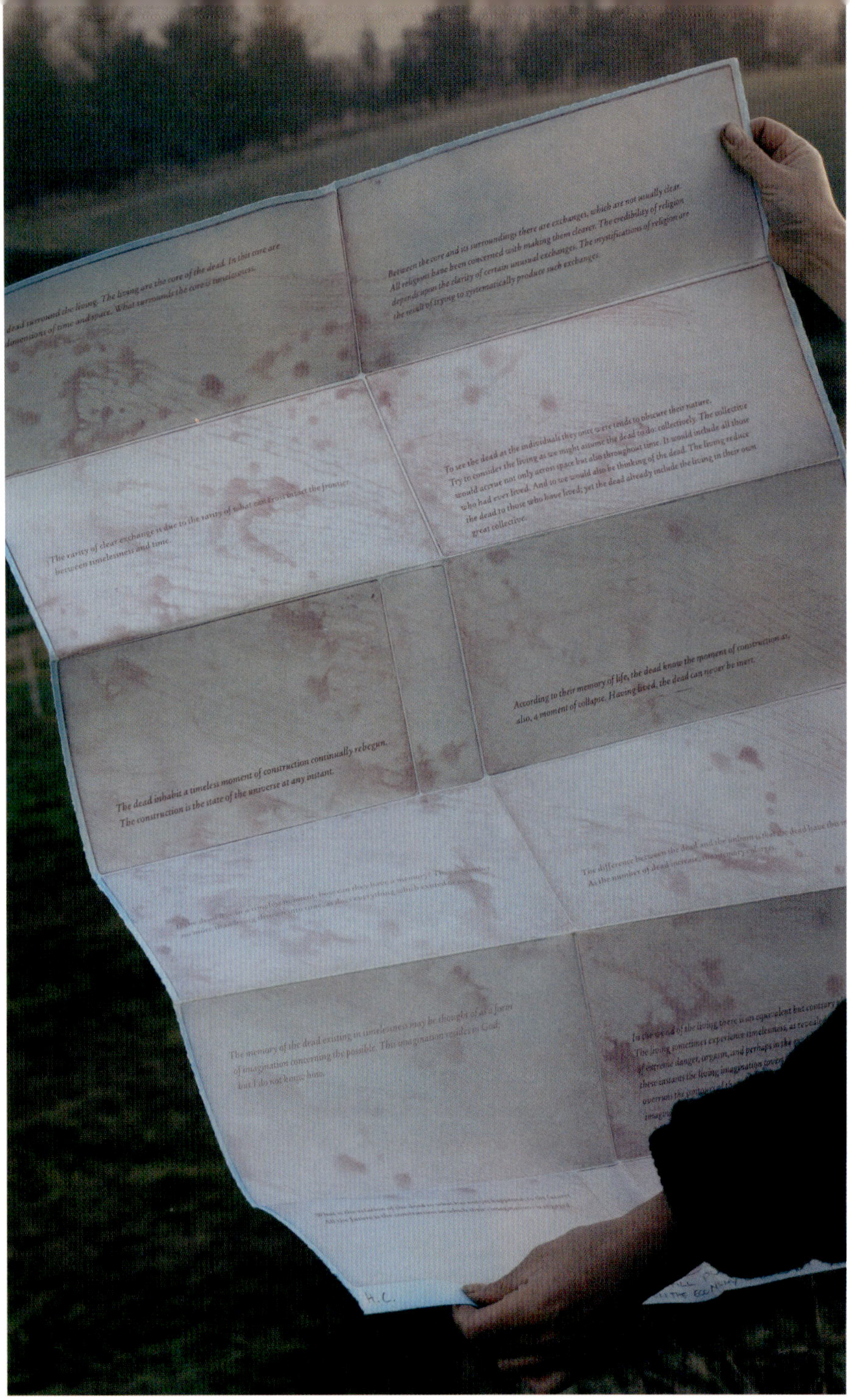

left John Berger, Werner Schmidt, *The Eskhill Plate – 12 Theses on the Economy of the Dead*, a folded etching in a slip case, printed on hand-dyed paper by Robert Adam at Graal Press, 66 x 93 cm (26 x 36⅝ in.), 2005. Schmidt envisaged that the print could be kept close to the owner and contemplated at any time in any place (see plate on p. 96 and detail on p. 157).

opposite Rossana Martinez (Puerto Rico), *Huaca, Sacred Place*, collagraph prints on paper and thread, 366 cm diameter (12 feet), 1996.

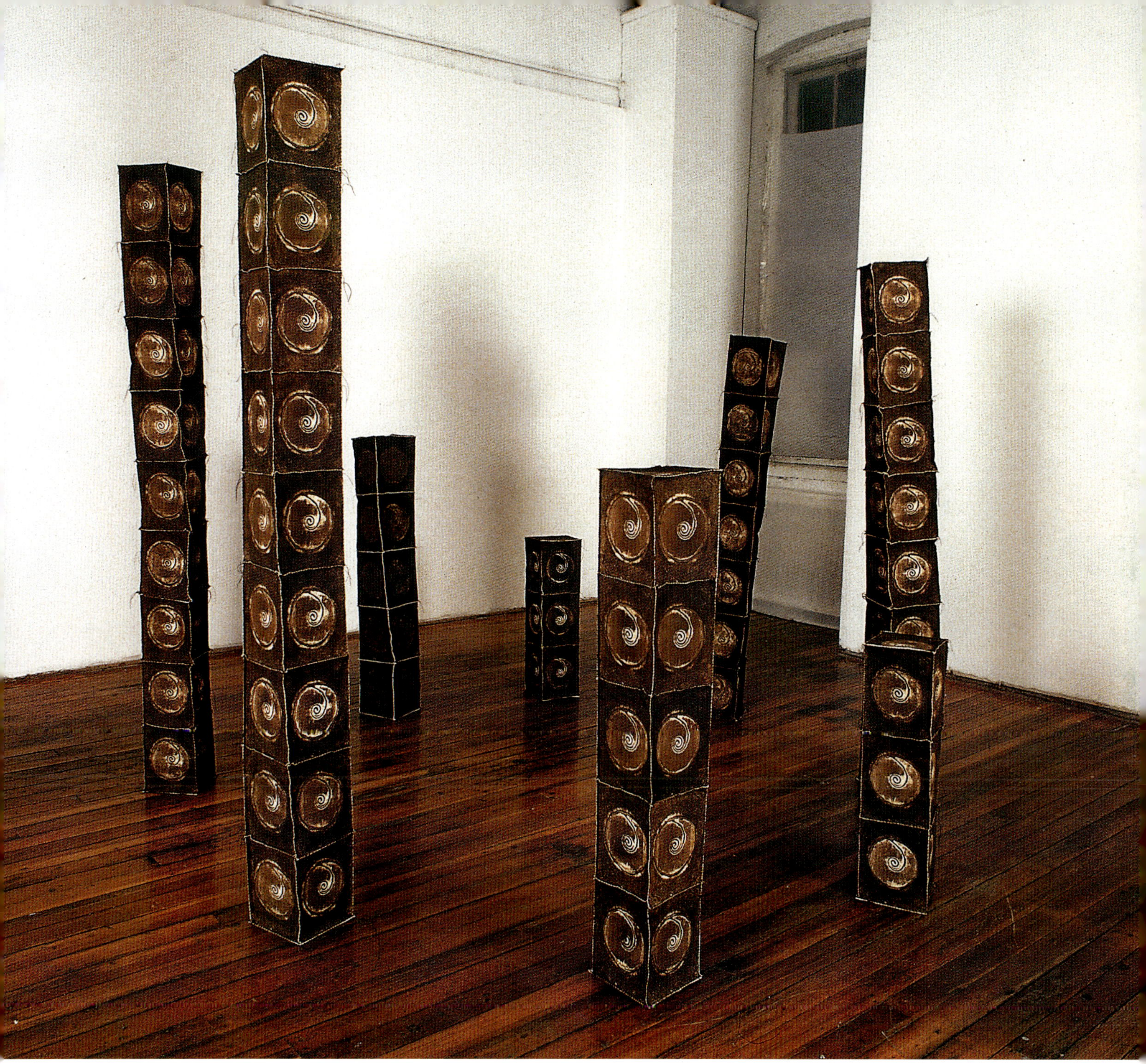

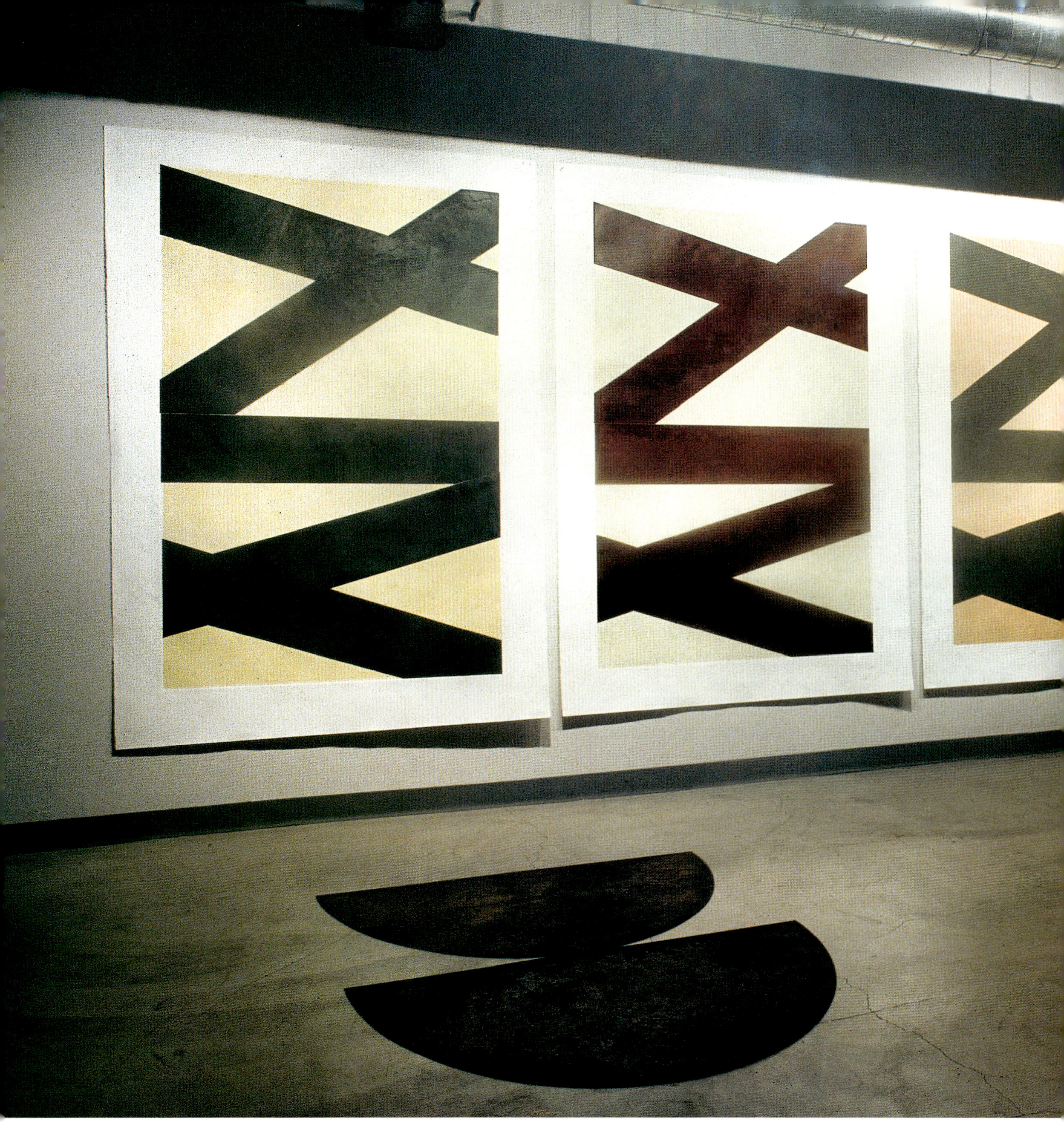

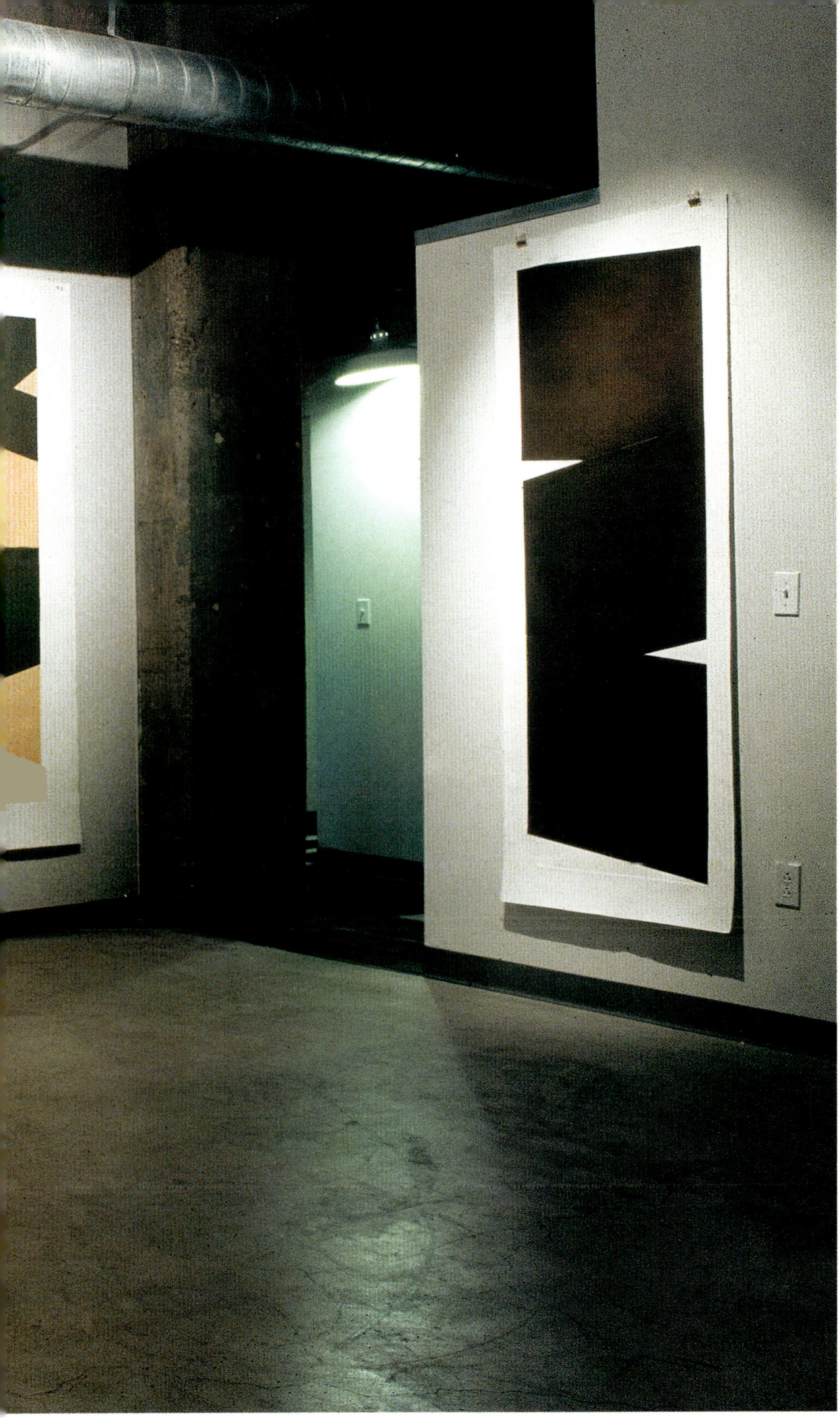

Michael Berkhemer (Netherlands), *Works in progress*, installation, 2002. Working at Wildwood Press, the artist made collagraph plates by painting with Rhoplex and carborundum onto Sintra plates. These were then printed with etching inks on an intaglio press. Berkhemer has printed from laser-cut steel plates and he has also made sculptural pieces from his steel plates after allowing these to weather outside for two years.

INTERNATIONAL SUPPLIERS OF MATERIALS

Abrading equipment
RapidMask
PhotoBrasive Systems
4832 Grand Avenue
Duluth, MN 55807
USA
Tel: +1 218 628 2002/+1 800 643 1037
Fax: +1 218 628 2064
Website: www.photobrasive.com

Airbrushes, compressors, spray booths and spare parts
The Airbrush Company Ltd
Unit 7 Marlborough Road
Lancing Business Park
Lancing
West Sussex BN15 8UF
UK
Tel: +44 (0)8700 660 445
Website: www.airbrushes.com

Badger Air-Brush Co.
9128 W. Belmont Ave
Franklin Park, IL 60131
USA
Tel: +1 847 678 3104/+1 800 247 2787
Fax: +1 847 671 4352
Website: www.badgerairbrush.com

Akua water-based inks
Rostow & Jung
USA
Tel: +1 212 473 4670/+1 888 473 4670
Website: www.waterbasedinks.com

Cardboard tubes and foam sheet
Sonoco Industrial Products
Unit 2 Brechin Industrial Estate
Montrose Road
Brechin
Angus DD9 7RU
UK
Tel: +44 (0)1356 625161
Fax: +44 (0)1356 625620

Uline
2105 S. Lakeside Dr.
Waukegan, IL 60085
USA
Tel: +1 800 958 5463
Fax: +1 800 295 5571
Website: www.uline.com

Chemicals: ferric chloride solution, P-grade (45 BE), citric acid powder, copper sulphate and 25 kg bags of sodium carbonate crystals
Gower Chemicals Ltd
Crymlyn Burrows
Swansea SA1 8PT
UK
Tel: +44 (0)1792 473344
Fax: +44 (0)1792 456578
Website: www.gowerchemicals.ltd.uk

Scientific Laboratory Supplies Ltd
Coatbridge Business Centre
204 Main Street
Coatbridge
Lanarkshire ML5 3RB
UK
Tel: +44 (0)1236 431 857
Fax: +44 (0)1236 431 050
Website: www.scientific-labs.net

Alcan Chemicals Division
Stamford Harbor Park
North Tower
333 Ludlow Street
Stamford, CT 06902
USA
Tel: +1 203 541 9190
Fax: +1 203 541 9191
Website: www.chemicals.alcan.com

Fox-Chemicals
Bockstalstr. 10 A
D-76327 Pfinztal
Germany
Tel: +49 (72 40) 92 71 51
Fax: +49 (72 40) 92 71 50
Website: www.fox-chemicals.com

Cleaning and degreasing products
The Clean Environment Company
8609 "I" Street
Omaha, NE 68127
USA
Tel: +1 800 266 2353
Fax: +1 402 537 0014
Website: www.cleanenvironmentco.com

Dishwashing liquid, vinegar, vegetable oil, salt, cleaning materials, basins, spatulas, jugs, mixing bowls, drying cloths, sandpaper, pot scourers, sponges, Miracle Lady non-scratch cleaning pads, cleaning brushes, masking tape and parcel tape, shelving, storage units, filing systems
Home improvement stores, supermarkets and household stores such as IKEA

Drafting film and Clear-lay
Grafix Plastics
19499 Miles Rd
Cleveland, OH 44128
USA
Email: filminfo@grafixplastics.com
Website: www.grafixplastics.com

Etching blankets (alternative materials)
Memory foam sheeting (5 cm thick) for etching blankets; Vilene sew-in interfacing (size catcher for etching blanket)

Etching presses
Harry F. Rochat Ltd
15a Moxon St
High Barnet
Herts EN5 5TS
UK
Tel: +44 (0)20 8449 0023
Fax: +44 (0)20 8449 6132
Website: www.harryrochat.com

Printmakers Machine Co (presses made by Polymetaal, Sturges and Conrad)
724 North Yale Avenue
PO Box 7191
Villa Park, IL 60181
USA
Tel: +1 630 832 4888/+1 800 992 5970
Website: www.printmakersmachine.com

Takach Press Corporation
3207 Morningside NE
Albuquerque, NM 87110
USA
Tel: +1 800 248 3460
Fax: +1 505 888 6988
Website: www.takachpress.com

Exposure units (self-contained)
Natgraph Ltd
Dabell Avenue
Blenheim Industrial Estate
Nottingham NG6 8WA
UK
Tel: +44 (0)115 979 5800
Fax: +44 (0)115 979 5700
Website: www.natgraph.co.uk

Amergraph Corporation
520 Lafayette Road
Sparta, NJ 07871
USA
Tel: +1 973 383 8700/+1 800 526 2852
Fax: +1 973 383 9225
Website: www.amergraph.com
US distributors: www.amergraph.com/distributors.aspx

Falcon Clear PVC sheets
Robert Horne Group
Huntsman House
Mansion Close
Moulton Park
Northampton NN3 6LA
UK
Tel: +44 (0)1604 495333
Fax: +44 (0)1604 491909
Website: www.roberthorne.co.uk/product_page.asp?prod_id=203

Files, clamps, sanders and other tools
Building and home improvement stores

Floor polish
JohnsonDiversey
8310 16th Street
PO Box 902
Sturtevant, WI 53177
USA
Tel: +1 262 631 4001
Website: www.johnsondiversey.com

Lascaux resists, tusches and remover
Lascaux Colours & Restauro
Barbara Diethelm AG
Zürichstrasse 42
CH-8306 Brüttisellen
Switzerland
Tel: +41 1 807 41 41
Fax: +41 1 807 41 40
Website: www.lascaux.ch
International retailers: www.lascaux.ch/english/vertrieb/index.html

Lascaux resists, Lascaux tusches, carborundum, pumice and pigments
A. P. Fitzpatrick
Fine Art Materials
142 Cambridge Heath Road
London E1 5QJ
UK
Tel: +44 (0)20 7790 0884
Fax: +44 (0)20 7790 0885
Email: apfcolours@aol.com

Mystrol cleaner (5 litre containers)
Evans Vanodine International plc
Brierley Road
Walton Summit
Lancs PR5 8AH
UK
Tel: +44 (0)1772 322 200
Fax: +44 (0)1772 318 844
Website: www.evansvanodine.co.uk

Overhead projector film (OHP)
Office stationery stores

Particulate respirators, eye protection, aprons, gloves, waste containers and janitorial supplies
Home improvement stores, agricultural stores and laboratory equipment wholesalers

3M Health Information Systems worldwide service
Website: www.3mhis.com

Photec dry film photoresist
Sally Dyas
Rocquette Villa
Rocquettes Lane
St Peter Port
Guernsey GY1 1XT
UK
Tel: +44 (0)1481 711130
Website: www.sdyas.demon.co.uk

Photec dry film photoresist (bulk purchase)
Enthone, Inc.
350 Frontage Road
West Haven, CT 06516
USA
Tel: +1 203 934 8611
Fax: +1 203 799 1513
Website: www.enthone.com/docs/FS-PHOTEC-6200.pdf
International suppliers: www.enthone.com/contacts.aspx

Pigments
Dr Georg F. Kremer
Hauptstrasse 41–47
D-88317 Aichstetten
Germany
Tel: +49 7565 1011
Fax: +49 7565 1606
Website: www.kremer-pigmente.de/englisch/homee.htm

Plastic open-weave scouring pads
151 Products Ltd
Globe House
Southall Street
Manchester M3 1LG
UK
Tel: +44 (0)161 839 5949
Fax: +44 (0)161 839 5943
Website: www.151.co.uk

Polythene bags (32 x 55 in., 250 g)
A L King and Sons
Unit B
Sands Industrial Estate
Hillbottom
High Wycombe
Bucks HP12 4HJ
UK
Tel: +44 (0)1494 461 876
Fax: +44 (0)1494 451 881

Printer's wipes (Ultrawipe)
Business Textile Services Ltd
Units 7 & 8 Spring Mill Industrial Estate
Avening Road
Nailsworth
Glos GL6 0BS
UK
Tel: +44 (0)1453 832266
Fax: +44 (0)1453 836620
Website: www.bustex.co.uk/ultrawipe.html

Prolene One Stroke Flat paintbrush (109) and Connoisseur One Stroke (99)
Pro Arte Limited
Park Mill
Brougham Street
Skipton
North Yorks BD23 2JN
UK
Tel: +44 (0)1756 792929
Fax: +44 (0)1756 790909
Website: www.proarte.co.uk

Puretch, degreaser, Stouffer step guide
Puretch
Cape Fear Press
610 Atlanta Ave
Carolina Beach, NC 28428
USA
Tel: +1 910 458 4647
Website: www.capefearpress.com

R&F pigment sticks
R&F Handmade Paints, Inc.
84 Ten Broeck Ave
Kingston, NY 12401
USA
Tel: +1 845 331 3112/+1 800 206 8088
Fax: +1 845 331 3242
Website: www.rfpaints.com

Ramer sponges, Neptune oval sponges
Ramer Sponges
Suite 30, Craven Court
Glebeland Road
Camberley
Surrey GU15 3BU
UK
Tel: +44 (0)1276 63192
Fax: +44 (0)1276 62902
Website: www.ramersponges.com

Screenprinting degreasers and CPS degreaser
Screenchem
5 Telford Place
East Lenziemill
Cumbernauld
Glasgow G67 2NH
UK
Tel: +44 (0)1236 733276
Fax: +44 (0)1236 733276

CPS-Chemical Products & Services A/S
Hejreskovvej 22
DK-3490 Kvistgaard
Denmark
Tel: +45 49 13 8110
Fax: +45 49 13 8077
Website: www.cps.dk

Sheet metal
Building, sheet metal and roofing suppliers or specialist intaglio suppliers

WW Lampert (cold-rolled mild steel sheet: 18 gauge, 1 metre x 914 mm)
12 Mychell House
Pincott Road
London SW19 2NN
UK
Tel: +44 (0)20 8540 1161
Fax: +44 (0)20 8544 0018

CG Metals, Inc. (specialist metal suppliers for artists)
93 Christopher Street
Montclair, NJ 07042
USA
Tel: +1 973 783 5013
Fax: +1 484 727 5013
Website: www.cgmetals.com

Sinks and dip tanks
Richards of Hull
Unit 1 Acorn Estate
Bontoft Avenue
Hull HU5 4HF
UK
Tel: +44 (0)1482 44 24 22
Fax: +44 (0)1482 44 23 62
Website: www.richards.uk.com

Tri-Mer Corporation
1400 Monroe Street
PO Box 730
Owosso, MI 48867
USA
Tel: +1 989 723 7838
Fax: +1 989 723 7844
Website: www.tri-mer.com

Specialist intaglio suppliers: equipment, press blankets, plates, needles and tools, magnifying glasses, acrylic and other resists, light-sensitive plates, dry film resists, contact/dot screens, mordants, inks, paper and graining, polishing, degreasing materials, etc.

Intaglio Printmaker
9 Playhouse Court
62 Southwark Bridge Road
London SE1 0AT
UK
Tel: +44 (0)20 7928 2633
Fax: +44 (0)20 7928 2711
Website: www.intaglioprintmaker.com

T. N. Lawrence & Son Ltd
208 Portland Road
Hove BN3 5QT
UK
Tel: +44 (0)1273 260260/0845 644 3232
Fax: +44 (0)1273 260270/0845 644 3233
Website: www.lawrence.co.uk

Rudolph Faust, Inc.
542 South Ave East
Cranford, NJ 07016
USA
Tel: +1 908 276 6555
Website: www.faustink.com

Graphic Chemical & Ink Co.
728 North Yale Avenue
PO Box 7027
Villa Park, IL 60181
USA
Tel: +1 630 832 6004/+1 800 465 7382
Fax: +1 630 832 6064
Website: www.graphicchemical.com

E. C. Lyons Company
3646 White Plains Rd
Bronx, NY 10467
USA
Tel: +1 718 881 7270
Fax: +1 718 515 7790
Website: www.eclyons.com

Rembrandt Graphic Arts
PO Box 130
Rosemont, NJ 08556
USA
Tel: +1 609 397 0068/+1 800 622 1887
Fax: +1 609 397 0666
Website: www.rembrandtgraphicarts.com

Renaissance Graphic Arts, Inc.
69 Steamwhistle Drive
Ivyland, PA 18974
USA
Tel: +1 888 833 3398
Fax: +1 215 357 5258
Website: www.printmaking-materials.com

Melbourne Etching Supplies Pty Ltd
33A St David Street
Fitzroy 3065
Australia
Tel: +61 3 9419 5666
Fax: +61 3 9419 6292
Website: www.mes.net.au

Papermill NV
Begijnenvest 37
2000 Antwerp
Belgium
Tel: +32 3 226 35 74
Fax: +32 3 226 31 48
Website: www.papermill.be

Grafisk Eksperimentarium
Trepkasgade 8
DK-2100 Copenhagen
Denmark
Tel: +45 35 35 39 07
Fax: +45 35 36 38 21
Website: www.artbag.dk/ge/uk/index.html

Polymetaal
Evertsenstraat 69 C
Leiden
2315 SK
The Netherlands
Tel: +31 71 5222681
Fax: +31 71 5214244
Website: www.polymetaal.nl

Specialist printmaking papers
R. K. Burt
57 Union Street
London SE1 1SG
UK
Tel: +44 (0)20 7407 6474
Fax: +44 (0)20 7403 3672
Website: www.rkburt.co.uk

Hiromi Paper International
2525 Michegan Ave
Bergamot Station G-9
Santa Monica, CA 90404
USA
Tel: +1 310 998 0098/+1 866 479 2744
Fax: +1 310 998 0028
Website: www.hiromipaper.com

Twinrocker Handmade Paper Inc.
PO Box 413
Brookston, IN 47923
USA
Tel: +1 800 757 8946
Fax: +1 765 563 3119
Website: www.twinrocker.com

Specialist printmaking papers, acid-free tissue and Truegrain
John Purcell Paper
15 Rumsey Rd
London SW9 0TR
UK
Tel: +44 (0)20 7737 5199
Fax: +44 (0)20 7737 6765
Website: www.johnpurcell.net

Speedball Screen Filler
Speedball Art Products Company
2226 Speedball Rd
Statesville, NC 28677
USA
Tel: +1 800 898 7224
Fax: +1 704 838 1472
Website: www.speedballart.com

Spontex Handy Sponges
Mapa Spontex UK Ltd
Berkeley Business Park
Wainwright Road
Worcester
Worcs WR4 9ZS
UK
Tel: +44 (0)1905 450 300
Fax: +44 (0)1905 450 350
Website: www.spontex.co.uk

Sulphur powder
Garden centres

Syphon pumps
Justoffbase
Unit One
Harlequin Business Park
Kenny Hill
Bury St Edmunds
Suffolk IP28 8DS
UK
Tel: +44 (0)870 922 4114
Fax: +44 (0)870 922 3063
Website: www.justoffbase.co.uk

Toxic waste removal
Edelchemie (UK) Ltd
Holland House
Valley Way
The Welland Industrial Estate
Market Harborough
Leics LE16 7PS
UK
Tel: +44 (0)1858 469 001
Fax: +44 (0)1858 469 002
Website: www.edelchemie.com

Scientific & Chemical Supplies Ltd
Carlton House
Livingstone Road
Bilston
West Midlands WV14 0QZ
UK
Tel: +44(0)1902 402 402
Fax: +44(0)1902 402 343
Website: www.scichem.com

Toyobo, Solar, and photopolymer plates
Photo-Functional Material Department
Toyobo Co., Ltd
2-8, Dojima Hama 2-chome
Kita-ku, Osaka 530-8230
Japan
Tel: +81 6 6348 3059
Fax: +81 6 6348 3099
Website: www.toyobo.co.jp/e/

Gene Becker Photopolymer Plates
73-48 183rd Street
Flushing, NY 11366
USA
Tel: +1 718 454 0654
Fax: +1 718 454 0769
Website: www.photopolymerplates.com

Hampton Editions, Ltd
PO Box 520
Sag Harbor, NY 11963
USA
Tel: +1 631 725 3990
Fax: +1 631 725 8687
Website: www.solarplate.com

Z*ACRYL resists, dip tanks and equipment
The CRATE, Inc.
PO Box 3661
Oakland, CA 94609
USA
Tel: +1 800 651 7975
Website: www.zacryl.com

GLOSSARY

à la poupée use of small pads to apply different coloured inks to a single intaglio plate
abrading rubbing or spraying an abrasive grit onto an intaglio plate to create a scored or pitted surface which is able to hold ink
acid chemical substance with a pH less than 7, ranging from strong (which corrodes metal) to mild (such as lemon juice): cf. alkali
acid resist (acid-resistant material) material which is impervious to and unaffected by acids
acrylic resist acid-resistant material made from acrylic co-polymers
acrylic-resist etching etching process in which plates are protected by acrylic resists
additive process of adding media to an intaglio plate: cf. subtractive
alkali chemical compound with a pH greater than 7, ranging from strong and corrosive (such as sodium hydroxide and ammonia) to mild (soap): cf. acid
alkaline having the properties of (or containing) an alkali
aquatint method of creating tone by applying a multitude of tiny dots of resist to a plate: the metal is etched away around the dots to form a reticulated pattern in the surface, and the plate prints with a tonal effect resembling watercolour washes or tints
artist's proof test print made by the artist
autographic positive positive made by painting or drawing opaque marks on a transparent or translucent substrate
BAT perfect proof (*bon à tirer*, good to pull or print) passed by the artist as a standard against which prints in an edition will be compared
Baumé (Bé) unit of measurement of specific gravity used for ferric chloride
bite indentation on a metal plate resulting from corrosive action of mordant
bleed print printed image which covers the entire sheet, leaving no border
burnishing using a tool to smooth rough areas of a plate, reducing capacity to hold ink: cf. scraper
burr spur or ridge of metal created when the plate is worked into with a drypointing, engraving or mezzotint tool
carborundum very hard particles of silicon carbide, available in different grades
chine collé method of incorporating collage elements during the intaglio printing process
chop embossing or printing stamp applied by hand to finished prints, normally identifying the printer or studio
collagraphy method of creating an ink-holding surface on selected areas of an intaglio plate by adding media such as acrylic gesso, varnish, glue, carborundum, fabrics, paper or light-sensitive film; these media may be altered on the plate by painting, drawing or dissolving areas
collagraphic media additive materials used to make collagraph plates (sometimes used to alter other types of intaglio plate, e.g. mezzotinted, etched)
crosslink change which alters and strengthens polymers
deckled edge feathered edge of a handmade (or sometimes mouldmade) paper, caused during manufacture by pulp seeping between the mould and the removable frame (deckle)
degreasing removing any traces of oil or grease from the plate
de-oxidizing removing oxidization from the plate surface (caused by exposure to oxygen in air or moisture)
dermatitis inflammation of the skin
digital positive positive created and output using a computer
drypoint print taken from a drypointed plate
drypointing creating an ink-holding surface by working into the plate with a sharp tool which displaces the plate material: cf. burr
edition group of identical (or sometimes varied) prints, signed and numbered by the artist
electrolysis process of etching a plate by immersion in an ionized solution through which a low electric current is passed
emboss marks on paper or a print which stand out in relief
engraving creating an ink-holding surface by cutting with a sharp tool which removes the plate material; also a print taken from an engraved plate
etching action of a corrosive substance on a metal plate: cf. bite; also a print taken from an etched plate
etching needle pointed or shaped drawing tool used to remove areas of resist from a plate
fish eye unwanted open area which prints with the appearance of a fish's eye
flash bite initial immersion of a plate in a bath of mordant for a short period (one or two minutes) to determine that it is biting correctly
foul bite accidental etched marks on a plate

found materials collected objects which can be employed in printmaking
frottage rubbing taken from a textured surface
gesso acrylic medium containing white powder which dries to a hard, finely textured surface
ground term used in printmaking to describe a mezzotinted plate surface; also the name given to certain acid-resistant materials (e.g. hard ground, soft ground)
halftone tonal image broken into a structure of different-sized dots, which prints to give the optical illusion of continuous tonal change
lift solution mixture for painting stencils: these are then covered with a layer of resist and 'lifted' to expose areas of metal in the form of the painting: cf. sugarlift
MDF medium density fibreboard
mezzotint print taken from a mezzotinted plate
mezzotinting creating a textured, burred surface by working into the plate with a heavy toothed tool and then smoothing these ink-holding areas down with a burnishing tool in order to create whites and light tones
monotype single print made by drawing or painting onto a plate (or plates) and printing this onto paper
mordant corrosive substance used to etch plates
MSDS Material Safety Data Sheet
muller heavy flat-bottomed weight used for grinding pigment on a slab
offsetting using pressure to transfer media such as tusche or resist from one surface to another
open bite characteristic effect when broad lines or large open areas of metal are etched
photo-abrading laminating a special light-sensitive mask onto a plate, exposing this to a positive or a negative and then abrading the processed mask to create an ink-holding surface in the plate (the mask is stripped before printing)
photocollagraphy method involving laminating a light-sensitive layer onto a plate, exposing this to a positive and then developing and drying the layer to create an ink-holding surface in this added layer (pre-laminated plates may also be used)
photocopy positive positive created and output using a photocopier
photo-etching laminating a light-sensitive dry film resist onto a plate, exposing (to a positive), developing and drying this; the plate is then etched to create an ink-holding surface and the resist is stripped before working the plate further or printing
photographic positive positive created and output using a photographic process
photogravure early photo-etching process in which a plate is coated with a light-sensitive resist made from a bichromatized gelatin solution
photomask light-sensitive stencil designed to be used in conjunction with sprayed abrasives
photopolymer light-sensitive polymer
photoresist light-sensitive material which can be processed to become acid-resistant
pinhole unwanted small open area which prints as a dot or spot
positive transparent or translucent substrate supporting opaque marks which can be translated onto an intaglio plate using light-sensitive processes
proof test print
PVA polyvinyl adhesive
PVC sheet transparent sheet made from polyvinyl chloride
realia teaching aids which are objects and material from real life, e.g. proofs and plates
registration process of aligning the disparate elements (e.g. plates, registration sheet, positives, paper) which may be required to create a print so that the image on the plate or paper is positioned exactly as required
relief printing inking up the top surfaces of the plate and taking a print from this
resist material or coating that is able to withstand the effect or action of specific substances, e.g. protect metal from the action of a mordant: cf. acid resist
respirator close-fitting breathing mask designed to protect the user from airborne particles
reticulated like a net or network
rocker toothed tool with curved blade used for creating mezzotint
roulette mark-making tool with rotating spiked wheel or drum used to pit the surface of a plate; may be used to work into acrylic resists
scraper hard sharp tool which is pulled or pushed across the plate to remove unwanted rough metal before burnishing: cf. burnishing
scrobiculated a surface with numerous small pits or depressions
sizing part of the papermaking process which describes the addition of glue (size) to the paper pulp so that the resulting paper contains a homogenous mix of size within each sheet, increasing its strength and impermeability to water
spit bite etching by applying mordant to a plate (usually coated with an aquatint) using a paint brush or cotton wool
stage biting etching and stopping out a plate in a series of steps so that each bite is a different depth
stencil shaped mask or shield which is painted, sprayed or squeegeed over with paint to create an image: usually

made from paper but in printmaking processes a liquid may be applied to a screen mesh or an etching plate to form a stencil; a light-sensitive film or emulsion may be used to create a photostencil for screenprinting or a photomask for the spray abrading process in intaglio

step biting, see **stage biting**

stippling creating ink-holding indentations by using a hard sharp pointed tool to pit the surface of a plate

stop-out acid-resistant solution which can be painted onto the plate for creative purposes, alterations, stage biting or to protect the edges of the plate

subtractive process of removing material from an intaglio plate to create ink-holding marks: cf. additive

sugarlift super-saturated solution of sugar, water and dye used traditionally for painting stencils which can be 'lifted': cf. lift solution

tusche originally a greasy compound used for drawing or painting marks or washes such as peau de crapaud ('toad skin') on lithographic plates, later used as a 'lift' stencil for oil-based screenprinting, as an oily resist in etching, as an oily stencil in acrylic-resist etching and for painting marks on positives; since the 1980s also used to describe special opaque compounds used specifically for painting marks and washes (including the peau de crapaud effect) on positives

wiping removing ink from the smooth areas of an intaglio plate so that it is left only in the indentations

PICTURE CREDITS

All photographs courtesy of the authors except: p. 18 Desirée Alvarez; p. 9 Richard Årlin; pp. 10, 137, 205 Julie Arnall; p. 29 Blazej Baláz; p. 65 Alison Bracey; pp. 19, 183, 203 Bill Brady; p. 199 Robert Callender; p. 15 Carrie Clingan; pp. 86 right, 88 David DuBose; p. 223 Kari Holopainen; p. 204 Anita S. Hunt; pp. 86 left, 176, 202 Hiro Ihara of Ihara Studios, Inc.; p. 171 Frances Kiernan; p. 87 Mikael Kihlman; pp. 28, 192 Ryan Laurey; pp. 47, 48, 55 right, 56, 79, 131 top left Peter Mackertich (petermackertich.com); pp. 21, 227 Rossana Martinez; p. 201 Zea Mays; p. 225 Elizabeth Ogilvie; p. 141 right Jennifer Page; p. 209 David Jay Reed; pp. 92, 93 bottom Judith Rothchild; p. 177 Seacourt Print Workshop; pp. 53, 54 Penny Stanford; p. 91 Courtesy of Behr Thyssen, Ltd., NY, and the Francis Kyle Gallery, London; p. 198 Rebecca Vincent; pp. 80, 207, 228 Wildwood Press; p. 13 Yama Prints; pp. 22, 38, 109 above, below left and below right, 208 below Mark Zaffron

INDEX

Page numbers in *italics* refer to illustrations